KYOTO-CSEAS SERIES ON ASIAN STUDIES 23
Center for Southeast Asian Studies, Kyoto University

THE PHANTOM WORLD
OF DIGUL

KYOTO-CSEAS SERIES ON ASIAN STUDIES 23
Center for Southeast Asian Studies, Kyoto University

THE PHANTOM WORLD OF DIGUL

Policing as Politics in Colonial Indonesia, 1926–1941

Takashi Shiraishi

NUS PRESS
Singapore

in association with

KYOTO UNIVERSITY PRESS
Japan

NUS Press
National University of Singapore
AS3-01-02, 3 Arts Link
Singapore 117569
http://nuspress.nus.edu.sg

ISBN 978-981-325-141-0 (Paper)

Kyoto University Press
Yoshida-South Campus, Kyoto University
69 Yoshida-Konoe-Cho, Sakyo-ku
Kyoto 606-8315
Japan
www.kyoto-up.or.jp

ISBN 978-4-8140-0362-4 (Paper)

National Library Board, Singapore Cataloguing in Publication Data

Names: Shiraishi, Takashi, 1950–
Title: The phantom world of Digul: policing as politics in colonial Indonesia, 1926–1941/Takashi Shiraishi.
Other title(s): Kyoto-CSEAS series on Asian studies; 23.
Description: Singapore: NUS Press; Kyoto: in association with Kyoto University Press, [2021] | Includes bibliographic references and index.
Identifiers: OCN 1241242997 | ISBN 978-981-325-141-0
Subjects: LCSH: Boven Digoel (Concentration camp)--History. | Indonesia--Politics and government--History--20th century. | Political participation--Indonesia--History--20th century.
Classification: DDC 959.802--dc23

Cover: An inmate being examined for physical anthropological studies at the Wilhelmina Hospital at the Tanah Merah camp, this photo from *Boven-Digoel: het land van communisten en kannibalen* (Amsterdam: G. Kolff & Co., 1940), written by the former camp doctor, L.J.A. Schoonheyt. KITLV 19036, CC-BY license.

Printed by: Markono Print Media Pte Ltd

To

Ben, Jim and Ruth

CONTENTS

LIST OF IMAGES

(between pp. 98 and 99)

1. The Digul River, with Tanah Merah and Tanah Tinggi both shown.
2. Two boats on the Digul River, c. 1928. The *kapal putih* is the government ship *Fomalhout,* c. 1928.
3. The internment camp at Tanah Merah, shortly after its initial construction in 1927–28.
4. The military encampment at Tanah Merah, built between the designated areas for internees and staff.
5. Louis Johan Alexander Schoonheyt on the front porch of the doctor's house in the internment camp in Tanah Merah, with a political internee as a houseboy (rear) and two Papuans (front).
6. Children at the school of the Digul internment camp, January 1929. It was typical for soldiers to bring their families with them, even on such remote postings.
7. The Wilhelmina Hospital at the Tanah Merah camp conducted physical anthropological studies of inmates.
8. The Tanah Tinggi camp for the recalcitrant, the Digul within Digul, 40 kilometers and 5 hours by motorboat upriver from Tanah Merah.
9. Tanah Tinggi internees, around 1929. Aside from the regular food rations the government provided, detainees in Tanah Tinggi were left largely to themselves.

ACKNOWLEDGMENTS

This book, which I had long thought would never be finished, was completed thanks to the encouragement and support of Caroline Sy Hau, my partner, and Onimaru Takeshi, who invited me to join his project on comparative states and surveillance, which led me to revisit the issue of political policing in the Dutch East Indies. John Ingleson, Audrey Kahin, and Yamamoto Nobuto read the manuscript, entirely or in part, and offered many helpful and insightful suggestions that saved me from making elementary mistakes. I would like to thank Peter Schoppert and the editorial team of NUS Press for making this book a reality.

In many ways this book is a product of my years at Cornell University, particularly the intellectual stimulation and succor provided by the Southeast Asia Program and the wonderful Wason and Echols library collections. Portions of this book first appeared as articles and book chapter in the following publications: "The Phantom World of Digoel," *Indonesia*, no. 61 (1996): 93–118; "Policing the Phantom Underground," *Indonesia*, no. 63 (1997): 1–46; and "A New Regime of Order: The Origin of Modern Surveillance Politics in Indonesia," in *Southeast Asia over Three Generations: Essays Presented to Benedict R. O'G. Anderson*, ed. James T. Siegel and Audrey R. Kahin, 47–74 (Ithaca: Southeast Asia Program, Cornell University, 2003). I thank the Cornell Southeast Asia Program and Cornell University Press for permission to reprint these articles and book chapter.

I am fortunate to have come to know, and worked with, Benedict R. O'G. Anderson, Ruth McVey, and James Siegel, from whom I learned a great deal not only about Southeast Asia, especially Indonesia, but also about area studies. To these three people I would like to dedicate this book in friendship and gratitude.

INTRODUCTION

The waxing and waning of Indonesian anticolonial activity is the subject of Pramoedya Ananta Toer's 1950 short story "Kemudian Lahirlah Dia" (And then he was born). A nameless first-person narrator, "I" (aku), recounts his experiences of the so-called "movement" (*pergerakan*) as a child growing up in the small town of Blora:

> Mother said brother Hurip had joined a political party. How surprised I was to hear that he meddled in politics. In my understanding, politics is police, and everyone in our house was disgusted with anything that had to do with the police.
>
> "Is father not angry because he has joined the police?" I asked.
>
> Mother smiled sweetly, hearing my question. Then, with simple words [she] explained what politics meant, which was:
>
> "Those who join political parties are the enemy of the police."
>
> And I understood a little.

> Ibu bilang, kak Hurip sudah masuk partai politik. Bukan main kagetku mendengar dia campur tangan dalam politik. Menurut pengertianku politik adalah polisi, dan seisi rumah kami jijik pada apa saja yang berhubungan dengan polisi.
>
> "Tidak marahkah bapak karena dia masuk polisi?" tanyaku.
>
> Ibu tersenyum manis mendengar pertanyaanku itu. Kemudian dengan kata-kata sederhana menjelaskan apa artinya politik: "Mereka yang masuk partai politik adalah musuh polisi."
>
> Dan aku mengerti sedikit.[1]

---

[1] Pramoedya Ananta Toer, "Kemudian Lahirlah Dia," in *Cerita dari Blora: kumpulan cerita pendek* (Kuala Lumpur: Wira Karya, 1994), 49. Translation is mine.

The story most likely takes place in the years 1932–33, when the nationalist movement led by Soekarno's Partindo (Partai Indonesia, Party of Indonesia) gains momentum, only to fall flat under the weight of colonial government intervention. The setting is a small town in which life has changed suddenly with the arrival of the movement, which establishes art, sports, *ketoprak* (theater), *wayang* (shadow play), dance, and gamelan music associations. Residents become interested in *swadesi*, based on India's Swadeshi movement, which calls for the boycotting of foreign products and the revival of domestic production processes, and Japan's Asian Awakening. Soekarno himself comes to the town to deliver a speech. People join the scout movement and express hopes of a better future, of having their own national government, and of "easterners" (*orang timur*) no longer being looked down on by "westerners" (*orang barat*). People wear *lurik*, a locally produced coarse cloth. The narrator's father, together with his assistant, Hurip, runs his own private school and heads some of the associations. Father and his friends talk about *swadesi*, cooperatives, a people's bank, education, and fighting illiteracy. He offers party cadre courses. Many young people enroll in his school. He buys two stencil duplicators and five typewriters, producing thousands of copies of textbooks. The family's house becomes an office, a hive of intellectual and political activity.

Yet all the while, police officers are watching, and the government soon hires more police officers. One day, Father is banned from teaching. Textbooks are confiscated. School enrollment drops. People stop talking about *swadesi* and stop buying *lurik*. The ideals that have hitherto energized people's collective action and animated the movement are slowly dissipated. Individuals resort to different outlets: Hurip is gone, likely underground, while Father spends days, maybe months, gambling. In the meantime, the narrator's baby brother grows in their mother's womb and one day he is born. "Eventually, all went back as before. Our quiet and peaceful small town of Blora." (*Akhirnya: Semua kembali berjalan seperti tadinya. Tenang dan damai kota kecil kami Blora.*)[2]

---

[2] Ibid., 66. Pramoedya says elsewhere that his house was the center of activity for the PPPKI (Permoefakatan Perhimpoenan-perhimpoenan Politiek Kebangsaan Indonesia, Association of Indonesian National Political Associations) in Blora when he was small. Toer, ed., *Cerita dari Digul*, vii. See also John Ingleson, *Workers, Unions and Politics: Indonesia in the 1920s and 1930s* (Leiden: Brill, 2014), 184–90 about *swadesi* and its influence in the Indies.

One need not tax one's imagination to see that the phrase "quiet and peaceful (*tenang dan damai*)" is a play on the infamous Dutch mantra "*rust en orde*" (peace and order, or law and order) that the Dutch Indies government prized above all and tried to impose on the Indonesian people. Under specific circumstances that will be the subject of this study, the idea of politics came to be equated with its suppression by the police. As the nameless narrator in Pramoedya's story puts it, "politics is police," politics=police.

As Pramoedya tells us, the movement manifested itself in the form of associations, schools, publications, rallies, and language that expressed the hopes and dreams of the people. The rise of the movement marked the arrival of modern popular politics in the Indies in the early years of the twentieth century. Its activities were manifold, ranging from the founding of newspapers and journals to organizing rallies, meetings and strikes; from the establishment of trade unions and political parties to the composition of novels and songs and the staging of theatrical productions and revolts. The movement signified the arrival of something new, exciting, hopeful, and revolutionary, because the new forms and languages that the movement introduced enabled people to say what they could not previously say.[3]

The movement began in the early twentieth century when Tirto-adisoerjo (1880–1918), an OSVIA (Opleidingschool voor Inlandsche Ambtenaren, Training School for Native Officials) graduate who left government service to become a journalist, published *Soenda Berita* (Sunda News), the first Malay-language weekly established, funded, and run by natives. He also founded a commercial cooperative, the Sarekat Dagang Islamijah (Islamic Trade Association). Medical students from the STOVIA (School tot Opleiding van Inlandsche Artsen, School for Training Native Doctors) went on to establish the Boedi Oetomo (BO, Noble Endeavor) in 1908.

Another cooperative, the Sarekat Islam (SI, Islamic Association), was established by Javanese batik traders in Surakarta in 1911 to boycott the business of Chinese traders. In 1912–13 the SI expanded rapidly and enormously under the leadership of Oemar Said Tjokroaminoto (1882–1934) who learned the art and power of the rally from the first such rally organized by the Indische Partij (Indies Party), which was established by E.F.E. Douwes Dekker (1879–1950) and joined by Tjipto

---

[3] Takashi Shiraishi, *An Age in Motion: Popular Radicalism in Java 1912–1926* (Ithaca, NY: Cornell University Press, 1990).

Mangoenkoesoemo (1885–1943) and Soewardi Soerjaningrat (Ki Hadjar Dewantara, 1889–1959) as well as a number of Indo-Europeans (Indos).

The Indies government established the Volksraad, or Advisory Council, in 1918. Governor General Johan Paul van Limburg Stirum (1873–1948) appointed Tjipto and Tjokroaminoto as Volksraad members in the hope of steering the movement toward cooperation with the colonial government. In the immediate postwar years of economic prosperity, however, trade unions underwent radicalization, successfully agitating for improved labor conditions and increased wages for their members.

Until 1918, Surabaya was the center of this nascent movement. But an investigation into a 1919 incident in which Haji Hassan, a wealthy farmer in West Java, was shot and killed for his refusal to comply with government demands for rice delivery led to the "discovery" of a secret organization called the SI Afdeeling B (Section B). The Afdeeling B affair crippled the Central Sarekat Islam (CSI), resulting in the arrest of Tjokroaminoto's three lieutenants, secretary Sosrokardono, Alimin Prawirodirdjo (1889–1964), and Moesso (1897–1948), and, eventually, Tjokroaminoto himself. With its Surabaya-based leadership group under Tjokroaminoto in trouble, the CSI increasingly came under the influence of Soerjopranoto (1871–1959), an older brother of Soewardi Soerjaningrat, and Haji Agoes Salim (1884–1954), a Minangkabau who was known among Dutch liberals for his brilliance and who once worked in the Dutch consulate in Jedda. Soerjopranoto rode in on the rising trade union movement to emerge as the leader of both the PFB (Personeel Fabriek Bond, Sugar Factory Workers' Union) and the SI Yogyakarta. Agoes Salim and Soerjopranoto led the Yogyakarta group.

Another hub aside from the one centered on the Yogyakarta group emerged in Semarang, largely under Semaoen's leadership. In his mid-teens, Semaoen (1899–1971) had joined the Indische Sociaal Democratische Vereeniging (ISDV, Indies Social Democratic Association), a political party established in 1914 under the leadership of Henk J.F.M. Sneevliet (1883–1942), and within a few years he emerged as the leader of three major organizations: the SI Semarang, the trade union VSTP (Vereeniging voor Spoor- en Tramweg Personeel, Union of Railway and Tramway Workers), and the ISDV. In 1920, the ISDV was transformed into the Communist Party (initially called PKI, Perserikatan Komunis di India, League of Communists in the Indies, it was later renamed the Partai Komunis Indonesia, or the Communist Party of Indonesia). These organizations, headquartered in Semarang, with Semaoen as their leader, became the new center of radical forces in the movement.

The government responded to the radicalization of the movement with intervention—interning Tjipto Mangoenkoesmo in Bandung, suspending the rights of speech and assembly in Surakarta and other areas, arresting SI leaders and others, and clamping down on trade unionism—and effectively scared moderates away from the movement.

By 1921, the movement was splintered by open, bitter internecine rivalry and conflict between the Semarang group under Semaoen and the Yogyakarta group under Soerjopranoto and Agoes Salim. The CSI and all the local SI groups were legally separate entities, and a major issue of contention was whether the CSI and the SIs would allow members who also belonged to other parties to keep their membership.

In 1921, the CSI introduced party discipline to prohibit CSI members from belonging to another party. With this new regulation, the CSI purged PKI members from its roster. The 1923 CSI congress decided to establish the Partai Sarekat Islam (PSI, Party of Islamic Association), to transform the SIs into its branches, and to purge PKI members from its ranks. The "Red SIs," or the SIs that supported the Semarang group, had reorganized themselves into the Sarekat Rakyat (SR, People's Association). With the moderates having been scared away, the PKI as a vanguard party could not abandon the SR, which provided one of the two most important mass bases (the other being trade unions). Soon, the PKI and the SR attracted radicals and ventured further into daring, anarchic action. They teamed up locally with many different social groups, including those in the twilight zone between legality and illegality, even as the central leadership was decimated by government suppression, split over party direction, and unable to exert control over its local sections.

The PKI became even more deeply divided, after the party decision to rebel in 1925 between those who were for rebellion (represented by Sardjono, Winanta, Alimin, Moesso, and others) and who were against (led by Tan Malaka). With most of its leaders either in prison or abroad and facing disintegration, the PKI organized revolts in Java in November 1926 and in Sumatra in January 1927, only to be violently suppressed by government forces in a few days.

In the wake of the communist revolts the movement showed signs of revival under the leadership of a small group of Dutch-educated intellectuals who established the PNI (Partai Nasional Indonesia, National Party of Indonesia) under the leadership of Soekarno (1901–70) in 1927–29. After the PNI was dissolved, the Partindo and the New PNI (PNI Baru: Pendidikan Nasional Indonesia, National Education of Indonesia [Party]) were established in 1931–34.

The energies and excitement generated by the movement, especially the Partindo led by Soekarno, form the backdrop of Pramoedya's short story. Historians generally agree on the fact that the Indies government never tolerated radical anti-colonial movements for more than a brief period and never allowed urban-based political organizations to gain footholds in the rural areas. Retreating from the liberal hope of association between Dutch and Indonesians enshrined in the Ethical Policy (and called for by liberals called Ethici) in the early years of the twentieth century, the Dutch turned to the right and shifted the policy from constructive engagement with Indonesian nationalist intellectuals to containment. John Smail argues that "Indonesian political life in the 1930s took place in a context of rigorous police surveillance and infrequent but effective repression, which made mass movements impossible." In those years the Dutch were firmly in control of the Indies and determined to remain so. Indonesian political life was confined within a narrow political space, in which "great numbers of different organizations grew, split, merged, and quarreled among themselves."[4]

Building on studies of Indonesian nationalist politics and movements in the post-communist revolt years, this book examines how and why the Indies government came to the decision to deal with Indonesian nationalist movements in the way it did. What was its strategy? How was the government able to fashion its policing apparatus as the most potent instrument to achieve peace and order when the Great Depression hit the Indies, nationalist and communist forces were gaining strength in other places of the world and war was coming both in Europe and Asia? How did political policing shape Indonesian nationalist politics?[5]

If we look at other colonies in South and Southeast Asia, it is clear that the British in India and Malaya, the French in Indochina, and the

---

[4] David Steinberg, *In Search of Southeast Asia: A Modern History*, rev. ed. (Honolulu: University of Hawai'i Press, 1985), 309. See also George McT. Kahin, *Nationalism and Revolution in Indonesia* (Ithaca, NY: Cornell University Press, 1952), 94–100; John Ingleson, *Road to Exile: The Indonesian Nationalist Movement, 1927–1934* (Singapore: Heinemann Educational Books, 1979), 138–9; M.C. Ricklefs, *A History of Modern Indonesia since c. 1200*, 3rd ed. (Stanford, CA: Stanford University Press, 2001), 225, 231, 236.

[5] I rely heavily on work done by such scholars as Susan Abeyasekere, John Ingleson, Audrey Kahin, Jacque Leclerc, J.D. Legge, William J. O'Malley, Harry A. Poeze, and Kenji Tsuchiya on Indonesian nationalist politics and movements in the interwar years. I should also note the valuable contributions R.C. Kwantes and Harry A. Poeze made to the historical study of the Dutch Indies/Indonesia with their two important series of Dutch Indies historical sources.

Americans in the Philippines dealt with their nationalists differently than the Dutch. They also organized and deployed police forces differently. Policing did not always work as it did in the Dutch Indies.

Policing played a critical role in the colonial strategy that imperial centers and their colonial governments developed to secure their immediate and longer-term interests, especially when imperial legitimacy was under challenge and peace and order threatened by the rise of anti-colonial nationalist movements in the interwar years in Asia. Historians hold that the colonial police were fashioned for colonial rule and as such were expressly meant to be state servants and not public servants. As Georgina Sinclair put it, colonial police were "an armed constabulary with a limited civil police capability."[6]

Historians are also in general agreement that, with the rise of nationalism and communism, which questioned and challenged the legitimacy of colonial rule, policing expanded. They also agree that political policing and intelligence gathering became a crucial part of police work, that ideologies of policing shifted and evolved, and that the political intelligence apparatus was kept separate from the main body of the police and placed directly under the head of intelligence for the colony or region.

They note that as anti-colonialism went transnational, as evidenced by the growing network of the Communist International (Comintern) and the League Against Imperialism, imperial powers also found ways to cooperate with each other in political policing and intelligence gathering. Historians calling for a political-economy analysis of policing remind us that police forces were there to protect both the colonial political order and its economic structures and were therefore deployed unevenly—more densely in urban centers and in mines, plantations, railways, factories and workplaces, and less densely in the yet to be monetized countryside.[7]

---

[6] Georgina Sinclair, *At the End of the Line: Colonial Policing and the Imperial Endgame, 1945–80* (Manchester: Manchester University Press, 2006), 2. See also Georgina Sinclair and Chris A. Williams, "'Home and Away': The Cross-Fertilisation between 'Colonial' and 'British' Policing, 1921–85," *Journal of Imperial and Commonwealth History* 35, no. 2 (2007): 221–38.

[7] See David M. Anderson and David Killingray, eds., *Policing and Decolonisation: Politics, Nationalism and the Police, 1917–65* (Manchester: Manchester University Press, 1992); Sinclair, *At the End of the Line*; Martin Thomas, *Violence and Colonial Order: Police, Workers and Protest in the European Colonial Empires, 1918–1940* (New York: Cambridge University Press, 2012); Martin Thomas, Bob Moore, and L.J. Butler, *Crises of Empire: Decolonization and Europe's Imperial States*, 2nd ed.

Far more useful for our purposes of investigating colonial strategies to deal with nationalism, of which policing was only a part, however, are individual Asian cases for comparison. Colonial or imperial strategies often sought to legitimize themselves and court the support of the colonized population through ideas (and promises) of political education and eventual self-government. Domestic politics in the metropolitan center and the logistics and realities of colonial rule, however, imposed limitations on self-rule. Dutch colonial policy differed from the British and American colonial policies because domestic political developments in the Netherlands and the overweening economic and cultural importance of the Indies for the Netherlands made it impossible for the Indies government to grant any meaningful political concessions to coopt even moderate Indonesian nationalist forces. Instead, the Dutch relied increasingly on policing to contain nationalist forces. Policing was not just a question of isolating (and destroying) national political forces, but also setting the parameters of what the Dutch understood and allowed as "politics."

The United States took over the revolutionary Philippines as the second colonial power to replace the Spaniards and as such had to defeat, pacify, and colonize revolutionary Philippines over an extended period. The Americans understood that the success of their colonial pacification rested on coopting the established and emerging Filipino political leadership. They offered a deal to the Filipino elite to provide the chance to fill the vacuum the Spaniards left through collaboration with the US. The Americans ended friar power, guaranteed private property and acknowledged the social and economic realities of Philippine life. They also defined their colonial mission as providing tutelage to make the Philippines self-governing and independent in due course. Municipal and local elections were held with the Philippine Act of 1902. By the time the national assembly elections were held in 1907, the timing of independence had become an important issue.

Yet it took 15 years to "pacify" the Philippines. The Americans inherited the Spanish colonial police structure and married their own data management to the old system. In Manila, which in the early days

---

(London: Bloomsbury, 2015); Daniel Bruckenhaus, *Policing Transnational Protest: Liberal Imperialism and the Surveillance of Anticolonialists in Europe, 1905–1945* (New York: Oxford University Press, 2017).

of American occupation was called "this revolutionary and insurrectionary city of … 250,000 inhabitants," the Metropolitan Police was in charge of containing radical nationalists and militant workers.[8] It introduced advanced crime control technologies, a centralized phone network, police and fire alarms, a photo identification system, and finger printing —and in twenty years it amassed file cards on two hundred thousand Filipinos, the equivalent of 70 per cent of Manila's population. The constabulary, paramilitary police of Filipino soldiers and US officers, patrolled the countryside. Within five years after its foundation in 1901, it also developed its own covert capacity, including media monitoring, surveillance, disinformation, penetration, and manipulation. Moreover, the colonial state delegated part of its authority and informal immunity to parastatal elements—"bandits, warlords, smugglers, gambling bosses, militia chiefs, special agents, forest concessionaires, planters, industrialists, and vigilantes" for social control and created the "covert netherworld" in the twilight zone between legality and illegality.[9]

Different from British India and Malaya, French Indochina, and the Dutch Indies, where colonial officers from metropolitan centers spent their lives pursuing professional careers, American rule in the Philippines relied on the short-term seconding of consultants and contractors— "technical consultants in administration, agronomy, entomology, ethnography, economics, meteorology, plant biology, public health, urban planning, and zoology." Instead of the deep cultural knowledge and immersion their European counterparts cherished, American officials amassed contemporary "superficial" data for control from without, collected "through cadastral mapping, census taking, geography, photography, police surveillance, and scientific reconnaissance."[10] Police also gathered incriminating and potentially scandalous data on Filipino political leaders, whether radical or moderate, revolutionary or collaborator. Systematically collecting and selectively releasing such incriminating information, the colonial government protected its allies and destroyed its critics. To suppress criticism, the government enacted punishment for subversion and libel of its officials. The combination of police pressure and violence, on the one hand, and political cooptation, on the

---

[8] Alfred W. McCoy, *Policing America's Empire: The United States, the Philippines, and the Rise of the Surveillance State* (Madison: University of Wisconsin Press, 2009), 15.

[9] Ibid., 48–9.

[10] Ibid., 43–4.

other hand, turned some Filipino activists into spies and collaborators and caused confusion, suspicion, and betrayal in the radical nationalist movement, leaving conservative politicians in control of public space. The police thus emerged as a major force and factor in Philippine politics. Through the combination of law and policing, surveillance and scandal-mongering, the American colonial regime stifled political dissidence and constrained Filipino public discourse within colonial bounds. Filipino collaborators were rewarded with access to colonial offices, while radicals who resisted the American rule were punished with exile, imprisonment, and police surveillance. Filipino politicians learned the game, some better than others. Alfred McCoy argues that Manuel Quezon, who later became the President of the Commonwealth, played the game with consummate skill, defending radical leaders and winning nationalist credentials while simultaneously spying on them and courting American patronage.[11]

The interwar years were crucial for the decolonization process of British India. For the British, India's deepening integration into, and growing strategic and economic importance in, the "British world-system" meant that "India must play a larger but also more obedient part in imperial strategy."[12] Indian nationalists demanded self-rule on a par with the constitutional status of the white-settler societies.[13] In 1919 the Government of India Act introduced the principle of dyarchy. Indians acquired a considerable role in provincial government, while Britain retained responsibility for central administration, especially in the areas of security and finance. It is true that these concessions "had an iron limitation": "No change could be made that imperiled India's military budget (the largest item of spending), nor the huge remittance it made for hire of its garrison."[14] Nonetheless, the introduction of electoral politics opened up spaces for elite participation. Elections became a major concern for the enfranchised Indian elite and led to changes in the nature of its political organizations. The Indian National Congress was transformed into "a genuinely nationwide, mass-based party."[15]

---

[11] Steinberg, *In Search of Southeast Asia*; McCoy, *Policing America's Empire*.
[12] John Darwin, *The Empire Project: The Rise and Fall of the British World-System 1830–1870* (Cambridge: Cambridge University Press, 2011), 185.
[13] Ibid., 26.
[14] Ibid., 62.
[15] Thomas et al., *Crises of Empire*, 28.

Renouncing violence, the Congress under Gandhi led mass action such as strikes, demonstrations and commercial boycotts to expand its social base in 1920s and 1930s. The police were instrumental in defeating the mass action, especially the Civil Disobedience Movement of 1930–33. At the same time, the British were keen to avoid confrontation with Indian nationalist forces and hoped to persuade Indian politicians to share power and responsibility at the provincial, and not at the entire India, level. They offered power-sharing over the police as a bait to tempt the Congress away from civil disobedience and into the constitutional arenas. The Government of India Act of 1935 extended dyarchy to full provincial self-government. The British provincial governor was entrusted with special powers to uphold law and order in cases where his ministers proved unable or unwilling to do so. Some aspects of police intelligence work were also brought under the direct control of the central government. As far as the police were concerned, however, the Act clearly marked the beginning of a significant erosion of British control over the colonial police. The Congress ministries met British expectations: police power under their watch was deployed against such targets as communists, socialists, striking workers and communal rioters. In 1939 the Congress ministries resigned in protest against India's involuntary involvement in the war. By then, however, the decolonization process had gone far enough, only to regain momentum after the war.[16]

Compared to India and the Philippines, British Malaya—referring to the Straits Settlements, the Federated Malay States, and the Unfederated Malay States—in the interwar years was a more placid place until 1937 when the Sino-Japanese war broke out and an anti-Japanese national salvation movement gained momentum among the ethnic Chinese. Decolonization was not on the political agenda in the interwar years. The colonial authority rested on the judicious management of plural society which set the parameters of its communal politics. Policing reflected wider colonial practices. The police strength was about 10,000 for the population of five million in 1941, commanded by British officers who had Malay and were supported by "kindly and courteous" Malays

---

[16] David Arnold, "Police Power and the Demise of British Rule in India, 1930–47," in *Policing and Decolonisation*, ed. David M. Anderson and David Killingray (Manchester and New York: Manchester University Press, 1992); Thomas et al., *Crises of Empire*.

and the "military races of India."[17] The police monitored plantations and their Indian workers. But Chinese-speaking officers and constables were in short supply and the police had problems doing intelligence gathering among Chinese, even though Chinese were the most politically active and modern economic sectors in Malaya were largely dependent on Chinese, whether in mines on the west coast or in workshops, factories, transportation, ports and merchant houses in Singapore and Penang. The Special Branch was in charge of political policing. It went about its business under the premise of a continual flow of Chinese between China and Malaya and hence constant inflows of revolutionaries, both nationalist and communist, from China. The Special Branch in the Straits Settlements worked closely with its counterparts in Hong Kong and other British settlements in China and did its best to banish revolutionaries from Malaya. The Special Branch also watched transnational Muslim networks, because Singapore and Penang served as major shipping centers for haji from the Dutch Indies. In the wake of the 1926–27 communist revolts in the Dutch Indies, the Straits Settlements government started police cooperation with the Indies government and monitored Indonesian political fugitives closely. By the mid-1930s, the Special Branch also succeeded in putting its own agent high in the Malayan Communist Party leadership and effectively managing the communist threat with good intelligence gathering and timely, highly targeted intervention, even though the party regained momentum to expand its influence in the Chinese community after the Sino-Japanese war started in 1937.[18]

---

[17] A.J. Stockwell, "Policing during the Malayan Emergency, 1948–60: Communism, Communalism and Decolonization," in *Policing and Decolonisation*, ed. David M. Anderson and David Killingray (Manchester: Manchester University Press, 1992).

[18] Stockwell, "Policing during the Malayan Emergency"; Thomas, *Violence and Colonial Order*, 177–201. The security situation changed drastically with the Japanese invasion and occupation of Malaya and Singapore in 1941–42. For the postwar British defense and decolonization strategy of Malaya and Singapore and the role of the Special Branch in the Malayan Emergency, see Karl Hack, *Defense and Decolonization in Southeast Asia: Britain, Malaya and Singapore 1941–68* (Richmond, UK: Curzon Press, 2001); Simon Smith, "General Templer and Counter-Insurgency in Malaya: Hearts and Minds, Intelligence, and Propaganda," *Intelligence and National Security* 16, no. 3 (2001): 60–78; Leon Comber, *Malaya's Secret Police 1945–60: The Role of the Special Branch in the Malayan Emergency* (Clayton and Singapore: Monash Asia Institute and Institute of Southeast Asian Studies, 2008); Georgina Sinclair, "'The Sharp End of the Intelligence Machine': The Rise of the Malayan Police Special Branch 1948–1955," *Intelligence and National Security* 26, no. 4 (2011): 460–77.

In French Indochina, the interwar years opened with Albert Sarraut's republican-minded, but in the end, empty, policy of Franco-Annamese collaboration. It was welcomed by an emerging Vietnamese bourgeoisie in Cochinchina who established the Indochinese Constitutionalist Party in 1923 and trusted Sarraut to proceed in the collaboration to produce an Indochinese constitution which would expand colonial democracy. But the colonial authorities refused to give the native elite any real decision-making power. They imposed strict regulations on the opening of new secondary schools, maintained strict censorship and limits on freedom of travel, assembly and expression, did little to expand representative politics, and never considered expanding the Cochinchinese Colonial Council northward to establish a Vietnamese or an Indochinese colonial parliament. The French in Indochina, different from the Americans in the Philippines and the British in India, thus failed in developing or allowing representative institutions and mass parties capable of reaching into the countryside and hemmed in their loyal partners.

The educated youth, a product of the Franco-Indigenous school system, radicalized along with the decline of colonial reformism. By the mid-1920s, they came to the conclusion that the French promise of association was empty and that opposition to colonial rule required the creation of political parties that could operate clandestinely. The geopolitical location of French Indochina favored the Vietnamese revolutionaries. Because of the effectiveness of French repression inside Indochina, Vietnamese communities in southern China and northeastern Siam just beyond the direct reach of the Sûreté provided bases for the survival of anticolonial movements. In 1927 a group of teachers, students, journalists, civil servants, and merchants in the north established the Vietnamese National Party (VNQDD). Ho Chi Minh established the Vietnamese Youth League in 1925 in Guangzhou, which was transformed into the Indochinese Communist Party (ICP) in 1930. They built their bases in southern China and along the Mekong and recruited cadres from among Vietnamese abroad.

In 1930, the VNQDD organized an attack on the French garrison in Yen Bay, Tonkin. The ICP helped organize peasant revolts in Nghe An and Ha Tinh provinces, briefly establishing Soviets. French repression was violent. Governor General Pierre Marie Antoine Pasquier authorized the air force to bomb the protesters. In Nghe Tinh alone, 3,000 peasants are said to have died. French repression in 1930–31 destroyed the VNQDD and the ICP in Tonkin and Annam. The Siamese and the Chinese Kuomintang's anti-communist attitude also allowed the

French to cut links between the revolutionary movement inside Vietnam and the outside. These developments effectively pushed the center of gravity of the Vietnamese communist movement toward Cochinchina. In the wake of the revolts of 1930–31 the French sought to resurrect the monarchical authority. Christopher Goscha writes that a well-informed French police inspector already warned his superiors in 1931 that they "no longer have anyone with us" and that "something more than simple repression is needed here." Governors General in French Indochina had excellent intelligence at their disposal. But the problem was not there, but in "this closing of the French official mind."[19]

In a seminal work on the Dutch Indies colonial state, "The Pattern of Administrative Reforms in the Closing Years of Dutch Rule in Indonesia," Harry J. Benda argued that the Dutch Indies "may well have been a 'police state'" at "the harsh edge of a colonial system, but that the absence of a constant concern with Indonesian nationalist movements should not be misunderstood as the absence of a Dutch colonial policy in the final years of its rule." Benda pointed out that "[s]uch a colonial policy did exist," perhaps "to the detriment of political questions," and it was a policy to recreate "a virtually full-fledged *Beamtenstaat*," "apolitical, administrative polit[y] par excellence," "a colonial polity proper," the foundations of which were laid through a series of administrative reforms in 1930s.[20] In this polity, the problem of nationalism was "relegated to the police, leaving the administrators to devote their expert training and tireless energies to matters of administration."

The Phantom World of Digul is not concerned with the question of which administrative reforms led to the refashioning of the Indies *Beamtenstaat* in the 1930s, a question already addressed by Heather Sutherland in her excellent book.[21] Rather, this book looks at the ways in which the Dutch colonial polity sought to reduce the problem of

---

[19] Christopher Goscha, *Vietnam: A New History* (New York: Basic Books, 2016), 149. For Albert Sarraut, see also Martin Thomas, "Albert Sarraut, French Colonial Development, and the Communist Threat, 1919–1930," *Journal of Modern History* 77, no. 4 (2005): 917–55. See also Christopher E. Goscha, *Thailand and the Southeast Asian Networks of the Vietnamese Revolution, 1885–1954* (Nordic Institute of Asian Studies monograph series, 79, UK: Curzon, 1999).

[20] Harry Benda, "The Pattern of Administrative Reforms in the Closing Years of Dutch Rule in Indonesia," *Journal of Asian Studies* 25, no. 4 (1966): 590–1, 601, 603.

[21] Heather Sutherland, *The Making of a Bureaucratic Elite: The Colonial Transformation of the Javanese Priyayi* (Singapore: Heinemann Educational Books, 1979).

nationalism to the question of police, to the point where the Dutch and the Dutch Indies government could dismiss Indonesian nationalist forces as insignificant even as the Indies were hit by depression and faced the prospect of a looming war in Asia and Europe.

Dutch colonial policy on the nationalist movement in the interwar years was shaped, as Heather Sutherland put it, "by the tension between the liberal desire to allow limited free play of political forces and the conservative determination to retain a European monopoly of power."[22] It was built on three pillars: the first and least important was the Volksraad and regency councils established as an outlet for political pressure; the second was containing, isolating, and marginalizing nationalist political forces by encouraging "counter-forces"; and the third and most effective was policing and repression of the nationalist movement.

The Volksraad was established in 1918 with 39 members, approximately half elected by municipal and residency councils and half appointed by the governor general. Membership was on a racial basis, initially with 15 natives and 23 "Europeans" and "foreign Orientals." In 1931 membership was expanded to 60, with 30 natives, of whom 20 were elected. The number of council members who comprised the electorate for the Volksraad was very small. Native members in the Volksraad did not represent radical Indonesian political forces. Revolutionary nationalists were thus convinced that the government would never make any real concession to the nationalist movement.

In the early years of the Volksraad, however, there was a debate both in the Netherlands and in the Indies about its future. The Carpentier Alting Commission for Constitutional Revision called for the opening up of the political structure, limitation of Netherlands interference, and wider powers and new electoral procedures for the Volksraad in its report in mid-1920. But conservative Simon de Graaff who replaced liberal Alexander Willem Frederik Idenburg as minister of colonies in the Netherlands in 1919 and Dirk Fock who replaced van Limburg Stirum as governor general in the Indies in 1921 largely ignored the report. The 1925 Indische Staatregeling (Indies Constitution), which replaced the 1854 Regulation, redefined the relationship between the Indies and the Netherlands, but denied any meaningful native political participation. The governor general retained real power. This political

---

[22] Ibid., 87.

framework defined the limits, within which Governor General van Limburg Stirum and his successors had to deal with Indonesian nationalist movements.

The Indies government in the post-revolt years thus did not have the useful political instrument that the British Indian government and the American Philippine government had to offer meaning political concessions to moderate nationalist forces to coopt them. While the administrative reform law laid the basis for the administrative reforms of 1922–25 and the creation of regency councils, these local councils did not bring about decentralization. Rather, they represented a devolution of authority from the provinces to regencies with the government remaining fully in control. As J.S. Furnivall observed, the council's actual powers were far more constricted, closer to those of an Indian local board than a functional Indian Provincial Assembly.[23] Not surprisingly, popular nationalist parties opted for non-cooperation, that is, not participating in the councils and therefore being labelled by the government as radical and revolutionary, while "moderate" parties which opted for cooperation and participated in the councils often emphasized social and economic works outside the councils.[24]

The second pillar of government strategy was to contain, isolate, and marginalize "radical" and "revolutionary" nationalist political forces with "counter-forces." Ch. O. van der Plas, an adviser for native affairs to Governor General Andries Cornelis Dirk de Graeff, identified in 1927 as counter-forces Islamic social and educational associations such as Moehammadijah and Nahdatoel Oelama (Nahdatul Ulama), traditional leaders (*volkshoofden*) such as autonomous administrations in the Outer Islands, princely courts of Java's Principalities and *priyayi* (Java's internal administration corps), Javanese nationalists and other "local patriots" such as Boedi Oetomo and Pasoendan, as well as Soetomo's Indonesian Study Club (which would merge with Boedi Oetomo to form Persatoean Bangsa Indonesia [PBI], National Union of Indonesia, in 1931) and Soewardi Soerjaningrat's Taman Siswa nationalist educational institute,

---

[23] J.S. Furnivall, *Netherlands India: A Study of Plural Society* (Cambridge: Cambridge University Press, 1937, digitally reprinted 2010), 286.
[24] Robert Cribb and Audrey Kahin, *Historical Dictionary of Indonesia*, 2nd ed. (Lanham, MD: The Scarecrow Press, 2004), 448; Sutherland, *The Making of a Bureaucratic Elite*, 100–6; Susan Abeyasekere, "Partai Indonesia Raja, 1936–42: A Study in Cooperative Nationalism," *Journal of Southeast Asian Studies* 3, no. 2 (September 1972): 262.

and suggested that the government should support activities "for peaceful national construction of native society in all its forms." But the government action was half-hearted, and in late 1929 Governor General de Graeff decided to arrest Soekarno and other PNI leaders. The government policy under Governor General de Jonge shifted further into the conservative direction. After a brief attempt to impose its direct control of private schools with the wild school ordinance, the government decided to refrain from doing so on condition that the Taman Siswa, the Moehammadijah and other educational institutions police themselves to make sure that their teachers and students did not participate in "practical" nationalist party politics. The cooperation parties and their affiliated associations were allowed to work for "constructive" social and economic development, and royalist associations in Surakarta and Yogyakarta underwent huge expansions in the 1930s. Yet the government made the entire rural area off limits for any organizational action—loyalist, royalist, constructive, evolutionary, bona fide, destructive, revolutionary, and mala fide—because whatever their stated intentions were, political party and associational activities created a space for "criminal" and "recalcitrant" elements to assert themselves, mobilize the "emotional, primitive, and easy to incite" population and threaten peace and order.[25]

Dutch conservatives such as Hendrikus Colijn (prime minister, 1925–26 and 1933–39) insisted that the *volkshoofd* (traditional leader) was alive and well and that the government could count on *priyayi* as loyal *volkshoofd*. But *priyayi* as a social class and the native administrative corps were changing. Many Dutch-educated *priyayi* were culturally alienated from the population. As Heather Sutherland put it nicely, as their functions changed—"from local chief to security and crop overseer to bureaucrat"—so too did the ways in which they used "their following of relatives, allies, clients and spies." In the twentieth century many Dutch-educated regents did not consort with village *jago* (local toughs) and mystics, did not sleep with many village headmen's daughters, and could not give jobs, feasts, or floggings as they did in the past. They could still mobilize local toughs and kyai and organize counter-movements if supported by the state coercive power, as those in Priangan, West Java,

---

[25] See Resident of Surabaya to Governor of East Java, June 26, 1933, in *De Ontwikkeling van de Nationalistische Beweging in Nederlandsch-Indie, Bronnenpublikatie 3 de Stuk 1928–Aug. 1933*, ed. R.C. Kwantes (Groningen: Wolters-Noordhoff/Bouma's Boekhuis, 1981), 803–4.

did in 1925 to destroy local PKI organizations, but violence, irregularities and disturbances that might accompany a counter-movement un-
nerved the government. In the post revolt years, *priyayi* as the *volkshoofd*
was thus made more symbolic: the government made it clear that the
native administrative corps was subordinate to their Dutch counterparts,
that the administrative reform would never lead to Dutch withdrawal
from local administration, and that control over the municipal and
field police would remain vested with the assistant resident for peace
and order.[26] To put it differently, the government strategy to contain,
isolate, and marginalize nationalist political forces worked to the extent
that educational, religious and social organizations policed themselves to
prevent their members from joining radical and revolutionary nationalist
party politics and that rural action was made off limits for any organizational activity, including native officials' organizing counter-movements.

The Indies government thus ended up relying far more on policing
and repression—in lieu of allowing limited forms of meaningful political representation—as the most important strategy to deal with the
nationalist movement. The communist revolts in 1926–27 marked the
clear turning point in the evolution of this strategy. Conservatives had
been gaining ground since 1918 in a series of battles over constitutional
reform, the administrative reform, and the limits the government should
tolerate for the native political movement, but the revolts had a decisive
effect on the debate over the colonial strategy and tilted the balance in
favor of conservatives.[27]

The government attempted a series of measures to strengthen the
state capacity to quell revolts and resistance. It established a mass internment camp in Boven Digul on the edge of the empire. It policed the
political underground, erecting "no trespass" signs bearing such keywords
as "Tan Malaka," "Moscow," and the "Comintern" and exiling to Digul
anyone who dared to go into the zone. It also modernized and expanded
the police system to watch over and intervene in above-ground political
activities and to prevent the outbreak of any disturbance.

The most important innovation of this new policing and surveillance
system was Digul, which served as both a metaphor and ground for the
ideal colonial regime the Dutch wanted to build in the Indies. Digul

---

[26] Sutherland, *The Making of a Bureaucratic Elite*, 91, 120, 133–4.
[27] As Ruth McVey points out, the uprisings came as a surprise for the Dutch authorities and tilted the balance in favor of the conservatives. Ruth T. McVey, *The Rise of
Indonesian Communism* (Ithaca, NY: Cornell University Press, 1965).

also provided the organizational principles for policing and surveillance in the Indies. Their views were informed by the shifting and unstable parameters between civilization and wilderness. Such dichotomy provided its spatial/geographical as well as social maps. Internees in Digul were classified according to their degree of reformability and recalcitrance. Digul in this sense was a concentration camp for troublemakers. The most recalcitrant of Digul internees were banished to yet another Digul within a Digul, the camp in Tanah Tinggi, where they would be reduced to a state of nature. Digul's success as an internment camp was assured by its location on the margin of the empire. It had no need of barbed wires except to protect its own troops and their families. Instead, the physical limits were set by nature—a wilderness of malaria, crocodiles, hostile Papuan natives, forest, and Australian border patrols—to hem in its prisoners, who were allowed free movement within a 25 kilometer radius and encouraged to develop their own colony and thereby created a semblance of normalcy.

A similar preoccupation with creating and enforcing normalcy informed the Dutch efforts to police political activities, both above-ground and underground. Digul was no Taman Mini of the Indies, mainly because the Indies were far larger in geographical space and population. Recognizing the "national" reach of political organizations such as the Sarekat Islam, the Dutch reorganized their police force and created the institutional basis for political policing in the attorney general's office, which became the dominant player in the bureaucratic politics over native policy and whose political intelligence supplied most of the materials that served as the basis of native policy. Its main target was communism, but its notion of "revolutionaries" expanded quickly to encompass myriad forms of activism. Liberal Governor General De Graeff debated the merits of constructive engagement with nationalist forces through the creation of "no trespass" signs, impressing the awareness of danger zones on the population to tame their activities and encouraging "counter-forces" to contain them. The installation of a conservative governor general, de Jonge, coupled with the shock of the rebellion on the HM *Zeven Provincien*, resulted in the tightening of policing, surveillance, and repression that equated politics with police and circumscribed the space for nationalist political activities.

The Dutch largely succeeded in insulating the colony from the international network of communism, but they nonetheless recognized and worried about the power of charismatic leaders, men of authority such as Tan Malaka and Soekarno who led the underground and above-ground parties to mobilize resistance, not least because these figures of authority were gifted with a communicative power, enhanced through the media and technology of print and mass rallies and capable of unleashing "wild forces" within themselves and among their so-called followers. Tan Malaka saw his persona acquire its own potency as a political symbol and object of literary fantasy circulating through print, while Soekarno's skill in oration and the power of his voice could carry away himself and his listeners.

Despite the semblance of peace and order, the native terrain was never completely pacified. Activists linked up with each other in fluid networks that cut across spatial and ideational boundaries. Some of them were careful not to cross the no-trespass signs and stopped short of entering the danger zones, but others trespassed and traversed the danger zones of their own volition. In this sense, the political policing regime the Dutch Indies state created was both a success and a failure. The success is evident in the coining of the phrase *"zaman normal,"* a time of normalcy, with which Indonesians in the post-colonial era remember that period of time. The failure of Digul and the policing regime more generally is evident in the continuing, disruptive presence of "wild forces."

Comparing American Philippines, British India and Malaya and French Indochina, we can make the following general observations about the colonial strategy, political policing, and anticolonial movement in the Dutch Indies. First, even though the Dutch liberals and conservatives debated the extent to which they should allow native (and foreign Oriental) political participation in their colonial affairs, the framework for it was very narrowly defined by the 1925 Indies constitution and they had no intention of letting the Indies gain independence, not even in the "eventual," putative future. The colony was too important for the Dutch politically, economically, and culturally. Their golden past deeply embedded in the VOC, they could not imagine their empire without the Indies. The Indies contributed enormously to the Dutch economically: the colonial drain from the Indies to the Netherlands in 1921–39 amounted, in Angus Maddison's calculation, to 10 per cent of the Dutch NDP (net domestic product), far larger than that from India to Britain which was about 1.5 per cent of the British NDP.[28] Many of

---

[28] Angus Maddison, "Dutch Colonialism in Indonesia: A Comparative Perspective," in *Indonesian Economic History in the Dutch Colonial Era*, ed. Ann Booth, W.J. O'Malley, and Anna Weidemann (New Haven, CT: Yale University Southeast Asian Studies, 1990), 322–3.

the Dutch ruling elite, as represented by Colijn, made their careers in the Indies. American Philippines were not a model of the post-colonial future for the Dutch Indies. Neither was British India. Not only were no meaningful concessions given for Indonesian political participation; no opportunities were provided for any Indonesian nationalist party to grow into a Congress party. Unlike the Metropolitan police in Manila, the Indies police did not create an interlocking regime of vice prohibition and paramilitary policing that not only deployed police powers for repression, but also circulated incriminating scandalous information to punish its critics, regulate colonial politicians' behavior, and stifle political dissidence.

Second, the Dutch in the Indies were better positioned than the French in Indochina in policing and repressing communists and radical nationalists. The British in Malaya worked closely with the Indies government to surveil political fugitives from the Indies in Singapore. There were no substantial "Javanese (Indonesian)" communities outside the Indies in which Indonesian anti-colonial parties could establish their bases. (And not a few fugitives, mainly Sumatrans, who arrived in Malaya in the wake of the revolts, it seems, settled down quite comfortably there and no longer actively participated in radical politics.) The Indies economy was not as dependent on a constant and massive inflow of people from China. The Indies government could thus opt for quarantining the colony from international communism and place the nationalist movement in the Indies under close political surveillance. Nor for that matter did Indonesian nationalist forces pose as serious a threat to the regime as the Indian National Congress, the revolutionary nationalist forces in the Philippines or Vietnamese communists to force political concessions or elicit lethal violent repressions.

Peace and order or rather, the semblance of normalcy, thus reigned supreme in the Indies. The Dutch took this as a sign of popular acquiescence, if not popular support, for its rule. But such normalcy could only be maintained under a set of assumed conditions: the Netherlands would be able to stay neutral in the war in Europe; the Japanese would not invade as far down as the Indies; the British would remain hegemonic in the region; and Singapore would be invincible. All these assumptions collapsed with the Japanese invasion, and the myth of white supremacy, on which peace and order in the Indies ultimately depended, also collapsed. The time of normalcy was over, to be replaced by the time of occupation and revolution.

Conceived originally with the title of *A Time of Normalcy*, this book is not about policing per se, but about Dutch political strategies of imposing peace and order under conditions of unequal political relations that entailed, on the one hand, Dutch assertions of racial, civilizational, and moral superiority and, on the other hand, Indonesian responses and interactions that undermined, evaded, challenged, and went beyond Dutch attempts. The Dutch colonial attempt to impose *rust en orde* can only be understood and studied not simply as an administrative matter, but as a set of political strategies for enhancing state power vis-à-vis a "non-white" (non-Dutch, non-European) population. This book is indebted to Michel Foucault's insight on "policy [*police*]" as one of two "great ensembles of political knowledge and technology" (the other being diplomatico-military technology) for securing the state against its external and internal enemies.[29] In his seminar on the eighteenth-century German *Polizeiwissenschaft*, Foucault points out that the theory and analysis of statecraft were "above all," concerned with the "maintenance of order and discipline."[30] Colonialism, however, presented far more complicated challenges because of the logic of "difference" that colonizers used to distinguish themselves from, and rule, the colonized. *Rust en orde* was not just the principle by which the Dutch sought to regulate and repress the "natives" and "Foreign Orientals." The fact that, as Harry Benda argues, the Dutch colonial state appeared to be an "apolitical, administrative polit[y] par excellence" was arguably one of the key effects of its political strategies, as was *zaman normal*, the very "time of normalcy" now remembered by the Indonesians themselves.[31]

Not all scholarship on colonial policing avoids the trap of treating "policy [police]" as a question mainly of administration rather than a set of political strategies to enforce colonial rule against subject peoples. An example is Marieke Bloembergen's study of the Indies police as an

---

[29] Michel Foucault, "Security, Territory, and Population," in *Ethics: Subjectivity and Truth: The Essential Works of Michel Foucault 1954–1984*, vol. 1, ed. Paul Rabinow, trans. Robert Hurley et al. (London: Allen Lane, 1997), 69. See also Nick Cheesman, *Opposing the Rule of Law: How Myanmar's Courts Make Law and Order* (Cambridge: Cambridge University Press, 2015), 26–7.

[30] Ibid., 70.

[31] For a recent take on a time of normalcy, see Nicole Lamb, "A Time of Normalcy: Javanese 'Coolies' Remember the Colonial Estate," *Bijdragen tot de Taal-, Land-, en Volkenkunde* 170 (2014): 530–6.

institution.[32] Though useful and meticulously researched, the book remains heavily Dutch-centric and wedded to the Dutch colonial notion of *beschaving* (civilization). In examining the police reorganization in 1918–20, Bloembergen rightly points out that it was informed by the dual purposes of "control and civilization (*beheersing en beschaving*)," that is the pursuit of enhanced "European [Dutch]" control over the security apparatus and the effort to create "more civilized police (*een meer beschaafde politie*)."[33] *The Phantom World of Digul* interrogates the "civilization/civilizing" assumptions, the implications of which Bloembergen does not explore. It is true that the Dutch defined their mission as one of "civilizing" the natives. This notion in turn informed the government policy of modernizing, professionalizing and "civilizing" the police. Bloembergen notes, though with only a passing comment, that the Dutch deployed differential terms for training "native police recruits" and "cadres and middle cadres" (Dutch and presumably Dutch-educated senior native police officers) such as "posthouse commanders, detectives and mantri polisi." For training native police recruits, the Dutch used the term *africhting*, a word that also applied to the training of animals. In contrast, they used the word *opleiding* (educating) to refer to the training of cadres and middle cadres.[34] This differential use of terms demonstrates that the Dutch idea of their civilizing mission was built on the assumption that there was a fundamental dichotomy between *beschaving* (civilization) and *wildernis* (wilderness). This distinction was simultaneously geographical and racial, spatial and subjective, as it mapped onto the dichotomy between Dutch/European/white and native/Oriental/non-white. Put differently, such a distinction precluded the possibility of making the entire native population "civilized." The question, therefore, boiled down to one of how the Indies state went about containing what it saw as an ever-present, looming wilderness,

---

[32] Marieke Bloembergen, *De Geschiedenis van de Politie in Nederlands-Indie* (Amsterdam: University of Amsterdam Press, 2007).

[33] Bloembergen, *De Geschiedenis van de Politie*, 173.

[34] Bloembergen only says the use of *africhting* indicated "distrust of the possible civilization[al level] of indigenous police [*wantrouwen tegenover de mogelijke beschaving van inheemse politie*]." The Indonesian translators of Bloembergen's book more explicitly noted the differential terms applied to Dutch and Indonesian police officers. See Marieke Bloembergen, *Polisi zaman Hindia-Belanda: Dari kepedulian dan ketakutan*, trans. Tristam P. Moeliono et al. (Jakarta: Penerbit buku Kompas, 2011), 230.

and preventing natives from "going wild" and making them—as many as possible, that is—behave. *Phantom World* looks at policing from the perspective of an evolving set of colonial political strategies to deal with the rise and threat of Indonesian nationalism and probes both its effectiveness and its limits.

It should also be said that *Phantom World* is not concerned to revisit debates on the nationalist movement in historiography spelled out, for instance, in George Kahin's classic *Nationalism and Revolution in Indonesia* and John Smail's Indonesia section of *In Search of Southeast Asia*. Historians such as Susan Abeyasekere, Michael van Langenberg, and William J. O'Malley have done excellent work on the Indonesian nationalist movement, including the role of "moderates" in the late colonial peirod. *Phantom World* does not retread the paths these scholars have cleared. Nor does *Phantom World* revisit nationalist figures on the center stage such as Soekarno, Hatta, Sjahrir, Soetomo, and Thamrin, on whose life and activities many books and articles have been written.

Inspired instead by the work of John Ingleson, Kenji Tsuchiya, and Nobuto Yamamoto, this book asks the question of what it was like to be political in the post-revolt years. It attempts to narrate and analyze the political-policing regime of the Dutch Indies and how it shaped, and was simultaneously shaped by, the rise of Indonesian nationalism.[35] How nationalist politics came to be equated with the colonial police is both a sign of the success of this policing regime and a symptom of the failure of the colonial state's long-term policies and objectives. For it was precisely this time of normalcy that incubated the revolutionary generation of 1945.[36] These were formative years for once and future activists who would go on to play important roles in post-independence Indonesia. Some channeled their energies into literature and the arts, others joined political parties and trade unions, still others joined the military and the government.

Chapter 1 examines the political significance of Digul as an indispensable component of the political policing regime in the Indies after

[35] Ingleson, *Workers, Unions and Politics*; Kenji Tsuchiya *Indonesia Minzokushugi Kenkyu: Taman Siswa no Seiritsu to Tenkai* (Kyoto: Sobunsha, 1982); Nobuto Yamamoto, "Print Power and Censorship in Colonial Indonesia, 1912–1942" (PhD diss., Cornell University, 2011); Nobuto Yamamoto, *Censorship in Colonial Indonesia, 1901–1942* (Leiden: Brill, 2019).
[36] See Benedict R. O'G. Anderson, *Java in a Time of Revolution: Occupation and Resistance, 1944–1946* (New York and London: Cornell University Press, 1972).

the communist revolts and as a device on which the Indies colonial order was constituted. Chapter 2 looks at the evolution of political policing, with the *hoofdparket* (attorney general's office with the ARD [Algemeene Recherche Dienst, General Intelligence Service] as its core) in the center, and city and field police with their own investigation branches in the regions. This chapter highlights the importance of the communist bogey and the threat it posed to peace and order for the political policing regime. Chapter 3 explores the ways in which the Indies government went about policing the political underground. The government basically set the "outer limits" of the movement, a figurative "no trespass" zone, by clamping down on the workers' union SKBI, exiling Moscow returnee and activist Iwa Koesoema Soemantri (1899–1971), and suppressing Tan Malaka's party, Pari (Partai Republiek Indonesia, Republic of Indonesia Party), and sending its leaders and activists to Digul. Chapter 4 builds on the argument presented in chapter 3 by examining the debate within the government concerning its policy on the nationalist movement. It focuses on the strategy Charles O. van der Plas, an adviser to the governor-general for native affairs, mapped out to deal with the above ground revolutionary nationalist movement represented by the Indonesian National Party (PNI, Partai Nasional Indonesia). I argue that the *hoofdparket* misunderstood the development of revolutionary nationalist politics, mistakenly assuming that the nationalists were in alliance with the Communist International, and forced Governor General de Graeff to clamp down on PNI despite his policy of constructive engagement. Chapter 5 examines the policy shift under Governor General de Jonge and shows how the Indies government went about fashioning the terrain systematically, making a deal with the Taman Siswa, the Moehammadijah and other educational institutions, setting the rural area off the limits to any organizational action, and blurring the outer limits of government tolerance to subject the small space left for nationalist politics to intensive policing and thus establishing the equation of "politics=police" in the popular imagination. Chapter 6, the last chapter, examines what it was like for Indonesians to be active politically in this age of normalcy by following a small group of activists—Soemanang, Adam Malik, Sajoeti Melik and S.K. Trimoerti, Soekarni and Wikana. I underline the importance of network analysis in understanding the nationalist movement in the final years of Dutch colonial rule.

This book, a sequel to my earlier work, *An Age in Motion*, was originally intended in the early 1990s to provide a comparative historical case to understand Suharto's New Order regime. Struck by Suharto's open admission of unleashing state power to kill those in the "covert netherworld," I wondered how violence and the fear of it produced a mix of policing and self-policing and how the mix contributed to enforcing regime stability. I wanted to examine how the Dutch Indies government achieved and maintained "peace and order" in the post-communist revolt years of the late 1920s and 1930s.

The first three chapters of this book had been written by 1996 and two of them were published in 1996 and 1997 as journal articles, and the third in 2003. By late 1997, however, Suharto's New Order was in deep crisis and by May 1998, he was gone. I saw no point in offering a comparative case to understand a regime that had already collapsed and therefore shelved the project. In retrospect, I was too obsessed with Suharto's New Order and should have taken more seriously how different the Dutch Indies colonial regime was from Suharto's New Order regime. As Joshua Barker and James Siegel persuasively argue, Suharto built his authority as the principal anchor of social order.[37] Suharto was "sovereign" in the Schmittian sense of he who possesses the unlimited authority of deciding on the exception.[38] Suharto killed those, like *preman* "criminals," who dared to stare death in the eye and threaten social disorder. Suharto demonstrated what the state was capable of by establishing the equation, the state=death.

In contrast, neither Andries Cornelis Dirk de Graeff nor Bonifacius Cornelis de Jonge nor for that matter any Dutch governor general who served in the Indies in the 1910s to 1940s was "sovereign." De Graeff destroyed the Indonesian communist party and interned its leaders and cadres in the camp in faraway New Guinea. But he wanted the internees in the Digul camp to have a humane and normal life. De Jonge clamped down hard on nationalists and interned some more in Digul. But we can be sure that it never occurred to him to kill thousands of them in the name of peace and order. It is certainly not because these Dutch officials

---

[37] Joshua Barker, "State of Fear: Controlling the Criminal Contagion in Suharto's New Order," in *Violence and the State in Suharto's Indonesia*, ed. Benedict R. O'G. Anderson (Ithaca, NY: Cornell Southeast Asia Program, 2001), 20–53; James T. Siegel, "Thoughts on the Violence of May 13 and 14, 1998, in Jakarta," in *Violence and the State in Suharto's Indonesia*, 90–123. See also Freek Colombijn and J. Thomas Lindblad, "Introduction," in *Roots of Violence in Indonesia: Contemporary Violence in Historical Perspective* (Singapore: Institute of Southeast Asian Studies, 2002).

[38] Carl Schmitt, *Political Theology: Four Chapters on the Concept of Sovereignty*, trans. George Schwab (Chicago: University of Chicago Press, 1990), 5.

were more civilized and humane. Rather, it was because the brutal and terrifying part of Dutch conquest and pacification of the Indies, marked by large-scale killing and repression of tens of thousands of Indonesians, had been done before their terms of office and because the terror that had been impressed on the natives already underpinned the authority of the Dutch Indies state and the founding colonial myth of white supremacy.[39] The Indies government in the post-revolt years went about building and maintaining its order in a different way, shaping the native terrain to isolate the sphere of popular politics, watched anyone who entered it while making him/her aware that he/she was watched, and established the equation, police=politics.

The effect of policing was felt by Indonesians. In Pramoedya's story, in the face of government repression, the narrator Aku's father ends up dissipating the energy that had galvanized the movement in gambling and, it is strongly suggested, in child-making. But the story does not tell us what happened to the father's assistant Hurip, who disappears one day because he cannot stand the suffocating normality imposed by the Dutch policing regime. One can surmise that he had gone underground, as many young Indonesians opted to do to escape state surveillance.

This underground was shapeless, in the way that led Indonesian Armed Forces (ABRI) under Suharto to characterize the imagined latent communist threat as an "organization without form" (*organisasi tak terbentuk*).[40] The underground and aboveground activists were less a motley collection of organizations than a network that straddled and

---

[39] Petra Groen tells us that in 1899 to 1909 when J.B. van Heutsz served as military governor of Aceh and then as governor general (1904–09), 21,685 Acehnese were killed, according to official Dutch accounts. In the same years, the Indies army conquered and pacified other areas, Ceram, Jambi, south-eastern Borneo, southern and central Sulawesi, Bali, Sumba, Sumbawa and Flores. Petra Groen, "Colonial Warfare and Military Ethics in the Netherlands East Indies, 1816–1941," *Journal of Genocide Research* 14 (2012): 3–4, 289–90. H. Colijn who served in Aceh as a military officer under General van Heurtsz should have understood the very foundation on which both de Graeff and de Jonge went about their liberal and conservative native policy. See also Bart Luttikhuis and A. Dirk Moses, "Mass Violence and the End of the Dutch Colonial empire in Indonesia," *Journal of Genocide Research* 14 (2012): 3–4, 257–76.

[40] Jun Honna, "Military Ideology in Response to Democratic Pressure during the Late Suharto Era: Political and Institutional Contexts," in *Violence and the State in Suharto's Indonesia*, ed. Benedict R. O'G. Anderson (Ithaca, NY: Southeast Asia Program, Cornell University, 2001), 57.

moved between both grounds. A good way of understanding this network is to look at the lives and careers of activists who served as hubs,
people like Soemanang, Adam Malik, Sajoeti Melik and S.K. Trimoerti,
Soekarni and Wikana.

Colonial government documents, at least those that were not
destroyed by the Dutch, including police reports, intelligence analysis,
and interrogation records are indispensable for any study of the anti-
colonial movement. Pramoedya Ananta Toer warns us, however, in his
tetralogy, especially its fourth volume, *Rumah Kaca* (House of Glass),
that the state, as personified by Pangenamann, has its own story to tell
and that the state monitors, shapes, and if needed destroys the movement. Therefore, it is wrong to believe that we can rely exclusively on
documents to reconstruct Indonesian history without setting foot outside
the archives.[41]

This book heeds Pramoedya's cautionary tale, reading Dutch Indies
government and other archival documents, especially police reports,
intelligence analysis and interrogation records against the grain in order
to glean and affirm the agency of Indonesians who were both the objects
of scrutiny and surveillance yet often elided as subjects of history in
one-sided colonial and scholarly accounts. In this way, we learn something about how the Indies state went about fashioning a regime of
police=politics in the final decades of its rule and what it was like for
Indonesians to live, die, and, just as important, survive as political activists under the *Beamtenstaat* regime.

---

[41] Pramoedya Ananta Toer, *Rumah Kaca* (Jakarta: Hasta Mitra, 1988). See also Ann
Laura Stoler, *Along the Archival Grain: Epistemic Anxieties and Colonial Common Sense*
(Princeton: Princeton University Press, 2009), 18–19.

CHAPTER 1

The Phantom World of Digul

In the final years of its imperial rule after the communist revolts in Java in 1926, the Dutch East Indies colonial regime established the infamous mass internment camp, Boven Digul, in the heart of the malaria-infested New Guinea on the fringe of the empire. In this place inmates were forced to live normal lives under abnormal conditions. Boven Digul, or Upper Digul (so-called because it was located up the Digul river), was not a penal colony. As the Indies government studiously made clear, internment was not a penal sanction but an administrative measure, invoked by the governor general's extraordinary powers (*exorbitant rechten*), to require an internee to live in a certain place.

Internment, and for that matter externment, or exile, was a long-established practice of the Dutch East Indies state. In the twentieth century alone, Soerontiko Samin, a Javanese from Blora and the founder of the Samin religion, was interned in West Sumatra in 1907. Tjipto Mangoenkoesoemo, a Javanese medical doctor and a tough critic of the Dutch East Indies government, was banned from the Javanese language region of Central and East Java when he was still serving as a Volksraad member in 1920; in 1927, he was exiled to Banda Neira in the eastern part of the archipelago. Communist leaders, beginning with Henk Sneevliet and A. Baars and including Semaoen, Tan Malaka, Darsono, Hadji Misbach, and Aliarcham among others,[1] were either denied their

---

The chapter title is borrowed from Hannah Arendt, "The Phantom World of the Dark Continent" in her book, *The Origins of Totalitarianism* (New York: Harvest/HBJ, new edition, 1975), 186.

[1] Henk Sneevliet was a founder of the Indonesian Social Democratic Association (ISDV), the first Marxist party in Asia, which was transformed into the communist party in 1920. A. Baars was a top lieutenant of Henk Sneevliet's at the ISDV.

right to stay in the Indies or exiled to different parts of the eastern archipelago in the years 1919 to 1926. It was only later, from 1927 to 1940, that all internees were exiled in the same place, except "intellectuals," that is those university educated who the Indies government deemed to deserve better treatment.

To be clear, Digul was no concentration camp. As the Dutch historian J.M. Pluvier reminds us it was different from the Nazi concentration camps "in the way in which the inmates were treated: no one in Digul was mistreated or killed as in the German concentration camps."[2] Indonesians, however, well understood what it meant to be exiled in Digul. There was no shortage of information in the Indies about Digul. Virtually every new internment to Digul and every new release from it were reported in Malay language newspapers, often accompanied with internees' letters to their relatives and friends and interviews. The government let Indonesians know about Digul, no doubt, to teach them lessons. Soekarno, always imaginative, was so terrified in a Sukamiskin prison cell in 1933 at the thought of living in Digul, away from his mother and perhaps without his wife, that he asked for a government pardon in exchange for his quitting political activity and, if necessary, cooperating with the government.[3]

Darsono, born in 1897, joined the ISDV in its early days and, when its headquarters moved to Surabaya in 1918, was appointed its first full time propagandist. He was serving as party chairman when he was banished from the Indies. Semaoen was elected in 1920 as the first chairman of the Communist Party of Indonesia (PKI), but left the Indies in late 1921. Tan Malaka, who we will see often in the coming chapters, served as party chairman after Semaoen. Misbach was a leading Islamic communist in Surakarta. Aliarcham, "an extremely principled and courageous man," as Ruth McVey puts it, served as chairman of the SI Semarang and called for a purely proletarian action to prepare the party for a revolution in 1923–24. Ruth T. McVey, *The Rise of Indonesian Communism* (Ithaca, NY: Cornell University Press, 1965), 261–2.

[2] J.M. Pluvier, *Overzicht van de Ontwikkeling der Nationalistische Beweging in Indonesie in de jaren 1930 tot 1942* ('s-Gravenhage: W. van Hoeve, 1953), 42–3. For Boven Digul, see also Rudolf Mrazek, "Boven Digoel and Terezin: Camps at the Time of Triumphant Technology," *East Asian Science, Technology and Society: An International Journal* 3, nos. 2–3 (2009): 287–314; and Nobuto Yamamoto, *Censorship in Colonial Indonesia, 1912–1942* (Leiden: Brill, 2019), esp. chap. 6.

[3] See Soekarno's letters to Attorney General R.J.M. Verheijen in R.C. Kwantes, *De Ontwikkeling van de Nationalistische Beweging in Nederlandsch-Indie: Aug. 1933–1942* (Groningen: Wolters-Noordhoff, 1982), 37–43; Ingleson, *Road to Exile*, 218–21. For authenticity of the letters as well as questions raised about it, see Bob Hering, "From the Files of Empire," *Kabar Seberang* 13–14 (1984): 180–1.

It was Soebakat, however, who perhaps understood the political meaning of Digul best. A founder, together with Tan Malaka and Djamaloedin Tamin, of the revolutionary underground political party, the Pari, he invented a code for its internal communication, in which "General Hospital" signified Digul, while "Hospital" meant prison and "Abu" police.[4] In his imagined political landscape of the Dutch Indies policed by "Abu" and dotted with "Hospitals," Digul was the terminal destination for revolutionaries—in colonial Dutch parlance, *de onverzoenlijken*, the recalcitrant, the incorrigibles, the die-hards—suppressing the fear of which would make them real revolutionaries. Soebakat killed himself before being sent to Digul to deny the police an opportunity to extract from him any useful information about the party. But if he had not killed himself, he would have found that Digul, complete not only with its own prison, police, military garrison, vigilante groups, spies and informers, but also with its own second internment camp at Tanah Tinggi for the recalcitrant, could be considered a metaphor for the East Indies and the colonial regime that the Dutch fashioned in the final years of their rule.

Establishing a Camp in Digul

The establishment of a mass internment camp was decided on at an extraordinary meeting of the Council of the Nederlands-Indies (Raad van Nederlandsch-Indie) convened on November 18, 1926, less than a week after the communist rebellion started in West Java in the night of November 12.[5] The question Governor General de Graeff presented to the meeting was straightforward: whether, and if yes, what measures should be taken, "to fight the communist excesses which took place

---

[4] Assistant Commissioner of Police, Proces Verbaal (Soebakat), Vb. 6-8-30 B18.
[5] The meeting was chaired by Governor General de Graeff and attended by K.F. Creutzberg, vice-president of the Council; J.W. van der Marel, P.W. Filet, Ch. J.I.M. Welter, and A.M. Hens, council members; General Secretary (*algemeene secretaris*) G.R. Erdbrink; Governor of West Java W.P. Hillen; Director of Justice D. Rutgers; Director of Internal Administration (*binnenlandsch bestuur*) A.H. Maas Geesteranus; Attorney General (*procureur generaal*) H.G.P. Duyfjes; Government Representative for General Affairs at the Volksraad J.J. Schrieke; and Deputy Advisor for Native Affairs E. Gobee. R.C. Kwantes, ed., *De Ontwikkeling van de Nationalistische Beweging in Nederlandsch-Indie, Bronnenpublikatie 2e Stuk Medio 1923–1928* (Groningen: Wolters-Noordhoff, 1978), 475–80.

in the past week and to prevent [their repeat] in the future as far as possible."

He said that he had decided before convening the meeting that it was imperative to place "the dangerous communist leaders" in custody as soon as possible for the interest of public safety and had instructed the attorney general on November 17 to order the heads of regional administration in Java and Sumatra to act on his decision. In his view, however, arrest could serve only as a temporary measure, for upon completion of their investigation, the great majority of those arrested would have to be released for lack of legal evidence to support their prosecution and they might then renew their activities once again. "But there appears to be a way to prevent this from happening," he pointed out, "namely that of interning the principal communist leaders on a large scale." De Graeff assured the council that the measure would be applied only to "principal leaders" and promised that all internees would be taken to the same place as far as this was possible.[6]

The council supported his proposal and decided that internment should start with those arrested in West Java and that those held in custody elsewhere should follow as soon as the *hoofdparket*, the attorney general's office, received the necessary information for the measure. It was also decided that the procedure and formalities to be followed for internment be revised and simplified to expedite implementation—the reasons given in the draft internment decision should be succinct and limited to eight points, the essence of which was that the person to be interned was a member of the PKI, the party which joined the Third International, and was intent on overthrowing the established authority; that the PKI worked for the establishment of illegal organizations; and that its purpose was to recruit bad elements (*slechte elementen*) to commit crimes against the property and life of officials and against the safety of society.

The next day, on November 19, Attorney General H.G.P. Duyfjes sent a telegram to the heads of regional administration and informed them that "in connection [with] unrest [in] various regions, above all recent disturbances [in] West Java, the government is considering the application of internment on a large scale against communist leaders in [the] entire Dutch Indies, whose action poses serious threat to public

---

[6] "Verslag bg. vergadering van de raad van Nederlandsch-Indie, Nov. 18, 1926," in Kwantes, *De Ontwikkeling, medio 1923–1928*, 476–7.

peace and order." A slight but important change had taken place in one day to the category of people to be interned: it was no longer "the principal communist leaders" as de Graeff had put it, but "communist leaders" "whose action poses serious threat to public peace and order."[7]

On November 24, the list of questions to be asked at the interrogation of those to be interned was sent to the heads of regional administration. All over the Indies, would-be internees were to be asked the same questions: his/her name, age, birth-place, residence, education, and occupational career; whether he/she was aware that the principal aim of the PKI was to overthrow the established authority; that the PKI established illegal organizations; and that the objective of these organizations was to recruit criminal elements for committing all sorts of crimes; whether he/she was a member of the PKI and/or one of its illegal organizations; and whether he/she participated in an action that posed a threat to peace and order.[8]

These questions were based on the theory ARD chief A.E. van der Lely put forward about the communist rebellion. In a preliminary report he submitted to the attorney general he argued that "behind the seemingly clumsy and incoherent efforts of resistance against the established regime exists a central idea," as formulated in Tan Malaka's *Naar de Republiek Indonesia* (Toward the Republic of Indonesia), that guided the communist leaders and informed their actions. The attorney general, based on this theory, in his letter to the governor general dated November 21 argued for "an extensive application of extraordinary powers upon the core [*kern*], the principal leaders [*hoofdleiders*] working behind the scenes, to prevent a repeat of the recent events."[9] In the circular he sent to the heads of regional administration on December 31, he wrote that "this large-scale internment would lose its effectiveness, if a new group of leaders could come to the fore untroubled." It is the task of the administration and police, he continued, "timely to discern the significance and the threatening influence of new propagandists and to choose the best moment to neutralize them in the same way as their predecessors."[10] Depending on the interpretation of the

---

[7] Ibid., 478.
[8] Ibid., 480.
[9] PG to GG, Weltevreden, Nov. 27, 1926, Mr. 1174x/26.
[10] PG to heads of regional administration, Dec. 30, 1926, in Kwantes, *De Ontwikkeling, medio 1923–1928*, 520–1.

local chief, anyone identified as communist leader or propagandist could now be interned.

In the meantime, Digul, which Deputy Governor of the Moluccas J. Roest described as "an inhospitable barren environment not without danger," "isolated," "thinly populated," with "limited access routes," was identified as a place ideal for the mass internment camp "insulated as completely as possible from the rest of society, severed of contact with it as much as possible—and separate always and for life."[11] On December 10, 1926, the area up the Digul river was separated from the sub-division (*onderafdeeling*) of Southern New Guinea by government decree and was made a new administrative sub-division of Boven Digul with Tanah Merah as its center.[12] Shortly thereafter, Captain L.Th. Becking, instrumental in crushing the November revolt in Banten, West Java, was sent to Digul with his largely Ambonese soldiers and convict workers to build a camp in time for the arrival of the first batch of internees which was scheduled in March 1927.

While Captain Becking was on his way to Digul, the first government secretary sent a letter to the deputy governor of the Moluccas to spell out "the Digul regime of order":

> The purpose intended with this extraordinary measure is achieved with the arrival of the internees in the place designated as their residence and therefore any coercion with respect to their person which is inevitable in implementing [this] administrative measure should be terminated unless there arise special circumstances. In their place of residence these people enjoy the same rights and be subject to the same obligations which the law guarantees or imposes on all free residents and in normal cases the government and its organs should refrain [from doing more with respect to the internees] than keeping vigilant supervision [over them]...
>
> [On the other hand] it is the governor general's opinion that the abnormal circumstance that so many people ... are brought together in an as yet inhospitable place at the government order as well as

---

[11] The quotations are from the letter of the deputy governor of the Moluccas to the governor general dated Dec. 18, 1929, cited in Kwantes, *De Ontwikkeling, medio 1923–1928*, 521.

[12] "Overzicht van de Inwendigen Politieken Toestand (1924–15 Apr. 1928)," in *Mededeelingen der Regeering omtrent Enkele Onderwerpen van Algemeen Belang* (Weltevreden: Landsdrukkerij, Mei 1928), 9–10.

the government responsibility that goes with it[s order] for the life
and welfare of these people can be a legitimate ground for special
measures on the spot and in particular for more than normal police
power of the Captain-*gezaghebber* [administrator]. To this regime
of order should be subjected not only the internees themselves but
naturally also their families...

In this connection it should be advisable in His Excellency's view
that internees' families follow as soon as possible in case they have
not accompanied them yet in order to encourage a regular family life
and perhaps gradually to replace [their] present political ambition
with interest in affairs of more domestic and social kind.[13]

In this letter Governor General de Graeff's voice is muffled by the
government secretary's careful bureaucratic language. But substitute the
first-person pronoun for the government, the governor general, and
His Excellency, then we can hear his clearer voice. De Graeff says that
his goal is achieved with the internment of these communists and that
therefore the internees should be allowed to live a normal life in Digul
as elsewhere in the Indies. There is no reason to be cynical about his
concern for the internees' life and welfare. After all, it was his decision
to intern them, and he was aware that his decision would force on them
much suffering. He agreed with the deputy governor of the Moluccas on
the need to institute a special regime of order in Digul, but he made it
clear that it should be kept to a minimum. He wanted to see the internees and their families found a colony together with the government—
he talked about colonization in Digul elsewhere in the letter—and start
a new regular and normal family and social life. He was seeing Digul,
as J.J. Schrieke, government representative for general affairs to the
Volksraad, once wrote in early 1925, as a "humane" project to give a
way out to "communist leaders and propagandists for whom there was
practically no choice but that between propaganda and prison," to create
a little peaceful Indies, an outpost of civilization in the dark island,
insulated from the outside world, undisturbed politically, and closely
monitored by the state, where the internees could do something useful
and should not waste their life on untenable political dreams.[14]

---

[13] First government secretary to deputy governor of the Moluccas, Jan. 5, 1927, in
Kwantes, *De Ontwikkeling, medio 1923–1928*, 521–3.
[14] For Schrieke's proposal, see Shiraishi, *An Age in Motion*, 311.

Digul's History

Captain Becking with his men and convict workers arrived in Tanah Merah in January 1927 and built barracks, warehouses, a hospital, a radio station, a post office, and a large and solid bath raft on the river for soldiers and convicts in two months. The first batch of internees and their families arrived in March, fifty internees, including a Chinese, and thirty family members, everyone dressed for the occasion in colorful tropical clothing with clean socks and shoes, a felt hat and a briefcase, and an umbrella under the arm.[15]

The population in Digul increased steadily after that. When Controller M.A. Monsjou arrived, together with the seventh batch of internees, in Tanah Merah on October 30, 1927, to replace Captain Becking as the Digul administrator (*gezaghebber*), the camp population was 930, with 538 internees and 382 family members. It reached 1,139, that is 666 internees and 473 family members, in February 1928. When W.P. Hillen, member of the Council of the Netherlands Indies, visited Digul in April 1930, the camp population was at its peak, about 2,000 people, including 1,308 internees.[16]

Hillen's visit was the culmination of a series of government investigations into the conditions of Digul, triggered by the articles M. van Blankenstein published in *De Nieuwe Rotterdamsche Courant* in September and November 1928, in which he argued that there were innocent victims interned in Digul by error.[17] In response, the government announced in the Volksraad in November 1928 that the internees were classified into three categories, *de onverzoenlijken* (the recalcitrant), *de halfslachtigen* (the half-hearted), and *de welwillenden* (the well-meaning), and that it was prepared to release the third category of internees, the well-meaning, if their internment was not based on sound grounds and

---

[15] I.F.M. Salim, *Vijftien Jaar Boven-Digul: Concentratiekamp in Nieuw-Guinea, Bakermat van de Indonesische Onafhankelijkheid* (Amsterdam: Contact, 1973), 78–84; Verslaggever Boven Digul [Mas Marco Kartodikromo], "Riwajat Boven Digul (IV)," *Persatoean Indonesia* no. 36 (Jan. 1930).

[16] "Overzicht van de Inwendigen Politieken Toestand (1924–15 Apr. 1928)," 12, and "Rapport van het lid van de raad van Nederlandsch-Indie, W.P. Hillen, over de interneringskampen aan de Boven-Digul, July 22, 1930" (hereafter *Rapport Hillen*), in R.C. Kwantes, *De Ontwikkeling van de Nationalistische Beweging in Nederlandsch-Indie, Bronnenpublikatie 3de Stuk 1928–Aug. 1933* (Groningen: Wolters-Noordhoff/ Bouma's Boekhuis, 1981), 463.

[17] Kwantes, *De Ontwikkeling, 1928–Aug. 1933*, 165–6.

if they behaved well in Tanah Merah.[18] The governor general also instructed the governor of the Moluccas in December 1928 to report "on their behavior, their attitude, their mentality, in short on everything that can give an impression as regards the question of whether they can still be seen as a threat to public peace and order in case they are returned to their places of origin."[19]

Hillen's job was to observe the general conditions in Digul, to interview the well-meaning, and to identify those who could be released. He stayed in Tanah Merah for 49 days, visited Tanah Tinggi, and interviewed 20 to 25 internees a day, totaling 610. He wrote in his report that at a glance Tanah Merah looked prosperous—the houses looked well-kept, all covered with galvanized iron, the gardens well-tended, the roads well maintained, electric lighting along the main roads, two schools, a hospital, a small telephone link, and a simple movie theater. The native population he met behaved well, calm and orderly, though he noticed after a short while that there were some who he felt ignored him and did not want to have anything to do with him.

But the situation was not as idyllic as it looked, he wrote, because there were many who, opposing the government as a matter of principle, were unwilling to work for the government, even if they could improve their material conditions considerably by doing so. The camp population was divided into many different and shifting groups, cliques and parties along political and ethnic lines, and between those who refused to work, those half-hearted, and those willing to work. Digul reports local officials had sent to the central government were too optimistic, Hillen argued. Shortly after the resident of Amboina visited Digul and submitted an optimistic report on the internees' mentality, he pointed out, several internees had been punished for their refusal to perform corvee labor and all the bridges in the camp had been destroyed in retaliation. Governor of the Moluccas J. Tideman reported in March 1929 that "a good spirit" prevailed in the camp, but in the following month, 69 internees were sent to Tanah Tinggi, and in his subsequent August 1929 report Tideman himself had to admit that about half of the internees remained hostile to the government and that he was not sure whether the "conversion" of many of the well-meaning was genuine.[20]

---

[18] Ibid., 338, originally from *Handelingen Volksraad*, Nov. 8, 1928, 1649.

[19] First government secretary to governor of the Moluccas, Dec. 27, 1928, in Kwantes, *De Ontwikkeling, 1928–Aug. 1933*, 167.

[20] Rapport Hillen, in Kwantes, *De Ontwikkeling, 1928–Aug. 1933*, 460–3.

Hillen argued, however, that there were not a few former peasants and small traders in Digul who knew little about communism and what the PKI and the SR were all about. He recommended that 412 out of 610 internees he interviewed could be released, while suggesting the retention of Tanah Tinggi as the second internment camp for the recalcitrant. He also had a serious doubt about the future of the internment camp at Tanah Merah. He argued that its "great disadvantages" such as infertility of the soil and malaria should be weighed against the advantage of its isolation to decide on the future of Digul and that "a timely retreat appears to me politically sensible."

> After the well-disposed [*goedgezinden*] are returned, the settlement in Tanah Tinggi can be abolished and its population be combined with those in Tanah Merah. In the new place of internment, the process of selection should also continue of those whose mentality changes for the better, so that eventually the number of those who have to be kept in internment can be counted by tens and not by hundreds. Then, perhaps, this new place of exile can also be abolished in not too distant a future and the remaining incorrigible can be put in small groups in various places in the archipelago, where they can stay in the middle of a politically apathetic population.[21]

De Graeff clearly saw his "humane" project failing. He acted on Hillen's recommendations immediately. The camp in Tanah Tinggi was made an official internment camp for the recalcitrant. He agreed with Hillen about the desirability to transfer the internment camp to somewhere else under the government of the Moluccas and instructed the director of internal administration to appoint a commission to study the matter. In December 1930 he also decided to release 219 internees from Digul.[22] But the time left was too short for de Graeff to institute a new regime of internment. Appointed the new governor general in May 1931, Bonifacius Cornelis de Jonge came to the Indies to replace de Graeff in September 1931. In January 1932 de Jonge decided to retain Digul as an internment camp.[23]

---

[21] Ibid., 464, 469–70.

[22] Kwantes, *De Ontwikkeling, 1928–Aug. 1933*, 470.

[23] K.C. Kwantes, *De Ontwikkeling van de Nationalistische Beweging in Nederlandsch-Indie, Bronnenpublikatie 4de Stuk Aug. 1933–1942* (Groningen: Wolters-Noordhoff/ Bouma's Boekhuis, 1982), 319. It was perhaps one of the insignificant decisions de Jonge made as governor general. In his memoir, he does not mention the decision even in passing (Wal, S.L. van der, ed., *Herinneringen van Jhr. Mr. B.C. de Jonge met brieven uit zijn nalatenschap* [Groningen: Wolters-Noordhoff, 1968]).

Yet a bureaucratic precedence was set with de Graeff's decision to release internees. Notwithstanding the shift in Buitenzorg from liberal de Graeff to authoritarian and conservative de Jonge, internees were regularly released thereafter, and the internee population steadily declined from 1930 to 1936. J. Th. Petrus Blumberger, cabinet chief of the department of colonies in The Hague and the foremost expert on the native movement in the Indies in his time, gave the following statistics in the note he sent to the minister of colonies in October 1937.[24]

The Internee Population in Digul

As of	Total	in Tanah Tinggi
May 1930	1,308	70
Jan. 1931	1,178	82
Jan. 1932	793	69
Jan. 1933	553	66
Jan. 1934	440	60
Jan. 1935	416	60
Jan. 1936	419	71
Jan. 1937	446	64

Petrus Blumberger noted in his report that about three-quarters of the internees at Hillen's time had been released by January 1937, while about 100 new internees arrived in Digul in these years. We can tell from the new arrivals who the Indies government saw as most dangerous enemies of the state. In the years from 1930 to 1934 they still included "PKI and SR leaders and propagandists" interned after having served their prison sentences because of their involvement in the revolts in 1926 and 1927. But they were of increasingly less importance. As we will see in the following chapters, more prominent were leading members of the "red" trade union central, the Sarekat Kaum Boeroeh Indonesia (SKBI, Union of Indonesian Workes), interned in 1930, and Pari "leaders and agents" such as Mardjono, Sarosan, Djamaloedin Tamin, and Kandor, interned from 1931 to 1934. Indeed, after the government discovery of the Pari underground, its membership meant an almost sure one-way ticket to Digul in the 1930s. Then, in the wake of the government clamp down on the "non-cooperation" nationalists in 1933–34,

---

[24] The numbers for May 1930 are from Rapport Hillen in Kwantes, *De Ontwikkeling: 1928–Aug. 1933*, 463; the rest is from Nota van de afdeling Kabinet van het departement van kolonien, Oct. 15, 1937, in Kwantes, *De Ontwikkeling: Aug. 1933–1942*, 468–9.

non-communists such as Permi (Perhimpoenan Moeslimin Indonesia, Indonesian Muslims' Association) and PSII (Partai Sarekat Islam Indonesia, Indonesian Islamic Association Party) leaders from West Sumatra (Moechtar Loetfi, Ilyas Jacob, Jalaloeddin Thaib and several others), Hatta, Sjahrir, and their friends from the Pendidikan Nasional Indonesia (Indonesian National Education; PNI Baru/Young PNI), Partindo (Partai Indonesia, Party of Indonesia) leaders from North Sumatra (Moehidin Nasoetion, Abdul Hamid Loebis and some others) went to Digul. And finally, a new generation of the Pari, the Young PNI, and the Comintern linked Young PKI (PKI Muda) leaders—Jahja Nasoetion and Djaoes/ Dawood of the Pari, "Moscow agent" Amir Hamzah Siregar, Ahmad Soemadi, Djokosoedjono and Soenarmman of the Young PKI, Moerad and Bermawi Latif of the New PNI, among others—again swelled the rank of Digul internees in 1936.

In 1936–37 the Indies government also made two important decisions to fine-tune its internment policy and practice. First, in deciding to transfer Hatta and Sjahrir from Digul to Banda Neira in early 1936, the government in effect concluded that Digul was not appropriate for university-educated "intellectuals." As Tjipto Mangoenkoesoemo and Iwa Koesoema Soemantri, a Leiden University trained lawyer, were interned in Banda Neira and Soekarno, a graduate from the School of Technology, in Ende, this had been a practice as old as Digul, but with their transfer to Banda, this became an established policy. As the resident of the Moluccas observed in April 1936, those for whom the Digul regime was inappropriate "because of their education, refinement or birth" were to be interned somewhere else.[25]

Second, shortly after A.W. Tjarda van Starkenborgh Stachouwer replaced de Jonge as governor general, the attorney general's office investigated in August 1936 the situation of 800 ex-Digulists and 2,500 ex-communists released from prison. The study found that 45 ex-Digulists and 180 ex-PKI convicts were still under close police surveillance because of their potential threat to public order, but that few posed serious enough threat for internment/reinternment.[26] The attorney general concluded that it was desirable to release internees steadily, but made it clear at the same time that those who tried to develop the revolutionary

---

[25] Resident of the Moluccas to GG, Apr. 15, 1936, in Kwantes, *De Ontwikkeling, Aug. 1933–1942*, 337.

[26] This does not mean that no ex-Digulists were reinterned, as we will see in chapter 6.

underground even after the government measure against the communists
—namely Pari leaders and propagandists and Moscow-trained Comintern
agents—as well as the recalcitrant interned in Tanah Tinggi should not
be released from Digul at all.

By the time Petrus Blumberger submitted his note to Minister of
Colonies Ch. J.I.M. Welter for policy review, therefore, Digul had long
become an indispensable component of the Indies political policing
regime, an internment camp inappropriate for university-educated
"intellectuals," a correction camp for the recalcitrant who could hope
for their release only if they behaved well in the government's judgement
and demonstrated their willingness to cooperate with the government
day in day out for many years. By then Dutch officials had long stopped
talking about Digul as a project to create a normal colony in an isolated
outpost of the empire. Not very many perhaps bothered about it. It
was simply there, conveniently, to get troublemakers out of sight and
equally importantly to warn potential troublemakers not to become too
troublesome. Yet there was life in Digul, normal on the surface, but
in fact profoundly perverted, the sole meaning of which was given by
liberation from it one fine day.

A Tour of Tanah Merah

Digul was ideally isolated from the Indies policing point of view. Tanah
Merah, the administrative center and the site of the main internment
camp, was located 455 kilometers up the Digul river—from the river
mouth to Tanah Merah was as distant as from Batavia to Semarang
or from Amsterdam to Paris—in the heart of the thick and hostile
jungle and right in the middle of New Guinea, close to the border
with Australian New Guinea. Tanah Tinggi, the second internment
camp, was isolated yet further from Tanah Merah, located 50 kilometers
upriver from it. It took three-and-a-half days from the river mouth to
Tanah Merah by the police ship, Albatros, and five more hours from
Tanah Merah to Tanah Tinggi by motorboat.

The area was malaria-infested, hot and humid, barren, and very
sparsely populated—the internees' neighbors reported as being "head-
hunters" and "cannibals" in the jungle and crocodiles in the river.[27]

---

[27] Salim, *Vijftien Jaar Boven-Digul*, 68, 81, 125; Verslaggever Boven Digul, "Riwajat
Boven Digul (I)," *Persatoean Indonesia*, no. 33, Nov. 15, 1929.

In its early years two men were snatched into the water by crocodiles when bathing, one of whom was internee no. 528, Mangoenatmodjo, the former guru of Islam Abangan, who had emerged onto the center stage of the movement together with Hadji Misbach and Tjipto Mangoenkoesoemo in the Surakartan countryside in the heady days of 1919 and 1920.[28]

There was no barbed wire encircling the internment camp, no watch towers. On the contrary, soldiers and their families lived behind barbed wire. The internees were free to wander around and stay within a 25-kilometer radius of the camp. But one could go nowhere in the north, west and south, as anyone who ever attempted to escape learned from his "death march." If there was ever an even slight chance for escape, the route had to be to the east—overland through the thick jungle, avoiding any encounter with Papuans, crossing over the crocodile-infested Mandobo, Kaoh, and Muyu rivers, and reaching the Fly river in the Australian territory. There were 16 attempts at escape from 1929 to 1943, Salim says, in which 60 internees participated, about 40 from Tanah Tinggi and the rest from Tanah Merah.[29]

Najoan, a member of the PKI since the ISDV days who Salim calls the "Jungle Pimpernel," made altogether four attempts at escape, the last in 1942, less than a year before the camp was closed, only to disappear in the jungle. Dahlan and Soekrawinata, two former leaders of the revolutionary committee in Batavia, were killed by Mappi-Papuans in the jungle. One-third of the escapees were successful in reaching the Fly river, where most of them were arrested by the Australian police, sent to Thursday Island, handed over to the Dutch police there, and then shipped back to Digul on the police ship. The most successful was a group led by Sandjojo, a former SR propagandist in Surakarta, who crossed the Torres strait by boat and reached Thursday Island without an assistance of the Australian police. The group stayed there for some time and even opened a barber shop. But one of them sent a

---

[28] Mangoenatmodjo disappeared from the camp on November 13, 1928. See Mr. 1140x/1928. For his career as a leader of peasant protest, see Shiraishi, *An Age in Motion*, 197–203.

[29] Mrazek says there were twenty attempts at escape between 1927 and 1935. Rudolf Mrazek, *Sjahrir: Politics and Exile in Indonesia* (Ithaca, NY: Southeast Asia Program, Cornell University, 1994), 130. The section on Digul in his work (pp. 128–53) is one of the best available in English about Digul.

letter to his family in Java to ask for money. A secret police agent was sent from Batavia instead of money. With his assistance, the group was arrested by the Australian police, handed over to the Indies police, and shipped back to Digul.[30] None, therefore, succeeded in escaping Digul in its entire history. Freedom of movement for residents in Digul was a farce. It only lead to getting lost in a jungle inhabited by parasites and hostile Papuans.[31]

Tanah Merah consisted of three distinct areas separated by small rivers: the administrative terrain where the civilian officials lived, the military terrain, and the internment camp. For a tour of Tanah Merah, we have Chalid Salim as an excellent tour guide. He witnessed almost the entire history of Tanah Merah from July 1927 to its closure in 1943 and knew every corner of the place because he wandered about the camp every day for fifteen years as a worker for the malaria control service, looking for mosquito breeding grounds. In his memoir he starts his tour of Tanah Merah from the dock on the Digul river.[32]

From the dock ran a wide gravel road, gently sloping, up to the hill. Along the road was a long shed for staff for maintaining motorboats on the right-hand side, and after passing it by, there were several well-kept stone houses for the low-ranking civilian and police staff, all surrounded with neat small gardens, on the left-hand side. Then, there was a new guest house (*pasanggrahan*) for sailors, the building which used to be a civilian club house (*burgersocieteit*) where silent films were shown with a simple projector—like *Tarzan*, and films starring Tom Mix and Douglas Fairbanks.[33]

To the left of the guest house was a tennis court for civilians and soldiers, then the well-kept Oranje Park along the lane, where stood the

---

[30] Salim, *Vijftien Jaar Boven-Digul*, 293–304.

[31] Ibid., 144–5; Tim Penyusun Pembuatan Buku Sejarah Perintis Kemerdekaan Departemen Sosial RI Tahun 1976/77, *Citra dan Perjuangan Perintis Kemerdekaan Seri Perjuangan Ex Digul* (Jakarta: Direktorat Jenderal Bantuan Sosial Departemen Sosial, 1977), 75.

[32] Chalid Salim, born in 1902 in West Sumatra and a brother of anti-communist CSI-PSI leader Hadji Agus Salim, was arrested in Medan in October 1927, when he was serving as an editor of *Pewarta Deli*, and was banished to Digul in July 1927. Before his arrest and exile, he was active in the PKI and the SR, as an editor of the West Sumatran PKI organ *Halilintar Hindia* and then the Surabayan PKI newspaper *Proletar* (under Moesso's chief-editorship). Salim, *Vijftien Jaar Boven Digul*, 27–8.

[33] Ibid., 123.

large and pompous residence, almost a small palace, for the administrative head, an assistant resident in the 1930s, and next to it the more modest house for the military garrison commander, a captain.

To the right of the guest house ran a wide gravel road, along which stood a power station, a telephone office, a civil prison and a Catholic church with its mission center. Further up the gravel road was a shooting range on the right and a large empty field which bordered with the internment camp to the north and where in the late 1930s was built an airfield.[34]

At the small power center and the telephone office worked internees, their labor indispensable to their functioning. Discipline in the civil prison was lax and easy-going, Salim recalls. In the late 1930s when he was doing a routine round as a worker of the malaria control service, he saw one of two police agents on prison guard duty sitting on a mat playing the card game, "tjeki," with inmates, all the cell doors wide open, while the other man on duty was happily dozing. Shortly after that, the guard alerted the people that an officer was coming. In an instant the mat was rolled up and put away, the inmates were back to their own cells, and when the officer arrived and walked along the cells, he was greeted by the guard who reported in a routine tone: nothing special to report, sir.[35]

If we take the original wide gravel road to the north from the intersection where the guest house and the power station stood, there was a well-stocked Chinese store on the right-hand corner. Its first owner, Tan Toey, a small shopkeeper in Ambon, had obtained a concession from the government to open two stores, one in the administrative terrain and the other in the internment camp. Holding a monopoly, he had made a small fortune and returned to Ambon. Then were invited Two Chinese store owners were then invited to rectify the monopoly. One of them, Tan Tjo, inherited Tan Toey's stores and opened a "modern" restaurant with a pool table and served beer with ice.[36]

Next to Tan Tjo's store were residences for native officials, first built in 1927 for Sundanese *wedana* (district head) Soeria Atmadja and his Minangkabau assistant Bitek.[37] Further along the gravel road was

---

[34] Ibid., 124.

[35] Ibid., 125–6.

[36] Ibid., 126.

[37] This ethnic combination makes sense, given the fact that two largest ethnic groups of internees were from West Java and West Sumatra.

the administrative office, where several internees worked in addition to the administrative head, two officers, a few mainly Ambonese clerks, the *wedana* and his assistant. Criminal cases were tried in this building, too, with the administrative head as judge. These were mostly minor offenses, often matters involving women and once in a while more serious cases of violence. In the building was a special secluded room holding the Digul archives, where dossiers of all internees, fattened by constant streams of information provided by spies and informers on their conduct, were neatly and systematically classified and stored.[38]

To the north of the administrative building stood a protestant church in the middle of a grass field. In front of the church, where the gravel road turned east, were the houses for the only doctor in Digul and high-ranking civil and police officers. Further up along the road extended a large grass field, "reclaimed" originally from the jungle for rice cultivation at the order of an assistant resident to make Digul "self-supporting." It was disaster. It was left empty for many years, but in later years internees cultivated vegetables and plants there, which did make Digul self-sufficient in terms of vegetables.[39]

The gravel road then led to a large empty field, originally opened for an airfield in 1937. That year a mining company, Nederlandsch Nieuw Guinea, but known as "Goldmine," came to Digul to prospect for gold. This brought changes to Tanah Merah. It broke a "deadly calm" in which everybody in Digul had lived for ten years and opened a new window to the "civilized" world, a window previously provided only by visits from the *kapal putih*, the white police ship, which came to Tanah Merah once a month (and in 1933 once every six weeks). Many foreign ships now came to Tanah Merah for the Goldmine. Enormous quantities of material were unloaded at the dock and transported by lorries to the empty field. An airfield was built with hangars and houses for the staff. The Goldmine also built its own post office, radio station, and residential quarter, where about 230 people lived—Dutch officers, Javanese laborers, and Dayak gaugers—headed by Captain Becking, the first military administrator in Digul.

But Goldmine's exploration did not go well. In 1939, less than two years after its arrival, the company decided to pull out. Most of the buildings were dismantled and their material carried away. The airfield

---

[38] Ibid., 126–7.
[39] Ibid., 127–8.

once again became an empty grass field. Digul returned to a solitary, stiflingly calm, outpost of the empire in the middle of the primeval forest. The population of the administrative terrain was reduced again to about 120, although a number of Papuans visited over the years, usually wandering around the area for several months and then returning to the jungle.[40]

Following the gravel road to the north instead of going straight to the airfield, one passed a small bridge to reach the military terrain and further north the internment camp. The military camp was strategically located between two small creeks, one separating it from the administrative terrain and the other from the internment camp. An internee who went to the administrative terrain had to show his/her pass to an armed guard standing at the entrance post of the military camp. The entire camp, called *tangsi*, was encircled with barbed wire and guarded with a watch post at every corner. As Salim says, the military camp, more than the internment camp, looked like a concentration camp.[41] It was with good reasons. As a 1928 government report explicitly stated, the military terrain was demarcated with barbed wire from the internment camp to protect soldiers and convict laborers from internees' "extremist" propaganda and to prevent unwanted contact between internees and those who lived in the military and administrative terrains.[42]

In the military camp were barracks for soldiers, an office of the garrison commander, a sick ward, a munitions depot, a radio station, a canteen, a prison, kitchens, a women's quarter, and a small exercise field. The original camp facilities, made of wood and covered with thatched roof, had been built in haste in 1927 in time for the arrival of the internees. In 1932, however, Governor General de Jonge decided to make the camp semi-permanent, even as he was frantically cutting back on government expenditures elsewhere to cope with the financial crisis caused by the great depression. Though de Jonge's decision to retain Digul was not made known to the internees, they quickly learned from the renovations made to the military camp that the camp would remain semi-permanently.[43]

The force strength of the military garrison was originally 5 and later 7 infantry platoons, each platoon was comprised of 16 to 20 men

[40] Ibid., 129–31.
[41] Ibid., 132–3 and 144.
[42] "Overzicht van de Inwendigen Politieken Toestand (1924–15 Apr. 1928)," 13.
[43] Salim, *Vijftien Jaar Boven-Digul*, 133–4.

under a European or native sergeant. Their mission was to maintain local peace and order in Tanah Merah, to take a guard duty in turn at Tanah Tinggi, and to patrol the entire Digul region. Like anywhere else in the Indies, soldiers' families also lived in the camp, in a separate barrack, and European and native non-commissioned officers, soldiers, their wives and children, and convict laborers formed a small world of their own, apart from the rest of the population in Digul.[44]

Passing by the military camp and crossing another small bridge over a creek, the wide gravel road led to and ran straight through the internment camp, dividing it into two sections. Once in the camp, the first building on the left-hand side was a small clinic for the internees, Wilhelmina Hospital. Along the main street on the left-hand side, in-between the street and the Digul river were kampungs A, B, and, bordering the jungle to the north, C.

In the early years, internees lived separately along ethnic lines. To the north end of the camp, on the river side, was kampung Udjung Sumatra (Tip of Sumatra), whose inhabitants were predominantly Minangkabau. Acehnese and Lampongers lived separately. Peoples from Java—Madurese, Javanese, and Sundanese—gathered in their own quarters, while Bantenese, mostly participants in the 1926 revolt in Banten, formed yet another separate group. Conflicts often arose between Javanese and Sumatrans. Sumatrans found it ludicrous to see a Javanese internee-official insist on being followed by another internee with a parasol. They also dismissed Javanese *tembang* (recitation of Javanese poems), dance (*tandak*), *wayang* (shadow play), and *ketoprak* theater as feudal. As time went by and as more and more internees were returned home, however, ethnic differences became less pronounced in residential patterns.[45]

A community hall, *congresgebouw* (lit. "congress building"), was on the right-hand side of the main street, which was used for showing films and on festive occasions. In later years when internees became apathetic and deeply demoralized because of prolonged isolation, it was left unused and desolate.

Houses were relatively well-built, made of wood with zinc roofs, some with plastered walls and raised floors. One internee from Jepara

---

[44] Ibid., 135–6.
[45] Salim, *Vijftien Jaar Boven-Digul*, 225–6.

decorated his house with fine wood carvings. The school was in Kampong B, where internee teachers taught in Indonesian and Dutch. Salim often stood in front of the school and listened to school children singing "merry, typical Dutch, ballads."[46]

The main kampung administration office was in Kampong B. It was headed by Gondojoewono, who once served on the party central committee representing the Ternate section, and then Boedisoetjitro, a former party secretary, and had its own police force, the ROB, Rust en Orde Bewaarders (Peace and Order Guards).[47] The ROB worked closely with the local government and its police force and was headed in its early years by Soeprapto from Salatiga.[48]

A small mosque was built in 1928 in Kampung C. Shortly after their arrival, Haroenrasjid and Ahmad Dasoeki, both Hadji Misbach's proteges and former leaders of the Islamic communist mualimin movement in Solo, established a mosque committee (Comite Masigit) to open a nearby forest and build a mosque. Natar Zainoedin, Hadji Datoek Batoeah, Hadji Achmad Hatib, and other religious leaders from West Sumatra and Banten established another association, the Al Islam Association (Al Islamvereeniging) and supported the mosque committee. In Marco's words, "the AIV [Al Islamvereeniging] was an association to unify Muslims and the CM [Comite Masigit] became its executive committee." The local government then proposed to fund part of the project and made it a contentious issue among Muslims. The majority did not want to accept government money for building a mosque. The Al Islam Association was split and dissolved. But the minority went ahead anyway, accepted government subsidy, and built a mosque. Their leaders were appointed government officials, Marco wrote contemptuously. Haroenrasjid became penghulu, religious head, of the mosque.

---

[46] Ibid., 137–9.

[47] Gondojoewono, a descendent of the nineteenth-century Javanese rebel prince Diponegoro, served as a member of the party central committee from 1923 to 1926 and the first chairman of the seamen's and dockers' union established in 1924. According to Djamaloedin Tamin, he converted Moesso and Alimin to Communism in Cipinang prison in 1923. McVey, *The Rise of Indonesian Communism*, 155, 183, 424, 426, and 461.

[48] Ibid., 139; Verslaggever Boven Digul, "Riwajat Boven Digul (I)"; Tim Penyusun Pembuatan Buku Sejarah Perintis Kemerdekaan, *Citra dan Perjuangan Perintis Kemerdekaan Seri Perjuangan Ex Digul*, 75.

Hadji Emed became a "*tukang* [workman]" to swear in internees as government officials, and Ahmad Dasoeki a member of the ROB.[49]

Not far from the mosque was a tennis court that Boedisoetjitro had built to impress visiting Dutch officials, but which no one used. Along the main street were several stores run by Chinese. The largest in the camp was first owned by Tan Toey and later Tan Tjo, but there were smaller stores, *warung* (stalls), and photo studios owned by internees. English words were often used for signboards: "English teacher," "Barbershop," "Hairdresser," and "Laundress."[50]

In the evenings, people gathered here and there in front of their houses, enjoying cool air and smoking cornhusk-rolled cigarettes (*klobot*). The sounds of guitar, mandolin, and sometimes violin were heard. Salim's house was in Kampung B. It consisted of a small front verandah and a small room and a bedroom inside. There was a rattan chair on the verandah, a small table with two stools in the room, and a couch with a red-white-blue Dutch color mosquito net in the bedroom. Drinking water could be had from the water-butt nearby, but in the dry season one had to go to the river for bathing. In the evening, Salim recalls, he read books under the light of a petroleum lamp. He bought books at the auctions that departing civilians and military officers held regularly. He also benefitted from Hatta's arrival, for he brought 15 cases of books with him to Tanah Merah.[51]

An auction (*lelang*) was a great occasion for internees in Tanah Merah, like anywhere else in the Indies. They were always held in the evenings. After a day's work, internees, dressed as elegantly as they could, went to the military or administrative terrain in groups. On such occasions they did not need to show their passes to the armed guard at the entrance of the military camp. They were guests, and they merrily mingled with civilians and soldiers. Drinks were served. Cigars and

---

[49] Verslaggever Boven Digul, "Riwajat Boven Digul (IV)." Mas Marco Kartodikoromo is now remembered as the author of *Student Hidjo* (published in Semarang). He was serving as chairman of the Surakarta SR and was a leading member of the PKI in Surakarta when he was arrested and banished to Digul. Both Haroenrasjid and Ahmad Dasoeki were his comrades in Surakarta. For the mualimin movement and Marco, see Shiraishi, *An Age in Motion*.
[50] Salim, *Vijftien Jaar Boven-Digul*, 140.
[51] Ibid., 141.

cigarettes were passed around. The gramophone was played. And the host was always very nice and friendly.[52]

Another great occasion was Queen Wilhelmina's birthday. The Oranje house was a symbol of the empire, and in those days her portraits were hung all over the Indies, in government and business offices, in the houses of practically every European, Chinese, and native notable, and in many villages in the front verandah (*pendopo*) of the village headman. So were her portraits in Digul. On her birthday a delegation went to the house of the assistant resident early in the morning for honoring the day in the name of all internees. A soccer match would be held in the afternoon, and in the evening orange-color clad people would form a lantern procession and would go to the civilian club (*burgersocieteit*) to see a play. At the Oranje festivities in Tanah Merah, more than a few *naturalisten* who refused to work for the *governmen* also participated, together with those willing to work for the government.[53]

Internees established many associations: "Orient," an opera club; "Liberty," a music and opera group; Kebinangkitan Pasoendan, a Sundanese theatrical troupe; Langen Moedo Matojo, a Javanese *ketoprak* and *wayang orang* troupe (led by a Solonese internee); a *kroncong* group headed by Samsoedin Katjamata and Mohamad Jasin from Medan. The most important club, which lasted to the final days of Digul, was the Digul Arts and Sports Association (Kunst en Sportvereeniging Digul). It was established in 1928 under Winanta's leadership, and featured Abdoel Xarim's jazz band, Digul Concert.[54]

At the north end of the main street, bordering on the jungle, were remains of long abandoned Kampung Udjung Sumatra on the river side, and next to it, the graveyard which was kept well till the last days

---

[52] Ibid., 141–2. For the social and political significance of auctions, in which officials auctioned off their private possessions and household furnishings often at outrageous prices at the end of each posting, see James R. Rush, *Opium to Java: Revenue Farming and Chinese Enterprise in Colonial Indonesia, 1860–1910* (Ithaca, NY: Cornell University Press, 1990), 131–2.

[53] Ibid., 231–3.

[54] Ibid., 237–8; Verslaggever Boven Digul, "Riwajat Boven Digul (IV)"; Tim Penyusun Pembuatan Buku Sejarah Perintis Kemerdekaan, *Citra dan Perjuangan Perintis Kemerdekaan Seri Perjuangan Ex Digul*, 84. Winanta served on the PKI central committee and participated in the Prambanan decision in December 1925. Abdoel Karim was a leading PKI member in Medan and would emerge as a major figure in the social revolution in East Sumatra in the early days of the revolution.

of the camp. Those who died in Tanah Tinggi, including Marco and Aliarcham, were also buried there. Many were victims of malaria.[55]

The main street turned east there, along which were the remains of Kampungs D, E, F and G, by the late 1930s overgrown with weeds and being "reclaimed" by nature. These quarters were abandoned one by one in the early 1930s when internees started to be released regularly and the camp population declined from the peak of 2,100 in 1929 to less than 1,000 by the mid-1930s. The population of the internment camp at the end of 1939 was 580 in total, 355 men, 66 women, and 159 children.[56]

The Phantom World of Digul

Life in Digul was not easy, but it was life nonetheless: a social and family life with its own small happiness and messiness. Digul, with its own small palace, Oranje park, military garrison, and native quarters, looked like any other small town in the Indies, and even could be seen as a little Buitenzorg. But life in Digul was perverted. It was perverted normalcy, if we use Rudolf Mrazek's precise words, which was the hallmark of Digul.[57]

To see how perverted life was in Digul, we only need to think about Chalid Salim, our tour guide of Tanah Merah, who has left powerful descriptions of life in Digul which at times remind us of Garcia Marquez' *One Hundred Year Solitude*. A well-educated intelligent man in his mid-twenties when he was sent to Digul in 1927, he worked for the malaria control service, looking for breeding places of malarial mosquitos day in day out, from one ditch to another and from one water tank to another, for 15 years. It was certainly not what he wanted to do with his life—he was and perhaps wanted to continue to be a journalist—but he did so anyway because it was his way of keeping his sanity in Digul and disciplining himself both physically and mentally. No doubt he was aware that this might improve his chance to be released from Digul, but he long suppressed his hope of returning home because that would make his life in Digul even more unbearable. Salim was not an exception. Internees were in Digul in order not to be there, to return home one

---

[55] Salim, *Vijftien Jaar Boven-Digul*, 142.
[56] Ibid., 143.
[57] See Mrazek, *Sjahrir*, 141.

fine day. Or they were there to suppress their hope not to be there as the sign that they had not capitulated and to demonstrate to themselves that they had not given up something which made their life meaningful.

This pervertedness was not just psychological, but deeply institutionalized. Salim talks about a set of categories which structured the internee life in Digul. It consisted of four main categories in Tanah Merah.

The first was *de werkwilligers*, the willing-to-work. They worked in many different jobs, as kampung chiefs and clerks in the local government office, nurses in the hospital, workers for the malaria control service, clerks and coolies in the harbor warehouses, technical workers in the power center and the telephone office, and manual laborers in the fields. All in this category were government employed. The lowliest paid were field workers, their wage being 40 cents a day, about f.10.50 a month, for work from 7:30 a.m. to 1:00 p.m. Clerks and technical workers were better paid, a monthly salary from f.18.75 to f.30, and the best paid was a clerk in the government office who obtained f.90 a month. The great majority of the internees were willing to work for the government, because they believed from the beginning—and their expectation was confirmed after Hillen's visit—that it would improve their chances of release from Digul.[58]

The second category of internees, who had less of a chance of being released, was *de eigenwerkzoekenden*, the self-employed: fishermen, vegetable farmers, store and *warung* (stall) owners, barbers, bakers, tailors, shoemakers, photographers, private teachers. They were given food rations, 18 kilograms of rice per man per month, until they could support themselves. The third category was *de steuntrekkers*, the relief-recipients or invalids—people with serious chronic illnesses such as incurable malaria and tuberculosis, or mental illnesses caused in most cases by their long isolation, great solitude, and homesickness.

The final category was *de naturalisten*, the naturalists, so called because they refused to perform any work for the government and received free food rations in *natura* from the government. Since the local authorities regarded them as undesirable "extremists," they were natural targets of spies who were many, and their conduct, both fabricated and real, was regularly and systematically reported to the local government. In the early years of the camp, a number of naturalists were suddenly arrested

---

[58] Ibid., 217–8.

and sent to the second internment camp for the *onverzoenlijken*, the recalcitrant, in Tanah Tinggi. The naturalists had no chance of returning
home, and they were aware of it. As such men of "principle," their presence reminded the rest of the internees, above all those willing-to-work
that they had somehow "capitulated"; they were sometimes admired and
more often resented.[59]

Salim divides the group into four categories and because he writes
about the internees in Tanah Merah, he does not discuss the *onverzoenlijken*, or recalcitrant, held in Tanah Tinggi. If we include this category,
however, his explanation is remarkably similar to that given by Hillen
in his 1930 report. According to Hillen, the Digul internees were classified into five categories: the willing-to-work (*de werkwilligers*), which
included the employed (*geemploieerden*), 110 in total, who worked as
policemen, telephone workers, teachers and so on, and were paid monthly
salary and the day-laborers (*dagloners*), 380 men and women, who worked
for the government, mainly in agriculture; the naturalists (*naturalisten*),
225 in total, who refused to work and received food rations; the recalcitrant (*onverzoenlijken*), 70 men, interned in Tanah Tinggi; the self-
employed, 350 men and women; and finally the invalids, 40 in total.[60]

This classification, shared both by the government and the internees,
evolved early in the history of Digul. When the camp was still under
construction, the first administrator, Captain Becking, was invested with
a number of powers, among which were to search internees, to hold
morning roll calls, and to require each internee to perform corvee labor
every day with a pay of f.31.50 a month. After the visit of the governor
of the Moluccas in July 1927, however, this regime was changed, perhaps
to keep "special measures" to a minimum, following de Graeff's instruction more strictly. In a new regulation which was to remain in place until
the camp's closure, the internees were allowed to choose whether or not
to work for the government; each internee was to be given allowance of
f.0.72 a day in *natura*; and only those willing to work for the government were paid additional f.0.30 a day in cash.[61] The two categories,

---

[59] Ibid., 221–5.
[60] Rapport Hillen, in Kwantes, *De Ontwikkeling: 1928–Aug. 1933*, 463. See also
Ongko D's statement in Sudijono Djojoprajitno, *PKI-SIBAR contra Tan Malaka*
(Jakarta: Jajasan Massa, 1962), 71–2; Soetan Sjahrir, *Out of Exile*, trans. with intro.
by Charles Wolf, Jr. (New York: John Day, 1949), 53–4.
[61] Verslaggever Boven Digul, "Riwajat Boven Digul (IV)"; Salim, *Vijftien Jaar Boven-
Digul*, 237.

those willing to work and the naturalists, as well as the other two auxiliary categories of the self-employed and the invalids, resulted directly from this regulation.

The new regulation, however, was met with internee resistance. Under the leadership of former PKI central leaders, a kampung council (*kampungraad*) was organized in each kampung and as their central body, the CRD (Centraal Raad Digul or the Digul Central Council) was formed by the kampung council representatives with Sardjono as chairman and Soemantri as the executive head. Sardjono had been elected PKI chairman at the Kota Gede, Yogyakarta, conference in December 1924, and he was part of the group that decided to make concrete plans for insurrection in December 1925 in Prambanan. Soemantri was a former leader of the PKI Semarang section and the author of the novel, *Rasa Merdeka* (Taste of freedom). Marco wrote his report, which was smuggled out in 1929 and published in the PNI organ *Persatoean Indonesia* in late 1929:

> When controller Monsjou replaced Captain Bekking [sic.] as administrator [in November 1927], the CRD and the kampung councils demanded: 1. Give us sufficient allowances; 2. Give us sufficient work tools. Such were the people's demands. They could put Digul in good order by themselves.
>
> The only duty of the government is to provide its budget; the doctor [should be] responsible for health. For [our own] domestic affairs we appoint officials. To [our] schools the government may only provide subsidy. At that time people understood and wanted not to receive allowances permanently but wanted to live as free men [orang merdeka]. Their position was that they did not want to become workers of any kind.
>
> [Their] good intention was always obstructed from within and without like Cooperatie CD [Cooperatie Digul], PVD [Particuliere Veiligheids Dienst, Private Security Service] and so on...[62]

If we borrow Abdoel Xarim's words, the CRD and the kampung councils thus wanted to create "New Australia—New America," a colony of free men, in Digul.[63] But not all internees supported the CRD, as Marco

---

[62] Verslaggever Boven Digul [Mas Marco Kartodikromo], "Riwajat Boven Digul (III)," *Persatoean Indonesia*, no. 35, Dec. 15, 1929.

[63] Abdoel Xarim M.S., *Pandoe Anak Boeangan* (Medan: Uitgevers Genootschap "Aneka," 1933), 4.

reported. Many *werkwilligen* felt threatened because they were under pressure to join the CRD and a kampung council but were afraid that it might jeopardize their chances of release. Gondojoewono established a vigilante group, PVD, and called for their cooperation with the government.

On May 1, 1928, Digul administrator Monsjou decided to destroy the CRD and the kampung councils. Marco again writes:

> People who could develop Digul without relying on the government power were arrested and are now in exile because of slander [*fitnahan*] ... by people who are prepared to develop Digul while leaning on the government power and flattering [*mendjilat*] so that they are soon returned to their old places by the government.[64]

As Marco says, leading members of the CRD and the kampung councils, including Sardjono, Soemantri, Boedisoetjitro, Aliarcham, Dahlan, and Marco himself, were arrested and sent to a temporary internment camp, Gudang Arang, south of Tanah Merah. Sardjono, Boedisoetjitro, and Aliarcham were on the PKI central committee elected at the Kota Gede conference in December 1924 and that two, Sardjono and Boedisoetjitro, together with Winanta, Moesso and some others, were part of the group who made the fatal decision to launch an insurrection at Prambanan in December 1925. In any event, Gudang Arang was not a good location for a camp, for it flooded whenever the water level of the Digul river rose. Nor was it isolated enough from Tanah Merah. It was also possible for internees to demonstrate their resistance against the government there. One day in March 1929, the governor of the Moluccas, Monsjou's boss, was on his way to Tanah Merah for an inspection tour. When his ship approached Gudang Arang, its internees stood on the riverbank in a row, with their backs to the river, pulled down their pants, and greeted him with their bare buttocks. Shortly after that, Gudang Arang internees were transferred to Tanah Tinggi, 40 kilometers upriver from Tanah Merah and thus comfortably out of sight.[65]

With the destruction of the CRD, the backbone of internee resistance was broken. "A normal village administration" was introduced soon thereafter and kampung chiefs were appointed from among the leading cooperationists by the local government: Gondojoewono, Hamid

---

[64] Verslaggever Boven Digul, "Riwajat Boven Digul (IV)."
[65] Salim, *Vijftien Jaar Boven-Digul*, 269–70.

Soetan,[66] Soehirman, Daris, and Soeprapto for Kampungs A, B, C, D, and E respectively. Gondojoewono's PVD, Private Security Service, was transformed into the ROD, Peace and Order Guards, and attached to the kampung chiefs. It placed internees, especially naturalists, under surveillance and informed the government of potential troublemakers, *onverzoenlijken*, leading to their arrest and second internment at Tanah Tinggi.[67]

From the government's perspective, the whole point of the matter was how to enforce the new regulations and introduce "a normal village administration" to the internment camp. In its eyes, those who offered resistance to its effort were *onverzoenlijken*. From Marco's perspective, the question was how to create a space and order for the internees' own free lives (*hidoep merdeka*) in Digul, and their enemy was the government as well as those who cooperated with the government, flattered it, and slandered them. Either way, the dividing line was drawn between the recalcitrant (*onverzoenlijken*)/principled and the willing-to-work (*werkwilligers*)/ass-lickers/slanderers. The constitution of the category, the recalcitrant —and the second internment camp for this category of people in Tanah Merah—was indispensable for introducing "normalcy" in Tanah Merah. As Digul was instituted for restoring order in the Indies and making it normal, so was Tanah Tinggi needed for reordering Tanah Merah and making it normal.

It is no surprise, then, that entirely different perspectives made up life in the two camps. In Tanah Merah those willing-to-work formed the great majority. They desperately wished to be released from Digul. The better they behaved and the more they cooperated with the government, the better chances they believed they had to return home. Their expectations were met by the government. After Hillen's visit, those who contributed most to the introduction of normalcy in Tanah Merah, Gondojoewono, Soeprodjo, and Soeprapto among them, were released as early as 1931. Boedisoetjitro, who repented his incorrigibility in Tanah

---

[66] Soetan Hamid was one of the members of Komite Pembrontak (Insurrection Committee), a committee established by the Batavia PKI in September 1926 for the insurrection, along with Soekrawinata and Heroejoewono who we met earlier. Michael C. Williams, *Sickle and Crescent: The Communist Revolt of 1926 in Banten* (Ithaca, NY: Southeast Asia Program, Cornell University, 1982), 70.

[67] The phrase, a "normal village administration" (*een normaal dorpsbestuur*) comes from "Overzicht van de Inwendigen Politieken Toestand (1924–15 Apr. 1928)," 15. See also Verslaggever Boven Digul, "Riwajat Boven Digul (IV)"; and, also, the statements of Ongko D and Nurut in Sudijono, *PKI-SIBAR*, 68–9, 92–3.

Tinggi, returned to Tanah Merah and replaced Gondojoewono as kampung chief in 1931. In a few years he too was allowed to return home.[68]

Life in Tanah Merah in the post-Hillen days thus centered on the tense moments when the list of names of those to be released was posted in front of the kampung administration office. As the list was put up, internees crowded around to read it. Occasionally jubilant voice was heard, but many more went home disappointed, feeling they were "forgotten," and then waited for the next tense moment to occur in the next few months.[69]

The internee mentality in Tanah Tinggi was entirely different. It was the place for the recalcitrant, *de onverzoenlijken* or as Salim put it more neutrally, those who were *nekat*, determined, principled, stubborn, and recalcitrant. They suppressed their desire to return home and persevered in the hellish life in order not to capitulate. Aside from the regular food rations the government provided, they were left entirely to themselves. There was no kampung administration. In 1930 there were 115 inhabitants, 70 internees and 45 family members in Tanah Tinggi. The houses, 43 in total, Hillen wrote, were built "in places wherever they chose, separate from each other, in the forest, surrounded by badly kept gardens." The only road there was the one built by the government, a short entrance road leading to Tanah Tinggi, and since the internees refused to make roads on their own, there were no paths to link houses with each other. An official sent from Tanah Merah stayed in a simple guest house to keep his eyes on the internees, but they shunned him except when they received food rations twice a week.[70]

When Hillen visited Tanah Tinggi, he had an occasion to talk with Najoan, a former leader of the VSTP railway union and a member of the PKI since its ISDV days. He wrote:

> The notorious Najoan declared in earnest: "Life is really quiet here." This man has lived in many places in the Archipelago in various jobs and has also visited the Netherlands. Now he finds it "really quiet" in Tanah Tinggi. This shows an abnormal psyche, and perhaps there are various psychopaths among the recalcitrant.... Whatever they may be, the residents of Tanah Tinggi do not come into consideration for the moment for return to the free society.[71]

---

[68] Wiro S. Miardjo's statement in Sudijono, *PKI-SIBAR*, 73.

[69] Salim, *Vijftien Jaar Boven-Digul*, 254.

[70] Rapport Hillen, in Kwantes, *De Ontwikkeling: 1928–Aug. 1933*, 467–8.

[71] Ibid., 470.

No doubt Hillen thought Najoan was crazy, he eventually disappeared in the thick hostile jungle in 1942 in his fourth and last attempt at escape. Perhaps Hillen thought that Najoan and his fellow inmates had succumbed to nature and had been reduced to becoming a part of nature. Undoubtedly, nature was the undisputed master in Tanah Tinggi. Hillen must have felt that the inmates could not possibly create a human world, a human reality there and that nature remained, in all its majesty, the only overwhelming reality—compared to which they appeared to be phantoms, unreal and ghostlike. Damped in Tanah Tinggi, these internees appeared to Hillen to be reduced to natural human beings devoid of the specifically human reality, real *naturalisten*, not very different from their Papuan neighbors, though without their freedom and innocence. But they were not. They kept their ghostlike human reality in that phantom world of Digul.[72]

The internees in Tanah Tinggi were divided into three "cliques" in the mid-1930s. There were people who continued to see Aliarcham as their leader, an example of what a communist man should be like, long after his death in 1931. Another group was led by Sardjono, Ngadiman, and Winanta, who ran their own communist cadre training courses in this phantom world. The third group was led by three Moscow returnees, "Hadji Moskow," Waworoentoe, Daniel Kamoe, and Clementi Wentoek, who were proud of their Moscow training and insisted that all books other than those published in Russia were fakes. In 1935 the three groups met, and after a long discussion, concluded "conventie anti-penDigulan [anti-Digul-internment convention]," in essence a pledge, despite their mutual antagonisms, not to capitulate. But Sardjono repented his recalcitrance in 1937, and, arguing that "the goal justifies the means," his group asked for a transfer to Tanah Merah. The Moscow returnees followed suit shortly thereafter. Thus, there remained in Tanah Merah only those "true followers of Aliarcham." They somehow managed to survive until the camp closure; there were 25 in total who were evacuated to Australia in 1943.[73]

---

[72] This paragraph, slightly revised, is from Arendt, *The Origins of Totalitarianism*, 192.
[73] The statements of Wiro S. Miardja and Nurut, in Sudijono, *PKI-SIBAR*, 74–6, 96–8. Wiro S. Miardja and Nurut, as well as Ongko D., whose statement is also included in Sudijono's book, survived in Tanah Tinggi until its closure and came back to Java in the early days of the revolution.

It should be clear by now why Digul with its perverted normalcy could be seen as a metaphor for the Indies themselves. As we have seen, Tanah Tinggi was needed to create normalcy in Tanah Merah as Digul was instituted to establish normalcy in the Indies. Normalcy was achieved in the Indies and in Digul because of an isomorphic structure in which the insertion of Digul in the Indies resembled that of Tanah Tinggi in Digul. One wonders then what constituted normalcy in the Indies if the normalcy created in Digul was fundamentally perverted, for if one cannot say that Tanah Merah was normal while Tanah Tinggi was abnormal, then similarly one cannot say that the Indies was normal while Digul was abnormal. Instead, normalcy appeared in relativity: The Indies appeared normal compared to Digul, as Tanah Merah appeared normal compared to Tanah Tinggi. It was not just isolation in general, but isolation in the heart of a hostile, overwhelming, majestic nature that threatened to reduce anyone to a part of nature, to natural human beings devoid of any human character, as in Tanah Tinggi, where Hillen thought psychopaths were the only form of human existence. Compared to Tanah Tinggi, Tanah Merah was infinitely more human, more civilized, and more normal, and so was the Indies compared to Digul. In this sense, the Indies colonial order was constituted on the phantom world of Digul; therein lay the most important meaning of Digul.

It should not be surprising, then, that this isomorphism of the Indies/Digul and Digul/Tanah Tinggi was accompanied with another isomorphic social mapping. We have seen that the internees were classified into the three categories of *de werkwilligen* (the willing-to-work), *de naturalisten* (the naturalists), and *de onverzoenlijken* (the recalcitrant) and that the insertion of Tanah Tinggi in Digul and the creation of normalcy in Tanah Merah compared to the phantom world of Tanah Tinggi was made operative on the basis of this classification. We have also seen that this set of categories emerged in Digul in negotiations between the Indies state and the internees. In the Indies outside Digul, another set of categories—those who were willing to cooperate and not to cooperate with the government, that is cooperationists and non-cooperationists, as well as moderates and revolutionaries/extremists/recalcitrant—evolved during the same years, once again in negotiations between the Indies government and Indonesian nationalists, without which the insertion of Digul in the Indies for the creation of normalcy would not have been as effective and operative as it did. This means that we can understand aboveground Indonesian nationalist politics, both cooperationist and non-cooperationist, in the Indies only if we also look at revolutionary underground politics, however phantom-like it was, for we can understand Tanah Merah, with its *werkwilligen* and *naturalisten*, only if we also look at Tanah Tinggi and its ghostlike *onverzoenlijken*. Life in Digul was perverted in a profoundly politicized way, and it is in the mirror of its pervertedness where we can see the perverted normal order in the Indies reflected.

Closing Years

When Tjarda van Starkenborgh Stachouwer replaced de Jonge as governor general in 1936, and especially after Welter became minister of colonies in 1937, Digul after so many years once again became a major issue in The Hague and Buitenzorg. It was partly because Digul was part of Welter's past—he had participated in the decision to create the mass internment camp in late 1926 when he was a member of the Council of the Netherlands Indies, and he was its vice president when the Council discussed Hillen's report in 1930—but more importantly because the international situation was changing fast, with the Nazis in power in Germany and the Japanese military invasion to China and because he wanted to make sure the Netherlands would not be criticized for its moral rectitude in the colonial rule. The note on Digul which Petrus Blumberger submitted to Minister Welter was the earliest sign of his active interest in the question.

In December 1938, Welter sent a note to Petrus Blumberger for drafting his letter to the governor general, in support of his recent decision to release twenty internees from Digul as "a step further on the way to abolish this place of exile except for the '*onverzoenlijken*'." He then wrote:

> That in my view the effort should be made to liquidate this place of exile as fast as possible. That ... I am of opinion that the establishment of a distinct internment camp should be regarded as permissible only as an exceptional measure...
>
> That I am of opinion that the Netherlands authority over the Indies derives its great moral prestige in the world from its effective and humane administrative methods and [therefore I believe that] the sooner it can do without the exceptional means of a special place of internment, the better.

Welter thus suggested that Digul should be replaced with the traditional method of internment in not too distant a future, with internees to be dispersed widely in many areas where they could not hope to have any political influence because of their linguistic differences and that the internment camp in Digul should be abolished "with the exception of that of the 'onverzoenlijken'."[74]

The Indies government, however, was unenthusiastic about his suggestions. The attorney general argued that the traditional method would not work as effectively as it used to, because of the spread of Malay (Indonesian) in the Indies and the increased possibilities of contact with the outside world once the internees were placed outside the camp.[75] The retention of Digul was decided on at a meeting of the Council of the Netherlands Indies in December 1938, though in the first half of 1938, 118 more internees were released, reducing the internee population in Digul to 345 by July 1938, including 42 internees in Tanah Tinggi.[76]

In May 1940 Welter once again wrote a note, expressing his disappointment in the slow progress in liquidating Digul.

> A departure was made in 1927 [from the long-established internment practice] because hundreds of people had to be interned simultaneously then. Thus was born, perforce, the camp in New Guinea. But it is in contravention with a long tradition and with the experiences gained thereby, to use the Boven Digul concentration camp again for "normal" internment, normal in the sense that they always took place and will take place for now and perhaps permanently. In my view the old tradition should be followed for such internment.[77]

Fourteen years after its establishment, one of the founders admitted that Digul was a concentration camp, not even for "normal" internment, let alone for a normal life. Yet it survived for three more years, until 1943, two years after most of the Indies was occupied by the Japanese. That year, the Indies government in exile in Melbourne became sufficiently worried about the possibility of the internees being liberated by the Japanese that it decided to liquidate the camp altogether and to evacuate

---

[74] Notitie van de minister van kolonien, Dec. 23, 1937, in Kwantes, *De Ontwikkeling: Aug. 1933–1942*, 474–85. Based on this note, a letter was sent to the governor general, dated Dec. 29, 1937.

[75] Procureur-generaal aan gouverneur-generaal, Nov. 9, 1938, in Kwantes, *De Ontwikkeling, Aug. 1933–1942*, 552–4.

[76] Kwantes, *De Ontwikkeling, Aug. 1933–1942*, 552 and 556.

[77] Notitie van de minister van kolonien, May 6, 1940, in Kwantes, *De Ontwikkeling, Aug. 1933–1942*, 744–5.

all internees to Australia. Evacuation was carried out by Ch. O. van der Plas and the camp closed in 1943.[78]

Thus, the history of the Digul concentration camp to an end and with it the last remnant of the political policing regime the Indies government fashioned in the final years of its existence. The post-revolt years, 1927 to 1942, can be understood in this sense as the age of Digul, for the normalcy in the Indies in these years was constituted fundamentally on the phantom world of Digul. Digul and its camps functioned both to refract and to reflect the normal, that is Digul by definition demarcated the boundaries between the normal and abnormal, the willing-to-work with the government and the recalcitrant, thereby separating the rational colonial order and the psychopathic fringe population, and in doing so mirrored the very regime that institutionalized and marginalized it. Normalcy was contingent on a complex apparatus of policing that marked and partitioned colonial territories, subjects, and signs.

---

[78] Van der Plas. in his letter dated on Apr. 18, 1943, wrote to Minister of Colonies H.J. van Mook about his visit to Digul thus: "[T]he atmosphere among the internees was horrible.... [Y]ou may see men aged twenty-seven years, who are grey and broken after ten years of internment. Very old looking men, using walking-sticks, in reality have not even reached the age of fifty. There is a lot of mutual hatred and envy; the people of Tanah Tinggi are lunatics, all living in barricaded houses, armed with wooden spears, who are out for each other's lives.... I spend a lot of time with the internees, was available day and night for discussion and went through the complete evacuation." Harry A. Poeze, "From Foe to Partner to Foe Again: The Strange Alliance of the Dutch Authorities and Digoel Exiles in Australia, 1943–1945," *Indonesia* 94 (Oct. 2012): 62.

CHAPTER 2

A New Regime of Order

Creating a regime of order in Digul was easy. It was isolated. It had no history. And each of its small internee population was fully identified— his/her name and aliases, identification number, birthplace and birth-date, marriage status, educational and occupational background, poli-tical career, fingerprints, photographs, and other information in one file; all the files were stored in one room. Fashioning a new regime of order in the Dutch East Indies was far more complicated. It was a vast archipelagic empire. It had a population of sixty million (in 1930) that included many different histories, languages and cultures. Its state insti-tutions evolved over centuries with many regional variations. Nonethe-less, a new, fairly uniform regime of order was established in the 1930s, with prisons and the internment camp, a relatively small modern police force (34,000 strong in 1930), and a small colonial army (37,000 strong in 1930).[1]

Crucial in this development was the creation of a modern political policing apparatus, nestled in the police, led by career professional Dutch and native police officers, and autonomous of the Department of Internal Administration. Its arrival was marked by the 1919 establishment of a General Investigation Service (Algemeene Recherche Dienst [ARD]) in the attorney general's office called *hoofdparket*. Its reach expanded more widely over the empire and penetrated more deeply into the native world in the 1920s with the creation of a regional intelligence apparatus in each residency. Indonesians called the political intelligence apparatus the Politieke Inlichtingendienst (PID, Political Intelligence Service), because

---

[1] *Indisch Verslag 1931: II. Statistisch Jaaroverzicht van Nederlandsch-Indie over het Jaar 1930* (Batavia: Landsdrukkerij, 1931), 14, 405–6.

its local manifestations, city and regional intelligence units, were often called political intelligence or political investigation (politieke inlich-tingen, politieke recherche).

The PID was a machine with its own history. It grew up with the PKI as its enemy. Its tradition—its mentality, its thinking, its way of seeing the native world, and its mode of operations—was shaped by this history. It carried this tradition with it to create a normalcy after it destroyed its communist enemy. It was an answer on the part of the Dutch Indies state to the rise of modern popular politics in the Indies. As such it signified the coming of age of modern surveillance politics in the Indies. How did this machine evolve? What were its mechanics? What mentality and thinking informed the machine? How did it work and with what consequences?

The Coming of Modern Policing

The history of the Indies police is as old as Dutch colonialism. As virtually every writing on the Dutch Indies/Indonesian police history tells us, the first police officer in the Indies was a man called Jan Steijns van Antwerpen who Jan Pieterszoon Coen appointed as *baljuw*, officer of justice and head of police, when he took Jakatra from the Bantenese king and founded Batavia in 1620.[2] But we do not need to go back to the VOC prehistory of the Indies state to understand the modern police that came into being in the early twentieth century. The foundation of future modern police was laid in the early nineteenth century, when the bankrupt VOC was transformed into a state under Napoleon Bonaparte-appointed old Jacobin Governor General Herman Willem Daendels

---

[2] See, for instance, A. Neijtzell de Wilde, "De Nederlandsch-Indische Politie," in *Koloniaal Tijdschrift* 13 (1924): 115; Abdulkadir Widjojoatmodjo, *Riwajat Kepolisen di Hindia Ollanda dengan Ringkas: Lezing dengan hadlirat j.m. toen Resident Prijangan Tengah dalam Congres Inlandsche Politie Bond ke-tiga di Bandoeng pada boelan April 1927 tanggal 17* (Semarang: Typ Khouw Beng Wan, 1927), 5; "Uit de Voorgeschiedenis der Politie," in *Vereeniging van Hoogere Politie-Ambtenaren, 1916–1936: Jubileum-Nummer van de Nederlandsch-Indische Politiegids bij Gelegenheid van het 20 Jarig Bestaan van de Vereeniging* (Batavia: n.p., 1936), 17; P. Dekker, *De Politie in Nederlandsch-Indie: Hare Beknopte Geschiedenis, Haar Taak, Bevoedheid, Organisatie en Optreden* (Soekaboemi: Drukkerij "Insulinde," Tweede Druk, 1938), 3. As a recent good his-torical work on the Indies police, see Marieke Bloembergen, *De Geschiedenis van de Politie in Nederlands-Indie* (Amsterdam: University of Amsterdam Press, 2009).

(1808–11) and his successor British liberal Governor General Thomas Stamford Raffles (1811–16).

Daendels did away with the government of Java's North East Coast and divided the area into five prefectures. He organized a corps of *djajangsekars*, native light dragoons, in each prefecture as an instrument of power of the prefect. *Djajangsekars* were also organized in Cirebon and Banten when their sultanates were reduced to residencies under Raffles. Thus began the tradition of paramilitary armed police to maintain peace and order in Java's countryside.[3]

Raffles' contribution was greater. He discovered, in Herman W. Muntinghe's words, "the ancient institution of village administration which had existed since before the times of the Mohammedan domination along the entire coast of Java." In his regulation of February 11, 1814, Raffles made the village headman responsible for policing in his own village and required him to organize a regular night watch for maintaining order, preventing crimes, and arresting criminals. Raffles also divided the territory into areas (residencies), each area into districts (regencies), and each district into divisions headed by an officer of division. In each division, the regulation stipulated, was a police station to be established with several subordinate officials called *mantri* and other police officers. With the promulgation of this regulation in February 1814, Raffles laid on paper the foundation of two most enduring Dutch Indies/Indonesian police institutions, village police (*desapolitie*) and administrative police (*bestuurspolitie*).[4]

When the Dutch were returned to the Indies in 1818, these police institutions were inherited by the Dutch Indies government. In 1819, however, Governor General G.A. Baron van der Capellen made yet another institutional innovation. With two regulations on criminal justice and the administration of police and criminal justice, he made the attorney general (*procureur generaal*) central head of justice and police and the resident regional head of administrative police. But the residents were not under the attorney general. Though he had his own regional representatives, officers of justice, they had fewer powers than the residents. This created a dualism. The attorney general and the officers of justice in effect became responsible for European justice and police, while

---

[3] Dekker, *De Politie*, 35; See also Sutherland, *The Making of a Bureaucratic Elite* (Singapore: Heinemann Educational Books, 1979), 7–8.
[4] Dekker, *De Politie*, 37–8; Sutherland, *The Making of a Bureaucratic Elite*, 8–9.

the residents were in charge of native justice and police. The dualism survived into the twentieth century.[5]

This regime remained in force throughout the nineteenth century with minor modifications. In the years from the 1870s to the 1890s *djajangsekar*, *pradjoerit* (literally, soldier) and other para-military armed police forces, which had been part of the colonial army and led by non-commissioned army officers, were phased out and replaced by corps of police agents. It was organized out of police *oppasser* (opas/upas, messenger/attendant/policeman) of administrative police, attached to Dutch and native administrative officials—residents, assistant residents, schouten (sheriffs, chiefs of administrative police in major urban centers), regents (*bupati*), regent's chief deputy (*patih*), district heads (*wedana*) and subdistrict heads (assistant *wedana*). In Java's three urban centers of Batavia, Semarang, and Surabaya, this police organization was placed under the assistant resident for police, while in the rest of the Indies the police agents were attached, like previous police *oppasser*, to administrative officials. The police force was made responsible for prison and treasury guard duties, transportation of prisoners and government money as well as for maintaining order and carrying out normal police duties.[6]

The establishment of the corps of police agents marked the beginning of professional police (*beroepspolitie*) in the Indies, the fourth type of Indies police, along with armed police, village police, and administrative police. In the early twentieth century, however, the combined force strength of administrative and professional police remained small. In 1907–08, it was about 9,500 men strong, including police agents in charge of prison guard, transportation of prisoners, forest policing, and salt and opium monopoly policing, led by about 700 police *mantri*. According to the estimate of A. Neijtzell de Wilde, who served as member of the welfare commission for a study of the police situation in those days, at least 4,000 more police agents and *oppasser* were needed for the 25,000 villages in Java and Madura.[7]

---

[5] Dekker, *De Politie*, 39.

[6] Ibid., 40–4. See also Marieke Bloembergen, "The Dirty Work of Empire: Modern Policing and Public Order in Surabaya, 1911–1919," *Indonesia* 83 (2007): 119–50.

[7] Neijtzell de Wilde, "De Nederlandsch-Indische Politie," 119–23. Neijtzell de Wilde says that each resident and regent was allocated four *oppasser* in 1907–08; assistant resident three; *patih* one; *wedana* four; assistant *wedana* two; and police *mantri* two police *oppasser*. Ibid., 119.

The government also became concerned about police corruption as pointed out in many studies on police about that time. In the early twentieth century, as in the previous century, administrative officials from residents and regents down to police *mantri* and *oppasser* relied heavily on "henchmen and spies," variously called such as *palang* (literally, junction), *weri* (spy), *jagabaya* (police), and *jago* (literally, fighting cock). These networks of administrative and police officials and their henchmen and spies formed a twilight zone linking the official state sphere and the Java's village world. James Rush describes this twilight zone thus:

> Jagabaya distinguished themselves from ordinary villagers by their supra village experience and an aptitude for intrigue ... Their métier was crime, its perpetration and detection, and their services were for hire. Thus they frequently appear alongside other local functionaries as village police (*kapetengan*), appointed by headmen to protect villages from banditry and arson, and as detectives and "secret police" in the service of headmen, *priyayi* officials, and Dutch administrators.... The social environment of the *jagabaya* was much broader than that of the ordinary villager. Jagabaya gathered in opium and gambling dens and consorted among the fringe elements of Javanese society: dancing girls, prostitutes and pimps, traveling show folk, magicians and con-men, brigands, fences, and thieves. It was their familiarity with these elements and their equal familiarity with the village world that made them such valuable resources. Jagabaya were, therefore, enlisted in the service of not only the native and Dutch authorities, but also a variety of other individuals and groups whose interests penetrated the village world.[8]

---

[8] James R. Rush, "Social Control and Influence in Nineteenth Century Indonesia: Opium Farms and the Chinese of Java," *Indonesia* 35 (April 1983): 59. Also see his *Opium to Java: Revenue Farming and Chinese Enterprise in Colonial Indonesia, 1860–1910* (Ithaca, NY: Cornell University Press, 1990); Onghokham, "The Inscrutable and the Paranoid: An Investigation into the Sources of the Brotoningrat Affair," in *Southeast Asian Transitions: Approaches through Social History*, ed. Ruth T. McVey (New Haven: Yale University Press, 1978); Neijtzell de Wilde, "De Nederlandsch-Indisch Politie," 122; "Nogmaals Politiespionnen," in *De Nederlandsch-Indische Politiegids*, no. 7 (1932): 51–3; "Uit de Desa II: Spion," in *De Nederlandsch-Indische Politiegids*, no. 12 (Dec. 1934): 283–293; *Onderzoek naar De Mindere Welvaart der Inlandsche Bevolking op Java en Madoera: VIIIb. Overzicht van de Uitkomsten der Gewestelijke Onderzoekingen naar 't Recht en de Politie en daaruit gemaakte Gevolgtrekkingen. Deel II. Slotbeschouwingen* (Batavia: Ruygrok, 1912).

In the nineteenth century, Dutch administrative officials were part of this twilight zone and the government had to live with this reality to maintain peace and order and to raise revenues. In the early twentieth century, however, when "progress" and "promotion of native welfare" became watchwords for the new Ethical era, the government could no longer afford to tolerate police corruption, and police reform became a major political issue of the day. In 1904 Assistant Resident L.R. Priester was commissioned by the government for a study of police reform in Java's three major urban centers of Batavia, Semarang and Surabaya, and experimented his reform in Semarang to create a police organization led by a professional chief commissioner of police who was autonomous of the administrative officials in its everyday operation.

Two years later, W. Boekhoudt was commissioned for a study of police reform in Java and Madura outside the three major urban centers. Not surprisingly, his major concern was the "penetration" of underworld networks of *guru weri* ("spy master," adept of magical lore) and their disciples into local administrative and police officials. He therefore argued in his 1907 report for the centralization, institutional autonomy and professional leadership of police under the chief commissioner of police and the retention of administrative police under the resident, while suggesting the surveillance of rural supra village underworld figures from *guru weri* and hermits down to gold and silver smiths, heads of dancing girl groups, brothel owners and so on.[9]

The first major police reorganization was introduced in 1911 on the basis of these studies. The most important in this reform was the organization of city police (*stadspolitie*) in Batavia, Semarang and Surabaya, led by professional police officers. The Batavia city police force was 600 men strong, while the Semarang and Surabaya police forces combined were 675 men strong. City police were organized in several other municipalities—Medan, Bandung, Yogyakarta, Surakarta, Malang, and Makassar—in 1914.

In the 1910 plan the government also decided to appoint a second advocate general for police leadership under the attorney general and an

---

[9] W. Boekhoudt, *Rapport Reorganisatie van het Politiewezen op Java en Madoera (Uitgezonderd de Vostenlanden, de Particuliere Landerijen en de Hoofdplaatsen Batavia, Semarang en Soerabaja), 1906–07* (Batavia: Landsdrukkerij, 1908), 6–9 and 18–19. For succinct explanation of Priester's and Boekhoudt's studies, see Dekker, *De Politie*, 47–54.

inspector of police for police management under the director of internal administration to strengthen the central police leadership. But the budget for these measures was not approved by the Dutch parliament, making it a major issue for police reform in the 1910s.[10]

In 1912, armed police forces, *gewapende politie*, were established out of the remaining *pradjoerit* (soldier) and other local para-military police units. One division each was given to a region (*gewest*, i.e., residency) and each platoon-size detachment to a division (*afdeeling*, i.e., regency/kabupaten). Each division was commanded by a captain seconded from the colonial army and the entire armed police was placed under the department of internal administration. Its force strength, initially 5,000, reached 10,000 men in a few years.[11] The police school was opened in 1914 for training police commissioners and inspectors to mark the completion of police reform planned in the 1910s.[12]

By the time the police reorganization was completed in 1914, however, its shortcomings had become apparent to the Indies government and the ministry of colonies in The Hague. One can see why it had if one recalls its timing. All the studies on which the reform was based were carried out in the 1900s, the last major study being Boekhoudt's, which was completed in 1907. This means that the reform had not anticipated the rise of the movement as represented in the early 1910s by Sarekat Islam which started in early 1912 and whose expansion like "flood" in 1912–14 was accompanied in many places by street fighting, disturbances, boycotts, beatings, killings, "improper" attitude toward government officials, and other acts of "undermining" state authorities.

Boekhoudt wrote in 1907 that "the national feeling seems not to exist with the Javanese, at least it is fast asleep." In his view, disturbances among Javanese derived from "Pan-Islamism" and/or "fanaticism for the restoration of a Javanese kingdom," but they were local and did

---

[10] Dekker, *De Politie*, 55–60; Neijtzell de Wilde, "De Nederlandsch-Indische Politie," 124–5. In 1911 the force strength of the entire police in Java and Madura (i.e., city, professional, and administrative police combined) was about 11,000 men. Neijtzell de Wilde, "De Nederlandsch-Indische Politie," 125.

[11] A. Hoorweg, "Gewapende Politie," in *Vereeniging van Hoogere Politie-Ambtenaren 1916–1936: Jubileum-Nummer van de Nederlandsch-Indische Politiegids bij Gelegenheid van het 20 Jarig Bestaan van de Vereeniging* (Batavia: n.p., 1936), 41–4.

[12] "De Opleidingsschool van het Personeel der Politie," in *Vereeniging van Hoogere Politie-Ambtenaren, 1916–1936*, 49–50.

not constitute a threat to the state. *Ratu adil* (just king) movements, which could be easily dealt with by the police court as holding meetings without permission, did not have any deep political significance. More worrisome was Pan-Islamism, especially international networks of *tarekat* (sufi order) spanning over Java, Singapore, and Mecca.[13] It does not mean that Pan-Islamism worried him about subversion of the authority by an internal enemy, he wrote, but he feared for the life of officials and private citizens in the interior who would have to rely on their own until the arrival of the military force from the nearby regional capital to quell the revolt.[14] Boekhoudt argued for the need of better armed police and political police to alert administrative officials of potential troubles in their localities.[15] The reorganized police in the early 1910s could adequately handle problems he had anticipated.

The problem the SI presented to the government, however, was different. It was not because it was subversive, as Governor General Alexander Willem Frederik Idenburg well understood, even though many Dutch and native administrative officials in the field believed it was. But it was national, not local, in scope. It did not come from Pan-Islamism and/or *ratu adilism*, but was built on Malay language newspapers and rallies and led by journalists-turned-movement-leaders. Besides Idenburg did not want to destroy the SI. He understood it as a sign of native awakening and as Advisor for Native and Arabic Affairs D.A. Rinkes put it, he wanted to guide it "onto the path we hope or at least not objectionable to our authority."[16] The government had to deal with the SI differently from the way in which it dealt with native disturbances that derived from Pan-Islamism and fanaticism for the restoration of a Javanese kingdom.

To understand the thinking of senior government officials in the Indies and The Hague about police reform in the mid-1910s, it is useful to examine what P.H. Fromberg Sr. wrote about it. Former member of the supreme court and foremost expert on modern Chinese popular movement in the Indies, Fromberg was consulted by the minister of

---

[13] Boekhoudt, *Rapport Reorganisatie*, 3–5. See also Bloembergen, *De Geschiedenis van de Politie in Nederlands-Indie*, 47–51, for the fear of "white haji."

[14] Boekhoudt, *Rapport Reorganisatie*, 5.

[15] Ibid., 5.

[16] Shiraishi, *An Age in Motion*, 69. For the government policy on the SI in its early days, see 68–9.

colonies about "who should lead the Indies police?" He addressed the question in light of the rise of modern popular politics in the Indies in 1915.

In his view, there was no legal ambiguity about the central leadership of the attorney general in the matter of policing. The problem was that he was not in a position institutionally to exert his leadership. The adviser for native and Arabic affairs, he said, was playing an important role in the policy making to the popular movement in Java. The adviser had an enormous knowledge about religious trends and native languages, kept good relations with prominent people in the native society, attended SI rallies and conferences, and read native newspapers. No doubt his reports should be valuable for the attorney general to evaluate the situation. Fromberg reminded the minister, however, that the adviser belonged to the department of education and religion and that his reports did not reach the attorney general regularly. It also was the case with the adviser for Chinese affairs, he said. His reports should be important for the attorney general to evaluate the Chinese situation in the Indies in the wake of the revolution in China in 1911, but they did not regularly reach their destination because they were submitted to the governor general through the director of internal administration and bypassed the attorney general. As a result, Fromberg argued, the attorney general was left without important information about "natives, Indos [Indo-Europeans], anti-government Muslims, Chinese boycott organizations, rival Chinese *kongsi* [by which he meant secret societies], ethnic rivalries, etc.," and knew little more than was reported in Dutch language newspapers. This was the reason in his view that the attorney general could not provide any central leadership when for instance applying the regulation of associations and assemblies on the SI. In the early days of the SI, each local chief took his own measures without consulting the attorney general. This was the source for confusion. One resident banned even the smallest SI meeting, while another resident let the SI hold rallies and meetings more liberally. So too was the confusion in the government handling of Chinese "agitation" in the wake of the revolution. The resident of Surabaya gave permission to the Chinese to hoist the Chinese national flag after he consulted with the attorney general, while the resident of Batavia banned it after he talked with the governor general.[17]

---

[17] P.H. Fromberg Sr., "Nota-Fromberg," in Dekker, *De Politie*, 62–4.

Fromberg concluded that "there is practically no chief of police in the Netherlands Indies." But there should be a central leadership for providing the general guidelines and instructions for policing and for maintaining general supervision over the entire police, because "rebellious movements, racial conflicts, boycott organizations etc., are not normally confined to a municipality, a division or a region." The same argument can be made, he added, for policing counterfeit money, piracy, and sugar cane burning. There should be no confusion on the part of the government in the regulation of associations and assemblies, processions and demonstrations, theaters and films and so on.[18] He stated thus:

> He [attorney general] should get to know the reports of the adviser for native affairs, of the officials for Chinese affairs, of the inspectors of the opium monopoly as regards smugglings, political reports and communications of the residents as far as they have to do with security police [*veiligheidspolitie*], crime statistics as needed for the supervision of district and village policing ... Police authorities (chief commissioners, residents, and assistant residents) should be required to put [regulations they issue] on record and send [their written reports] to the attorney general if they affect general police regulations, for instance, regulations concerning the curbing of cattle theft, sugar cane burning....[19]

It was not until late 1919, however, that Governor General van Limburg Stirum decided to take measures initially on an emergency basis to make the attorney general's office a functioning central police leadership. The reason was perhaps straightforward. Van Limburg Stirum had created a central political intelligence agency, the Politieke Inlichtingendienst (PID), in May 1916 in view of the war in Europe. Its task was to place foreigners and socialists under surveillance and to investigate revolutionary trends in the Indies. It was a small operation headed by W. Muurling, former captain of the general staff of the Indies army with one officer each stationed in Batavia, Semarang and Surabaya. But it reported directly to the governor general and had regular access to the reports the adviser for native affairs, the adviser for Chinese affairs,

---

[18] Ibid., 67.
[19] Ibid., 75. Also see Nijtzell de Wilde, "De Nederlandsch-Indische Politie," 151.

the residents and city police chiefs sent to Buitenzorg. Van Limburg Stirum could rely on the PID for directing the police. With the end of the War, however, there was no longer any official justification for its continuation. Muurling himself recommended its disbandment in November 1918. In April 1919 it was formally dissolved, and its functions were transferred to the military intelligence.[20]

But the internal security situation, seen from the government perspective, started to deteriorate precisely in these months. There was a massive anti-Chinese riot in late 1918 in Kudus, a major center of kretek cigarette production in Central Java, led by Muslim producers and traders.[21] The movement also started to revive in late 1918, for the first time since the heady days of the early SI in 1912 and 1913. Its radical wing, represented by the Insulinde and the "red" Semarang SI, expanded its influence. A series of peasant strikes took place in the Surakartan countryside, led by Haji Misbach and local Insulinde activists. Strike actions also mounted in Central and East Java, especially among sugar factory workers who joined the Sugar Factory Workers' Union, PFB (Personeel Fabriek Bond), led by Yogyakartan CSI leader Soerjopranoto. In Toli-Toli, Central Sulawesi, a Dutch controller was killed in June 1919 when he visited the area to enforce corvee duties, after Abdoel Moeis, loyalist CSI leader, made a propaganda tour there and unwittingly sparked popular enthusiasm for the movement.[22]

More important was the incident that took place in West Java in July 1919. In Garut, Hadji Hasan and his family who resisted forced rice delivery were shot to death by armed police led by the assistant resident. Investigating the shooting, the local authorities "unearthed" the existence of a secret SI organization, SI Afdeeling (branch) B, with "subversive" purposes. In a symbolic way, the Afdeeling B affair exposed the contradiction inherent in the Ethical Policy. Its basic idea was that

---

[20] For the PID, see R.C. Kwantes, *De Ontwikkeling van de Nationalistische Beweging in Nederlandsch-Indie: Eerste Stuk 1917–medio 1923* (Groningen: H.D. Tjeenk Willink, 1975), 134; Theodore Friend, *The Blue-Eyed Enemy: Japan against the West in Java and Luzon, 1942–1945* (Princeton: Princeton University Press, 1988), 35; Mr. 209x/1919, Vb. 10-7-19 No. 45.

[21] For the riot in Kudus, see Lance Castles, *Religion, Politics and Economic Behavior in Java: The Kudus Cigarette Industry* (New Haven: Southeast Asia Studies, Yale University, 1967).

[22] For the movement in 1919, see Shiraishi, *An Age in Motion*, chaps. 3 and 4.

the natives could be guided onto the path of progress under Dutch tutelage. It was this idea on which was built the government policy to the movement as shown in Governor General Idenburg's recognition of the legal status of the SI in 1913. But the Afdeeling B affair demonstrated, so it was argued by conservatives, that Dutch tutelage was a fantasy of liberals and that the hidden mysterious and wild forces in the native society had found new outlets to exert themselves in the movement. This deeply worried the government. All of Java's residents were instructed to investigate the existence of SI Afdeeling B in their own regions. Dutch newspapers in the Indies went hysterical about native conspiracies.[23]

Immediately after the Afdeeling B affair, Advocate General H.V. Monsanto warned the governor general of the movement's "decay," its "getting wild (*verwildering*)," and suggested that a central investigation bureau attached to the attorney general's office and supported by a regional intelligence network should be created to assume the functions the PID had performed in the war years. "Many factual materials are there," he argued, "scattered all over the government bureaus and regional and local chiefs' offices, but they need to be pieced out, brought together, sorted out, and ordered from the policing point of view ... in order to know with more certainty than [we do] now how extensive a revolutionary drive of various associations has become, what influence this [revolutionary drive] has over the population, ... what dangers of excesses threaten the country, people, and ultimately the authority."[24]

The governor general announced in his opening address to the Volksraad on September 1, 1919, that "where the movement exceeds the bounds it will bite iron."[25] In the same month, he decided on organizing field police, *veldpolitie*, to deal with "local excesses" and creating a general investigation service, *algemeene recherchedienst*, attached to the attorney general's office. As he informed S.J. Hirsch, the chairman of

---

[23] Ibid., 113–14. Also see William A. Oates, "The Afdeeling B: An Indonesian Case study," *Journal of Southeast Asian History* 9, no. 1 (March 1968): 107–16; Elsbeth Locher-Scholten, "State Violence and the Police in Colonial Indonesia circa 1920: Exploration of a Theme," in *Roots of Violence in Indonesia*, ed. Freek Colombijn and J. Thomas Lindblad, 81–104 (Singapore: Institute of Southeast Asian Studies, 2002).

[24] Kwantes, *De Ontwikkeling, 1917–medio 1923*, 133.

[25] "Redevoering van zijne Excellentie den Gouverneur Generaal bij gelegenheid van het openbaar gehoor op 1 September 1919," *De Indische Gids* 41 (1919): 1438–9.

the powerful sugar syndicate, the first task of the ARD was to investigate the Afdeeling B affair.[26]

With this decision, the political policing apparatus was born. In the center the attorney general was there to lead and supervise the entire police, while the director of internal administration, assisted by the inspectors of general police (*algemeene politie*) and armed police (*gewapende politie*), was made responsible for the central management of police. In the regions, regional police chiefs—chief commissioner of police in Batavia, Semarang, and Surabaya; adjunct chief commissioner of police in Medan, Bandung, Yogyakarta, and Surakarta; and commissioner of police first class in the rest of the colony—were made responsible for the leadership and management of general police, which included city police with its investigation branch (*stadsrecherche*), field police with its embryonic regional investigation service (*gewestelijke recherche*), administrative police with its local investigation service (*plaatselijke recherche*), and village police (*desapolitie*).[27]

Mechanics of Political Policing

The ARD was established by the government decree of September 24, 1919, with A.E. van der Lely, commissioner of police first class, as its chief and with the budget of f.4,680. Its office was located at Waterlooplein Oost No. 1. Van der Lely, who had served as commissioner of police first class in the Batavia city police from 1915 to 1919, moved to the attorney general's office in late November 1919, though he was formally appointed the ARD chief on December 27. His day-to-day task was "to gather, order, sort out and link" "the almost constantly arriving

[26] First government secretary to chairman of the general syndicate of sugar factories in the Netherlands Indies, March 5, 1920, in Kwantes, *De Ontwikkeling, 1917–medio 1923*, 214. It should be noted that police reform was suspended during the war and that all the strikes, riots, and disturbances in the immediate postwar months served as another compelling reason for the reform. As Bloembergen reminds us, Governor General van Limburg Stirum had complained about the paucity of information about the native world in a few months after his arrival in Batavia in 1916. Neijtzell de Wilde presented the postwar police reform plan which A. Hoorweg formulated to the Volksraad on July 21–22, 1991, on behalf of the government. Bloembergen, *De Geschiedenis van de Politie*, 171–2, 181, 186–97.
[27] See the organizational chart included in Neijtzell de Wilde, "De Nederlandsch-Indische Politie"; Dekker, *De Politie*, 179 and 191.

stream of official reports and records as well as the daily news reports" and "to give instructions and order investigations with reference to the information."[28] To assist his work, two more officers were appointed in July 1920: Mohamad Jatim, previously with the political intelligence section of the Batavia city police, as native officer with the rank of wedana and B.R. van der Most, previously with the Semarang city police as commissioner of police second class, as deputy chief, though his appointment was not formally announced until February 1925.[29]

Along with the ARD, a new post of the second advocate general for police was created with A. Neijtzell de Wilde, who served as a leading expert in police reorganization and previously with the attorney general's office (since July 1916), as its first incumbent. The advocate general for police was responsible for the daily supervision of the ARD, but the ARD chief reported directly to the attorney general.

Attorney General G.W. Uhlenbeck informed the heads of regional administration of the creation of the ARD and its task in his secret circular dated April 16, 1920, where he assured the residents that it was not meant to form a second body for the local police leadership or to change the daily police practice. He continued:

> But there should be a center informed of the trends and symptoms in the Indies society.... The task of the general leader of police should be to make the local leaders of police follow the governmental principles known to him, to test the regulations proposed or taken by the local police authorities not only and exclusively out of utility considerations but also in terms of legal provisions, and thus to exercise control over the local leaders of police [to ascertain that] the police not run the risk of going astray of the legal framework. The task of the central leadership is to provide general [guide]lines.

This power was now vested in the attorney general, he said, and the advocate general for police and the ARD were to assist him in exercising the central leadership in policing. He then went on to describe the mechanics:

---

[28] PG to GG, March 20, 1920, Mr. 520x/20.

[29] Uittreksel uit het Register der Besluiten van den Gouverneur Generaal van Nederlandsch-Indie, Buitenzorg, May 15, 1920, No. 2x, Mr. 520x/20. Mohamad Jatim was promoted to the rank of patih in August 1927. Van der Most served most likely as chief of political intelligence, Semarang city police, from July 1919 to July 1920.

(a) In the three urban centers in Java [Batavia, Semarang, and Sura-
baya] and in several other places there now exists a city investigation service on a more modern basis. Elsewhere investigation
personnel are now very much being strengthened. We now intend,
starting with Java and Madura, to attach to the heads of regional
administration who are and remain responsible for the daily exercise of police [power] in their area a technical leader of police
(one leader for two residencies for the moment) with the rank of
at least commissioner of police first class, who aside from taking
care of the training of police personnel and good cooperation between various police units in the designated domains, must be
responsible for an effective division and work of the investigation
over the regions concerned.

Finally [the technical leader of police] should [be responsible]
for giving more support in their investigation to the intelligence
[units of administrative police] which for now must remain in
the hands of the European and native administration, and where
necessary and feasible should establish a regional investigation
depot [*gewestelijke recherchedepot*] to provide assistance in the
region wherever local investigation [units] are insufficient for [the
investigation of] certain cases.

(b) The regional investigation service … must report to the central
leadership of police [i.e., attorney general] information it obtains
which may be of interest to him; It [ARD] has as its special task
to gather, order, and sort out what the regional and local investigation [services] track down and what is reported to it by the
local service as interesting for the general leader and furthermore
to draw attention of the general leader of police to that which can
be useful as information for the regional investigation. The ARD
therefore forms an integral part of the central police exercise
without which a good general leadership would not be possible.[30]

It should be clear from this circular what institutional shape the political policing apparatus was about to take. In the center, there was the
attorney general, the central leader of the police, assisted by the advocate
general for police and the ARD. The task of the ARD was to gather,
piece together, order, and sort out constant streams of information sent
by the regional investigation service and alert the attorney general of

---

[30] Parket van den Procureur Generaal, Rondschrijven aan de Hoofden van Gewestelijke
Bestuur, Weltevreden, April 16, 1920, Mr. 503x/20.

problems he should look into and directives and information he should give to the regional investigation service. The *hoofdparket* was the name given to this unit.

In major cities, which included not only Batavia, Semarang, and Surabaya, but also Medan, Padang, Palembang, Bandung, Yogyakarta, Surakarta, Malang, Makassar, and several others by 1920, there were city police, led by a chief commissioner of police, adjunct chief commissioner of police, or commissioner of police first class. The city police consisted usually of four branches: secretariat or general affairs; investigation with a photographic and dactylographic studio and a police library; general control over street patrol, uniform, firearms, book-keeping, and treasury; and traffic police. Each branch was headed by a commissioner of police first class.[31]

The investigation branch, also called city investigation service in contrast to regional investigation service or central investigation service to distinguish it from the ARD, consisted of several sections, each headed by a commissioner of police second class or police *wedana*: general administrative affairs, responsible for gathering and processing criminal data, keeping registers and dossiers, compiling statistics, managing special intelligence archives, and storing information on persons and cases not under investigation; criminal investigation; moral police in charge of prostitution, trade in women, coolie recruitment, gambling, exploitation of children and women, hotel control, and others; Chinese affairs; surveillance of immigrants and foreigners; opium police; photographic and dactylographic studio; and most importantly, political investigation or intelligence (*politieke recherche* or *politieke inlichtingen*). Sub-sections were normally headed by police assistant wedana or police mantri.[32]

The political intelligence, so called officially after 1926, initially formed a section in the investigation branch, but after 1926–27, a branch in itself, often combined with the policing of immigrants and foreigners and in close communication with the Chinese affairs section. Its task, even defined in general terms, was very extensive. It was responsible for control over the exercise of the right of association and assembly; surveillance of meetings (*vergaderingen*); registration and reporting on meetings (*bijeenkomsten*); handling the request to hold a rally open to

---

[31] Dekker, *De Politie*, 197–9.

[32] Ibid., 203–5 and 211–2; Neijtzell de Wilde, "De Nederlandsch-Indische Politie," 126.

the public; reporting on rallies and associations; alerting the resident and the *hoofdparket* of an association which is in conflict with the public order; investigation of secret associations (associations without legal status of incorporation); investigation and recommendation for externment and internment; surveillance over the press; issuance of press cards; surveillance over the import of dangerous printed material and other propaganda means; immigration and emigration; surveillance over stations, hotels, ports, and other public places; control over weapons trade.[33]

The relationship of the city investigation service with the regional and the local investigation service differed from one region to another. In one residency, it was headed by its own chief under the chief of city police and separate from the regional investigation service attached to field police and local investigation units of administrative police. In another it was combined with the investigation units of administrative police to form a central investigation service. And in yet another residency the central investigation service was combined with the regional investigation depot and was led directly by the city police chief who also acted as technical leader of field police.[34]

The organization of the regional investigation service was more complicated. It consisted of the local (*plaatselijk*, i.e., regency, district, and sub-district) investigation units nestled in administrative police, the investigation units attached to field police detachments, and the regional investigation depot led directly by the technical leader of field police. The most important, however, was the regional investigation depot, which according to Neijtzell de Wilde, the first advocate general for police, was created to serve as the backbone of the regional political policing and to assist the work of field and administrative police.[35]

Field police started to be organized in 1919. Its initial force strength in 1923 was 3,000 field police agents, with 780 horses, 2,500 bicycles, and 420 motorcycles, but it expanded to about 10,000 men in a few years. Each unit, called a detachment or brigade, was on average 30 men strong; they were led by a posthouse commandant or group chief, and stationed in 90 barracks all over the Indies.[36]

---

[33] For the whole list of the task of the political intelligence section, see Dekker, *De Politie*, 205–6.
[34] Ibid., 206.
[35] Neijtzell de Wilde, "De Nederlandsch-Indische Politie," 129.
[36] Ibid., 227. Hoorweg, "Gewapende Politie," 44–6. Neijtzell de Wilde, "De Nederlandsch-Indische Politie," 133.

Field police agents were recruited from outside the region but from the same linguistic area. Two hundred inspectors and 60 chief agents were recruited from the Netherlands, while many others were recruited from among non-commissioned officers and soldiers of the former German colonial army in Kianchow. Nine army officers were appointed commissioners of police first class to act as regional leaders. In Java, field police were placed under the technical leader responsible for two residencies and where there were city police, its chief doubled as technical leader.[37]

A small intelligence branch was attached to each field police detachment. It was staffed by one or two police *mantri* and several agents, who worked in close communication with local investigation units under European and native administrative officials and the regional investigation depot under the field police technical leader.[38]

The regional investigation service was responsible both for criminal investigation and political policing. After the PKI emerged as the leading force in the movement, more emphasis was placed on political policing at the attorney general's direction. The regional investigation depot was expanded, and its agents were sent to local investigation units to lead their activities.[39] This shift was so complete, future Batavia police chief P. Dekker wrote in retrospect, that the regional investigation service became synonymous with the political intelligence service by the mid-1920s.[40]

The expansion of general police (city, field, and administrative police combined, but excluding village and armed police) is seen in the tables that follow.

---

[37] "De Opleidingsschool" and "De Veldpolitie," both in *Vereeniging van Hoogere Politie-Ambtenaren 1916–1936*, 51, 60. The chief commissioner of police in Batavia, Bandung, Semarang, and Surabaya acted as technical leaders for the field police units in Batavia and Banten, Priangan, Semarang, and Surabaya and Madura respectively; the adjunct chief commissioner of police/commissioner of police first class of Yogyakarta, Surakarta, Madiun, Kediri, and Malang served simultaneously as technical leaders of field police for Yogyakarta, Surakarta, Madiun, Kediri, Pasuruan and Besuki.

[38] Neijtzell de Wilde, "De Nederlandsch-Indische Politie," 129.

[39] Cornelis Gijsbert Eliza De Jong, *De Organisatie der Politie in Nederlandsch-Indie. Proefschrift ter verkrijging van den graad van doctor in de rechtsgeleerdheid aan de Rijksuniversiteit te Leiden* (Leiden: "Luctor et Emergo," 1933), 46.

[40] Dekker, *De Politie*, 230. See also Neijtzell de Wilde, "De Nederlandsch-Indische Politie," 134, 159; "De Veldpolitie," in *Vereeniging van Hoogere Politie-Ambtenaren, 1916–1936*, 60.

Table 1: General Police, ranks

	1921	1925	1928
Europeans	362	1,092	1,346
Commissioners	28	86	110
Inspectors	130	443	611
Chief Agents	194	526	574
Chief Detectives	10	37	51
Natives	18,341	25,704	31,644
Police Wedana	–	5	8
Police Assistant Wedana	2	29	54
Police Mantris	859	1,198	1,495
Posthouse Commandants	72	524	1,353
Detectives	111	720	1,668
Police Agents	17,657	23,223	27,018
Total	18,703	26,796	32,990

Table 2: General Police, regional distribution

	1921	1925	1928
Java and Madura Total	14,226	20,824	22,148
Batavia**	1,438	3,079	5,960
Priangan	1,294	1,406	–
Pekalongan	1,052	1,284	1,349
Semarang	1,782	2,752	2,678
Surabaya-Bojonegoro	1,334	2,475	2,657
Kediri	999	1,480	1,575
Pasuruan (Malang)	1,333	1,588	1,838
Yogyakarta*	208	533	788
Surakarta*	264	628	792
Sumatra's West Coast	554	579	1,432
East Coast of Sumatra	608	661	2,206
The Rest of Outer Isl.	3,315	4,732	7,204
Total	18,703	26,796	32,990

Notes: * The police forces of Kasultanan, Pakualaman, Mangkunegaran, and Kasunanan are not included in the statistics.
** Batavia for 1921 and 1925 includes Buitenzorg and Kwawang; Batavia for 1928 signifies the entire West Java.

Source: Calculated from: *Handelingen Volksraad, 1920, Begrooting 1921, Stuk O, Afdeeling IV, 5*, pp. 2–3; *Handelingen Volksraad, 1924, Begrooting 1925, Stuk O, Afd. IV, 6*, pp. 2–3, and *Afd. IV, 7*, pp. 2–3; *Handelingen Volksraad, 1927, Begrooting 1928, Afdeeling IV, Stuk 13*, pp. 1–3.

Government statistics do not tell us how many police officers were in charge of political policing. But it is safe to assume that the majority of native police officers in the ranks of *wedana*, assistant *wedana*, police *mantri*, and detectives, as well as a substantial number of police agents were in political policing. (In the principalities of Surakarta and Yogyakarta, where general police forces as shown in the table consisted solely of the city and regional investigation service and the field police units, almost half of police agents were with the investigation service.) As more than six-fold expansion of native detectives from 1921 to 1925 illustrates, the political policing apparatus was no doubt significantly beefed up in these years. Indeed, if we take police *wedana*, assistant *wedana*, *mantri* and detectives as the core of the political policing apparatus, its strength, 1,952 men in 1925, was substantially larger than the core of the PKI the attorney general deemed imperative to intern in Digul in 1927.

Regional distribution showed heavy concentration of police forces in Java, especially urban centers of Batavia, Bandung, Semarang and Surabaya and sugar plantation regions of Pekalongan, Kediri and Pasuruan (Malang). (Police strength in Surakarta and Yogyakarta were not pronounced, because principality police forces were not included in the statistics. If they were included, their force strength should be on a par with Priangan/Bandung).

Growing up with the Indonesian Communist Party

After the creation of the political policing apparatus in the early 1920s, the *hoofdparket*, the attorney general's office with the ARD as its core, soon emerged as the dominant player in native policy making and remained so until the end of the Dutch era. One main loser of this development was the office for native and Arabic affairs. In the first two decades of the twentieth century, it was the most important office for native policy making, but in the 1920s it was reduced into such insignificance that the question was raised in the highest circle of the government in the early 1930s whether to replace it with two new agencies, a bureau for political affairs under the director of internal administration and a bureau for Mohammedan religious affairs under the director of education and religion. Part of the reason for this shift was organizational. While the office for native and Arabic affairs was small without any regional outfit, the *hoofdparket* was supported by the Indies-wide infrastructure which passed on to it the constant streams of reports and records the city and regional political policing apparatus sent. But the shift signified more than the way the government gathered intelligence on the movement, for it was accompanied with an important change in the way in which it saw native politics. To see this point, we need to examine the ARD in comparison with the office for native affairs, above all their different modes of operations, expertise, mentalities, and fantasies.

The office for native and Arabic Affairs was established in 1899 with Dutch Islamologist Dr. Christiaan Snouck Hurgronje as its first adviser (in office 1899–1906), and was subsequently headed by Dr. G.A.J. Hazeu (1907–13, 1917–20), Dr. D.A. Rinkes (1914–16), E. Gobee (1927–37), and Dr. G.F. Pijper (1937–42), all trained in Indology with good Arabic and native languages.[41] In 1933, Director of Education and Religion B.J.O. Schrieke, who had served as deputy adviser for native affairs in 1917–20, put the question this way: This office served as government adviser for native and Arabic affairs in a time "when the native world was still silent" and it was important to "fathom the deeper currents" among natives. In the beginning of this century arose the movement, which broke the silence in the native world. Native political associations came up, and with them a native press. Their opinions were remarkably different from those in earlier times: "the more good-natured forms

---

[41] For Christiaan Snouck Hurgronje, see Michael Francis Laffan, *Islamic Nationhood and Colonial Indonesia: the Umma below the Winds* (London: Routledge Curzon, 2003). Laffan says that Snouck Hurgronje was consulted about the appointment of both the adviser for native affairs and the placement of consular staff in Jeddah, Cairo and Singapore (ibid., 95). No adviser was appointed from 1920 to 1926, when the office was run by deputy adviser, R.A. Kern (1921–22, 1924–26) and E. Gobee (1923). G.A.J. Hazeu (b. 1870) who obtained a doctorate at Leiden University in 1897 was an expert on Javanese language and culture. H. Aqib Suminto, *Politik Islam Hindia Belanda: Het Kantoor voor Inlandsche Zaken* (Batavia: LP3ES, 1985), 125; G.W.J. Drewes, "Balai Pustaka and its Antecedents," in *Papers on Indonesian Languages and Literature*, ed. Nigel Phillips and Khaidir Anwar (London: Indonesian Etymological Project, SOAS, University of London, 1981), 101. See also Doris Jedamski, "Balai Pustaka: A Colonial Wolf in Sheep's Clothing," *Archipel*, no. 44 (1992): 23–46. D.A. Rinkes (b. 1878) obtained a doctorate at Leiden in 1906 and served as deputy adviser for native affairs from 1911 to 1913 and head of Balai Poetaka (Pustaka) from 1917 to 1927. R.A. Kern (b. 1875) studied Indology in Delft in 1893–95 and later became a lecturer of Sundanese at Leiden in 1927–42. E. Gobee (b. 1881) studied Indology at Leiden in 1906–08 and Arabic in 1915 and served as consul in Jeddah from 1917 to 1921. G.F. Pijper (b. 1893) obtained a doctorate in Arabic and Islamology in 1924. Suminto, *Politik Islam*, 132, 128, 141, 147.

in the past gave way to more or less extremist forms of opinions"
such as "communism, extreme nationalism, and non-cooperation."
Under these circumstances, other government organs have come to pay
attention to the spiritual trends of the native society. The political intelligence service was established during the war, whose function is now
transferred to the [hoofd]parket, while the post of government representative for general affairs to the Volksraad was created, along with the
government representative for the police, to handle the general political
situation in the Volksraad. The heads of regional administration, responsible for peace and order in their regions, keep themselves and their
subordinates informed of the trends in the native world. The question
may therefore arise whether there still exists a need for yet another body,
in this case the office for native affairs.[42]

As Schrieke points out, the office for native and Arabic Affairs was
created before the rise of the movement, when in Boekhoudt's words,
"the national feeling seems not to exist with the Javanese, at least it is
fast asleep." This does not mean that the native world was calm and that
there were no disturbances, riots, and revolts. The question, rather, was
how to make sense of the natives, their mentalities, their thinking, and
their society, for there was a deep sense of mystery among the Dutch
about natives, Chinese, and Arabs in the Indies at the turn of the twentieth century.[43]

In the early twentieth century, however, any threat to the order
seemed to come, as Boekhoudt said, from "Pan-Islamism" and "fanaticism for the restoration of a Javanese kingdom." This perception of
threat informed the establishment of the office for native and Arabic
affairs. Its founder, Christiaan Snouck Hurgronje, argued that "most of
kyai, ulama, and haj were otherworldly, most of whom desired nothing
better than to serve Allah in peace, but fanatical ulama dedicated to the
notions of Pan-Islam had to be watched. The enemy was not Islam as a
religion, but Islam as a political doctrine, both in the shape of agitation
by local fanatics and in the shape of Pan-Islam, whether or not it was
in fact inspired by Islamic rulers abroad, such as the Caliph." The office
was responsible for "fathoming the deeper currents" among natives
and watching local and international subversive networks of Muslim

---

[42] Director of education and religion to GG, Oct. 28, 1933, in Kwantes, *De Ontwikkeling, Aug. 1933–1942*, 95–6.
[43] See, for instance, Louis Couperus, *De Stille Kracht* (1900; reprint L.J. Veen, 1989).

fanatics—religious scholars and teachers (*kyai* and *ulama*), religious schools, sufi order (*tarekat*) leaders, haj, Indies Arabs, and the Kampung Jawi in Mecca.[44] The target to watch thus defined, it was natural that those who ran the office as advisers and deputy advisers were trained in Islamology and Indology, had expert knowledge of Islam and Indies natives, had good Arabic and local native languages, and maintained good relations with prominent members of the native and Indies Arab communities.

Its expertise, however, also led to its eventual marginalization, for once the movement arose and government agencies other than the office for native affairs started to watch the native world, it soon became clear that Pan-Islam was a bogey, that there was no international Islamic conspiracy, and that disturbances, revolts, and rebellions derived not from Pan-Islamism but from something else. In his defense for the office for native affairs, Schrieke therefore stressed not Islam but a unique contribution the office had made to the government: The officials of the internal administration can only be local-oriented, the *hoofdparket* mainly see the native society with a limited objective, and it is the task for the office for native affairs to provide the overall picture, maintaining both official and more personal relationships with those who occupy prominent places in the political and religious fields in the native society and obtaining information from those the internal administration and the intelligence service can hardly have access to. "The adviser for native affairs is the trusted man from the early days, to whom the more prominent members of the native society expressed [their] feelings and opinions (also criticisms of the government policy), who normally keep silence to other officials."[45]

Schrieke did not say that the adviser for native affairs as the "trusted man" for the native society had long been suspect because of the radicalization of the movement. To see why, we only need to recall one major development in the movement in the early 1920s, what Schrieke calls the rise of "more or less extremist forms" of opinions such as "communism, extreme nationalism, and non-cooperation."

---

[44] Harry J. Benda, *The Crescent and the Rising Sun: Indonesian Islam under the Japanese Occupation, 1942–1945* (The Hague: W. van Hoeve, 1958), 23–4. See also Suminto, *Politik Islam*, 52–8, 64–70, 78–97, 99. For the haj scare toward the end of the nineteenth century, see Bloembergen, *De Geschiedenis van de Politie*, 22–4.

[45] Director of education and religion to GG, Oct. 28, 1933, in Kwantes, *De Ontwikkeling: Aug. 1933–1942*, 96–7.

As Advocate General Monsanto wrote to the governor general in proposing the creation of the ARD, the movement then was showing signs of "decay" and "getting wild" in its radicalization, if seen from the government perspective. Interestingly, however, he did not, and perhaps could not, theorize on the "decay," because although the Islamic bogey was gone, a new communist bogey had not arrived yet on the scene. The situation, however, changed soon in his favor. In less than half a year after the creation of the ARD, the ISDV was transformed into the Perserikatan Kommunist di India (PKI), League of Communists in the Indies, with Semaoen as chairman in May 1920. The SI split, which started to spread from the central leadership to local SIs in October 1920, became definite with the CSI congress in Madiun in February 1923 and the PKI congress in Bandung and Sukabumi in early March 1923. By early 1924, the PKI and red SIs affiliated with it had emerged triumphant in their contest with the non-communist CSI for the leadership of the movement. This development made the office for native affairs far less useful that it used to for the government, because its officials simply did not have any access to the PKI and red SIs/SRs.

The expansion of the regional investigation apparatus, as we have seen, took place in response to this development. Equally important, the political policing apparatus found in the PKI and red SIs/SRs its first enemy. Police officers from the ARD down to local investigation units developed their expertise while policing the PKI and red SIs/SRs. They did not need to have expert knowledge in Indology, Islamology, and native languages. Most of local police agents were natives anyway, normally operating in the areas of their own origin, relied on spies and informers for intelligence gathering, and accumulated knowledge about local party figures and organizations: identities and personalities of local leaders and activists, their places of residence and possible hideouts, their aliases, their relatives and friends, their meeting places, couriers, identities and places of their sympathizers, and so on so forth.

These myriads of information were constantly fed into the *hoofdparket.* In order to piece out, sort out, order, link, and make sense of these disparate and often contradictory information, the ARD under van der Lely needed a "theoretical" framework. Thanks to the rise of the PKI, the ARD found it in the fantastic international communist conspiracy. It saw Moscow's hands everywhere behind the scenes, understood often poorly coordinated and sometimes purely individual, anarchistic terrorist actions as part of a grand communist plan directed by the Comintern. It thus developed its own expertise for policing domestic and international communist networks: identities and aliases of leading PKI members in the regions and abroad, of those in communication with the Comintern, their possible travel routes, their hideouts, their meeting, staying, and eating places in Singapore, Penang, and the Netherlands, their contacts, their secret codes, secret directives the party central committee sent to the branches, their secret mail addresses, identities of couriers between the party headquarters and branches, spies and informers with access to the party leadership.[46]

In short, the ARD created its own *topographie* and *biographie*, if we use the terms the founding father of modern secret police, Joseph Fouche, coined.[47] Nothing demonstrates the steady accumulation of political policing expertise more graphically than the increase in the number of fingerprint slips and identifications (i.e., photographs) stored in general police. The number of fingerprint slips increased from 19,077 in 1924, 24,605 in 1925, 29,467 in 1926, to 36,862 in 1927, while the number of identifications (photographs) grew from 1,469 in 1924, 2,402 in 1925, 3,030 in 1926, to 3,710 in 1927.[48]

---

[46] See, for instance, how two police agents from Semarang in August 1926 penetrated PKI networks in Singapore. They went straight to the food stall at Arab Street No. 131 where communist fugitives from West Sumatra frequented. Introducing themselves as PKI fugitives from Yogyakarta, they were easily accepted as such and in a few weeks one was made responsible for receiving and sending off communist representatives from Java to a meeting place in Batu Pahat, while the other became secretary of the Sarekat Dagang Indonesia, Indonesia Commercial Union, established by West Sumatran communists without Tan Malaka's knowledge and in support of Alimin and Musso. They could operate as spies until they inadvertently met with Soebakat, who also came from Semarang and knew their identities. See Geheim Rapport, Pinang, Sept. 9, 1926; Sept. 13, 1926; and Sept. 30, 1926, all in Mr. 971x/26.
[47] Eric A. Arnold, Jr., *Fouche, Napoleon, and the General Police* (Washington, DC: University Press of America, 1979), 154.
[48] Centraal Kantoor voor de Statistiek in Nederlandsch-Indie, *Statistisch Jaaroverzicht van Nederlandsch-Indie: Jaargang 1925* (Weltevreden: Landsdrukkerij, 1926), 172; *Jaargang 1926* (Weltevreden: Landsdrukkerij, 1927), 174; and *Jaargang 1927* (Weltevreden: Landsdrukkerij, 1928), 207. Note, however, how small-scale it was in comparison with the American operation in the Philippines. See for example Alfred W. McCoy, *Policing America's Empire: The United States, the Philippines, and the Rise of the Surveillance State* (Madison: University of Wisconsin Press, 2009). John Ingleson reminds us that the size of the ARD database pales in comparison with the database the Sugar Syndicate, which maintained files on about 160,000 workers in 1929. One wonders whether the ARD shared information on its files with the Sugar Syndicate and other private employer organizations, either systematically or on a case-by-case basis. Personal communication with John Ingleson, July 1, 2019.

This history shaped the tradition of political policing in the Indies —its expertise and the way it saw the movement.[49] With the rise of revolutionary nationalism the ARD would be forced to change its way of seeing the movement, and it was the moment as we will see when the government started to undergo a major shift in its native policy. For now, however, it is important to remember that its founding fathers, men such as van der Lely and van der Most, were convinced of the importance of their work and entertained quiet pride about their achievement. Van der Lely wrote after his retirement in the Netherlands:

> Having played a role behind the scenes, naturally I cannot go into detail over my ten-year experience as Chief of the General Investigation Service and over nature and priorities of the "finer" detective work the police there has to perform. It will suffice, therefore, to underline that because foreign influences on the currents in the Far East are very remarkable, but mainly underground, the significance of that "finer" detective work should not be underestimated in any means. The modern police perform this task in a capable way....[50]

The New Regime of Order

The political policing apparatus was thus very much in place when the revolts took place in late 1926 and early 1927. There was no break in its evolution with the revolts, even though the government was caught by surprise by the revolts.[51] It only developed along the logic inherent in its original design: more control and leadership of the *hoofdparket* over the regional investigation service; streamlining the communications between the ARD and the regional investigation service; regularization and expansion of the regional investigation service; more control and leadership of the regional investigation service over the local investigation units; deeper penetration of the local investigation units into the village

---

[49] The ARD's focus on communism was shared by its sister agencies in the Netherlands. See Constant Willem Hijzen, "The Perpetual Adversary: How Dutch Security Services Perceived Communism (1918–1989)," *Historical Social Research* 38, no. 1 (2013): 166–99.

[50] A.E. van der Lely, "Handhaving der openbare rust, orde en veiligheid," in *De Nederlandsch-Indische Politiegids* (June 1932): 191–3, originally published in *Rijkseenheid* in January 1932. Italics are original.

[51] See McVey, *The Rise of Indonesian Communism*, 323–46; Bloembergen, *De Geschiedenis van de Politie*, 255–60.

sphere. Two points deserve consideration. One is organizational, which is discussed below. The other, which concerns its political effects, will be addressed in the following chapters.

Let us start with the *hoofdparket*. Whether there took place revolts or not, attorney generals and advocate generals changed regularly. In 1926 to 1942, seven officials served as attorney general: D.G. Wolterbeek Muller (in office 1922–26); H.G.P. Duijfjes (1926–28); J.K. Onnen (1928–29); R.J.M. Verheijen (1929–34); G. Vonk (1934–38); H. Marcella (1938–40); A.S. Block (1940–42). In contrast the ARD had only two chiefs, deputy chiefs, and chief native officers in its entire history: A.E. van der Lely (1919–29) and B.R. van der Most (1929–42) as ARD chief; van der Most (1920–29) and H.J.A. Vermijs (1929–42) as deputy; and Mohamad Jatim (1920–35) and Raden Hermansaid (1935–42) as chief native officer.[52] The ARD was run in the post-revolt years by those who had personal memories about the revolts. It was suffused with the mentality, "it should never happen again," and its vigilance against the movement, whether communist or nationalist, going "wild."

In the provinces, the city and regional investigation apparatuses were beefed up. In the countryside, investigation cores (*recherche kernen*, also called special intelligence service), that had been established as regional investigation depots in the early 1920s, were expanded in the regions of West Java, Pekalongan, Semarang, Kedu-Banyumas, Yogya-karta, Surakarta, Madiun, Surabaya-Bojonegoro, Pasuruan (Malang), and Sumatra's West and East Coast. Smaller investigation cores were established in Kediri, Besuki, Tapanuli, Palembang, Jambi, Benkulen, Lampung, Bangka, Riau, the Moluccas, and two regions of Borneo. The police school also started a new course for the training of political intelligence staff.[53] As Tables 1 and 2 show, the force strength of general police increased from 26,796 in 1925 to 32,990 in 1928, while the number of detectives was expanded from 720 to 1,668 in the same period.

---

[52] See *Regeeringsalmanak*, 1919–41. In the regions, the continuity of intelligence personnel is less pronounced. The political intelligence branch of the Batavia city police had four native chiefs: Mohamad Jatim (1920–22), Naipin (1923–29), Mas Rangga Soetandoko (1929–40) and Mas Moehammad Jasin Partadiredja (1940–42). Bandung and Semarang had three each and Surabaya four. But the political intelligence of the Surakartan police was run by one chief, R. Ramelan, throughout its entire history.

[53] *Mededeelingen der Regeering omtrent enkele onderwerpen van algemeen belang (Mei 1928)*, (Weltevreden: Landsdrukkerij, 1928), 2–3. See also PG to GG, Jan. 10, 1927, Mr. 66x/1927.

This expansion of the political policing apparatus took place in 1927. The governor general instructed the attorney general to present his recommendations for the reform of political policing on December 7, 1926. Attorney General Duyfjes in turn sent a secret circular to the heads of regional administration on December 29, 1926 with the instruction to report on the organizational structure of political policing in their respective regions, the number and ranks of intelligence personnel, and their reform plans. In the same circular Duyfjes also ordered the residents to instruct their subordinate administrative and police officers to report directly to the *hoofdparket*, cutting short the administrative hierarchy, on anything that might seem of more than local significance by telegraph and, if possible, by telephone.[54]

Another important development, logical in light of the PKI's international connections and the presence of communist leaders and fugitives abroad, especially in British Malaya, was international police cooperation of the Indies government and the British Straits Settlements government. Informal police cooperation started in July 1926, when the British authorities in Singapore agreed to allow two police agents sent by the ARD to spy on Indies communists in British Malaya. Pretending to be communist fugitives from Yogyakarta, they successfully penetrated into local networks of communists from West Sumatra and reported back to the ARD, before their identities were exposed by Soebakat in September, about the schism which was developing between Tan Malaka, Soebakat, and Djamaloedin Tamin on the one hand and the PKI central committee led by Sardjono and Boedisoetjitro as regards its plan for revoltion and the visit of Alimin and Moesso to Moscow.[55] The existence of "a propaganda center" of Indies communists in Singapore confirmed, the attorney general suggested to establish an intelligence unit to watch their activities in Singapore.[56] Negotiations took time, however, and it was only after the revolts in West Java that the Straits Settlements police chief gave the Dutch deputy consul general "a strictly personal and confidential report":

---

[54] First government secretary to PG, Dec. 7, 1926, Mr. 1225x/1926; PG to heads of regional administration, Rondschrijven-Spoed-Geheim, Dec. 29, 1927 and PG to GG, Jan. 10, 1927, both in Mr. 66x/1927.

[55] See Geheim Rapport, Sept. 13, 1926, Mr. 971x/1926; Geheim Rapport, Sept. 30, 1926, Mr. 1031x/1926.

[56] First government secretary to deputy consul general of the Netherlands in Singapore, Oct. 25, 1926, Mr. 1031x/1926.

Our policy at the present moment is to prevent any known Javanese communist from landing in Malaya. Unfortunately, ... we are only able to recognize two or three leaders, so that if the blockade is to be made effective it would be necessary for the Government of the Netherlands East Indies to send over unofficially at least two men, one for Singapore and one for Penang, who could board vessels coming from Java and Sumatra, etc., and warn the police of the presence of extremist leaders or well-known communists.[57]

M. Visbeen, assistant commissioner of police at the Batavia city police, was sent to Singapore with two native detectives in early December. He established a close working relationship with Harold Fairburn, the inspector general of the Straits Settlements police, and Rene Onraet, the chief of its criminal investigation department (future special branch). The high point, and ultimate failure, of Visbeen's investigation work in Singapore was the arrest of Alimin and Moesso and their subsequent banishment from British Malaya in December 1926. Visbeen was back to Batavia by July 1927, but important personal connections had been established by then and in the subsequent years he emerged as the expert on Indies communists abroad.[58]

On the more formal level, the Indies government first recognized the need for international police cooperation in late 1924 and asked British India and French Indochina for intelligence exchange on "the colonial propaganda of the Soviet government" in January 1925. The French did not respond, but the negotiations between the Indies government and the British Indian government eventually resulted in an agreement in February 1927 on direct intelligence exchange between the ARD chief and the director of the intelligence bureau of British India.[59]

---

[57] Deputy consul general to GG, Singapore, Nov. 25, 1926, Mr. 12x/1927. See also Deputy consul general to GG, Singapore, Nov. 22, 1926, Mr. 12x/1927.
[58] For Visbeen's activities in Singapore, see Mr. 811x/1927, 902x/1927, and 1104x/1927.
[59] See PG to GG, July 15, 1926, Mr. 754x/1926; Deputy first government secretary to PG, Aug. 3, 1926, Mr. 754x/1926; Viceroy and Governor General of India to Governor General of the Dutch East Indies, Simla, Sept. 26, 1925, Mr. 70x/27; Viceroy and Governor General of India to Governor General of the Dutch East Indies, Delhi, Dec. 28, 1926, Mr. 70x/27; PG to GG, Feb. 24, 1927, Mr. 380x/1927. See also Anne L. Foster, *Projections of Power: The United States and Europe in Colonial Southeast Asia, 1919–1941* (Durham, NC: Duke University Press, 2010), especially chap. 1; Nobuto Yamamoto, "Teikoku Seiji kara Kokusai Seiji he: 1920-nen dai Tonan Ajia ni okeru Chiiki Kokusai sistemu no tankan," *Hogaku Kenkyu* 86, no. 7 (2013): 67–92.

This arrangement, however, turned out to be unsatisfactory, because intelligence exchange did not take place regularly.[60] When Governor of the Straits Settlements Sir Cecil Clementi visited Batavia in August 1930, Governor General de Graeff again raised and discussed with the British governor "the question of a closer and more direct and more systematical cooperation between our governments with the aim of controlling and preventing communist agitation." They reached an agreement.[61] Advocate General for police G. Vonk visited Singapore in October 1930 and worked out an arrangement with the Straits Settlements police for the "systematic" exchange of:

> a. photographs and descriptions of suspected agitators; b. communist manifestos, posters, and handbills, if needed in photographic reproduction; c. copies of important reports and sentences concerning communist agitation and of important communist correspondence in photographic reproduction; d. information about plans for extremist action in our mutual territories, the latter should be given with all possible diligence.[62]

It was also agreed that this exchange take place directly between the *hoofdparket* and the inspector general of police in Singapore as regards communist activities and between the adviser for Chinese affairs and the Straits Settlements secretary for Chinese affairs as regards matters pertaining to the Chinese.

Vonk was euphoric when he returned to Batavia. In his report to the governor general, he wrote that he received for examination "a great number of bundles [of documents] and reports" about "the political policing trends in the Malay peninsula." With Soekarno's PNI obviously in mind, Vonk also found useful "several issues of very secret reports of the British Indian intelligence bureau" to understand the kind of political policing problems "a preponderantly nationalistic rebellious movement" can pose. But his main interest lay in international communism, in the

---

[60] See Kwantes, *De Ontwikkeling, 1928–Aug. 1933*, 486.

[61] GG to Governor of the Straits Settlements, Sept. 16, 1930, in Kwantes, *De Ontwikkeling, 1928–Aug. 1933*, 486.

[62] GG to Governor of the Straits Settlements, Sept. 16, 1930, in Kwantes, *De Ontwikkeling, 1928–Aug. 1933*, 486–7. See also Uittreksel uit het Register der Besluiten van den Gouverneur Generaal van Nederlandsch-Indie, Sept. 26, 1930, Mr. 936x/1930; First government secretary to PG, Oct. 23, 1930, Mr. 1035x/1930.

activities of "Semaoen, Darsono, Alimin, Tan Malaka, Moeso [Moesso], and others" and he was euphoric because Fairburn, Singaporean police chief, sounded positive to his request for "the British authorities in Singapore to ask their police organizations elsewhere to cooperate for the promotion of this specifically Netherlands Indies interest."[63]

We will see in the following chapters why Vonk was so interested in the activities of Indies communists abroad. What needs to be noted for now is that the British government in Singapore had its own need for intelligence exchange. In British Malaya, the Straits Settlements Police Criminal Intelligence Department (CID-SS, reorganized into and renamed Special Branch in 1933) had been in place since 1918 to deal with political affairs, but it was not until after "a Chinese communist-led riot in Singapore" in March 1927 that the government became serious about communist activities and beefed up its police organization, in the words of CID chief Onraet, with "better pay, better buildings, more equipment, a training depot worthy of a force over four thousand strong, sufficient money for secret service, expansion of certain departments, and undivided authority for the police in certain Chinese activities hitherto partly controlled by other Government departments."[64] In British Malaya, however, communists were mainly Chinese, and as Tan Malaka rightly predicted in 1925, Malays were only marginally involved

---

[63] Rapport advocaat-generaal over besprekingen met engelse autoriteiten te Singapore van 10–17 okt. 1930, Oct. 18, 1930, in Kwantes, *De Ontwikkeling, 1928–Aug. 1933*, 487–8.

[64] Rene H. Onraet, *Singapore: A Police Background* (London: Dorothy Crisp, 1947), 96–7. While the ARD was a culmination of years of police modernization and professionalization, the CID-SS was led from the beginning by professional police officers. Its first chief, V.G. Savi, who spoke Malay, Fukien, Hindustani, and Punjabi, was one of the first "schoolboys," graduates of police cadet service for Hong Kong and Malaya established in 1903. Onraet, also a schoolboy who obtained an intensive language training in Amoy, was the second CID-SS chief and as such worked closely with Visbeen in hunting Indies communist fugitives in the early years of formal and informal Anglo-Dutch police cooperation. The Special Branch had 25 officers in 1935 and 43 in 1936, and consisted of five sections responsible for communist, Japanese, security, political (i.e., non-communist political activities), and alien affairs. For the history of secret police in British Malaya, see also Alun Jones, "Internal Security in British Malaya, 1915–1935" (PhD diss., Yale University, 1970). See also Ban Kah Choon, *Absent History: The Untold Story of Special Branch Operations in Singapore 1915–1942* (Singapore: Raffles, 2001).

in the communist movement.[65] This was the reason the adviser for Chinese affairs and the Straits Settlements secretary for Chinese affairs were brought into intelligence exchange. But there is no question the *hoofdparket* benefitted a great deal from the reorganization and expansion of the British Malayan political intelligence apparatus as we will see in the destruction of the Pari's Singaporean base in 1932.

Politics of Political Policing

We have now arrived at a point to consider the general nature of the political policing in the Indies, the kind of politics that the political policing brought forth in the post-revolt years. Let us dwell on one question, its effect on its client, the Indies government, for now, while examining another question, its political effect on the native society, in the following chapters.

The political policing had its own way of watching the population which not only shaped popular politics as we will see, but also shaped the way in which the government saw the native society. To see this point, we only need to look at a few paragraphs randomly taken from the ARD's monthly political policing survey, *politieke-politioneel overzicht*.[66] The ARD started to compile the survey in March 1927, in the wake of the revolts, with very limited circulation. It was sent to the governor general, select department chiefs, the heads of regional administration (32 in total), the minister of colonies, and Dutch diplomatic representatives

---

[65] See Cheah Boon Kheng, *From PKI to the Comintern, 1924–1941: The Apprenticeship of the Malayan Communist Party: Selected Documents and Discussion Compiled and Edited with Introductions* (Ithaca, NY: Southeast Asia Program, Cornell University, 1992), 50–1.

[66] Harry A. Poeze, ed., *Politiek-Politioneele Overzichten van Nederlandsch-Indie, deel I, 1927–1928* (The Hague: Martinus Nijhoff, 1982); *Politiek-Politioneele Overzichten van Nederlandsch-Indie, deel II, 1929–1930* (Holland and USA: Foris Publications, 1983); *Politiek-Politioneele Overzichten van Nederlandsch-Indie, deel III, 1931–1934* (Dordrecht, Holland and Providence: Foris Publications, 1988); *Politiek-Politioneele Overzichten van Nederlandsch-Indie, deel IV, 1935–1941* (Leiden: KITLV Uitgeverij, 1994). It should be acknowledged that Harry A. Poeze has done a great service to Indonesian studies by editing the four volumes. See also Harry A. Poeze, "Political Intelligence in the Netherlands Indies," in Robert Cribb, ed., *The Late Colonial State in Indonesia: Political and Economic Foundations of the Netherlands Indies, 1880–1942* (Leiden: KITLV Press, 1994), 229–45.

in Peking, Tokyo, Bangkok, Washington, Cairo, Singapore, Shanghai, Hong Kong, Calcutta, Manila, Sydney, Saigon, and Jedda.[67]

The survey consists of five sections: extremist movement, the national and Islamic movement, Chinese movement, trade union movement, and abroad. Let us look at the December 1927 survey for an example. The sixth and ninth paragraphs in the first section, "Extremist Movement" run as follows:

> In Kisaran (East Coast of Sumatra) arose a new association, Moehammadijah, which calls for communism but has nothing to do with the organization with the same name located in Java. At a rally held on November 17, a certain H. Saleh, who carried on a campaign in 1925 in Bengkulen [Bengkulu], explained how the people were oppressed by the government. It was decided after that [meeting] to establish an organization which is reportedly denoted with the initials A.W. (whose meaning is not known so far) with the purpose of recruiting "brani [brave]" members secretly. The association is said to have a substructure [onderbouw] with the name of Djamatoerhamah.
>
> In the village of Tjipanokolan (in the regency of Bandung), there reportedly exists a PKI branch under the leadership of a certain Iskak, which is said to have 50 members already. In the Tasikmadoe plantation (in Surakarta) there exists an association called Soerjo Moeljo, which reportedly wants to buy firearms to offer resistance to the authority and to kill police officers. The leader, called Irosemito, is under arrest.[68]

No longish analysis will be needed. The paragraphs tell us very little. The first paragraph tells us that a rally was held in Kisaran on November 17 and that a man called Haji Saleh gave a speech. We can be reasonably sure this much took place, but nothing more. The second paragraph tells us even less. We may be sure, perhaps, that there was an association called Soerjo Moerjo in the Tasikmadu plantation and that a man called Irosemito was under arrest. But this can be expected of any intelligence report. More important is the way in which the terrain was watched. It is clear there is only one thing that matters in the report. Whether factually correct or not, there seems to be a danger out there, in Kisaran, in a village near Bandung, and in the Tasikmadu plantation in Surakarta,

---

[67] Poeze, *Politiek-Politioneele Overzichten, 1927–1928*, vii–viii.
[68] Ibid., 188.

that there might be subversives there. Irosemito was already under arrest. H. Saleh and Iskak might also be picked out soon. If not, H. Saleh's file would become thicker and a new file would be created for Iskak.

What is missing is the sociological and cultural terrain in which those people lived. Try to imagine Kisaran, a small provincial town in Asahan, a four-hour drive even now from Medan, in the middle of rubber plantations and thick forest, back in the late 1920s. Try to visualize a man called Haji Saleh, addressing the audience at a meeting one fine day in November. We do not know where the meeting was held—at a mosque, in a religious school, or a town square?—what he said, who came to the meeting, let alone who he was, what he did in everyday life, what was his upbringing and so on. But these things did not matter, because the ARD was watching out for subversives, threats to the state, of whatever persuasion and color. The terrain was rendered flat, where a man called Haji Saleh stood alone as a subversive.

Let us also take a look at a few paragraphs from the section, the National and Islamic Movement. In November 1927, a new national united front, the PPPKI (Permoefakatan Perhimpoenan-Perhimpoenan Politiek Kebangsaan Indonesia, Association of Political Organizations of the Indonesian People), was in the making, which naturally drew a lot of attention of the ARD.

> In this report month the federation of political-national-native parties was officially founded, the foundation of which was laid at the recent P.S.I. [Partij Sarekat Islam] congress ...
>
> At the initiative of Dr. Soekiman it was decided to publish its own national newspaper, for which a committee was established— according to Sin Po [a Chinese Malay newspaper published in Batavia]—with Parada Harahap and Mr. Sartono as its members. The advisory committee consists of Mr. Iskaq Tjokrohadisoerjo, chairman, Dr. Samsi Sastrowidagdo, secretary-treasurer and Dr. Soekiman and Ir. Soekarno, commissioners.
>
> With the establishment of this federation the influence of the (extreme-national[ist]) intellectuals, who are the promoters of this movement (see the September survey), has made a step forward and the plans to attain an *anti-imperialist (national-religious) bloc* discussed in chapter 4 of the secret political note on the PKI and the July survey will become a bit clearer.[69]

---

[69] Ibid., 189–90.

Here we are perhaps on a firmer ground factually. There is no reason to doubt factual data reported in the paragraphs, not only because they can be cross-checked with newspaper reports but also because we know the ARD was intensely interested in the PPPKI and the young "intellectuals" as mentioned in these paragraphs and that the ARD was obsessed with facts in its own way. Yet all the same, these men and their actions are read in a special political policing perspective, where what matters boils down on a set of practical questions—whether the *hoofdparket* should intervene in the PPPKI and if yes when and at what timing, whether the *hoofdparket* should arrest these men, if yes when and for what reasons, and whether the *hoofdparket* should intervene in the publication of the PPPKI organ and if yes when and at what timing.

The ARD was watching out for subversives. It was as if only subversives and potential subversives inhabited the terrain under its surveillance, because the ARD only saw them and no one and nothing else. The ARD thus provided the government with the map which told the government where to hit and who to eliminate as a threat to peace and order, and equally important the government would eventually shape the terrain in light of the map the ARD was to produce for the purpose of the political policing of the Indies.

Long after the empire was gone, P.J.A. Idenburg, son of ethical Governor General A.F.W. Idenburg, who served as secretary of the Council of the Netherlands Indies (1926–34), wrote an article, "The Dutch Answer on the Indonesian Nationalism," which inspired Harry J. Benda to understand the Indies state as a *beamtenstaat* in his essay, "The Pattern of Administrative Reforms in the Closing Years of Dutch Rule in Indonesia."[70] After explaining how thorough the PID intelligence work was and how its monthly and quarterly reports were distributed by the *hoofdparket*, Idenburg wrote thus in this article:

One is hard pressed to assess what influence such an intelligence reporting, sound in itself, must have had on the policy of regional and

---

[70] P.J.A. Idenburg, "Het Nederlandse Antwoord op het Indonesisch Nationalisme," in *Balans van Beleid: Terugblik op de Laatste Halve Eeuw van Nederlandsch-Indie*, H. Baudet and I.J. Brugmans (Assen: van Gorcum, 1961), 144–5. See also Harry J. Benda, "The Pattern of Administrative Reforms in the Closing Years of Dutch Rule in Indonesia," *Journal of Asian Studies* 25, no. 4 (1966): 589–605; C. Fasseur, "Nederland en het Indonesische nationalism: de balans nog eens opgemaakt," *Bijdragen en medeelingen betreffende de geschiedenis der Nederlanden* 99, no. 1 (1984): 21–44.

local government officials. After all, there was no regular political
information [coming] from the government, which [could] serve as
the policy guidelines for the administrative heads ... Those who followed this intelligence reporting cannot but recall with appreciation
the soundness with which the data were processed and the sobriety of
explanation it provided ... Nonetheless the police could not get out
of its own skin: the considerations naturally came from a thought
world, which was typically police, and when one compares this steady
stream of considerations and reports with what the government representative for general affairs stated about the government policy in the
Volksraad, one could also say that the police intelligence reporting
did not—and also could not—make good the real policy of the
governor general.[71]

This is an important insight. The government was as much a hostage of
its own political policing as the Indies population, for without any other
intelligence reporting, the *hoofdparket* with its monthly and quarterly
reports provided the governor general and his senior officials, both in the
center and the provinces and residencies, with the only map that guided
their native policy making.

---

[71] Idenburg, "Het Nederlandse Antwoord," 149.

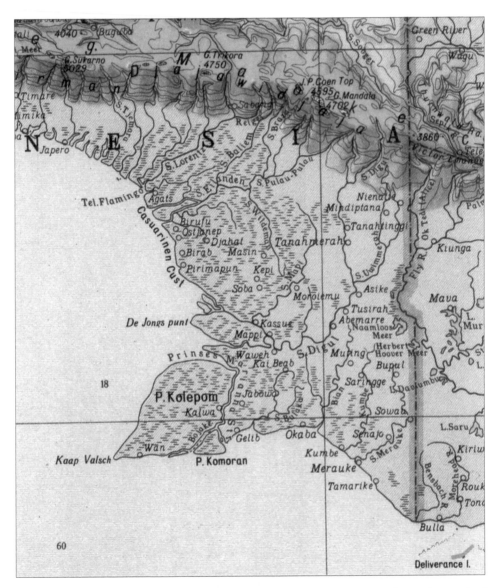

1. The Digul River, with Tanah Merah and Tanah Tinggi both shown, from plate 335 of *The Atlas of the World,* 2nd Edition. Moscow: Chief Administration of Geodesy and Cartography under the Council of Ministers of the USSR, 1967.

2. Two boats on the Digul River, c.1928. The *kapal putih* is the government ship *Fomalhout*, c.1928. KITLV 153813, CC-BY license.

3. The internment camp at Tanah Merah, shortly after its initial construction in 1927–28. From a photo album labelled J.J. Duyverman, 8 December 1930, KITLV 55463.

4. The military encampment at Tanah Merah, built between the designated areas for internees and staff. Photo by H. Witkamp, 1938, KITLV 25929, CC-BY license.

5. Louis Johan Alexander Schoonheyt on the front porch of the doctor's house in the internment camp in Tanah Merah, with a political internee as a houseboy (rear) and two Papuans (front). KITLV 19021, CC-BY license.

6. Children at the school of the Digul internment camp, January 1929. It was typical for soldiers to bring their families with them, even on such remote postings. KITLV 153787, CC-BY license.

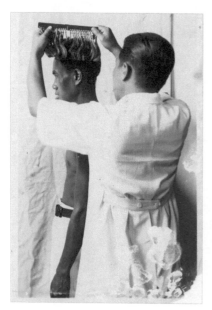

7. The Wilhelmina Hospital at the Tanah Merah camp conducted physical anthropological studies of inmates, this photo from *Boven-Digoel: het land van communisten en kannibalen* (Amsterdam: G. Kolff & Co., 1940), written by the former camp doctor, L.J.A. Schoonheyt. KITLV 19036, CC-BY license.

8. The Tanah Tinggi camp for the recalcitrant, the Digul within Digul, 40 kilometers and 5 hours by motorboat upriver from Tanah Merah. From a photo album labelled J.J. Duyverman, 8 December 1930,

9. Tanah Tinggi internees, around 1929. Aside from the regular food rations the government provided, detainees in Tanah Tinggi were left largely to themselves. KITLV 153792.

CHAPTER 3

Policing the Phantom Underground

When the communist revolts took place, the government's reaction was swift and drastic. On November 17, five days after the revolt started in West Java on November 12, 1926, the governor general decided to place "the dangerous communist leaders" in preventive custody for the interest of the public safety.[1] The next day, the Council of the Netherlands Indies decided to intern "the principal communist leaders on a large scale." In early December, the government decided not to seek the Indies Supreme Court to declare the Indonesian communist party illegal. Whether legally banned or not, the party had gone underground, and its activities had been "camouflaged in all sorts of smaller associations with apparently innocent purposes." Declaring the PKI illegal, it reasoned, was pointless.[2] And finally, On December 30, 1926, the attorney general instructed the regional chiefs "to discern timely the significance and the threatening influence of new propagandists and to choose the right moment to render them harmless in the same way as their predecessors." If not, he wrote, this policy of "eliminating the dangerous core of the movement" by mass arrest and internment would lose its effectiveness.[3]

---

[1] Verslag bg. vergadering van de raad van Nederlandsch-Indie, Nov. 18, 1926, in R.C. Kwantes, ed., *De Ontwikkeling van de Nationalistische Beweging in Nederlandsch-Indie, Bronnenpublikatie 2e Stuk Medio 1923–1928* (Groningen: Wolters-Noordhoff, 1978), 476.

[2] For the internal debate on this question, see PG to GG, Dec. 2, 1926 and Director of Justice to GG, Dec. 10, 1926, both in Kwantes, *De Ontwikkeling, 2e Stuk Medio 1923–1928*, 494–508.

[3] PG to heads of regional administration, Kwantes, *De Ontwikkeling, 2e Stuk Medio 1923–1928*, 520–1.

The policy adopted in late 1926 to combat communism was thus one of political expediency. The government took administrative and police measures to wipe out communist party cadres and not to allow the party to exist any longer. In connection with the revolts, 13,000 persons were arrested. A few of them were shot for their involvement in killings; 4,500 were sentenced to prison after trial; 1,308 were sent to Digul.[4] As the attorney general wrote to the chiefs of regional administration on July 30, 1927, "practically speaking the PKI is thus a banned association: there is nothing to speak of any more about an open action of the communists in connection with this association and wherever [there is an attempt to revive] the movement by propaganda among the population, sale of membership cards, etc., ... it can be put to an end by arresting the agitators, followed by a proposal for internment, if a criminal prosecution does not seem possible." This was the policy, and the attorney general reminded the regional chiefs, "this government standpoint should be impressed on the consciousness of the population."[5]

The question of how "this government standpoint" was to "be impressed on the consciousness of the population" was not specified by the attorney general because it was self-evident: arrest, imprisonment, and internment. More problematic was the question of what the government standpoint was. In the short term, it was clear: the government would not tolerate the PKI and its affiliated organizations and trade unions such as the SR and the VSTP (railway workers' union). The government's actions in 1927 and 1928 further impressed this position on the popular mind. The Soediro's Sarekat Rakjat, the PKI section in Pematang Siantar, East Sumatra, and the Trisnoadiasmoro's Centralisatie Indonesia in Surabaya were destroyed one after another in 1927. Numerous arrests and house searches were carried out in 1927 and 1928 in connection with local, isolated, largely individualistic attempts to revive SRs and other "communist," "magico-religious," "terrorist," or "criminal" organizations such as Djadjar, Sarekat Item, and Korban Diri.[6]

In the longer term, however, the government standpoint was not as clear-cut, because once the PKI and its affiliated associations and

[4] Ruth T. McVey, *The Rise of Indonesian Communism* (Ithaca, NY: Cornell University Press, 1965), 353.

[5] PG to heads of regional administration, July 30, 1927, Mr. 945x/1927.

[6] Harry A. Poeze, "Inleiding," in Poeze, *Politiek-Politioneele Overzichten, 1927–1928* (The Hague: Martinus Nijhoff, 1982), lxviii–lxix.

unions were destroyed, there were no longer any organizational foci for governmental policy. The enemy became diffuse, hidden, and no longer easily identifiable. This problem was further complicated by Governor General De Graeff's liberal policy of constructive engagement with Indonesian nationalists, a policy that was combined with tough measures of repression against "underground destructive action." (To see this point, one only needs to ask what the government standpoint might have been if former PKI and SR activists had established a party or a trade union with an explicitly non-communist, nationalist cause or if non-communist nationalists cooperated with international organizations under communist influence.) How did the government police the movement? How did the government remind Indonesians that there were limits beyond which they had to risk internment to Digul?

Lessons of the Revolts

One important task that ARD chief A.E. van der Lely performed in the busy days in late 1926 and early 1927 while directing the entire PID apparatus to destroy the PKI was to write a "detailed and pragmatic [*zakelijk*]" report on "the PKI organization and its ramifications" to "give a clear picture of the politically dangerous character of this association and its leaders," as instructed by the governor general on November 24, 1926.[7] As it turned out, van der Lely wrote three different versions of this report over several months. The first version, a rough draft written in haste, was submitted to de Graeff on November 27, and on the basis of this report the attorney general argued for "an extensive application of the extraordinary powers upon the core [of the party], the principal leaders working behind the scenes, to prevent a repeat of recent events."[8]

The second version, fatter and much better organized, but still retaining the basic argument of the first, was compiled in early January 1927 and submitted to the governor general on January 11. It had a long title: "Political Note concerning the Indonesian Communist Party: Report wherein is a Summary of Information that has Come to Light

---

[7] Kwantes, *De Ontwikkeling, medio 1923–1928*, 525–6. The governor general also established two committees, one to study the situation in Banten in January 1926 and the other to investigate the situation in West Sumatra in February 1927. But their more regionally focused reports are of less relevance for our discussion.

[8] PG to GG, Nov. 27, 1927, Mr. 1174x/1926.

Concerning the Actions of the Partij Komunist Indonesia (Netherlands Indies Communist Party), a Section of the Third International, from July 1925 Up to and Including December 1926." De Graeff liked it and instructed the attorney general to make 150 copies for internal use; he commended van der Lely for his work, which "gives such a clear insight into the general situation and shows that the complaints repeatedly raised these days about the inadequate functioning of the central political intelligence are generally unfounded."[9]

The third and final version, similarly titled to the second but fatter still, with some chapters substantially expanded and four new chapters added, was submitted to the governor general in April 1927. It was also printed for internal use, but this version served a different political purpose. As the immediate crisis was over, van der Lely looked to the future in this third version and spelled out his political policing strategy against communism.[10]

As the second version is available in English thanks to Harry J. Benda and Ruth T. McVey, it will suffice to only briefly summarize van der Lely's thesis on the communist revolts.[11] In a nutshell, his thesis was that local actions were part of an international communist conspiracy. He opened his second and third report with this paragraph:

> The action carried out by the Communist leaders in the period from July 1925 to the end of December 1926 may chiefly be regarded as in rigid compliance with the resolutions adopted at the fifth world congress of the Communist International in Moscow ([in] mid-1924) and at the Djogjakarta [Yogyakarta] conference of Communists ([in] December 1924).[12]

Having thus stated his basic position, van der Lely developed his thesis this way:

1. The Comintern (Communist International) decided at its fifth congress on reorganization of the parties by means of the cell

---

[9] Kwantes, *De Ontwikkeling, medio 1923–1928*, 466–7.
[10] Geheim Rapport, Waarin Is Samengevat Wat Gebleken Is omtrent de Actie der Partij Kommunist Indonesia (Nederlandsch-Indische Kommunistische Partij), Sectie der 3de Internationale, vanaf Juli 1925 tot en met December 1926, Mr. 497x/1927.
[11] Harry J. Benda and Ruth T. McVey, eds., *The Communist Uprisings of 1926–1927 in Indonesia; Key Documents* (Ithaca, NY: Southeast Asia Program, Cornell University, 1960).
[12] Ibid., 1; Geheim Rapport, Mr. 497x/1927.

system (in trade unions, political organizations, factories, workshops, villages, native residential quarters [kampungs], etc.) and Bolshevization of the parties.

2a. In compliance with this decision, the PKI decided at the Yogyakarta conference, and instructed its sections in the first half of 1925, to organize criminals in the illegal groups and to carry out propaganda by means of cells and closed meetings and cadre training courses.

2b. In the second half of 1925, the propaganda was carried out mainly in trade unions. "This activity was first and foremost a logical consequence of the decisions taken at the Pan-Pacific Labor Conference held in Canton [in June 1924]." After they met in Yogyakarta and Surabaya in December 1924, the PKI leaders decided to expand trade union activities, intensified propaganda in the unions under their control, and established new unions such as sugar workers' union, dockworkers' and seamen's union, and machine-shop workers' union. Surabaya was made the center of communist trade union activities with the establishment of Indonesian Red Trade Union Secretariat [Secretariaat Vakbonden Merah Indonesia] as a section of the Pan-Pacific Trade Union Secretariat in Canton. This propaganda drive led to the outbreak of numerous strikes in 1925.

2c. The PKI leadership also decided at the Yogyakarta conference to establish a secret propaganda center in Singapore, again in line with the Comintern decision to create a combined bureau of the Comintern and the Red International of Trade Unions [Profintern] there.

2d. The organization of criminals into anti-ruffian leagues [anti-riboet bonds] proceeded in the meantime, leading to disturbances such as strikes, riots, arsons, murders, and other terrorist actions. The DO, Double or Dictatorial Organization, was also organized without doubt linked with an order probably emanating from the PKI executive in the middle of [1925].

3a. The communist leaders in the Indies and in the Straits had an undeniable hand in the course of events leading to the revolts. This was demonstrated by the fact that at their meeting in Surakarta [Prambanan] in December 1925 they decided in expectation of financial aid from Moscow to provoke disturbances (revolution) which were to begin in Padang and to spread to Java. This decision was opposed by leaders abroad, above all Tan Malaka who argued that making a revolution did not depend on the acquisition of money but on the strength of the people, which was insufficient, and which had to be created by means of mass action, an uninterrupted series of strikes, demonstrations, and so on. But their difference lay in the timing of a revolution, and both were fundamentally in agreement about strikes, riots, and revolution.

3b. The PKI largely succeeded in strengthening its disciplined core after the Yogyakarta conference as demonstrated by the fact that the PKI expanded from 36 sections with the total membership of 1,140 in December 1924 to 65 sections in May 1926.

3c. In the East, unlike in the West, a small group of well-disciplined and well-organized communists can create [enough] discontent to cause spontaneous outbursts and mass rioting against the established state of affairs with misleading slogans and promises such as freedom from taxation and forced labor and distribution of property. This was the case with the revolts, and to this end terrorist means such as threats and mistreatment was not neglected as a way of forcing the population to join the party.

4. The serious disturbances that took place in West Java as well as outrages elsewhere should therefore be considered as a conse-quence of the decision taken at the Surakarta [Prambanan] meeting by the PKI executive to create disturbances. It was this decision which directly led to violent propaganda for illegal terrorist action, which was carried out intensively in the areas where the disturbances took place.[13]

Briefly this was the thesis van der Lely sketched out in the first version, fully developed in the second, and retained in the third. This thesis has long been debunked by Ruth T. McVey in her now classic *The Rise of Indonesian Communism*.[14] For the purpose of our discussion, however, what matters is not its historiographical truthfulness but the fact that it formed the base line from which a new political strategy of the govern-ment evolved, initially against the communist movement, but eventually against any movement in the Indies.

There were two major lessons, the report suggested. The first was the international nature of communism. The report understood the communist movement in the Indies as externally induced, transmitted from Moscow to the PKI central leadership, and then to the native society. It did not see the movement—which manifested itself in many

---

[13] Benda and McVey, *The Communist Uprisings*, 1–18.
[14] See McVey, *The Rise of Indonesian Communism*, chaps. 9–12.

different forms such as rallies and cadre training courses, newspapers, theaters, school education, trade unionism and strikes, "terrorist" actions, and revolts—as embedded in colonial, racial, and class relations in the Indies. For the government, it was "the phantom of external agitation" that was capable of being political and hence threatening.[15] It is only logical, then, that the basic government strategy put forth was to insulate the Indies from the international communist conspiracy and never to allow communist cadres to regroup and revive the party.

This became increasingly clear in the third version of the report. There, two chapters were expanded substantially: chapter 3, "Contact between the Third International and the PKI via the East, with Singapore as Principal Liaison Center," and chapter 6, "The Mohammedan Religion in the Service of Communist Propaganda." In addition, four new chapters were added. Chapter 7 emphasized the importance of the Perhimpoenan Indonesia (PI, Association of Indonesia) and left-oriented intellectuals and nationalists to the Comintern strategy for creating "an anti-imperialist bloc" of communists and nationalists. Chapter 8 discussed the communist propaganda activity through cells in the army and the police. Chapter 9 focused on the influence that developments in China might have on the communist movement in the Indies, above all in terms of the relationship between the PKI and the KMT, and the need for vigilance against the cooperation between Chinese "Soviet propagandists" and natives. And finally, chapter 11 discussed "the disturbances in November 1926, the communist organization and leadership, its drive for the party discipline, and how party leadership in Moscow tried to fan the stoked fire."

The chapters that van der Lely expanded or added in the third version of his report were all concerned with international links through which the Comintern might penetrate into the Indies. Not surprisingly, the anti-communist strategy he spelled out was that of quarantine, insulating the Indies from the Moscow-centered Comintern, with the destruction of communist propaganda centers in Singapore and Mecca, vigilance against any sign of "an anti-imperialist bloc" between the Comintern and young Indonesian intellectuals and nationalists, vigilance

---

[15] The phrase, "the phantom of external agitation," is taken from Ann Laura Stoler, *Capitalism and Confrontation in Sumatra's Plantation Belt, 1870–1979* (New Haven, CT: Yale University Press, 1985), 55, 79.

against Indies communist fugitives abroad, and surveillance of Chinese "Soviet propagandists."

The other point van der Lely emphasized was the central importance of Tan Malaka in the communist movement in the Indies. In the first version of his report, van der Lely argued that "behind the seemingly clumsy and incoherent efforts of resistance against the established regime exists a central idea," and quoted two sections—"Tactics and Strategy" and "Concentration of Forces in the Place and Time Advantageous for Us"—almost in their entirety from Tan Malaka's *Naar de Republiek Indonesia* (Toward the republic of Indonesia); this comprised 6.5 pages of the 15 page report.[16] In the second and third version of his report, van der Lely argued that "insight into the danger of the actions carried out by the Communist leaders is given" by Tan Malaka's writings; he retained the quotation about the "Concentration of Forces" from *Naar de Republiek Indonesia*, while replacing the quotation on "Tactics and Strategy" with an excerpt from Tan Malaka's another work, *Semangat Moeda* (The young spirit).

To understand the "central idea" and "insight" that van der Lely found in Tan Malaka's writings, it is useful to look, briefly, at what Tan Malaka wrote in those quoted passages. In the selection from *Naar de Republiek Indonesia*, Tan Malaka discussed his revolutionary strategy:

> If we choose Indonesia as our battlefield, then we will find that the full force of the enemy (economic, political and military) is not gathered together in one place, but dispersed. The military forces are centered in Priangan. The political center is now in Batavia, but this may soon be united with the military forces in Priangan. One can say that the economic center is the Surakarta [Solo] valley, i.e., the residencies of Yogyakarta, Surakarta, Madiun, Rembang, Kediri and Surabaya, where there are large numbers of sugar mills, railroads, ships, palm oil refineries, machinery shops and other concerns.

To carry out a successful attack on Dutch imperial power, Tan Malaka said, "we must divide our revolutionary forces and select the place which is most important for our victory." The question was where. Tan Malaka proposed the Solo valley.

---

[16] Compare PG to GG, Nov. 27, 1927, Mr. 1174x/1926 and Tan Malaka, *Menudju Republik Indonesia* (Jakarta: Jajasan "Massa," 1962), 42–6 and 48–51.

There we may more readily expect to be victorious and to be able to hold our position than in Batavia or Priangan. The industrial workers are concentrated in the Surakarta valley, and also the economic resources which can make the victory more permanent. We can consolidate a political victory if it goes hand in hand with an economic victory (embracing factories, agriculture, transport, and banking institutions).

This does not mean that places such as Priangan, the East Coast of Sumatra, Palembang, and Aceh were considered unimportant. Successful attacks on these places were seen to be extremely important in terms of diverting and misleading the enemy. The strategic blow could then be arranged to occur at a suitable moment in the Surakarta valley. Therefore, in accordance with this strategy, the party should concentrate its strength, energy and conviction "to put our army into action in factories, workshops, mines, plantations and such concerns, with a view of training our army for the future struggle."

All the troops under the command of the PKI must be subjected to a central authority... They must advance if the central authority deems it necessary... [I]f the general staff considers it advisable that the troops withdraw then they must not be ashamed of withdrawal.

If after skirmishes small and large, today in Java, tomorrow in Sumatra, today in the trade unions, tomorrow in the political parties, we have proved that we possess insight, determination, ability and enthusiasm, then the last blow to be dealt with will be dealt by us, with such force, in the right place and at the right time, that Dutch imperialism will fall, and its fall will be heard in all the other colonies in the East.

In the final version of his report, Van der Lely then quoted a few passages from *Semangant Moeda* to show "a clear picture of the propaganda methods indirectly recommended by the writer [Tan Malaka] for illegal terrorist actions" and "the poisonous character of his propaganda":

But even if we do not place much hope in freeing Indonesia by means of anarchism, anarchism can arise in connection with the people's attitude in Indonesia...

[I]f the government blocks up the crater of the movement the revolutionary fire will break out elsewhere, e.g., the sugar cane will burn, bridges will be destroyed, trains will be derailed, and the Europeans will be murdered.

It is not the PKI that wants this to happen, it is exclusively the will of the people who have been made desperate and have fled from our organization.

For instance, when the people, who are 55 million strong, choose death rather than life as slaves and laugh when they see the mounted police with their billy clubs; when the prisons are broken open and the leaders freed; when the railroad-workers and the ships' crews refuse to transport their leaders to places of exile; when the soldiers refuse to suppress the movement and to shoot at the innocent unarmed masses, when the Europeans go to sleep with a revolver in their hand and do not dare to eat before their food has been examined by a doctor.

This is all proof of the fact that the spirit of revolution has taken firm root, is spreading everywhere and can only be cured by freedom.

Tan Malaka wrote *Naar de Republiek Indonesia* in early 1925 and published it in Canton in April to criticize the PKI plan to abandon the SR after the Yogyakarta conference in December 1924 and to give his own view on a party program.[17] The passages van der Lely quoted were meant to reveal his revolutionary strategy centered on an attack on the Solo valley, to emphasize the importance of retaining the PKI as a cadre party and the SR as a mass base, and to argue for training "our army" in mass action, not for making a revolution.

Semangat Moeda was written somewhat later the same year, and it was published in Manila in 1926. McVey says that Tan Malaka was more cautious in this tract than in *Naar de Republiek Indonesia* and argued here that although the party should prepare for revolution, it could not consider beginning one until it was sure the entire population was behind it: "Any Indonesian revolt will be in vain unless the people are ripe for revolution. We must distrust and oppose ... all forms of 'putsch'."[18] These passages were not meant to be a call for anarchist actions, but instead were meant to describe the revolutionary conditions towards which mass action should lead.

However, van der Lely was not interested in the historical context of what Tan Malaka wrote in these passages. He was interested in gaining

---

[17] McVey, *The Rise of Indonesian Communism*, 316.
[18] Ibid., 317.

insight into "the seemingly clumsy and incoherent efforts of resistance against the established regime," finding the "central idea" that would not contradict his own thesis of an international communist conspiracy. It is no coincidence that van der Lely found what he was looking for in Tan Malaka's writings. Tan Malaka had all the credentials that van der Lely deemed important. He was the Comintern representative for the Far East. He was the most sophisticated and prolific of the PKI leaders. He wrote in Dutch. And he wrote quotable, graphic passages that nicely captured the substance of van der Lely's nightmares. In the political policing world in which van der Lely lived, he found his double in Tan Malaka, the worthy enemy sharing fantasies in common, glorious to one and nightmarish to the other yet inhabiting the same world. Among all Indonesian communist fugitives abroad, Tan Malaka was thus made the number one enemy, and the passages van der Lely quoted from his writing became well known and important in providing Dutch officials with information about the revolutionary strategy and vision of the Indonesian revolutionaries.

These were the lessons that formed the baseline from which the government embarked on setting outer limits for the movement. As long as the PKI was the target, there was nothing problematic with the strategy derived from these lessons. But these lessons continued informing the government even after the PKI was destroyed and the organizational foci for the target of repression became increasingly diffuse. How then did the government set outer limits for the movement and how did the political underground emerge in the face of this new government policy in the late 1920s and early 1930s? To address these questions, we need to turn to the examination of three major cases the attorney general's office handled: the Sarekat Kaoem Boeroeh Indonesia (SKBI, Union of Indonesian Workers) affair, Iwa Koesoema Soemantri's internment, and the Pari (Partai Republik Indonesia, Republic of Indonesia Party) underground.

The SKBI Affair: Setting an Outer Limit

The SKBI was established formally on July 8, 1928, at a meeting held in Surabaya under the leadership of Soenarjo, editor of Malay language newspaper *Indonesia Baroe* (New Indonesia). Soenarjo said, according to ARD chief van der Most, that the SKBI was a continuation of the communist Persarikatan Kaoem Boeroeh (SKB, Workers' Union) but now under nationalist leadership and that its purpose was to achieve better working conditions and not to carry out any political activity.[19]

The SKBI held its first public rally on August 5, 1928, in Surabaya, where Soedjiman, former PKI member and then commissioner of the PNI Surabaya branch, was elected its chairman. Other SKBI leaders the PID identified in these early days included: treasurer Soenarjo, former SR member, former secretary of the chauffeurs' union in Surabaya and the machine-shop workers' union (SBBE) in Malang, and then (in late 1928) secretary of the administrative committee of the "Bersatoe [Unite]" Commercial Press Co. and editor of *Sinar Indonesia* (Ray of Indonesia, former *Indonesia Baroe*) which "Bersatoe" published; secretary Hadji Mohamad Abas, former PKI member and former chairman of the Red SI in Banyuwangi; commissioner of the central committee and chairman of its printers' branch Goenardjo, former PKI member and then (in late 1928) commissioner of the administrative committee of the Bersatoe Commercial Press; and Askandar, state railway Surabaya station clerk.[20]

In September 1928, however, Soedjiman was ousted as chairman and replaced by Marsoedi, former PKI member and former secretary of the postal workers' union. A founder of the Bersatoe Commercial Press and the editor-in-chief of its newspaper, *Indonesia Bersatoe* (Indonesia Unite, future *Sinar Indonesia*), he was released from prison in August 1928, after having served eight months in prison for the transgression of press laws. After Marsoedi took over the SKBI leadership, its central committee was reorganized, separate branch committees were established for railway workers, printers, dockers, coachmen and others, member training courses were started, and statutes and a working program were written and published in its new monthly journal, *Sinar Kaoem Boeroeh* (Ray of Workers), in November 1928. Member training courses were run under the tight control of the SKBI leadership. Members of the executive committee read such texts as *Pedoman PKI* (PKI Directives),

---

[19] Wd. Hoofd van den Dienst der Algemeene Recherche, Rapport over de resultaten van het tegen de Sarekat Kaoem Boeroeh Indonesia (S.K.B.I.) ingesteld onderzoek, ten vervolge op mijn voorloopig rapport van 30 Juli 1929, Oct. 17, 1929, Mr. 1017x/1929. For more on the SKBI, see John Ingleson, *Workers, Unions and Politics: Indonesia in the 1920s and 1930s* (Leiden: Brill, 2014), 105–17.

[20] Wd. Hoofd van den Dienst der Algemeene Recherche, Rapport over de resultaten van het tegen de Sarekat Kaoem Boeroeh Indonesia (S.K.B.I.), Mr. 1017x/1929. See also Bijlage III (Staat van leiders en hun antecedenten), Mr. 627x/1929.

The Pan-Pacific Worker, and Soemantri's *Rasa Merdika* (Taste of Freedom), and discussed topics such as "imperialism" and "party discipline."[21] Texts were then written by first and second secretary of the executive committee, which leaders read aloud at the courses. Branches were established in Bangil and Banyuwangi, East Java, in December 1928.[22]

The attorney general wrote in his May 1929 letter to the governor general that SKBI branches were in Surabaya, Banyuwangi, and Bangil, that a new branch had been recently established in Medan by Iwa Koesoema Soemantri, and that preparations were reportedly under way for the establishment of branches and circles in Magelang, Purworejo, Kutoarjo, Malang, Probolinggo, Kertosono, Mojokerto, and Kotaraja. The largest SKBI base was in Surabaya, the attorney general reported, with 450 members, 175 of whom belonged to the branch for railway workers, 81 to the branch for dockworkers, and 52 to that for printers. A new organ, *Sendjata Indonesia* (Indonesia's Weapon, former *Sinar Indonesia*) started in April 1929 with Marsoedi as editor-in-chief.[23]

Most SKBI leaders were ex-PKI/SR/trade union activists and led the SKBI as PKI/SR/trade union activists used to lead unions in 1924 and 1925. But there were two crucial differences between the SKBI and the trade union movement in "the communist period." First, SKBI leaders knew the government would never tolerate any attempt to revive a "communist" movement. They also associated anything "communist" (such as PKI, SR, VSTP and other communist trade unions) with Digul. Second, many of these leaders had been marked as "communists" by the PID even before they established the SKBI. Led by such "communists," the SKBI was watched closely by the PID and penetrated by spies and informers from the beginning. The SKBI chairman, Marsoedi, epitomized the problems. He had been under Surabaya PID surveillance since at least 1927. He was mentioned three times in 1927 alone by van der

---

[21] For *Rasa Merdika*, see Shiraishi, *An Age in Motion*, 246–8.

[22] Wd. Hoofd van den Dienst der Algemeene Recherche, Rapport over de resultaten van het tegen de Sarekat Kaoem Boeroeh Indonesia (S.K.B.I.), Mr. 1017x/1929. John Ingleson says that SKBI activists also linked the union to the radical tradition of the labor movement in Surabaya and held up Semaoen as a model. Ingleson, *Workers, Unions and Politics*, 109–10.

[23] Advocate general to GG, May 15, 1929, in R.C. Kwantes, ed., *De Ontwikkeling, 1928–Aug. 1933 De Ontwikkeling van de Nationalistische Beweging in Nederlandsch-Indie, Bronnenpublikatie 3de Stuk 1928–Aug. 1933* (Groningen: Wolters-Noordhoff/ Bouma's Boekhuis, 1981), 212–21.

Lely in his monthly political police survey as editor-in-chief of *Sinar Indonesia*, as leader of its largely "communist" publication committee (by which he apparently meant "Bersatoe" Commercial Press Co.), and as a man who tried to establish a new political party, National Party of the Indonesian People (Nationale Partij Rajat Indonesia). He was also a tainted man. When he was arrested in November 1926, he provided the regional intelligence with important information that led to the arrest of "several PKI leaders who had eluded the police till that moment." He was released as a reward.[24] He was arrested again in 1927 for the transgression of press laws in connection with *Sinar Indonesia*. He served eight months in prison but was then allowed to return home. Perhaps people did not know that he had betrayed his friends in November 1926, but they naturally wondered why such a known communist had not been sent to Digul.

The governor general was alerted about the SKBI by his adviser, Charles O. van der Plas who was convinced of its communist character. In a report he submitted to de Graeff in April 1929, he referred to a decision at the recent Comintern congress in July 1928 to revive the communist trade union movement in the Indies. He also mentioned, based on ARD monthly surveys, that a branch was established in Medan by Iwa Koesoema Soemantri, "former chairman of the SPPL [Seamen's and Dockers' Union] and the Perhimpoenan Indonesia and former representative of Semaoen in the Netherlands, who stayed in Moscow for some time, now more or less aligned with the PNI," and that the SKBI was in communication with the Pan Pacific Trade Union Secretariat in Canton.[25]

Van der Plas knew that the SKBI was not successful as a movement. Most trade unions shunned the SKBI, he wrote to de Graeff, and its leaders had asked the PNI to take over its leadership. But nationalists, Surabaya Study Club and PNI members, distrusted "the SKBI promotors and leaders, all somewhat shady figures."

> Their communist past, their action first in *Sinar Indonesia*, later in *Indonesia Bersatoe*, and then in the SKBI, do not tally with the impunity they seem to enjoy, people say. "If they are bona fide

---

[24] Poeze, *Politiek-Politioneele Overzichten, 1927–1928*, 21, 50, 118; Resident of Surabaya to Governor of East Java, Sept. 20, 1929, Mr. 1191x/1929.

[25] Nota van Ch. O. van der Plas (td. wd. adviseur voor inlandse zaken) April 1929, in Kwantes, *De Ontwikkeling, 1928–Aug. 1933*, 207–12.

communists," people told me, "we should be crazy to let them take us in a tow and it does not make any sense at all that the government, which sent so many hundreds to Digul, does nothing against them or they are spies—as we believe—but then we are not so damn as they think."

SKBI leaders were seen by some nationalists as "agents provocateurs, at least as spies," van der Plas continued, but still there was a possibility for the PNI to take over its leadership and eliminate elements they distrusted.[26] His report was inconclusive. He did not suggest any definite course of action against the SKBI, but he advised the governor general to instruct the *hoofdparket* to submit a detailed report on the SKBI and its leaders and to explain how it was going to deal with it.

Advocate General Verheijen sent a letter to the governor general on May 15, 1929.[27] He agreed with van der Plas that the SKBI was being built "along the lines stipulated by the Third International" and that there was "no certainty that the action of the SKBI would remain within the boundaries set for the maintenance of public peace and order." But there was no evidence, he argued, that SKBI was established "at the instigation of Moscow" or that it had any relationship with the Anti-Imperialist League, the Pan Pacific Labour Union Secretariat, or other foreign organizations. Besides, he pointed out, the SKBI "had carried out no anti-government propaganda and made little effort to move the employees to a recalcitrant attitude against the employers, so that it cannot be attested that the leaders' conduct now provides danger to public peace and order." He also dismissed as irrelevant van der Plas's worry about the PNI taking over the SKBI leadership, saying that the PNI would go into trade unionism anyway and that the destruction of the SKBI might make it easier for the PNI to carry out trade union activities. His position was clear: no intervention for now, enough to keep the SKBI under surveillance.[28]

Verheijen then dwelled long on van der Plas's assertion that "the entire Surabaya group, the PNI members there included, do not trust

---

[26] Ibid., 209–10. Ingleson says that Soetomo was warned by the Surabaya PID in late 1928 about associating with the SKBI chairman Marsoedi and that Soetomo told Soekiman Marsoedi was a spy. Ingleson, *Workers, Unions and Politics*, 111.

[27] Advocate general R.J.M. Verheijen served as de facto attorney general from May to November 1929 when he was formally appointed attorney general.

[28] Advocate general to GG, May 15, 1929, in Kwantes, *De Ontwikkeling, 1928–Aug. 1933*, 212–21.

the promoters and leaders of the SKBI and that they are now seen by a part of nationalists as agents provocateurs, at least as spies." He pointed out that "the majority of the leading figures of the SKBI" were "members, even commissioners, of the PNI [Surabaya] branch" and that "it is not clear at all to me on what ground people can suspect that the government is using the leaders of the SKBI as agents provocateurs or as spies."[29]

It is odd enough for the advocate general to argue that the SKBI leaders were not agents provocateurs or spies but genuine activists. Odder still, he submitted two Surabaya PID reports to the governor general on May 24, 1929, to show that measures were being taken by the SKBI executive to purge police spies and that there was no evidence as Surabaya nationalists argued "that the promoters and the leaders of the SKBI acted as a group of spies or agents provocateurs of the government."[30] The first report, written by police *mantri* Soesilo and dated May 15, 1929, said that according to information he obtained from "spies S1 and S2," an executive committee meeting held on May 11, "attended by the executive committee members and several trusted members of the SKBI," decided to purge Marsaid, chairman of the SKBI council, "because he mingled too much with PID agents and was suspected of being a police spy." The other report, written by police *mantri* Oemar on May 16, said that according to "an informer's information," Marsaid was dismissed from the SKBI on May 12 at a members' meeting "attended by forty people."[31]

These reports show how deeply the SKBI was penetrated by spies. One wonders why Verheijen was so incensed at van der Plas's allegation and so insistent on the SKBI being genuine and not a group of agents provocateurs and spies. Partly, this can be seen as a matter of semantics. Verheijen said that the SKBI leaders were not a group of agents provocateurs, but he never denied that spies and informers had indeed penetrated into the SKBI. But one suspects that there was more to it. The *hoofdparket* knew that many SKBI leaders such as Marsoedi, Mohammad Abas, and Soenarjo were former PKI members. It must have been easy to intern them to Digul as "PKI and SR leaders and propagandists" if it

---

[29] Ibid., 220–1.
[30] Adovocate General to Governor General, May 24, 1929, Mr. 485x/1929.
[31] Mantri Politie afd. PID Soesilo, Geheim Rapport, May 15, 1929, and Mantri Politie Oemar, Geheim Rapport, May 16, 1929, both in Mr. 485x/1929.

so desired. But there were at least three important factors the *hoofdparket* had to weigh in deciding "the right moment to intervene" in the SKBI.

The first was the memory of the militancy of Indonesian trade unions in the late 1910s and early 1920s. Before the revolts, the VSTP (the railway workers' union) was the most powerful and best organized union under the communist leadership. It was devastated in the 1923 strike, but revived in two years, with 77 branches and 8,293 members by November 1925. It was led by young, militant branch leaders who were also involved in the PKI and the SR as well as other trade unions. As a result, Surabaya emerged in 1925 as a major center of communist trade union activity, with 900 members in the VSTP, 450 in the postal workers' union, 1,500 in the dockers' and seamen's union, and 2,000 in the machine ship workers' union.[32] With the destruction of the PKI, the VSTP and other unions under the communist leadership collapsed. Instead, a new union, PBST (Perhimpoenan Beambte Spoor dan Tram, Railway and Tramway Officials' Union) was established in July 1927, with a membership of 5,500 in August 1927. But it was no VSTP. When its first congress was held in January 1928, a proposal was made to attach the word, Indonesia, to its name. It was turned down on the ground that it was not "official." As Petrus Blumberger wrote in 1931, it "keeps itself aloof from the political and strives to stay in the terrain of pure union activity."[33] Given its past history, however, no one could easily dismiss the possibility for the revival of a militant railway union, all the more so because the SKBI succeeded in less than a year in organizing 150 railway workers in Surabaya and its propaganda was being carried out among railway workers in many cities in Java.

The second factor, related to the first, was the question of a trade union central. With the collapse of the Red Trade Union Central headquartered in Surabaya in 1926, there was no trade union central left. But efforts were being made to establish one, both by the PSI and nationalists. As Petrus Blumberger says, the SKBI positioned itself right in the middle of "the silent struggle for the hegemony over the trade union movement between the Sarekat Islam members and Indonesian

---

[32] John Ingleson, *In Search of Justice: Workers and Unions in Colonial Java, 1908–1926* (Singapore: Oxford University Press, 1979), 269, 271, and 296.

[33] J. Th. Petrus Blumberger, *De Nationalistische Beweging in Nederlandsch-Indie* (1931; repr. Dordrecht: Foris Publications, 1987), 362. See also Ingleson, *Workers, Unions and Politics*, esp. chap. 3.

nationalists."[34] The *hoofdparket* was watching carefully what position other unions would take toward the SKBI, as shown in van der Most's report dated October 17, 1929, in which he said that the PBST, the pawnshop workers' union (led by Soerjopranoto, PSI leader), the postal workers' union (Midpost), and the chauffeurs' union stayed away from the SKBI.[35]

And finally, there was the question of PNI-led trade unionism as van der Plas mentioned. The PNI congress held in Batavia in May 1929 decided to place greater emphasis on establishing trade unions and peasant organizations. This was a great concern for the *hoofdparket*, all the more so, because its Surabaya branch under Anwari's leadership took trade unionism more seriously than the central leadership in Bandung.[36] It was most likely this move on the part of the PNI that prompted van der Plas to alert the governor general of the SKBI. Verheijen dismissed the importance of the SKBI for the PNI, but this does not mean that he took PNI-led trade unionism lightly. It was only that he believed the PNI would go into trade unionism in any case, whatever might happen with its relationship with the SKBI.

As we have seen, Verheijen concluded his letter to the governor general dated May 15, 1929, saying that "I am of opinion that the time for the government measures to set bounds to the effort of the SKBI, that is to prevent this altogether, has not come yet, in any case for now." He knew that the SKBI was not a group of agents provocateurs and spies. But he also knew that police spies penetrated in the SKBI. He knew the *hoofdparket* would be informed about important decision the SKBI leadership might make. There was no reason to worry that the SKBI might hatch a plot in the dark. It could be destroyed at any moment the *hoofdparket* so pleased. He could choose the right moment to destroy it and to impress the government's standpoint on the people. Besides, it could serve as an ideal bait. Leave it for a while. If railway workers, dockers, printers, and others wished to join the SKBI, let them. If the PBST, the Midpost, and other non-communist unions wished to join the SKBI, let them. If the PNI agreed to take over the SKBI leadership, let them. The *hoofdparket* would intervene at the right moment,

---

[34] Ibid., 363.

[35] Wd. Hoofd van den Dienst der Algemeene Recherche, Rapport over de resultaten van het tegen de Sarekat Kaoem Boeroeh Indonesia (S.K.B.I.), Mr. 1017x/1929.

[36] John Ingleson, *Road to Exile: The Indonesian Nationalist Movement, 1927–1934* (Singapore: Heinemann Educational Books, 1979), 90–4.

and destroy any militant union, any political trade union central, and the PNI once for all. The only thing Verheijen wanted to avoid for the moment was a premature intervention at the instruction of the governor general, alerted by the meddlesome van der Plas, because he knew de Graeff did not want to destroy the PNI, especially if it was provoked by agents provocateurs and spies.

The *hoofdparket* thus kept watch on the SKBI. In a report submitted to the governor general on July 18, 1929, ARD chief van der Most noted a stagnation of SKBI activity: no public rallies or member training courses had been held since June; its organ, *Sendjata Indonesia*, had stopped publication because of financial difficulty; and workers were in no mood to join the SKBI under Marsoedi's leadership. In Bangil, the branch membership reached 40. A circle was established in Sidoarjo, supported mainly by state railway and sugar factory workers. Another branch was established in Yogyakarta, van der Most continued, mainly with tailors, batik printers, and smith as members. The Persarekatan Sophir Mataram (PSM, Mataram chauffeurs' union) also participated in the SKBI. The central figure in Yogyakarta was Moeljono alias Tarmoedji, former PKI and SR leader and propagandist in Kediri, who was not interned to Digul because he was in prison in November 1926 and released in August 1928. He participated in the establishment of the PSM, became its vice-chairman, joined the SKBI, and was appointed SKBI commissioner for Central Java. In Surakarta, Surabaya SKBI leaders contacted with "communist" Siti Aminah alias Woro Trisoelo, wife of Trisoelo from Surabaya now in Digul, who in turn introduced them to Sadino Martopoespito and Soemokasdiro alias Rasimin, both PNI candidate members. They formed a provisional committee in Solo. This was about all. Rumor had it that the SKBI had found no success other places such as Cepu, Semarang and Pekalongan. Verheijen again advised the governor general that there was no need to clamp down on the SKBI, it was enough to watch it closely.[37]

---

[37] Wd. Hoofd van den Dienst der Algemeene Recherche to PG, July 17, 1929, and PG to GG, July 18, 1929, both in Mr. 695x/1929. Also see Wd. Hoofd van den Dienst der Algemeene Recherche, Voorloopig Rapport over de tegen de Sarekat Kaoem Boeroeh Indonesia (S.K.B.I.) getroffen maatregelen, July 30, 1929, Mr. 731x/1929; PG to GG, Nov. 15, 1929, Mr. 1192x/1929; Adjunct Chief Commissioner of Police, Surakarta, to Resident of Surakarta, Aug. 10, 1929, and PG to GG, Nov. 15, 1929, both in Mr. 1193x/1929.

On the same day, July 18, 1929, however, the resident of Surabaya sent to the advocate general a secret police report of Surabaya PID assistant *wedana* Soentoro dated July 16. In this report, Soentoro wrote that "Spy S3 showed me a letter dated May 30, 1929, which originated from the Secretariat of the Anti-Imperialist League and addressed to the central executive committee of the SKBI." In this letter the Anti-Imperialist League Secretariat informed the SKBI that it was admitted to the League "as the first Indonesian member." With his report, Soentoro submitted a photographic reproduction of the envelope and the letter.[38]

Upon receiving this report, the *hoofdparket* decided to act. On July 24, the advocate general sent a telegram to the resident of Surabaya as well as the other regional chiefs in Java and Madura and the governor of the East Coast of Sumatra to carry out "police searches of SKBI offices and houses of its leaders and propagandists" on July 26 and to report to the *hoofdparket* by telegram on "any SKBI contact with other associations and who formed the linkage between the League and the SKBI in Holland."[39] In the police sweep, SKBI activists marked by the PID were arrested in such places as Batavia, Bandung, Semarang, Yogyakarta, Surakarta, Kediri, Malang, Surabaya, Bangil, Banyuwangi, and Makassar, including 25 in Surabaya, 20 in Surakarta, and 20 in Yogyakarta. Most of them were released soon afterward, but the government eventually decided in December 1929 to intern six "SKBI leaders and propagandists" to Digul: Marsoedi (chairman), Goenardjo alias Hardjosepoetro (commissioner of the executive committee and chairman of the branch for printers and chauffeurs), Ahija Soepardi alias Ahjadiredjo (former VSTP member and chairman of the branch for railway workers) in Surabaya; Sadino Martopoespito (SKBI propagandist and batik trader) and Soemokasdiro alias Kasimin (SKBI propagandist and former station clerk at the Solo-Balapan station) in Surakarta; and Moeljono alias Tarmoedji in Yogyakarta. Interestingly, SKBI secretary Askandar was not

---

[38] Assistant Wedana of the PID branch, Geheim Rapport, Surabaya, July 16, 1929, Mr. 731x/1929. Marsoedi, who John Ingleson describes as "poorly educated, opportunistic, hot-headed and too closely attached to the language and the ideology of the PKI," applied for the SKBI membership in the League without informing the central executive. Ingleson, *Workers, Unions and Politics*, 115–6.

[39] The hoofdparket soon learned from the Dutch Intelligence Service that Roestam Effendi and Ticoalu Pandean, who ran a press bureau for colonial politics in The Hague, form the link between the SKBI and the Anti-Imperialist League. PG to GG, Aug. 27, 1929, Mr. 812x/1929.

interned, even though he was responsible for SKBI correspondence with the League. Perhaps he was assistant *wedana* Soentoro's "Spy S3."[40]

On August 6, 1929, the government representative for general affairs made an announcement in the Volkraad on the Anti-Imperialist League that "the government would not tolerate any direct organizational contact between associations and persons in the Indies and the League or any other association under strong communist influence. As soon as enough evidence is available for such contact, the government will intervene. This has always been the standpoint of the government, and it will always remain so." He also offered "an explanation for the government standpoint on the trade unions" on the same occasion. He stated that "he did not want to deny the desirability of a healthy trade union," but made it clear that "all dogmas derived from the West" should be shunned and that "the government does not regard the so-called strike article in the criminal code (art. 161 bis) as damaging for the bona fide trade union activity in any respect, but as indispensable against the mala fide unions." As Petrus Blumberger interpreted, the message was clear: stay away from "party political, socialist and nationalist dogmas about 'capitalism' and 'imperialism,'" "work with the government to look after economic interests of the employees in harmonious agreement with the general interest of the land and people."[41]

The SKBI was neither illegal nor clandestine. Because it was led by former PKI/SR/trade union activists and penetrated by spies and informers, however, it was seen as "shady" from the beginning by nationalists and its shadiness was confirmed by the government clamp down. Its significance lays in the opportunity it provided the government to make its standpoint clear: no direct organizational contact with the Anti-Imperialist League or any other organization under communist influence;

---

[40] Deputy chief of the ARD, Voorloopig Rapport, July 30, 1929, Mr. 731x/1929; Deputy chief of the ARD, Rapport over de resultaten van het tegen de Sarekat Kaoem Boeroeh Indonesia (S.K.B.I.) ingesteld onderzoek, ten vervolge op mijn voorloopig rapport van Juli 30, 1929, Oct. 17, 1929, Mr. 1017x/1929; PG to GG, Generaal, Oct. 21, 1929, Mr. 1017x/1929; PG to GG, Nov. 13, 1929, Mr. 1191x/1929; Resident of Surabaya to Gouvernor of ast Java, Sept. 20, 1929, in Mr. 1191x/1929; PG to GG, Nov. 15, 1929, Mr. 1192x/1929; PG to GG, Nov. 15, 1929, Mr. 1193x/1929; Adjunct chief commissioner of police, Surakarta Branch, to resident of Surakarta, Aug. 10, 1929, Mr. 1193x/1929; Uittreksel uit het Register der Besluiten van den Gouverneur Generaal van Nederlandsch Indie, April 5, 1930, Mr. 393x/1930.
[41] Blumberger, *De Nationalistische Beweging*, 369, 374.

no politically inspired "dogmatic" trade union movement; and finally, a warning to the PNI regarding its own trade unionism, though the *hoofdparket* did not find any direct link between the SKBI and the PNI in the July police searches.

Iwa's Internment: Setting an Outer Limit

Framing Iwa Koesoema Soemantri

Mr. Iwa Koesoema Soemantri was also arrested on July 26, 1929, in the police sweep against the SKBI, but his case was dealt with separately from the beginning, even though the *hoofdparket* believed in December 1929 that he was a central figure in the SKBI Medan branch.[42]

"Former chairman of the SPPL and the Perhimpoenan Indonesia [PI] and former representative of Semaoen in the Netherlands, who stayed in Moscow for some time, now more or less aligned with the PNI," as van der Plas put it, Iwa had long been under surveillance, at least since 1924, when he became secretary of the newly established SPLI (Sarekat Pegawai Laoet Indonesia, Indonesian Seamen's Union) under Semaoen in Amsterdam.[43] When he returned to the Indies with the law degree from Leiden University (hence his title, Meester in de Rechten, Mr.) on November 11, 1927, the attorney general reported on the same day to the governor general that Iwa had returned to Ciamis, his home town in West Java where his parents lived (his father was a retired school inspector). The attorney general also mentioned again that Iwa had belonged to the left wing of the PI in the Netherlands, had stayed briefly in Moscow, and had been appointed PI representative to the Comintern.[44] After Iwa's return, he often appeared in ARD monthly survey. The survey for November 1927, for instance, noted that Iwa was planning to move to Medan. In February 1928 it was reported that he remitted money to Ahmad Soebardjo, then working at the Anti-Imperialist League Secretariat in Berlin. The survey for March 1928 noted his attendance at PNI closed meetings held in Bandung under Soekarno's leadership.[45] And when he moved to Medan on April 3, 1928,

---

[42] Advocate General to GG, Oct. 21, 1929, Mr. 1017x/1929.

[43] In other words, van der Plas made a mistake, mixing up the SPPL the PKI established in Java in 1925 and the SPLI Semaoen established in Amsterdam in 1924.

[44] PG to GG, Nov. 11, 1927, Mr. 1341x/1929.

[45] Poeze, *Politiek-Politioneele Overzichten, 1927–1928*, 169, 267, 274.

the chief commissioner of the Batavian police informed his counterpart in Medan of Iwa's departure by telegram.[46]

That Iwa moved to Medan was most likely not because of his politics. No doubt he was a nationalist like many of his friends who had studied in Holland. When he returned to Java, he worked briefly at Iskaq Tjokrohadisoerjo's law firm in Bandung and then at Sartono's in Batavia. Both had known Iwa since their Holland days. Both were working as leading PNI members. He also came to know Soekarno, PNI chairman, in late 1927 when he was in Bandung. But he went to Medan, as he says in his autobiography which he never intended to publish, because his uncle, Abdul Manap, told him that there were no Indonesian lawyers in Medan and invited him to Medan.[47] Seen from the *hoofdparket*'s perspective, however, he belonged to a specific group of "intellectuals," and might even be considered one of the most dangerous among them given his Moscow past, given that the Comintern encouraged the Indonesian communists to seek cooperation for the formation of "an anti-imperialist bloc." He would not have come to Medan, the *hoofdparket* was convinced, for any other reason than a political one.

A burgeoning "frontier" town and a European-dominated commercial enclave in the late nineteenth century, Medan had by the late 1920s become the "Paris" of the Indies with the population of 76,600 in 1930, of which natives were 41,300, Chinese 27,300, and Europeans 4,300. It was the capital of the residency of the East Coast of Sumatra, and more importantly the commercial center of Deli, a shorthand term for the plantation belt centered in Deli, Serdang, and Langkat, an area that Tan Malaka called "a land of gold, a haven for the capitalist class, but also a land of sweat, tears, and death, a hell for the proletariat."[48] The population of East Sumatra in 1930 was 1.69 million, of which Javanese with 600,000 (35.0 per cent) formed the majority, while other major racial and ethnic groups were Malays (335,000; 19.9 per cent), Chinese (193,000; 11.4 per cent), Karo Bataks (145,000; 8.6 per cent), Simalungun Bataks (95,000; 5.6 per cent), Toba Bataks (74,000; 4.4 per cent), Mandailing and Angkola Bataks (60,000; 3.5 per cent), Minangkabau

---

[46] Rapport No. 2, in Chief of intelligence, Algemeene Politie Batavia, Extra-Rapport, Sept. 10, 1928, Mr. 315x/1930.

[47] Iwa Koesoema Soemantri, *Indonesia Minzoku Shugi no Genryu: Iwa Kusumasumantori Jiden* (Tokyo: Waseda University Press, 1975), 65–6.

[48] Tan Malaka, *From Jail to Jail, Volume 1*, trans. with intro. by Helen Jarvis (Athens: Ohio University Press, 1992), 43.

(51,000; 3.0 per cent), Sundanese (44,000; 2.6 per cent), Banjarese (31,000; 1.9 per cent), and Europeans (11,000; 0.7 per cent).[49]

The central institution in East Sumatra was not the state, a conglomeration of the Indies regional administration, local sultanates, principalities, statelets and other "autonomous" units, but the Western (i.e., European and American) tobacco, rubber, palm oil and other plantations that had been were developed since the 1870s in this sparsely populated but fertile region with imported white planters and imported Chinese and Javanese coolies, and which developed in turn a network of roads, a railway line linking Langkat, Deli, and Serdang, a telegraph line, harbors, waterworks, and schools. As Rob Nieuwenhuys aptly said, "Deli was an island." "In Deli everything had to be imported, the employees as well as coolies. The staff came directly from Europe, the coolies from Java. Deli was a conglomeration of white settlements with Chinese and Javanese colonies encircling it. But they were all foreigners, no one had roots."[50] Tan Malaka who lived in Deli in 1919–21 would only add:

> The conflict between the white, stupid, arrogant, cruel colonizers and the colored nation of driven, cheated, oppressed, and exploited slaves ... fouled the atmosphere in Deli and gave rise to constant attacks by the coolies on the plantation Dutch. Frequently just one insult or criticism was enough to cause a coolie to draw his machete from his belt and attack the Tuan Besar [plantation administrator] or Tuan Kecil [white assistant] then and there, for his heart was filled with such a hatred for it all.[51]

Indeed, collective labor protests and physical assaults on management were common, though never with such organizational sophistication, frequency, and political inspiration as the planters claimed; they increased in the late 1920s. From 1925 to 1930, Stoler says, reported assaults on overseers (whites and non-whites) rose from 31 to 220, and the number perpetrated specifically against European staff more than doubled for the same period. In 1924 it was calculated that in fifteen years of service,

[49] Michael van Langenberg, "National Revolution in North Sumatra, Sumatra Timur and Tapanuli, 1942–1950" (PhD diss., University of Sydney, 1976), 959–60; Anthony Reid, *The Blood of the People: Revolution and the End of Traditional Rule in Northern Sumatra* (Kuala Lumpur: Oxford University Press, 1979), 43, 58.
[50] R. Nieuwenhuys, *Oost-Indische Spiegel* (Amsterdam: Querido, 1978), quoted in Stoler, *Capitalism and Confrontation*, 14.
[51] Tan Malaka, *From Jail to Jail*, 1: 47.

an assistant had a 3 per cent chance of being killed by a worker and at least a 50 per cent probability of being physically assaulted.[52]

The regional administration and plantation industry were highly sensitive to any sign of unrest in plantations and blamed communist agitators, extremist elements, and nationalist troublemakers for the increase in physical assaults and labor protest. The Deli Planters Association (DPV, Deli Planters Vereeniging) and the General Association of Rubber Planters in the East Coast of Sumatra (AVROS, Algemeene Vereeniging van Rubberplanters ter Oostkust van Sumatra) jointly established a private intelligence service in October 1927, which was headquartered in Medan and headed by a former East Sumatran PID chief. It worked closely with the regional intelligence to gather information on "the religious and political trends among the plantation workers" and track down runaway contract coolies.[53]

This does not mean that the movement was strong in Medan and made significant inroads in "politicizing" plantation workers. Whether in the name of the Boedi Oetomo (BO), the SI, the Insulinde, the PKI, or the Sumatera Thawalib, a modernist Islamic school association with its base in West Sumatra, the movement, which was largely confined to Medan and other East Sumatran small towns and expressed most lively in native journalism, hardly touched on plantation workers and found its main support among a small group of native civil servants, railway workers of the Deli Sumatran Railway, Mandailing and Minangkabau Islamic reformists, and urban "middle class" native professionals. Besides, its radical wing represented by largely Mandailing and Minangkabau PKI activists and Sumatera Thawalib militants was destroyed in the wake of the revolts with the internment of about thirty people from East Sumatra, including Abdoel Xarim M.S. (of future Digul Concert), Chalid Salim (our tour guide in Digul), and Urbanus Pardede, leader of the PKI Pematang Siantar section.[54]

When Iwa arrived in Medan in April 1928, the movement in East Sumatra was hardly lively, with at most a few hundred people active in political, religious, social, youth, and other associations, closely watched by the PID and the DPV-AVROS intelligence, and hemmed in by the opposition of the regional administration, the plantation industry, the

---

[52] Stoler, *Capitalism and Confrontation*, 42, 53, and 62.
[53] Onderzoek inzake het opvatten van gedroste contractanten door den te Medan gevestigden inlichtingsdienst der DPV en AVROS, Mr. 145x/1929.
[54] Langenberg, "National Revolution," 120–31; Reid, *Blood of the People*, 59–61.

hereditary rulers and chiefs, and conservative religious leaders. Yet all the same Iwa found himself right in the middle of this small movement world as soon as he settled down there. With his Leiden University law degree, his past as PI chairman, and his friendship with such PNI luminaries as Soekarno, Sartono, and Iskaq Tjokrohadisoerjo, Iwa was looked up to as a leader by activists and was seen by the PID as "PNI propagandist" "to win over the majority of the population to his political line to achieve 'free from the Netherlands' in an illegal way."[55]

To see how extensively he was involved in Indonesian associational life in East Sumatra, above all in Medan, and how closely he was watched by the PID, we only need to look at "hard facts" contained in the summary of regional intelligence reports the East Sumatra PID chief compiled after his arrest.

1928
April 3: Arrived at Belawan on board "Plancius" from Batavia; stayed with municipality veterinarian Abdul Manap.

April: "Mr. Iwa Koesoema Soemantri has opened a law firm at 12 Huttenbach street, here [in Medan]. The chairman of the Jong Islamieten Bond, named [Mohammad] Dasoeki, a family member of Mr. Iwa Koesoema Soemantri's, works there as a clerk."

May 19: a members' meeting held by the BO in its club house at the Tjong Yong Hian street, Medan, for the 20th anniversary; attended by about 80 people, including representatives of Minangkabau Saijo [Minangkabau friendship association] and the Journalists' Union; "Mr. Iwa Koesoema Soemantri, the well-known nationalist from Weltevreden, was also present."

July 20: The first issue of Malay language daily *Matahari Indonesia* [The Sun of Indonesia] appeared under Iwa's chief editorship.

Oct. 21: The BO held a meeting in its club house to establish a branch of youth organization Pemoeda Indonesia [Indonesian Youth]; Iwa appointed as adviser.

Nov. 6: Harijo Soedjono, director of the Nationale Bank established by the Surabaya Study Club, arrived in Medan and stayed at the Grand Hotel; he contacted with Iwa and Abdul Manap.

---

[55] Chief of the regional intelligence, Medan, East Coast of Sumatra, to Governor of the East Coast of Sumatra, July 22, 1929, Mr. 315x/1930.

1929

Jan. 8: The Medan branch of the Jong Islamieten Bond held a slametan [ritual feast] in its club house at the Oranje Nassau street; attended by 70 people, including Iwa and Abdul Manap.

Jan. 12: A meeting was held in the club house of Minangkabau Saijo to establish a branch of youth organization Pemoeda Indonesia [Indonesian Youth] formally; about 250 people attended, including Iwa, Abdul Manap, Mangaradja Ihoetan [editor-in-chief of *Pewarta Deli*], and Mohammad Dasoeki.

Jan. 31: *Matahari Indonesia* ceased publication.

Feb. 3: The Kaoetamaan Istri, a women's branch of the BO, celebrated its first anniversary in the BO club house; attended by 200 people; Iwa and Abdul Manap, BO Medan branch chairman, both gave a speech.

Feb. 24: Chauffeurs' Union Persatoean Motorist Indonesia (PMI) was established in the BO club house with Iwa as "provisional adviser."

March 16 and 17: The Opium Regie Bond Loear Djawa dan Madoera [Government Opium Monopoly Workers' Union outside Java and Madura] held a congress, attended by 45 branch representatives; Iwa elected its chairman.

March 24: The Persatoean Motorist Indonesia held a member meeting in the BO club house; Iwa attended the meeting as adviser. On the same day, Executive members of the BO, the Persatoean Motorist Indonesia, the Pemoeda Indonesia, the Nationaal Indonesische Padvinderij [National Indonesian Scout Movement] met at Iwa's office to discuss the establishment of a club house.

April 14: The Tebing Tinggi Sepakat [Tebing Tinggi Agrees] held a public meeting in Tebing Tinggi; Iwa gave a speech.

May 4: The Pemoeda Indonesia held a party in the BO club house; Iwa gave a speech.

May 26: Two branches of the Opium Regie Bond held a joint meeting at the club house of Taman Persatoean Indonesia [Garden of Indonesian Unity], under Iwa's leadership.

June 1: Mr. Soenarjo, a "well-known PNI leader," arrived in Medan.

June 16: A meeting was held under the leadership of Mr. Iwa Koesoema Soemantri and Mr. Soenarjo in the club house of Taman

Persatoean Indonesia to discuss the establishment of a "Volksuniversiteit [People's university]" in Medan.[56]

It should be kept in mind that any information derived from spies and
informers, what Iwa "reportedly" said, and/or any speculation on the
part of PID officers about his activity are not included in the above. In
other words, the above includes only those "events" we can reasonably
be sure happened (that which the PID officers could see with their own
eyes and had no reason to fake) and which Iwa admitted or at least
did not explicitly deny in his interrogation or stated or implied in his
autobiography. We can say this much with confidence: Iwa was active
in the BO and Pemoeda Indonesia circles, which is not surprising given
his Dutch education, his activist past as a leading member of Tri Koro
Darma (youth organization close to the BO, future Yong Java) and the
PI, and the fact that he was personally close to his uncle and Medan
BO chairman Abdul Manap. He met his future wife, Kuraisin, Abdul
Manap's niece and Iwa's cousin, at Manap's house and married her in
Medan at his encouragement.[57] He was also active in the PMI (Persatoean Motorist Indonesia) and the Opium Regie Bond, again not surprisingly, because Iwa like many other PNI leaders saw trade unionism
as a way for the PNI to reach out to "peasants and workers." Finally,
he was active in journalism and publishing and, for a while before J.
Manoppo joined him, edited *Matahari Indonesia*. And he would likely
have participated in the establishment of a Volksuniversiteit, People's
university, with Soenarjo, had he not been arrested in July 1929.

As the Medan PID chief suspected, Iwa might have been preparing
the ground for a PNI branch in Medan, establishing networks among
BO and Pemoeda Indonesia members, trade union activists, and journalists. If this was the case, however, he did not make any real progress.
On December 29, 1929, the governor of the East Coast of Sumatra
ordered the regional intelligence to carry out extensive house searches as
part of an Indies-wide clampdown on the PNI, to learn "how far the PNI
political propaganda [that] the above-mentioned agitator [Iwa] carried
out secretly had taken roots in the bosom of above-mentioned associations [BO, Jong Islamieten Bond, etc.], in this case [in the bosom] of

---

[56] This is based on the summary of East Sumatra PID reports compiled by the Leader
of the Regional Intelligence in Mr. 315x/1930.
[57] Iwa Koesoema Soemantri, *Indonesia Minzoku Shugi*, 72–3.

their leaders." Eighty-eight places were searched, including the houses of Soenarjo, Abdul Manap, Mohammad Dasoeki, Mohamad Samin (former Medan SI chairman), and Taman Siswa schoolteachers. "No positive results" were obtained, but the house searches were successful nonetheless, Governor van Sandick reported to the attorney general, in "raising the self-confidence administrative and police officials so needed."[58]

But it was what the government learned later, after it had made up its mind to intern Iwa to Banda Neira, that sealed its case. When Iwa was free in 1928 and 1929, both the *hoofdparket* and the regional intelligence suspected him not only of PNI propaganda but also and more seriously of clandestine, underground activity. And spies and informers supplied more than enough information to support their suspicion. Though there must have been not a few in Iwa's circles who worked for the PID, we know for sure of only one who was a spy. Mohamad Joenoes is included in the list of names of those who were interrogated and whose houses were searched in the police sweep on December 29, 1929, with this note attached:

> Is in constant contact with all political leaders in Medan; is collaborator of the Regional Intelligence; house search conducted in order to avoid suspicion. Editor of *Benih Merdika* (1920). President of the chauffeurs' union in Medan (1920). Leader and agitator in the D.S.M. [Deli Sumatran Railway] strike (1920). Editor of *Benih Timor* (1925). Commissioner of the journalists' union in Medan (1925). Former editor of *Matahari Indonesia*. Editor of *Bintang Sumatera* (1929).[59]

Being an editor of *Matahari Indonesia*, Mohamad Joenoes was in Iwa's inner circle, along with Mohammad Dasoeki, Abdoel Hamid Loebis (also an editor of *Matahari Indonesia*; Iwa served as his defense attorney when

---

[58] Governor of the East Coast of Sumatra to PG, Medan, March 7, 1930, and the list of people whose houses were searched, both in Mr. 381x/1930.

[59] See the list in Mr. 381x/1930. Mohammad Said says that Mohamad Joenoes started his activist career as vice chairman of the Asahan SI in Tanjung Balai and editor of *Benih Merdika* (Medan SI organ under Mohamad Samin's chief editorship) in 1916. Mohammad Said, *Pertumbuhan dan Perkembangan Pers di Sumatera Utara* (Medan: Waspada, 1976), 16. Hasboellah Parindoeri, better known for his pen name Matu Mona, was born in Medan in July 1921. Graduating from St. Anthony's International School, he worked as editor for *Pewarta Deli* (1930–38) and after traveling a year in Malaya in 1939, served as editor for *Penjedar* and *Tjendrawasih* (1940–41). See Matu Mona, *Akibat Perang* (Jakarta: Gapura, 1950).

he was prosecuted for the transgression of press laws for *Pertja Timoer* in 1928), and Hasboellah Parindoeri (Matu Mona, correspondent of *Matahari Indonesia*), among others.[60] It was most likely Joenoes who informed the PID about the meeting at Iwa's office on December 20, 1928, "to establish an SKBI branch," attended by Mangaradja Ihoetan (editor-in-chief of *Pewarta Deli*), Hasan Noel Arifin (editor of *Pewarta Deli*), Tan Tek Bie (editor-in-chief of Tjin Po), Mohammad Said (editor of *Oetoesan Sumatra*), and Mohamad Dasoeki.[61] The PID also obtained information from spies that Iwa appointed his solicitors—Pematang Siantar, Tebing Tinggi, and Tanjung Balai—PNI propagandists in late 1928, and that Iwa was trying to establish "a central trade union" with the assistance of two propagandists from Java, Soetarmono and Hardjo-soekarto, who "disguised" themselves as peddlers of "Indonesia" brand cigarettes and made connections with contract coolies; and that Iwa tried to establish "cells" of DSM workers.

As the governor reported to the attorney general in March 1930, the PID eventually learned there was nothing clandestine about Iwa's activity and that most if not all of these and similar reports received from their spy network were unfounded. But in 1928 and 1929, the PID trusted the reports and found them alarming. The PID officers believed, like other administrative officials and planters, that collective labor protests and physical assaults on the plantations were "politically" induced from the outside.

And there were plenty of reasons for the government to find the situation on the plantations alarming. Dutch language newspaper *Java Bode* reported on May 7, 1929, for example, that sixteen contract coolies were arrested on the Kotari tobacco plantation in Serdang for establishing "a Javanese nationalist association" and planning an insurrection on May 1, 1930. The next day, the advocate general sent a telegram to the governor of East Sumatra, inquiring about the *Java Bode* report. The governor sent back a telegram to Verheijen on May 10, reporting the arrest of seven "executive members [of PNI]" and eight "propagandists" and stating that this group had carried out "illegal activities" in Kotari

---

[60] Mohammad Said, *Pertumbuhan dan Perkembangan Pers*, 34; Iwa Koesoema Soemantri, *Indonesia Minzoku Shugi*, 71.

[61] See the summary of East Sumatra PID reports compiled by the Leader of the Regional Intelligence in Mr. 315x/1930. Judging from the participants, the meeting was more likely held by the journalists' union. Tan Tek Bie was its chairman in the mid-1920s. See also Mohammad Said, *Pertumbuhan dan Perkembangan Pers*, 46.

and that Iwa was "behind the secret nationalist action." The next day, Verheijen again sent a telegram to van Sandick, instructing him to consult him before taking any measure against Iwa.[62]

Then, van der Plas, as adviser for native affairs to the governor general, also raised concerns about Iwa. In his letter dated June 22, 1929, he mentioned "the underground action" among workers in Serdang and other places in East Sumatra and speculated that Iwa might be behind the movement. He then wrote:

> Besides, if Mr. Iwa Koesoema Soemantri's contact with the underground action in Serdang can be established and the grave character of this [contact] confirmed, I would suggest Your Excellency to intern this former chairman of the SPPL in the Netherlands, former representative of Semaoen, former resident of Moscow to Digul. Not only because the East Coast of Sumatra forms a very vulnerable point, but also because this is in line with the liberal policy of construction the government has followed along with stern measures against underground destructive action and because the arrest of one of the intellectual leaders, based on adequate reasons, will have its favorable influence on Java in general, on the PNI in particular, and call to mind in a convincing way the limits which the government wishes to set.[63]

Just like the question of the SKBI, then being debated by van der Plas and Advocate General Verheijen, the question of Iwa's arrest and internment was also raised by van der Plas who advocated setting an outer limit and thereby signaling to the PNI that the government would only tolerate it to a limited extent. But Verheijen did not immediately respond to van der Plas's report on Iwa. He was interested not only in setting an outer limit but also in determining the right moment to act.

That moment came perhaps earlier than he had expected. In early July 1929, an assistant's wife was killed by a contract coolie on the Parnabolan plantation in Simalungun, East Sumatra. News of the murder spread throughout the Indies and instantly became a cause célèbre for those who had long criticized what they regarded as the government

---

[62] PG to Governor of the East Coast of Sumatra, Medan, May 8, 1929; PG to Governor of the East Coast of Sumatra, Medan, May 11, 1929; PG to GG, May 13, 1929, all in Mr. 449x/1929.
[63] Tijd. wd. adviser voor inlandse zaken aan gouverneur-generaal, June 22, 1929, in Kwantes, *De Ontwikkeling, 1928–Aug. 1933*, 239.

leniency toward the native population. The funeral was widely attended. Telegrams of outrage were sent by Europeans to the governor general and the Queen. Newspapers in Java speculated on a "Moscow-Deli connection." Army troops were sent from Java to Deli to "restore order." The European protest climaxed with a privately convened meeting in Medan on July 16, 1929, attended by 2,300 "Fatherlanders" demanding sterner measures to protect their interests. A Dutch private person even sent a letter to the Queen and created a commotion at the highest level of the Dutch government.[64] Less than a month after that, a local branch of the right-wing Vaderlandsche Club (Fatherland Club) was established in Medan. In the meantime, the laborer Salim's trial started within a week of the incident, five days later he was sentenced, and on October 23 he was scheduled to hang.[65]

In the middle of this mounting European hysteria, Advocate General Verheijen sent a telegraph to the governor of East Sumatra on July 13 and instructed him to send a report on the secret nationalist propaganda he mentioned in his May 10 telegram and to tighten police surveillance over Iwa. Two days later, on July 15, he wrote a letter to the governor, suggesting him that he should consider taking stern measures against Iwa if necessary. He then said:

> His records, however, are such that enough terms are there to take into consideration administrative measures in his case, as soon as it can be deduced out of specific indications with probability bordering on certainty that he has a hand, directly as well as indirectly (through intermediary of henchmen, for instance), in a secret action, from which irregularities can be expected to result.[66]

What the advocate general meant by administrative measures was, of course, internment. Governor van Sandick sent his report to Verheijen on July 24, stating what he would have known already from ten-day and monthly East Sumatra PID reports: that Iwa and "two propagandists from Java," Soetarmono and Hardjosoekarto, were involved in "secret illegal associations and meetings in the sub-district of Serdang," that two propagandists from Java, "disguised as cigar and cigarette peddlers,"

---

[64] See GG to minister of colonies, Oct. 26, 1929, Lt. H. Origineel, Vb. 29-22-29 lr. Y23.

[65] Stoler, *Capitalism and Confrontation*, 75, 82–3; Reid, *The Blood of the People*, 39.

[66] Advocate General to Governor of the East Coast of Sumatra, July 15, 1929, Mr. 672x/1929.

visited almost all plantations and carried out propaganda activities, that Sailan, a former police agent from Surabaya, had established a Ketoprak troupe on the Kotari plantation and collected money, reportedly for the purchase of weapons, and that the police had arrested 20 and prosecuted 4, including Sailan.[67] The governor also sent a telegraph to the advocate general on the same day, reporting that the police arrested eight people on July 15 on the Sibogot plantation for their role in the establishment of a local SR.[68]

The information was nowhere close to what Verheijen called "specific indications with probability bordering on certainty," but by the time van Sandick sent his report to Verheijen, he had already decided to take action on the SKBI and Iwa simultaneously. In a July 24 telegram, he instructed the governor to arrest Iwa and to carry out police searches on July 26.

Iwa was arrested because of "his record," because his central position in Indonesian associational life in Medan made him a suspect, and because the government found in him an easy target to placate the European community in Deli as well as elsewhere in the Indies. On July 29, the advocate general asked the governor general's authorization to keep Iwa in preventive custody "in connection with the communist propaganda he carried out since 1924 in Amsterdam, his continued political activity in East Sumatra, and his relations with the League."[69] Thus framed, the administrative process to intern Iwa started.

The Meaning of Moscow

From the beginning, the advocate general only wanted to make a strong enough case for Iwa's internment on the basis of "his records." He was little interested in his activity in East Sumatra, so little, in fact, that the Council of the Netherlands Indies wondered why Iwa was not questioned about his activity in East Sumatra when it met to deliberate on his internment on March 7, 1930.[70] But as the advocate general wrote, his records looked strong enough.

---

[67] Governor of the East Coast of Sumatra to Advocate General, July 24, 1929, Mr. 757x/1929.
[68] Governor of the East Coast of Sumatra to PG, July 24, 1929, Mr. 712x/1929.
[69] Chief of the ARD, Voorloopig Rapport, July 30, 1929, Mr. 731x/1929.
[70] Council of the Netherlands Indies, Advies van de Raad van Nederlandsch Indie, March 7, 1930, Mr. 315x/1930.

Iwa Koesoema Soemantri, born in Ciamis in 1899, went to Holland in 1922 after graduating from the law school (*rechtschool*) in 1921. Active in the PI, he joined Semaoen in the establishment of the SPLI in Amsterdam in 1924 and became its secretary, and then vice chairman. In 1925 he served as PI chairman. After graduating from Leiden University in 1925, he was appointed PI representative to the Comintern and went to Moscow with Semaoen.

There was a letter Iwa sent from Moscow to "Saudara Baron van Bour de Platte (Soeleiman)" in Leiden, its photographic reproduction in the hand of the ARD, in which he told Soeleiman that Iwa and Semaoen disagreed so much that they no longer saw each other, that the Eastern University in Moscow (KUTV) was like an elementary school, and that he was teaching other Indonesian students. There was a picture of Iwa, taken in Moscow and in the possession of the ARD, who two Moscow returnees, Daniel Kamoe and Mohamad Saleh identified as "Dingli." In his interrogation, Iwa initially denied that he had been in Moscow, but confronted with this letter and this picture, he admitted that he had been there.

He also admitted that he had written a pamphlet, "Statement of the Anti-Ribut," at Semaoen's request. There was also a letter "Dingli" sent from Moscow, via Soeleiman in Leiden, to "Soedara A dan M," asking their help to get an exit permit from the Soviet authorities. It was in the envelope addressed "Saudara Toean Hadji Muchtar" at "Tuan Faddulah, c/o Dewanpengtahwan, Singapore" and dated December 17, 1926, which Visbeen most likely received because "Soedara A dan M," Alimin and Moesso that is, were arrested on December 18, "Saudara Toean Hadji Muchtar," that is Soebakat, fled to Bangkok shortly thereafter, and the CID-SS knew that "Tuan Faddulah" had been used as a secret mail post for PKI correspondence. Iwa had also written a booklet in 1926, *The Peasants' Movement in Indonesia*, under the name of S. Dingley and at the request of Th. Dombal and N.L. Mercheriakov of the Farmers and Peasants International. He obtained his exit permit from the Soviet authorities with Dombal's help. He returned to Berlin with the money he earned by writing the booklet.

He joined with Gatot Mangkoepradja in Berlin, and after a brief stay in Paris, they returned to the Indies in November 1927. He moved to Medan in April 1928, and he continued to correspond with his friends in Western Europe. There were two letters the PID confiscated from his house and office: one from V. Chattopadhyaya, international secretary of the Anti-Imperialist League, to the editor-in-chief of *Matahari Indonesia*, and the other from Nazir Pamoentjak to Iwa, introducing Prof. Dr. Freundlich as "a League man." Iwa admitted that he had spoken with Freundlich when he had visited Medan at the invitation of the Indies government and that he had introduced Freundlich to Soenarjo and Sartono. There was another letter that the PID found in Iwa's house, a letter from Berlin, dated February 25, 1929, which Iwa received from "Abdul Rahman," that is Soebardjo, then working at the Secretariat of the Anti-Imperialist League in Berlin. A notebook was also confiscated in his house, in which two addresses were written in cipher, which the military intelligence decoded as Frau Rose Berlin Ost zv Rigaerstrasse 60 Manfred and Hellm Muller Berlin Nord Ost Langenbeckstrasse 4 Georg.[71]

All of this evidence was convincing enough to persuade the governor general and the Council of the Netherlands Indies that "Iwa played a socially dangerous political extremist role since 1923," as a "communist propagandist for the Far East," "paid by Russia for his participation in the action of the Red Peasants' International," in contact with the Anti-Imperialist League and with trusted men (*vertrouwensmannen*) "secretly," and active in East Sumatra "behind the scenes.[72] It should be underlined, however, that central to the "records" was Iwa's stay in Moscow. There were other Indonesian students who worked with Semaoen and other communists and socialists in the Netherlands and with the League. But only Iwa went to Moscow. How could he not be a communist, a Communist International agent, if he stayed in Moscow for one and a half year, attended the Eastern University, and worked for the Farmers' and Peasants' International? This was the fundamental reasoning. But if we read his interrogation carefully, while keeping in mind what he has to say about his Moscow days in his autobiography, a different picture emerges about him.

Iwa was interrogated by Controleur W.J. Leyds on September 25–28, 1929. Initially, as noted above, he denied his stay in Moscow,

---

[71] Magistraat te Medan en Hoofd van Plaatselijk Bestuur, Proces Verbaal (Mr. Iwa Koesoema Soemantri), Sept. 25–28, 1929; ibid., Dec. 20, 1929; Het Hoofd der VIIde Afdeeling A, namens den Legercommandant, aan Procureur Generaal, Oct. 31, 1929, all in Mr. 315x/1930.

[72] PG to GG, Dec. 3, 1929, Mr. 315x/1930.

but confronted with his letter from Moscow to Soeleiman and his picture taken in Moscow, he admitted, most likely on September 28, that he was indeed in Moscow. Perhaps because the memory of his Moscow days welled back to the fore once he admitted that he had been there, he continued talking about his life in Moscow even after Leyds finished asking all the questions prepared beforehand, so much so that he made a supplementary notation dated September 28. In this part, Iwa told his story while Leyds apparently just took notes without asking any question.

> I must indeed admit that I was in Russia.... Semaoen had departed there earlier, I think at Russian expense, he wrote me from Russia that if I was willing to pay the cost of travel myself, I could study at the Eastern University and there I could get free meal and lodging. Semaoen said that I could not get the travel free because I was bourgeois, at least not a member of the communist party. I wanted to go there for a few months to have a look, and the plan to study there free was tempting. I left for Russia after I succeeded [in obtaining the law degree at Leiden University], at the end of 1925, I believe in December. It was terribly cold. I had a Dutch passport, with a Russian visa, [which I obtained] at the Russian Consulate in Berlin. I got a visa because Semaoen probably had written [to the consulate] for that. Semaoen also introduced me to the University in Moscow as a nationalist who was sympathetic with the Soviet. I went to Moscow with the authorization of Perhimpoenan Indonesia, but did not discuss its matter. Semaoen wanted to do that alone.

> ... At the Eastern University the Administration gave me a pseudonym, S. Dingley. Semaoen was called Serphon, this name was not official, Semaoen had little to do with the University, he was more [like] "Counselor for Indonesian students."

> ... I took a course in Russian, [taught in] Berlitz's method, and a couple of courses on Communism, historical materialism, and French, [taught] by an Austrian ... After a few weeks I had had enough and did not go there regularly anymore. I kept myself busy with teaching other Indonesian students in the dormitory, geography, general history, and newspaper reports. When people noticed that, I was appointed a teacher, but I remained a student. There were then four other Indonesians: Moelia, Minahasa, Celebes, and Oesman; Minahasa was probably Waworuntu [Johannes Wawoeroentoe]; and also there was Pakih.

> I gave no lectures in communism, people did not trust me to do that, I was a student there myself, and did not mind much about that.

I wanted to know more about communism then, but I have never been a convinced communist, and the more I knew about the theory and practice, the more I found it repugnant. I did not like the party men, either: authoritarian, fanatic and one-sided, I was generally greeted with mistrust. I could not move around in Moscow freely; all offices and so on were guarded by soldiers. No one could go in without his membership card with picture, and I was not a member. I wanted to leave altogether, but I had come to know Anna Elinischna Iwanna [Ivanova], who was going to give a birth to my child, she was a student in medicine and worked then as nurse in an orphanage, was not a member of the party and had a very difficult life; she was an intern in the orphanage. I was accommodated badly, slept with eight men in one room, Chinese, Persian, and Caucasian, a changing company, often ill-mannered, uncultured men. The meal was also bad. After a few months ... I did not attend the lectures regularly, and my lectures in history were bourgeois-minded, so they heard from my students who learned a little Russian. I was kicked out of the University, and Semaoen was angry because I did not want to get registered as party candidate... I had no place to stay, in the summer of 1926 I stayed in a village with Anna, 30 [miles?] from Moscow, and lived there among peasants, my wife paid for that, and I gave [her] whatever salary I [earned] as a teacher. I became acquainted with the chairman of the cooperative of peasants' associations, Dombal, and he introduced me to Michiarof [Mercheriakov], a colleague of his in [its] executive [committee]. Through their mediation I became [a] correspondent. Semaoen was no longer willing to help me then.

I became correspondent of a monthly journal for peasants... I also got Dutch and Malay newspapers from Dombal which he got from Semaoen and Dombal paid me. I did that for a couple of months. When my wife's delivery approached, I wrote home, via Soeleiman, [asking] for money to travel home, and in case it was not enough I wrote that brochure [*The Peasants' Movement in Indonesia*] which was published in Russian under Dombal's editorship... I earned pretty good [money]. Then, after the baby was born, I departed. The only connection I still have with Russia is the child. I have not sent money very often, twice fifty guilders each, once one hundred guilders...

I admit to have written this letter "to Soedara A and M." It is Alimin and Moesso. I knew them when they came to Moscow in the summer of 1926; I was then already in the countryside, but visited Moscow once in a while. They were sent as representatives of the communist party in the Indies. They were not that open to me, because I was not [a member] of the party.

They came in August and left in October and left me their address: c/o Tuan Faddulah Singapore, [who] this Tuan [is] I do not know.

The meaning of the letter is: I sent this letter in the envelope [addressed] to Hadji Muchtar, whether it is a pseudonym of Soebakat, I don't know.

A and M are Alimin and Moesso.

I reported there [in the letter] that I only received one letter from them [from Shanghai] ... [then I wrote] that I am no longer a friend of my "kawan [friend]," that is Semaoen, who did not want to work in Moscow but was always intriguing.

He did nothing for the Indies. He wanted to keep the position as representative of the party in the Indies for himself while he was out of the Indies all too long. Besides, he had promised me to write to Kijaji (i.e. the commissaris for eastern affairs, that was Petrowski for some time, then [M. N.] Roy, a British Indian), because I wanted to arrange my departure, but since I fell out with Semaoen he did not want to cooperate [with me to get] a visa, and I could not obtain a visa myself, because I was not trusted; Petrowsky did not want to let me go. I wanted them [Alimin and Moesso] to write to Petrowsky to let this Soemantri go. I had to write them anyway, because I had to know whether the address was still good, after the revolt, for "kedjadian [event]" [in this letter] means revolt. They had already told me in Russia about the plan to begin a revolt after their return, if those in Moscow at least agree with that.

But they told me that Moscow did not agree ... Moscow was afraid of a failure. When they arrived in Shanghai, the revolt had already taken place. Probably Soebakat had speeded it up, and the people who were in the Indies.

I did not get any answer to this letter. But I got a visa later, that is, by Dombal's mediation, I was sent to the border as a sort of prisoner.

I was in Russia from the end of 1925 to the middle of 1927.[73]

---

[73] Chief of Local Administration, Medan, Vervolg Proces Verbaal (Mr. Iwa Koesoema Soemantri), Sept. 28, 1929, Mr. 315x/1930.

Iwa's recollection of his Moscow days in his autobiography is not very different from what he says above, though warmer and more detailed, more resigned to the fact that people easily believed him to be a communist or at least a socialist because he was in Moscow, his bitterness towards Semaoen more low-key, Alimin and Moesso not mentioned, and his memory of Anna Ivanova and their child, Sumira Dingli or Mira, ssweeter. In one respect, however, it is useful to see the time frame in the autobiography. According to that, he arrived in Moscow in October 1925. He married Anna in early January 1926. Their daughter, Mira, was born in October 1926.[74] If his statement is located within this time frame, it becomes clear how quickly he became disillusioned with Moscow: in less than two months, he was kicked out the university. He fell out with Semaoen and became Dombal's protege by the summer of 1926. And after Mira was born in October, he was doing everything he could to obtain a visa to get out of Russia. It is hard to believe that Iwa became "a communist propagandist for the Far East" with this experience, let alone working with Semaoen, Alimin, and Moesso, who did nothing to help him obtain an exit permit. But Iwa's Moscow stay was enough to convince Verheijen, van der Plas, and other high-ranking government officials that he was a communist. On March 22, 1930, the governor general decided on his internment. Iwa went to his place of exile, Banda Neira, not Digul, in June 1930, because he was an "intellectual."

The Pari Underground

Its History

If the SKBI affair and Iwa's internment tell us how the government impressed an association between things "communist" and Digul on the popular mind and posted "no trespass" signs to set outer limits, we can learn from the Pari, the only real, albeit ghostlike, revolutionary underground party, and the way the government handled it what it was like to be in a "no trespass" zone and what was at issue. The Pari, Partai Republiek Indonesia, was established in Bangkok in June 1927 by three

---

[74] Iwa Koesoema Soemantri, *Indonesia Minzoku Shugi*, 43–55. Iwa visited Moscow for the second time in early 1958, but Anna had died just before his visit, in late 1957.

communist fugitives, Tan Malaka,[75] Soebakat,[76] and Djamaloedin Tamin. It grew out of "the communist propaganda center" in Singapore which opposed the Prambanan decision in 1926. It was small, clandestine, and tightly knit. Its purpose was "to achieve the most complete freedom of Indonesia as soon as possible" and "to establish a Federal Republic of Indonesia" by means of "*massa actie* [mass action]."[77]

The original Pari manifesto, which Tan Malaka wrote in Dutch and Soebakat translated into Malay in June 1927, seems no longer available. What we have is a Dutch language summary of the manifesto dated May 1929 and addressed to "supporters of the Comintern in Indonesia." In this manifesto, as far as we can tell from its summary, Tan Malaka and Soebakat located the meaning of Pari in the lessons they drew from the destruction of the PKI. They announced, first of all, that the most important goal for the Indonesian people was to achieve

---

[75] Tan Malaka was born in Padang Gadang near Suliki, West Sumatra, in 1894. Educated in the teachers' training school in Bukittinggi, he went to the Netherlands to obtain a license to teach at Dutch schools in the Indies. He became socialist in the Netherlands, in part because of his encounter with Christiaan Snouck Hurgronje. Upon his return, he worked briefly in a plantation in East Sumatra, the experiences of which hardened him as a communist. He moved to Semarang in 1920, joined the PKI and established Sekolah Ra'jat (people's school). In 1921 he succeeded Semaoen as PKI chairman. He was arrested and banished from the Indies in March 1922. In 1923 he was appointed as the Communist International's representative for Southeast Asia. He established his first base in Canton, moved to Manila in 1925, and moved again to Singapore in 1926. It was in Singapore where he repudiated the party central committee's decision for a rebellion. Party members who followed his instruction to flee the Indies, including Djamaloedin Tamin and Djamaloeddin Ibrahim, were soon to constitute the core group of Pari. See Audrey Kahin, *Rebellion to Integration: West Sumatra and the Indonesian Polity 1926–1998* (Amsterdam: Amsterdam University Press, 1999), 46.

[76] One of the party's chief theoreticians, Soebakat (Axan Zain) contributed an introduction to *Manifest Kommunist oleh Karl Marx dan Friedrich Engels* (Communist Manifesto by Karl Marx and Friedrich Engels) the VSTP press published in 1925. "One of the older and more responsible PKI members," as McVey put it, he fled the Indies to escape internment, established an office in Singapore in 1925, and served as liaison with Sumaun and Tan Malaka, but not with Moscow or with the Comintern representatives in China. He was one of the three leaders, along with Tan Malaka and Suprodjo, to sign a set of theses to reject the Prambanan decision for revolution in June 1926. McVey, *The Rise of Indonesian Communism*, passim.

[77] Unless otherwise noted, for this section on the Pari I rely on Djamaluddin Tamim, *Sedjarah PKI* (n.p.: n.d., Mimeo), Poeze, *Tan Malaka*, 354–446, and Helen Jarvis, "Introduction," in Tan Malaka, *From Jail to Jail*, vol. 1.

"Indonesian national and social liberation" and that the Pari was established to achieve this purpose. As "veterans of the [now] destroyed PKI," they also announced that they had decided not to establish the PKI anew in order to avoid any misplaced hope the people might have about the Comintern. "There exists a bureaucratic leadership even in Russia," and they argued that "after the example of China, Stalin will send his Borodins, van Galens, Cheka, military and other numerous advisers to revolutionary Indonesia." That would not be in the interest of Indonesia, for "there are things the Indonesian people have to do other than waiting for the outcome of the struggle between Trotsky and Stalin." The Pari is a revolutionary workers' instrument to solve these problems.

Second, the collapse of the PKI was due to more than one weakness as explained in Tan Malaka's *Semangat Moeda* and *Massa Actie*. The PKI was not a "strong machine." Its more fundamental weakness, however, lay in the popular belief in "Ratoe Adil [just king] or Mahdi." "The rebellions in 1926 were in essence a copy of what had happened in Aceh and Jambi." Members of the party central executive thought they could start a communist revolution that way. "Lia [Boedisoetjitro]" wrote to "Hasni [Tan Malaka]" in "Tokyo [Manila]" in January 1926 that the eleven leaders had decided to observe "a big feast [revolution]." Men in the underground and talisman [djimat] dealers took the situation into their own hands, and the official party executive in Bandung became isolated. The Pari should never repeat this mistake and become "a proletarian revolutionary party, which cannot agree with the action of Moscow and the Third International."[78]

The Pari statutes stipulated that its sections were to be established in "places which are regarded as important economic, political, and transportation centers" and "where there are at least five members." But it was never meant to be a mass party. As Mardjono, a leading Pari propagandist, said in his interrogation in 1930, Tan Malaka told him that it was "to form cells in various political parties and trade unions to bring these associations under the influence of the Pari."[79] It was meant to be a small, disciplined, clandestine, cadre party. And, indeed, it kept its activity so secret that the *hoofdparket* did not know its existence for more than two years after its establishment. But in late 1929 Soebakat was arrested in Bangkok and the government obtained Pari correspondence

---

[78] Korte Inhoud van het Manifest der Partij Republiek Indonesia (PARI), Vb. 6-8-30 B18.
[79] Proces Verbaal (Mardjono), Mr. 509x/1931.

and literature in his possession from the Siamese authorities. It published no party literature publicly; its organ, *Obor*, was hand-written and circulated from one person to another. Its correspondence was maintained through couriers and secret mail posts, letters written in cipher, all Pari members mentioned in code names, and its manifestos and brochures sent by mail, hidden in newspapers.[80]

Its central leadership consisted of Tan Malaka (chairman), Soebakat (secretary), and Djamaloedin Tamin (commissioner), and was called Kongsi Tiga, committee of three. They never met together after they established the party in Bangkok. Tan Malaka went from Bangkok to Manila, and after he was deported from Manila in August 1927, he stayed in Amoy and its vicinity until 1931, when he moved to Shanghai.[81] Soebakat remained in Bangkok for most of the time until he was arrested in October 1929. Tamin went back from Bangkok to Singapore and stayed there, though he was often away on board as seaman whenever he sensed danger.[82]

We know little about what Soebakat did in Bangkok, except that he was in regular communication with Tan Malaka and Tamin. Tan Malaka was more like a teacher and party theoretician than party chairman, training Pari cadres Tamin sent to him and writing "theses" and *Obor* articles. Central to the Pari activity was Djamaloedin Tamin, who

---

[80] Chief of the ARD, De Partai Republiek Indonesia (Pari), Geheim Rapport, March 4, 1930, Mr. 509x/1931.

[81] Tan Malaka, seriously ill when he arrived in Shanghai, was taken care of by the Comintern Far Eastern Bureau under Hilaire Noulens. As Poeze says, rightly I believe, Tan Malaka was with Alimin in Shanghai. Poeze, *Tan Malaka*. See also Ban Kah Choon, *Absent History*; Takeshi Onimaru, *Shanghai Noulens Jiken no Yami: Senkanki Ajia ni okeru Chika Katsudo no Network to Igirisu Seiji Joho Keisatsu* (Tokyo: Hayama Shuppan Kobo, 2014). One wonders how Tamar Djaja got it right in his otherwise fantasy story of Tan Malaka as Patjar Merah (Red Pimpernel) that Alimin spent a year before he found Tan Malaka in Shanghai in 1931. See Tamar Djaja, *Trio Komoenis Indonesia: (Tan Malaka, Alimin, Semaoen) berikoet Stalin dan Lenin* (Bukit Tinggi, Penjiaran Ilmoe, 1946).

[82] When Djamaloedin Tamin went to Bangkok in May 1927, he contacted Syekh Ahmad Wahad, who had studied with the three older generation of modernist ulama from West Sumatra. Syekh Wahab had known of Djamaloedin Tamin through his articles in *Al Munir* published in Padang Panjang in 1918–21, while Tamin had known the name of Syekh Wahab who had established modernist schools in Siam similar to those Zainoeddin Labai established in Padang Panjang. Syekh Ahmad Wahab was helpful for Djamaloedin Tamin and his colleagues to obtain funds, friends, food and lodging while they were in Bangkok. Wahab was especially close to Soebakat. Kahin, *Rebellion to Integration*, 63.

ran its network in the Indies almost single-handedly from Singapore until his arrest by the British CID-SS in September 1932.

No doubt Tamin was a consummate underground operative, even perhaps the best that Indonesia produced in the Dutch era. He had many names. Aside from Djamaloedin Tamin and Bakri, by which he was known in Singapore, he also used other names such as Gow, Abdullah/Dollah, Si Badu, Lookman/Lohman, Si Besar, Jozeph/Josefo, Sulaiman/Salomon, A. Jacob, Joesoef, Boediman, Iskandar, and Alex in Pari correspondence. He was cautious: whenever he sensed danger, he never hesitated to leave Singapore, often as a seaman on the Singapore-Mindanao-Zamboanga and the Singapore-Bangkok line. He was fortunate: he was protected by a retired CID-SS agent, Pak Said, who told him who were CID agents and informers. Having been trained at the Sumatra Thawalib Islamic school in Padang Panjang and assisted many PKI fugitives in finding jobs and settling down in Malaya, he had extensive network of non-Pari people to rely on among largely Minangkabau religious teachers, especially Sjech Taher Djamaloeddin Al Azhari and his disciples in Perak, Negri Sembilan, Johor, and Penang. And he was supported by a small group of Pari cadres and supporters, the core of whom seems to have evolved from among PKI fugitives who fled to Singapore in 1926 and 1927.[83]

Born in Padang Panjang, West Sumatra, in 1900, Djamaloedin Tamin graduated from government elementary school in 1913. He then studied under Haji Abdoel Karim Amroellah, popularly known as Haji Rasoel, at the Sumatra Thawalib School in Padang Panjang. One of his brightest students, Tamin was a founder of the Sarekat Islam in West Sumatra and joined the PKI in 1922. He cooperated with Haji Dt. Batoeah in editing the newspaper *Pemandangan Islam* (Islamic viewpoint). Arrested for articles published in *Pemandangan Islam* in December 1923, he spent 15 months in prison in 1924–25 and was released in September 1925. He joined Tan Malaka in Singapore in July 1926.[84] Shortly thereafter, in September 1926, PKI members in Singapore under Tan Malaka decided to repudiate the party central committee call for a rebellion. Tan Malaka sent orders to West Sumatra that all of his followers should flee the region.

This might explain, at least in part, why the Pari network was deeply embedded in the Minangkabau society. Basa Bandaro, who brought SI to

[83] See Tamin, *Sedjarah PKI.*
[84] Ibid. See also Kahin, *Rebellion to Integration*, 38–40, 46.

West Sumatra and was the principal financial supporter of *Djago-djago,*
Pemandangan Islam and other newspapers SR published in Padang Panjang in the early 1920s was one of Tan Malaka's key supporters and a
prime conduit for distributing his works and pamphlets to his followers
on Java. Leon Salim and Darwis Thaib, two founders and leaders of the
West Sumatra branch of the New PNI in the early 1930s were followers
of Tan Malaka. When Hatta was in Bukittinggi in November 1932,
a local businessman, Anwar Sutan Saidi introduced him to Kandoor
(Kandur) St. Rangkayo Basam, an emissary from Tan Malaka, who
brought him a copy of the Pari's political organ, *Obor.* Personal and
family ties between Tan Malaka's followers and New PNI leaders were
also close: Anwar was younger brother of Djamaloeddin Ibrahim, former
teacher in the Padang Panjang schools and the main Pari contact between Singapore and Java, and Djazir, younger brother of Djamaloedin
Tamin became chairman of the Padang Panjang section of New PNI in
mid-1934.[85]

In his autobiographical *Sedjarah PKI* (History of the PKI), Tamin
says that he helped more than one hundred PKI fugitives find jobs and
settle down in Malaya in late 1926 and early 1927, but only expected
much from the following ten people for the revolutionary cause: Djamaloeddin Ibrahim (also called Rahman Djamal), Daja bin Joesoef (Tenek,
Aliyasin), and Mohamad Arief Siregar (Mohamad Ajoob Siregar), from
West Sumatra; Maswar Madjid from South Sumatra; Tjek Mamad
(Mansur) from Banten; Kasim (Emang) from Ciamis; Agam Poetih
(Mahmoed) from Aceh; Mardjono (Djohan), Sarosan (Saroso, Agoes),
and Soewarno (Achmad), from Java.[86] Since he wrote *Sedjarah PKI* in
the 1960s, one may wonder whether he simply mentioned those who
stayed with him and played important roles in the Pari and its postwar,
post-independence successor, Partai Murba. In fact, this is not the case.
Tjek Mamad, Kasim, and Soewarno seem to have played hardly any role
in the Pari. Agam Poetih, the bodyguard Moesso brought with him to

---

[85] Djamaloeddin Ibrahim emerged out of young IPO activists as a foremost PKI
leader in West Sumatra. After the government clamp down on Sumatra Thawalib
radicals in 1924, Sekolah Rakyat (People's School) was established in Padang Panjang,
patterned on Tan Malaka's school in Semarang. Barisan Muda (Youth Front) was
organized as the youth arm of SR, which the PKI congress in Semarang in 1925
decided to transform into International Padvinder Organisatie (International Scouts
Organization, IPO). Kahin, *Rebellion to Integration,* 40–1, 62.
[86] Ibid., 47 and 57.

Singapore in early 1926, was close to Soebakat and Tamin, but remained on the margin of the Pari network. The rest as well as several others (such as Umar Giri/Abdoel Rahman, Kandoor/Kandur, and Dawood/ Djaoes) formed what was mentioned in Pari correspondence as the "young men of Tamin's university." All of them were eventually arrested, and, except Djamaloeddin Ibrahim who was kept in Onrust, a prison island off Batavia, then in Cipinang prison, and then in a Bogor hospital because of his tuberculosis, all were interned to Digul. Maswar Madjid was arrested by the CID-SS in September 1928 and interned to Digul. Sarosan and Mardjono were arrested in July 1930; Umar Giri in April 1931; Mohamad Arief Siregar and Daja bin Joesoef in September 1931 shortly after Tamin's arrest in Singapore; Kandoor in June 1933. And finally, Djamaloeddin Ibrahim together with Dawood/Djaoes—who had been briefly arrested with Tan Malaka by the British in Hong Kong in October 1932—formed the bridge to a new generation of Pari activists by the time they were arrested in Batavia and Surabaya respectively in 1936. The history of Pari was therefore that of failure, a series of arrest and internment that befell on Pari cadres one after another. Yet it tells us how the *hoofdparket* got them, what the Pari was all about, and what it meant to be in the underground.

The Detection of the Pari Underground

The first Pari activist interned to Digul was Maswar Madjid. He was arrested in Singapore by the CID-SS in September 1928, after the CID-SS learned that he gave Indonesian students stopping over Singapore Tan Malaka's writings—*Naar de Republik Indonesia, Semangat Moeda, Goetji Wasiat Kaoem Militer* (Jar of Military Testaments), and *Massa Actie*—which he obtained by mail from Amoy, hidden in *North China Daily News*. He was handed over to the Indies government in February 1929 and interned to Digul in October. But he did not reveal anything about the Pari to the police, and the Indies government remained ignorant of the Pari.

ARD chief van der Lely learned, however, that there was a secret mail post in Amoy, "Esquire Lawson, c/o Pit Sang Dispensary, Chan Chuang, Amoy," and believed that it belonged to a core of men that Tan Malaka and/or Alimin and Moesso organized.[87] The Dutch consul

---

[87] Poeze, *Tan Malaka*, 390, 396.

in Amoy learned at the Amoy post office in February 1929 that letters came from Bangkok to Esquire Lawson, and were sent by Viggo-Lund. The Dutch consul in Bangkok then located an Indonesian, Mohamad Zain, working at Viggo-Lund, and sent his picture to the governor general. The *hoofdparket* identified Zain as Soebakat. The attorney general asked the governor general in April 1929 to instruct the Dutch consul to negotiate with the Siamese government for the arrest of Soebakat and recommended his internment to Digul upon his extradition.[88] ARD staff were sent to Bangkok in October 1929 and confirmed that Mohamad Zain was Soebakat. The Siamese authorities arrested Soebakat and confiscated Pari literature and correspondence in his possession.[89]

The ARD succeeded in breaking the Pari code by December 1929 and learned for the first time that there was a party, Partij Republiek Indonesia, founded as an Indonesian revolutionary workers' party somewhere near the Indies. Here, the timing was important. The police clamp down on the SKBI and Iwa Koesoema Soemantri had taken place in July 1929. In early December, the advocate general had proposed Iwa's internment to the governor general. In his letter to de Graeff dated December 17, Verheijen reminded him that in proposing Iwa's internment he wrote that "Iwa intentionally and consciously took the side of those who plotted a deliberate attack on the Netherlands Authority and now seem to plot anew." Whether they participated in the revolts or not, there remained people around, he argued, who were "still working together and trying from abroad to sow the seed for a revolutionary movement in the regions in illegal ways." He had now found evidence, he wrote, which was the Pari, led by Tan Malaka, Soebakat, and Alimin [sic.], with the purpose of achieving Indonesian independence "by means of mass action" and, obviously recalling passages van der Lely quoted from Tan Malaka's *Naar de Republiek Indonesia*, with its sections to be established in places "which are regarded as important economic, political, and transportation centers." Many of its members, however, remained unidentified, he continued, because they were mentioned in code names such as Kan, Joseph, Mandar, Marwal, Ogiri & Co.[90]

The *hoofdparket* also learned from the confiscated documents and letters in Soebakat's possession, Verheijen reported to de Graeff, that

---

[88] PG to GG, April 25, 1929, Mr. 404x/1929; Poeze, *Tan Malaka*, 396–7.
[89] Poeze, *Tan Malaka*, 397.
[90] PG to GG, Dec. 17, 1929, Vb. 6-8-30 B18.

the Pari had sent Tan Malaka's letters to such nationalists as Soekarno, Singgih, and Soetomo to seek cooperation and that the Pari had planned to hold a conference in September 1929, to be attended by twelve participants, six from Java, three from Sumatra, and three from abroad. Based on "Boediman's" letter to Soebakat dated August 10, the advocate general speculated that one of the participants from Sumatra, "Ramantuan," was probably Iwa and that "Jono" and "Nar" who Boediman said were involved in that "eskabei ziekte [SKBI zaak, i.e., SKBI affair]" were Sediono and Soenarjo. He concluded that there was contact between Alimin on the one hand and the SKBI in Java and Iwa in Sumatra.[91] In his fantastic political policing world, Tan Malaka's Pari was joined with the SKBI, Iwa, and Alimin, forming the one, unified, revolutionary underground informed by Tan Malaka's revolutionary vision and strategy.

Soebakat was interrogated by Visbeen in January 1930. Visbeen was most interested in Pari codes. But Soebakat told him little more than what Visbeen had already known from the documents and letters. He told Visbeen that "Boediman" was Bakri and that Alimin was not involved in the Pari. Visbeen did not believe him.[92] Soebakat killed himself on February 2, 1930.

With further investigation, the ARD chief completed his first major report on the Pari in early March. He concluded in this report that the Pari was independent of the Comintern, that there was no connection between the Pari and the PNI, and that it had no connections with any foreign revolutionary parties. The ARD also identified "Jono" and "Nar" as Mardjono and Soenarjo, because they had left for Singapore in August 1929 shortly after the police clamped down on the SKBI and learned for the first time that Maswar Madjid was a Pari member. But it still believed that Boediman/Bakri was Alimin.[93]

---

[91] Ibid. Verheijen's speculation that "Ramantuan" was Iwa might be correct, but it does not mean that Iwa was involved in the Pari. Tamin most likely knew Iwa had been in Moscow, and he must have believed as the *hoofdparket* did that he was a communist. Given his position in the *pergerakan* world in Medan, it is not surprising that Tamin tried to get in contact with him as he did though in vain because of his arrest. Iwa mentions neither Tan Malaka nor Tamin nor the Pari in the pre-war section of his autobiography.

[92] Visbeen, Proces Verbaal (Soebakat), Jan. 13, 1930, Vb. 6-8-30 B18.

[93] Chief of the ARD, Geheim Rapport: Onderwerp Pari, March 4, 1930, Mr. 509x/1930.

The Pari Underground's Network

The detection, and subsequent destruction of the Pari network in Central and East Java in the summer of 1930, however, was not due to this fine detective work. Major hubs in this network were Mardjono and Sarosan. Mardjono (b. 1909 in Kediri), who studied at private Dutch native school (HIS) in Surabaya for six years and then graduated from the Semarang Rajat school in 1925, was a student of Tan Malaka's. He was active in the PKI-affiliated Indonesian Scout Organization (IPO) in Semarang and knew Soebakat personally.[94] In May 1926 he moved from Semarang to Banjarmasin with his friends, Moenandar and Sarosan, worked at the *Borneo Post* as a typesetter, and then went to Singapore in 1927 with an Arab entrepreneur, Said Djen Alsagaff, to work at his printing firm for six months. It was there that he met with Tamin and read Tan Malaka's writings. He joined the Pari, went back to Banjarmasin, and after a short while taught at a private school in Marabahan until Soenarjo came from Surabaya in March 1929 and replaced him.[95]

Soenarjo, one of the founders of the SKBI, had a longer career in the movement. Active in the SR and the chauffeurs' union in Surabaya in the "communist period," he changed from one job to another—a customs clerk in Surabaya, a clerk at the auction firm in Malang, a used book seller in Malang, a teacher at the school run by the Perserikatan Goeroe Bantoe, assistant teachers' union, in Surabaya—before he became secretary of the "Bersatoe" Commercial Press and editor of *Sinar Indonesia* and participated in the establishment of the SKBI in July 1928. In early 1929, however, he fell out with Marsoedi, moved to Banjarmasin in March 1929, became a teacher at Marabahan as Mardjono's replacement, and was recruited to the Pari by Sarosan.[96]

Sarosan (b. 1906 in Purworejo) came to Semarang in the early 1920s, shortly after his graduation from the HIS in Purworejo, worked

---

[94] Soebakat wanted to send him to the youth conference to be held in Shanghai in September 1926 because of his activity in Semarang, but for reasons not entirely clear (most likely because Soebakat could not get in touch with Mardjono in time) Tadjoeddin M.S., future Alphonso at the 1928 Comintern congress, was sent. See Tamin, *Sedjarah PKI*, 41; Poeze, *Tan Malaka*, 406–7.

[95] Visbeen and Mohamad Halid, Proces Verbaal (Mardjono), July 30, 1930, Mr. 509x/1931.

[96] Visbeen and Mohamad Halid, Proces Verbaal (Soenarjo), July 29, 1930, Mr. 509x/1931.

for *Sinar Hindia* as a typesetter, and then became a student nurse at the Semarang central hospital. He joined the SR and the Indonesian hospital workers' union in 1925, participated in the nurses' strike, lost his job, and worked for *Api*, Semarang PKI and SR organ, under Soebakat's leadership. He came to know Mardjono in Semarang, because both of them were active in the communist Indonesian Scout Organization (IPO). He moved with Mardjono to Banjarmasin in May 1926, worked for the *Borneo Post* as a typesetter, joined Mardjono in Singapore in February 1927, worked at Al Ikwan Press owned by Alsagaff, met Tamin, and joined the Pari.[97]

After working as a seaman on the Singapore-Australian line for some time, Sarosan went back to Banjarmasin by early 1928, met with Soenarjo, and then went to Java in April 1928 for Pari propaganda. His activity, it seems, went on smoothly. He first got in touch with Soedarmo, Mardjono's brother and NIS station clerk at Babat, Bojonegoro, who was not interested in the Pari but knew who would be active in trade unionism among railway workers. At his introduction, he met in Cepu with NIS conductor Danoewirjo and let him read the Pari manifesto and other Pari literature. Danoewirjo in turn introduced Soetedjo and Tjokrosoebono, both from Cepu, and Ngadimin from Semarang. All were NIS railway workers and joined the Pari.[98]

Here the timing was important. As we may recall, the SKBI was established in July 1928, when Sarosan was in Java and started Pari propaganda among railway workers. With the memory of VSTP still fresh, there must have been not a few railway workers who wanted to revive it, and rail workers certainly knew who were most likely to be active among them in this endeavor. Danoewirjo (born in c. 1900), NIS conductor since 1921 and a former VSTP member, should have been such an activist, for Marsoedi also asked him to join the SKBI in its early days. In his interrogation after his arrest, he admitted that he agreed to become a Pari propagandist and asked Ngadimin to make propaganda among "old friends," that is former VSTP members and SS (State Railway), NIS (Netherlands Indies Railway), SJS (Semarang Juana Railway) and SCS (Semarang Cirebon Railway) workers. If there

[97] Visbeen and Mohamad Halid, Proces Verbaal (Sarosan), July 25, 1930, Mr. 509x/1931.
[98] Visbeen and Mohamad Halid, Proces Verbaal (Danoewirjo), Aug. 3, 1930, Mr. 509x/1931.

is any truth in police reports that SKBI propaganda was being carried out in late 1928 and early 1929 among rail workers in Pekalongan, Cepu, Magelang, Purworejo, Kutoarjo, Malang, Probolinggo and other places in Central and East Java, some of it might in fact have been Pari propaganda as Tamin says in *Sedjarah PKI*, though neither Danoewirjo nor Ngadimin nor Soetedjo admitted that they had done any activity for the Pari.[99]

But this soon brought about a misfortune, for the Pari network in East and Central Java was badly shaken when the police clamped down on the SKBI and scared railway workers. Since Soenarjo had been marked by the PID as a SKBI activist, both Soenarjo and Mardjono (with whom Soenarjo stayed) were arrested briefly in Marabahan in the police sweep against the SKBI. Shortly after their release, both fled to Singapore in August 1929, and was soon joined by Sarosan. Mardjono was sent by Tamin to Amoy in September, stayed with Tan Malaka for a month, and came back to Banjarmasin in November. Perhaps because he was now marked by the PID as an activist, he was approached by a police *wedana* and started to work as "his spy to watch people coming from Java," while working as a clerk at the local Dutch controleur's office.[100] In the meantime, Soenarjo stayed in Singapore with Tamin, studied Tan Malaka's writings, and returned to Banjarmasin at the end of 1929 with Sarosan. But the resident now banned him to teach at the private school in Marabahan because of his SKBI past, and he was forced to return to Surabaya and became a "propagandist," that is commission agent, of *Soeara Oemoem*, the leading newspaper published there by Soetomo's Study Club.[101]

After joining Mardjono and Soenarjo in Singapore, Sarosan also went to Amoy in September 1929 and returned to Banjarmasin with Soenarjo in December. Shortly thereafter he went to Java, stayed with Danoewirjo, now in Surakarta, for a month, and then with Tjokrosoe-bono in Serang for three months. By this time, however, the situation

---

[99] See Tamin, *Sedjarah PKI*, 67; Visbeen and Mohamad Halid, Proces Verbaal (Soetedjo), Aug. 8, 1930; Visbeen and Mohamad Halid, Proces Verbaal (Ngadimin), Aug. 9, 1930; Visbeen and Mohamad Halid, Proces Verbaal (Danoewirjo), Aug. 3, 1930, all in Mr. 509x/1931.

[100] Visbeen and Mohamad Halid, Proces Verbaal (Mardjono), July 30, 1930, Mr. 509x/1931.

[101] Visbeen and Mohamad Halid, Proces Verbaal (Soenarjo), July 29, 1930, Mr. 509x/1931.

had changed. The SKBI affair scared railway workers. Neither Danoewirjo nor Tjokrosoebono was willing to make propaganda for the Pari any longer. Presumably Sarosan was there in Central Java with nothing to do. Eventually he ran away with Tjokrosoebono's wife in early July 1930, was caught by Tjokrosoebono, given money by Danoewirjo to go away, and then surrendered himself in Surakarta to police *wedana* Ramelan on July 10. He told Ramelan everything he wanted to hear, not only the identities of people involved in the Pari network in East and Central Java, but also its (false) connection with the Comintern.[102]

By early August, all men involved in the Pari network in East and Central Java were under arrest: Sarosan and Danoewirjo in Solo; Mardjono and Moenandar in Banjarmasin; Soenarjo in Surabaya; Soetedjo in Cepu; Ngadimin in Wonogiri; R. Moerdomo in Kediri; Soedarmo in Bojonegoro; Mas Soewarjo in Semarang. A year later, the governor general decided to intern eight Pari members, including Mardjono, Sarosan, Soenarjo, Ngadimin, and Danoewirjo to Digul. The rest were released but placed under strict police surveillance.[103]

From their interrogations, the ARD learned finally that Bakri/ Boediman was Djamaloedin Tamin, not Alimin, and concluded that the Pari network was run by "chief agents [*hoofdagenten*]" and "agents [*agenten*]."[104] The *hoofdparket* believed that Tamin was the chief agent for Sumatra and Iwa his supporter, while Mardjono was the chief agent for Java and Sarosan his agent. As far as we can tell from Tamin's *Sedjarah PKI* and several other sources, the Pari never used the words, chief agents and agents. The ARD projected its own organizational image of political policing onto the Pari, and believed that it had an isomorphic, albeit far smaller, structure with itself. As the ARD saw it, Tan Malaka was van der Most's counterpart, while Tamin was Visbeen's and Sarosan Ramelan's. But they did not just operate in thin air. Their "agents" and supporters were on murky ground, among activists, informers, and spies, sometimes like Mardjono, working as a spy for police *wedana* to protect himself as a Pari propagandist.

Yet in a curious way the words, chief agents and agents, captured an important feature of the Pari network. As we can see in the Pari

---

[102] Visbeen and Mohamad Halid, Proces Verbaal (Sarosan), July 25, 1930; Visbeen and Mohamad Halid, Proces Verbaal (Danoewirjo), Aug. 3, 1930, both in Mr. 509x/1931.

[103] PG to GG, March 21, 1931, Mr. 509x/1931.

[104] Chief of the ARD, Geheim Rapport, March 4, 1931, Mr. 509x/1931.

in East and Central Java, it was a very small network indeed. But the question is what it was supposed to do, if Sarosan, for instance, had succeeded in establishing a branch or two in East and Central Java. Ngadimin stated in his interrogation:

> Sarosan said then that he had come from abroad with his friends whose names he did not say in order to establish a new organization. He talked about the organizations abroad and said that the movement here did not have any success because the organization was not good, and the leaders made mistakes. Therefore, a new party has to be established, which has the purpose of organizing workers anew... The executive of the new party was established in Banjarmasin, [he said,] and branches should be established in Java. Each branch should consist of six persons divided into two sub-branches, namely A and B. The A branch should consist of one member who should lead the branch and come in direct contact with the executive in Banjarmasin. The B branch, comprising five persons, should receive instructions from member A and they have the task to try to expand the new party secretly by joining in various organizations, with the purpose that when mass action should take place, the new party can take over the leadership of the action. The members of the B branch may not know each other and should get in contact with only member A. They may not get in contact with the executive, either. All its work and also the names should be kept secret and especially the names of the executive members. The members of the executive in Banjarmasin should be in contact with the executive abroad, while the executive abroad should take care of the communication of the trade unions in the Indies with those in Europe. This way Sarosan hoped to be able to obtain improvements for the workers, and when the workers have formed a unity, the freedom should come of itself. Sarosan then asked me whether I was willing to become a member of the new party, to which I agreed.[105]

What Ngadimin talked about is the organizational structure of Pari, its shell, as he understood it from Sarosan's explanation. Ngadimin, or for that matter any other Pari member, never said anything about what they were supposed to do once they formed cells in other organizations

---

[105] Visbeen and Mohamad Halid, Proces Verbaal (Ngadimin), Aug. 9, 1930, Mr. 509x/1931.

but the moment for mass action had not arrived yet. Nor did Visbeen and Mohamad Halim, police wedana from the Batavia PID, ask this question, because the answer was self-evident. Recall what the Pari executive did when it sought cooperation with nationalists. It sent Tan Malaka's letters. Recall what Mardjono and Soenarjo did when Tamin persuaded them to join the Pari. They read Tan Malaka's writings such as *Naar de Republiek Indonesia* and *Massa Actie*. Recall what Sarosan did when he met with Danoewirjo. He gave him the Pari manifesto and other Pari literature. In short, the Pari was a group of Tan Malaka's disciples, and its network was that of distributing his writings. In this sense, the words, chief agents and agents, are apt for understanding the Pari, not in the sense the ARD used, but in the sense that commission agents of the Singer Company in the Indies were called agents and their supervisors chief agents.

The Meaning of the Pari Underground

The destruction of the Pari network in Central and East Java was followed, two years later, by the arrest of Djamaloedin Tamin, Mohamad Arief Siregar, and Daja bin Joesoef in the summer of 1932. This was mainly due to the improvement in political policing in British Malaya and the better police cooperation between the ARD and the CID-SS.

As Tamin recalls in *Sedjarah PKI*, Batavian PID chief Visbeen was back in Singapore about a month after the arrest of Pari activists in Java in July 1930. Tamin, always a cautious man, fled from Singapore in August. After that he was almost always on the run, except for several brief stays in Singapore, often shadowed by the CID-SS: as a seaman on board *Darvel* of the Singapore-Mindanao-Zamboanga line from August 1930 to January 1931; on board *Kistna* of the Singapore-Bangkok line with Daja bin Joesoef from January to July 1931; and, later, hiding out in Selangor, protected by Islamic teachers trained at Padang Panjang, from July to December 1931.[106]

By the time he was back in Singapore in December 1931, Arief Siregar and Daja bin Joesoef had obtained jobs at the Nederlandsch Koloniale Petroleum Maatschappij (NKPM, Netherlands Colonial Petroleum Corporation) in Sungai Gerong, Palembang, and the distribution of Pari literature in South Sumatra and Batavia had started to go well

---

[106] Tamin, *Sedjarah PKI*, 69–78.

once again. Daoed (Dawood or Davidson) had also joined the Pari at Tjek Mamat's introduction.[107] In early 1932, after Soekarno was released from prison and joined the Partindo (Partai Indonesia, Party of Indonesia), Tamin recalls, the demand for Pari books, pamphlets, and propagandists picked up. In February 1932, he sent Daoed to Tan Malaka for training, Tan Malaka had by then moved from Amoy to Shanghai. In March, Adam Galo from Padang Panjang got in contact with Tamin in Singapore. In May, he began to be tailed again by the CID-SS; he suspected that a former PKI fugitive that he had helped settle in Kota Tinggi had informed the CID-SS of his presence in Singapore. In July, Kandoor gelar Soetan Rangkajo Basa, who had been out of communication with Tamin for almost three years, came to Singapore and told him that he had been in contact with West Sumatran PSII leaders such as Hadji Djalaloeddin Thaib; he returned to West Sumatra with Pari literature. In August, Adam Galo sent two men, Loetan Soetan Basa and Loetan Madjid, from West Sumatra to Singapore for Pari cadre training. For the first time since 1929, there seemed to be a chance to establish a branch in Padang Panjang, West Sumatra, and perhaps in due course in Batavia and Palembang, too. Tamin bought a ticket to go to Batavia on September 15, 1932. Two days before his departure, however, he was arrested by the CID-SS, along with twelve other men, as they were producing Pari pamphlets at its hideout.[108]

In two days, the CID-SS learned from the Pari correspondence it confiscated that Mohamad Arief Siregar was in Sungai Gerong, working as a clerk at the NKPM and that Daja bin Joesoef was in Pasar Senen, Batavia. Alerted by the CID-SS by telegraph, the PID picked up both men on the same day. At their arrest, the police confiscated *Obor* at Arief

---

[107] Tan Malaka, *From Jail to Jail*, 3: 318.

[108] Tamin, *Sedjarah PKI*, 78–86. Leon Salim said in his interview with Audrey Kahin that toward the end 1928 Anwar St. Saidi, a brother of Djamaloeddin Ibrahim and director of Bank Nasional, introduced him to Kandoor in Bukit Tinggi and that Kandoor, a courier to smuggle Pari pamphlets and instructions from Singapore, identified him as his contact in West Sumatra. Leon Salim stayed in British Malaya for a year, most likely 1930–31 when he was 18/19 years old, and worked together with Djamaloeddin Ibrahim, Kandoor, and other Pari members. He met with Djamaloedin Tamin, but not Tan Malaka. Kandoor, originally from Bukit Tinggi, was a son of big merchant in Karimun, Riau, had a shop in Pekan Baru, and frequently visited Singapore with a merchant passport. I thank Audrey Kahin for sharing with me her Leon Salim interview notes.

Siregar's house and Pari Manifesto (one copy), Pari statutes (two copies), Pari Manifesto dated May 1929 (two copies), letters of Nadir (Tan Malaka) and Goenadhi (Soebakat) to Soekarno, Singgih, and Soetomo (two copies), and a picture of Tan Malaka at Daja bin Joesoef's place.[109] The ARD also learned that another man had been with Daja before his arrest, who was identifed later as Kandoor (Kandur, Mohamad Noer, Djamil, Tagong, Charles, and Tumbel). He was arrested in June 1933.

In the subsequent interrogations, Daja bin Joesoef and Tamin (who was handed over to the ARD in September 1932) said little about the Pari, but Mohamad Arief Siregar told an interesting story about his life, how he joined the Pari and what life was like in the Pari underground.

Mohamad Arief Siregar—to be more precise, Mohamad Arief Siregar alias Mohamad Ajoob Siregar alias Suntoo alias Suntok alias Noekman alias Hongko alias Mohamad Sidik alias Hamzah alias Menteri alias Adik Menteri alias John Little—was born in Beringin, sub-district of Sipirok, district of Padang Sidempuan, Residency of Tapanuli in c. 1908. A graduate from the second native school in Sipirok, he became a teacher-trainee for two years at the Moehammadijah school in Beringin, and then worked as an assistant teacher there until 1924. He then moved with his uncle to Pematang Siantar, to Singapore, to Indragiri, and back to Singapore, from 1924 to 1926. On his way from Rengat to Singapore in 1926, he met with Raoeb from Padang, who introduced him to Bakri (Tamin) in Singapore.[110] The interrogation continued:

6. What is the real name of Bakri?

I didn't know his real name until now. As a matter of fact, I didn't know that his name is Djamaloedin Tamin. The picture you show me (a picture of Djamaloedin Tamin held out to him) is that of Bakri I meant. Bakri often came by and borrowed money from me so that I had almost nothing left any more. On his advice I paid the remaining rent to Sjech Ibrahim with my money left and then went to stay with Hadji Akip, a man from Palembang, who lived at 7 Minto Road,

---

[109] See Hoofdparket, Opgave van te interneeren personen die daadwerkelijk deelgenomen hebben aan de actie van de geheime revolutionnaire "Partei Republiek Indonesia" (P.A.R.I.), Mr. 963x/1933.

[110] Visbeen and Mohamad Halid, Proces Verbaal (Mohamad Arief Siregar), Oct. 6, 1932, Mr. 963x/1933. Raoeb from Padang is most likely Madjid Rauf, who was working as a tapper at the rubber plantation in Kota Tinggi, together with Soebakat and Abdoel Rahman alias Umar Giri alias Idris in December 1926 when Alimin and Moesso were arrested there. See Tamin, *Sedjarah PKI*, 46.

Singapore. A man whose name was Masjwar [Maswar Madjid] was also staying there, a man from Padang, who is now in Boven Digul.

7. Who else stayed in that house?

Only Masjwar and I. At that time Bakri (hereafter named Djamaloedin Tamin in this document because this is his real name) also came once in a while, and I gave him some money. I stayed in the house of Hadji Akip for two months and then moved to 1 Rowell Road, where Chinese rickshaw coolies lived and I got a room with Adam, Moening, Timin, Zainoeng, and several others whose name I don't know, all peddlers from Padang. There also was a man whose name was Soelan, who had a small capital and let the other men from Padang hawk goods. It was the man, Soelan, to whom I was brought by Djamaloedin Tamin and for whom I hawked goods.

8. Where did Soelan come from and what is his real name?

He is from Padang and Soelan is his real name. I worked for Soelan for five months, and then told Djamaloedin Tamin that I was going to work [as a seaman] on board, because I couldn't [earn enough to] eat, could not buy anything anymore. I stayed in Singapore for three more months, got a job as postman at the central post office in Singapore, worked there for three months, and after that worked for nine months as postman at a sub-post office. Then I worked as a seaman on board steamship *Marella* of the [Singapore-]Australian line, made two trips which lasted for about three months. After that I was unemployed for three months, and I stayed with Soelan.

He went on board *Darval* of the North Borneo line as a seaman, stayed with Tamin for three months in Singapore, worked for Soelan, and for Adam after Soelan's departure, and finally in July 1929 he was sent by Tamin to Medan as a courier to deliver a letter to Iwa Koesoema Soemantri. By the time he arrived in Medan, however, Iwa had been under arrest. Arief destroyed Tamin's letter as instructed, stayed in Medan for two weeks, worked for four months in Pematang Siantar at a lodging his uncle owned, and then went back to Singapore. When he met with Tamin (most likely in December 1929 or January 1930), Tamin told Arief that they better keep quiet for some time (most likely because of Soebakat's arrest). Arief went to Pulo Sambu, worked at a BPM (Borneo Petroleum Maatschappij) for three months, and met with Abdoelrahim Siregar and Harahap. The three of them went to Palembang in March or April 1930 and got jobs at NKPM in Sungai Gerong. After working for seven months, Arief wrote to Tamin, asking him to send an assistant. Daja bin Joesoef, whom Arief had known from his Singapore days, came from Singapore.

17. How far did you go with your propaganda for the Pari then and how many members or candidate members did you get?

I did not do any propaganda myself because I had no time for that. I had to work hard from morning to evening, and then I was too exhausted to do anything for the Pari. So there were no members or candidate members for the Pari. Daja came about a month later [after he wrote to Tamin]. I had sent money for his travel...

After I was acquainted with Djamaloedin Tamin in 1926, he talked about political affairs regularly and gave me various books to read, such as *Semangat Moeda*, *Philippine Revolution* and *Chinese Revolution*. The first one was written by Tan Malaka. After Djamaloedin Tamin trained me in politics for about six months, which was when we were staying at 7 Minto Road, with Hadji Akip, he asked me what I thought about the various books, especially that of Tan Malaka. I answered that in my opinion it would be difficult to achieve the goal described in the book and that I thought I was not yet sufficiently informed of politics to understand everything. Djamaloedin Tamin laughed and did not say any more.

Tamin later told Arief about the Pari. He let him read its statutes and regulations. He also told him that "Tan Malaka used to receive f.400 a month from Moscow, but no more" and that "he broke his relationship with Moscow." The party was led by Tan Malaka, Soebakat, and Tamin, Arief said, and Sarosan, Soenarjo, Mardjono, Abdoelrachman (Umar Giri alias Idris, arrested in Riau in April 1931) and several others, all arrested by then, were its members. After he settled down in Sungai Gerong, Arief Siregar met with Pasariboe, a former PNI member and land register (*kadaster*) in Palembang, who introduced him to former chairman of the PNI Palembang branch Samidin.

25. Did you tell Samidin about your plan and did he agree with your ideas?

No. Well, I talked with him about holding rallies ... but he said that the local had to follow the instruction of the PNI central executive to hold no rallies. Samidin was planning at that time to establish [a branch of] the Pendidikan Nationaal Indonesia [PNI Baru or New PNI], but Noengtjik, a former PNI [local] executive member, was against it. I tried to reconcile each other, but without success.

Because I did not believe it right to have an PI [Parindra] and an PNI [Pendidikan Nasional Indonesia, New PNI] side by side, I conceived a plan with Theq Man and Soediardjo to establish the Taman Peladjaran [garden of learning], an association [reading club] which should not have anything to do with politics officially not to scare away government officials. But the plan was really political, was aimed at standing close to the PNI [Pendidikan]. As such, Samidin was to be asked to be its leader and the New PNI [i.e., Pendidikan] was to be born out of the Taman Peladjaran.

26. But the purpose of the Pari is not the same with the New PNI?

It doesn't matter. My purpose was only to form a political party in Palembang, and I first thought about the PNI which is closest to the Pari. Once the party is established in Palembang, it would be easier for me to advance my ideas. Djamaloedin Tamin also told me to try to establish trade unions and for that I asked Daja [bin] Joesoef's help. I don't know what he did in Palembang, but he once told me that he found someone in the inland who was willing to work for the Pari. Because of the party discipline, however, I was not allowed to ask who he was and to follow who he went about with.

... In Palembang I found no one who might agree with my idea and join the Pari. The members of Taman Peladjaran were all supporters of the PI [Partindo] and the [New] PNI. In Sungai Gerong I also had no success initially in establishing a cooperative because of the egoism of various people. When the pay was cut, however, a list went around to strike. I don't know who made the list. I said it was crazy to strike, because they themselves would become victims. Eventually I succeeded in establishing a cooperative. In Sungai Gerong, Palembang, and Plaju, I never talked about the Pari...

This was the story Arief Siregar told to Visbeen and Mohamad Halil. There is little reason to doubt his story. No doubt he spoke only about what he thought Visbeen and Halil already knew. He did not reveal anything about any Pari activists who he knew to be at large. Yet he admitted that he had been a Pari member and spoke about his life, how he met with Tamin and what his life was like after he joined the Pari.[111]

---

[111] See Yamamoto, "Print Power and Censorship," 344, for the two letters Arif Siregar wrote in September 1933, when he was about to be sent to Digul and which *Pewarta Deli* published in February 1934.

There is one striking thing about this story. Arief Siregar had had no stable jobs and no stable addresses since he left Tapanuli. He was free-floating from one place to another, working in one job or another, and meeting and establishing connections with many different people. In this respect he was perhaps not very different from many others he met such as peddlers from Padang who worked for Soelan in Singapore or two friends with whom Arief moved from Pulo Sambu to Sungai Gerong. He was wandering, like many other Sumatran *perantau* (wanderers). But he had a fatal encounter in his wandering. He met with Tamin and something happened. He did not say, and we do not know, what happened to him when he met Tamin. But he accepted his authority. He gave him money. He did what Tamin told him to do. He read Tan Malaka's *Semangat Moeda* because Tamin let him read it. He discussed politics with him. He warmly remembered his laughter when he said he did not fully understand politics. He remembered Tamin shared Pari secrets with him. He joined the Pari. But we do not know, and perhaps he himself was not sure, when he joined the Pari. Perhaps it was when he met Bakri/Tamin, perhaps it was when Tamin revealed Pari secrets to him.

His life did not change markedly after he became a Pari man. He kept wandering, moving from one job to another, from one place to another. Occasionally he worked as a courier, when Tamin told him to do so, as when he went to Medan to deliver the letter to Iwa. Once he settled down in Sungai Gerong, he also did what Tamin told him to do. He established a reading club with the hope that someday it would be a party. As he tells us, however, his political work did not go very far. He was exhausted after his work and people he came to know well were largely Partindo (PI) and New PNI supporters. But it did not matter. Important was the fact that he kept communicating with Tamin, in coded letters and coded names, which Tamin told him to use. To put it briefly, Arief accepted Tamin's authority in defiance of the Indies state authority and his fear of arrest and eventual internment, which was the most important meaning of the Pari underground for Arief.

It should be not surprising, then, that Visbeen and Mohamad Halil regarded the coded letters and coded names as the most important signs of the Pari underground. Recall what Arief said about Soelan. He said he was a man from Padang and that Soelan was his real name. As soon as he said this, Visbeen and Mohamad Halil understood what he meant: Soelan was not a Pari man. He did not use aliases, which meant he did not accept names given by Tamin. Coded names and letters were important, not only because they formed the key to expose Pari secrets, but also because they signified that there was a hierarchy built ultimately on the acceptance of Tan Malaka's authority, the very presence of which negated the established colonial order. It is symptomatic in this sense that Arief had *Obor* written mostly by Tan Malaka in his possession and Daja a picture of Tan Malaka.

Pari men knew they risked internment to Digul once they were arrested. They knew they were in a terrain the government had warned them not to "trespass" with signposts. They were there, because Tamin wanted them to be there and they knew he, and through him, Tan Malaka were watching them. This explains why Ngadimin said in his interrogation that "when the workers have formed a unity, the freedom should come of itself." They were talking about the emergence of a new hierarchy, independent of the Indies state, emanating from Tan Malaka and transmitted by Tamin, which somehow made their wanderings as well as their political liberation meaningful in a new way.

It should be clear by now why the internment of Pari men was never questioned by the government. The government knew that the Pari was small, politically insignificant, and unsuccessful as a revolutionary party. It also knew that most likely it had little to do with the Comintern and that it had few relations with any other political parties in the Indies. But these facts were irrelevant. The measures the government took in destroying the communist movement in the wake of the revolts, mass arrest, imprisonment, and internment, were meant to be both political and educational. It was political, as it aimed at destroying the core of the party. But it was also educational or *africhting* (training) as the Dutch might say, because the government intended to impress its standpoint on the popular mind with these measures. If there were recalcitrants who did not understand its standpoint, they too had to be arrested, imprisoned, and interned according to the seriousness of their delinquency. In this scheme of things, associating with Tan Malaka, an important "no trespass" sign, was very serious. As the resident of South and East Borneo wrote to the governor general in proposing Mardjono's internment, "every effort of this leader [Tan Malaka] to get in contact again with the population of the Netherlands Indies ... must be prevented at any cost, namely by rendering [his] contact persons harmless ... by the application of so-called extraordinary powers."

Thus, all Pari "agents" and "chief agents" had to go to Digul. And because they were associated with Tan Malaka and went into a "no trespass" zone knowingly, no chance was given for their release from Digul as Hillen and Welter wrote. Djamaloedin Tamin, Mohamad Arief Siregar, and Daja bin Joesoef were interned to Digul in August 1933 to Digul. More were to follow them in the coming years. For the purpose of our discussion, however, the important phase of the Pari was closed with the arrest of Tamin, because with his arrest there was no longer any contact left between Tan Malaka and remaining Pari activists, and with this loss of contact, Tan Malaka's legends started to replace his person and his writings as the source of authority and the most important meaning of the Pari was transferred from the Pari onto something else as we will see later.

We have now finally reached the point in which we might consider the questions raised in the previous chapter: how did the government police the movement and how did its policing shape Indonesian popular politics? To consider these questions, it is useful to step back somewhat from the immediate cases of the SKBI, Iwa's internment, and the Pari, and to think about the strategy the government adopted in the wake of the revolts. As we have seen, the government made large-scale arrests, imprisonments, and internments in connection with the revolts: 13,000 were arrested, 4,500 imprisoned, and 1,140 interned—massive in scale compared with arrests, imprisonments, and internments in the pre-revolt years. The immediate goal of this policy of repression was political, that is destroying the core of the Indonesian communist party. But it was only the immediate goal. More important from the government point of view was to teach/train Indonesians that there were limits for government tolerance, that they could go only so far, beyond which they should risk their internment. In this sense, the project was essentially educational: once "no trespass" signs such as PKI, SR, VSTP, Comintern (Third International), Pan Pacific Trade Union Secretariat, Anti-Imperialist League, Moscow, Tan Malaka were posted and their association with Digul impressed on the popular mind, Indonesians would remain within limits set by the government. In light of this project, it makes sense why the government dealt with the SKBI, Iwa, and the Pari in the way it did. The government decided to destroy the SKBI as soon as it learned that it was associated with the Anti-Imperialist League. Iwa had been a suspect even before his return to the Indies because he was in Moscow. And the Pari was a group of recalcitrant natives, because they were associated with Tan Malaka and disregarded "no trespass" signs.

Policing politics with erecting "no trespass" signposts, however, had its own problems. First of all, precisely because "no trespass" signs were posted, the entire PID apparatus—not only the *hoofdparket* with the ARD as its core, but also regional and local PID agents and their spies and informers—watched any trespassing intensely and placed under surveillance anyone who might even remotely come close to those signs. This was the reason that the murky twilight zone the PID was supposed to police for eliminating any "revolutionary" threat to peace and order kept expanding to penetrate ever more deeply into the more respectable, more "normal," political terrain. To see this point, one only need to recall what happened to Abdul Manap, Iwa's uncle, Medan municipal veterinarian, and BO Medan chairman: a moderate nationalist politically and a respectable man socially, he was nonetheless placed under police surveillance and his house searched at least once because of his association with Iwa. In raising the possibility of Iwa's internment, van der Plas refered to "the liberal policy of construction the government has followed along with stern measures against destructive underground action." As we will see, this was the essence of the policy Governor General de Graeff pursued toward the Indonesian nationalist movement in 1927–31. But it is useful to remember that its foundation was being undermined because the logic of political policing expanded the zone of suspicion.

The other problem created by posting "no trespass" signs was related to the nature of the underground. As we have seen, the political underground, a terrain beyond the "no trespass" signs, that emerged in the post-revolt years was very small. The Pari never succeeded in establishing any significant presence in the movement and certainly never offered a threat to the Indies colonial order. Yet it is important not only because it offered an opportunity for the government to erect another "no trespass" signpost like the SKBI and Iwa's internment, but also because it suggested that there was a problem for which no political policing could find a solution. The Pari in Singapore and Java, if not in West Sumatra, was a sect, a group of Tan Malaka's disciples, who believed that once it became large enough freedom would come of itself.[112] It was avowedly revolutionary, and so did the government see it. But it was in fact more educational than political, as Tamin's men were so aptly called "young men of Tamin's university" in Pari correspondence and Tan Malaka dutifully trained men Tamin sent to Amoy and Shanghai. In other words, the basic assumption on which the entire Pari was built was that

---

[112] See Kahin, *Rebellion to Integration*, chap. 2, for how socially embedded the Pari network was in West Sumatra.

if only there were millions of Tan Malakas and Tamins, freedom would come of itself. Tan Malaka and Tamin only succeeded in training at most thirty Tan Malakas and Tamins. The government therefore had no problem in interning Pari activists to Digul. But once "Tan Malaka" was divorced from his person and his writings and transformed itself into a sign as the government in fact did, it could appear in unexpected places. To put it in a different way, "no trespass" signs could be posted to warn Indonesians not to associate themselves with Tan Malaka and the Pari. But association could happen not only on a political-sociological terrain but also in a political-cultural sphere, in fantastic newspaper articles on the Pari and Tan Malaka and in spy and detective stories. That was what happened in the 1930s when the government succeeded in creating a normalcy. But before that, we have to examine the government policy to deal with above-ground nationalist politics.

CHAPTER 4

Managing Nationalist Politics

The historical contours of Indonesian nationalist politics in the immediate post-communist revolt years are well-known. The idea of *Indonesia
Merdeka*, Free Indonesia, caught on in the popular imagination from
the mid-1920s, especially among the school educated. It was pioneered
by Perhimpoenan Indonesia (PI, Indonesian Association), a small association of Indonesian students in the Netherlands, and study clubs
that ex-PI members and other intellectuals established in the Indies. In
the wake of the revolts these intellectuals, often marked by their titles
of Mr. (*meester in rechten*, attorney), Ir. (*ingenier*, engineer), and Dr.
(*doktor*, doctor), embarked on a new, mostly secular nationalist movement. The Indonesian National Party (PNI, established as Perserikatan
National Indonesia, Indonesian National League, and then changed to
Partai National Indonesia) was established in Bandung in July 1928 by
a small group of intellectuals led by Soekarno, and it soon dominated
nationalist politics. But it operated under tough police surveillance and
intervention. Soekarno and three other PNI leaders were arrested toward
the end of 1929. The PNI was disbanded in 1930. In its place came
two rival parties, Partindo (Partai Indonesia, Party of Indonesia), which
Soekarno joined shortly after his release from prison, and Pendidikan
Nasional Indonesia (Indonesian National Education or PNI-Baru, New
PNI), which was led by Mohammad Hatta and Soetan Sjahrir. Both
Partindo and New PNI tried to create a politically conscious mass
movement and to force concessions from the Dutch Indies government.
But "Indonesian political nationalism" was not allowed to go beyond
the stage of elite politics, because the Indies government made sure that
urban-based political organizations would not gain firm footholds in rural

areas.[1] With the change in leadership from liberal Governor General
A.C.D. de Graeff to conservative B.C. de Jonge, the government position on nationalist politics became tougher. In August 1933, the government clamped down on "non-cooperation" nationalist parties. Their
activities were banned. Soekarno was arrested, and this was followed by
the arrest of Hatta, Sjahrir, and other New PNI leaders.[2] Soekarno was
interned in Ende. New PNI leaders were sent to Digul.[3] The nationalist
movement never recovered from the blow under the Dutch. Its associational politics was largely confined to a narrow, secular, urban, elite
political terrain or, as Michael van Langenberg put it, to the Dutch-
educated, urban-based, nationalist establishment.[4] In the final years of
Dutch rule, it is generally understood, "great numbers of different organizations grew, split, merged, and quarreled among themselves," but
the members of the urban elite had come to share an Indonesian
national identity by the time that the Japanese arrived in the Indies in
early 1942 and "those same people who led the movement in the late
1920s and early 1930s were to lead Indonesian independence struggle
in the 1940s."[5]

---

[1] John Ingleson, *Road to Exile*, 138–9. See also Petrus Blumberger, *De Nationalistische
Beweging in Nederlandsch-Indie* (Haarlem: H.D. Tjeenk Willink & Zoon, 1931),
189–247.
[2] For Soekarno, see Sukarno, *Sukarno: An Autobiography as Told to Cindy Adams*
(Hong Kong: Gunung Agung, 1966); Bernhard Dahm, *Sukarno and the Struggle for
Indonesian Independence* (Ithaca: Cornell University Press, 1969); J.D. Legge, *Sukarno:
a Political Biography*, 3rd ed. (Singapore: Archipelago Press, 2003). For Hatta, see
Mavis Rose, *Indonesia Free: A Political Biography of Mohammad Hatta* (Ithaca, NY:
Southeast Asia Program, Cornell University, 1987); Deliar Noer, ed., *Portrait of a
Patriot: Selected Writings by Mohammad Hatta* (The Hague: Mouton, 1975); C.L.M.
Penders, ed., *Mohammad Hatta, Indonesian Patriot: Memoirs* (Singapore: Gunung
Agung, 1981). For Sjahrir, see Rudolf Mrazek, *Sjahrir: Politics and Exile in Indonesia*
(Ithaca, NY: Southeast Asia Program, Cornell University, 1994); J.D. Legge, *Intellectuals and Nationalism in Indonesia: A Study of the Following Recruited by Sutan Sjahrir
in Occupation Jakarta* (Ithaca, NY: Cornell Modern Indonesia Project, 1988); Soetan
Sjahrir, *Out of Exile* (New York: John Day, 1949).
[3] Hatta and Sjahrir were transferred to Banda Neira, a year after they were interned
to Digul as we have seen in chap. 1.
[4] Michael van Langenberg, "National Revolution in North Sumatra: Sumatra Timur
and Tapanuli, 1942–1950" (PhD diss., University of Sydney, 1976).
[5] The quotations are from David J. Steinberg, ed., *In Search of Southeast Asia: A
Modern History*, rev. ed. (Honolulu: University of Hawai'i Press, 1987), 307–11.

It is not the purpose of this chapter and the next to question the widely shared historiography of Indonesian nationalist politics in the final years of Dutch rule from the mid-1920s to the early 1940s. We will examine what it was like to be an activist in those days as a way to see what it meant to be political in a time of normalcy, but what needs to be underlined here for now is that this above ground politics took place in a terrain the Indies government carefully fashioned, watched and policed, while debating among themselves what to do with the native movement, how to guide it, and who to promote, who not to, and who to watch. It is this political space—how it was fashioned, managed and policed—that is the primary focus of our examination here.

Intellectuals in Action

Crucial in the rise of a new, secular, nationalist movement in the mid-1920s was the emergence of intellectuals who called for *Indonesia Merdeka* and spearheaded in the establishment of PI in the Netherlands and study clubs in the Indies. The significance of the western-style school education in the rise of Indonesian nationalism is well understood.[6] What needs to be underlined is the fact that university education came relatively late in the Indies. The first engineering faculty was established in Bandung in 1924. The law school (*rechtschool*) was converted into a faculty of law (Rechtshoogschool, RHS) in 1924. A new faculty of medicine was established in 1927. This development made it possible for a small number of Indonesians to obtain professional education in the Indies. Before these schools started, Indonesians had to go to the Netherlands for higher education, and not a few Indonesians, largely from aristocrat-turned-bureaucratic elite families, did study in Dutch universities. It was this group of university-educated who the Dutch called intellectuals. Their numbers were small. In 1924, for instance, there were more than 600 students from the Indies in the Netherlands,

---

[6] Benedict Anderson, *Imagined Communities: Reflections on the Origins and Spread of Nationalism*, rev. ed. (London: Verso, 1991), esp. chap. 7. Parada Harahap said in the mid-1920s that there should have been a reading public of five million among Malay-speaking Indonesians. Parada Harahap, *Journalistiek: Pers- en Spreekdelictenboek* (Weltevreden: Uitgevers Mij. "Bintang Hindia," 1924), quoted in Nobuto Yamamoto, "Print Power and Censorship in Colonial Indonesia, 1912–1942" (PhD diss., Cornell University, 2011), 171.

including Peranakan Chinese, Indo-Europeans, and Dutch. In 1929 they numbered 109. The number of native students trained at the institutes of higher education in the Indies was also very small—230 in total who had graduated from these schools by 1940. Intellectuals constituted a very small elite of the native society, conscious of their elite status and seen as such by the Dutch and hence treated differently from their less educated brothers and sisters.[7]

Structurally, the brief glory of PI in Indonesian nationalist politics in 1925–27 was a product of this educational development. Indonesian students came to the Netherlands for professional degrees, especially for law degree at Leiden University, before the opening of the faculty of law in Batavia in 1924. It was originally called the Indies Association (Indische Vereeniging) and its organ was titled *Hindia Poetra* (Indies Sons). It was renamed Indonesische Vereeniging (Indonesian Association) in 1922 when Iwa Koesoema Soemantri was its chairman and its organ *Indonesia Merdeka* (Free Indonesia) in 1924. It became an association primarily concerned with political issues in 1925 when Mohammad Hatta replaced Iwa as chairman. Its membership was tiny with 38 in 1926 and 26 in 1929. Its activists included R.M. Sartono (Law, Leiden University), Iwa Koesoema Soemantri (Law, Leiden University), Ali Sastroamidjojo (Law, Leiden University), Singgih (Law, Leiden University), Soenarjo (Law, Leiden University), R. Ahmad Subardjo (Law, Leiden University), Soekiman (Medicine, University of Amsterdam), Soejoedi (Law, Leiden University), Gatot Mangkoepradja (Law, Leiden University), and Mohammad Hatta (Economics, University of Rotterdam), all born in the late 1890s and early 1900s.[8]

The central figure in the PI was Hatta. He was in close contact with Semaoen and Darsono, the two leading PKI members in the Netherlands. Hatta called for Indonesian independence based on national unity, a national united front against the Dutch. His strategy was non-cooperation, that is ignoring the Volkraad and other colonial councils; self-help, self-reliance to develop an alternative national political, economic, and legal structure, in parallel with the colonial structure; and

---

[7] Ingleson, *Perhimpunan Indonesia and the Indonesian Nationalist Movement, 1923–1928* (Clayton, Victoria: Center for Southeast Asian Studies, Monash University, 1975), 2; Susan Abeyasekere, "Relations between the Indonesian Cooperating Nationalists and the Dutch, 1935–1942" (PhD diss., Monash University, 1972), 3–4.

[8] Ingleson, *Perhimpunan Indonesia*, 3–5.

massa actie (mass action) organized and led by politically articulate intellectuals.[9]

PI radicalized under Hatta's leadership. PI representatives attended the International Democratic Congress for Peace held in Bierville, France, in August 1926 and sponsored by the Comintern. Hatta, Ahmad Soebardjo, Gatot Mangkoepradja, and Nazir Pamoentjak also attended the Brussels Congress of the League Against Imperialism and Colonial Oppression, and PI joined its Netherlands section in July 1927. Its openly leftist, pro-communist activities attracted Dutch government attention which placed PI under the Dutch CID (Centrale Inlichtingendienst, Central Intelligence Service) surveillance.[10]

In the wake of the communist revolts, Hatta tried to seize the opportunity to create a new party, Indonesische Nationalistische Volkspartij (Indonesian Nationalist People's Party), in the Indies. Semaoen gave him his Organizational Plan for the new party. Hatta and Semaoen also signed an agreement in December 1926 on behalf of PI and PKI, in which it was agreed that PKI henceforth would accept PI leadership in the Indonesian nationalist movement. Semaoen's Organizational Plan, however, did not provide the base for Hatta's planned party, and Semaoen terminated the convention in two weeks after the signing per the instructions of the Comintern.[11]

Alarmed at the increasing radicalization of PI, the police raided the residences of PI activists in June 1927 and confiscated Semaoen's Organizational Plan, the agreement, and other PI documents and correspondence as "convincing" evidence that PI was under communist inspiration and influence. In September 1927, Hatta, together with Abdoel Madjid Djojoadhiningrat, Ali Sastroamidjojo and Nazir Pamoentjak, were arrested. Their trial began in March 1928.[12]

---

[9] Ingleson, *Road to Exile*, 5 and 9.

[10] Ingleson, *Perhimpunan Indonesia*, 33–4. The CID with its focus on revolutionary socialism and communism was established in the Netherlands in 1919, the same year when the ARD was established in the Indies. On the CID, see Constant Hijzen, *Vijandbeelden: De Veiligheidsdiensten en de democratie 1912–1992* (Amsterdam: Boom, 2016), 64–77.

[11] Ibid., 33–4. See Jacque Leclerc, "Aliran Komunis, The Communist Current: Sejarah dan Penjara, The Past and Prisons," *Kabar Seberang*, no. 17 (1986): 57.

[12] Ibid., 55–6. The police raided the residences of Hatta, Soebardjo, and Soepomo in The Hague and Darsono, Moehammad Joesoef, Abdoel Madjid, Ali Sastroamidjojo and Soelaiman in Leiden. Semaoen's Organizational Plan and the Convention led the government to conclude that the PI was "an extraordinarily dangerous organization."

In the meantime, other PI activists completed their studies and returned home.[13] Some joined established parties in the Indies. Soedjadi, Iskaq Tjokroadisoerjo, and Singgih joined BO, while Dr. Soekiman participated in PSI (Partai Sarekat Islam). Some also established study clubs. Soetomo established Indonesian Study Club (Indonesische Studieclub) in Surabaya in July 1924.[14] Bandung General Study Club (Algemeene Studieclub) was founded by Iskaq Tjokroadisoerjo, Sartono, Soenarjo, Boediarto, and Soekarno in November 1925.

Before Hatta's plan got under way, the initiative to establish a new party came from among intellectuals in Bandung. In July 1927, the Bandung General Study Club was transformed into a party, Perserikatan Nasional Indonesia (PNI, Indonesian National League) under the leadership of Soekarno and Sartono, and it was joined by Iskaq Tjokroadisoerjo, Soenarjo, Boediarto, Soedjadi, and Anwari, among others. It called for "a free and independent Indonesia" through "a conscious nationalist mass action." It started as a cadre party. Only three branches were established from July to December 1927 in Bandung, Yogyakarta (under the leadership of Soejoedi) and Batavia (under Sartono). Another branch was set up in Surabaya in February 1928. The party called for the creation of "a state within the state." Its major propaganda themes were the ruled against the rulers, a united brown front against the white front.[15]

The General Study Club also established a youth association, Jong Indonesia (Young Indonesia), in February 1927, which was soon renamed Pemoeda Indonesia (Indonesian Youth). It too remained small in its first year with its branches only in Bandung, Batavia, Yogyakarta, Surakarta, and Surabaya. Its organ, *Jong Indonesia*, was published with Soenarjo as editor in chief. Its sister association, Poetri Indonesia (Indonesian Girls), started in October 1927. The PNI Batavia branch founded a scouting

---

[13] Most of the core PI members returned home by the end of 1927, but Hatta remained in the Netherlands until 1931. Ingleson, *Perhimpunan Indonesia*, 63.

[14] On Soetomo (Sutomo), see Benedict R. O'G. Anderson, "A Time of Darkness and a Time of Light," in *The Spectre of Comparisons: Nationalism, Southeast Asia and the World* (London: Verso, 1998); Paul W. van der Veur, ed., *Towards a Glorious Indonesia: Reminiscences and Observations of Dr. Soetomo*, trans. Suharni Soemarmo and Paul W. van der Veur (Athens: Center for Southeast Asian Studies, Ohio University, 1987); John Ingleson, "Sutomo, the Indonesian Study Club and Organized Labour in Late Colonial Surabaya," *Journal of Southeast Asian Studies* 39, no. 1 (2008): 31–57; Savitri Scherer, "Sutomo and Trade Unionism," *Indonesia* 24 (1977): 27–38.

[15] Ingleson, *Road to Exile*, 32–4.

organization, which was soon to evolve into Nationale Padvinders Organisatie (National Scouting Organization). The driving forces were Faculty of Law students in Batavia active in the Perhimpoenan Peladjar Peladjar Indonesia (PPPI, Indonesian Students' Association).[16]

The PNI also took the lead in unifying the nationalist movement. Soekarno had been calling for the creation of a federation of Indonesian political parties since June 1927, even before the establishment of PNI. Under the leadership of Soekarno and Soekiman, Permoefakatan Perhimpoenan Perhimpoenan Politik Kebangsaan Indonesia (PPPKI, Association of Political Organizations of the Indonesian People) was formed in December 1927 to bring PNI, PSI, BO, Indonesian Study Club, Pasoendan (Sundanese Association) and others into a common front.[17]

By the time its inaugural congress was held in Surabaya in May 1928, the PNI, though small, had emerged as a dominant force in nationalist politics. It was renamed Partai Nasional Indonesia (PNI, Indonesian National Party). It had four branches with about 550 members: 250 in Batavia, 200 in Bandung, 40 in Yogyakarta, and 60 in Surabaya. The congress also decided to publish its party organ, *Persatoean Indonesia* (Indonesian Unity), the first issue of which appeared in July 1928 with Soekarno and Soenarjo as editors and Sartono as administrator.[18]

---

[16] Ibid., 35. For Pijper's observation on the PPPI and the general trend of using Malay instead of Dutch among young activists, see Verslag van G.F. Pijper van het congres van Jong-Java op 28–31 dec. 1927 te Semarang, in R.C. Kwantes, ed., *De Ontwikkeling van de Nationalistische Beweging in Nederlandsch-Indie, Bronnenpublikatie 3de Stuk 1928–Aug. 1933* (Groningen: Wolters-Noordhoff/Bouma's Boekhuis, 1981), 1–9. G.F. Pijper served under the adviser for native affairs during 1925–31.

[17] Ibid., 46–51. The establishment of the PPPKI was agreed on at the meeting held in Bandung on Dec. 17 and 18, 1927. The committee was constituted with Iskaq Tjokroadisoerjo as chairman, Samsi Sastrowidagdo as secretary-treasurer, and Soekiman and Soekarno as members. See Oprichting van de Permoefakatan Perhimpoenan Perhimpoenan Politiek Kebangsaan Indonesia (PPPKI): rapport van de Algemene recherchedienst, Jan. 23, 1928, in R.C. Kwantes, ed., *De Ontwikkeling van de Nationalistische Beweging in Nederlandsch-Indie, Bronnenpublikatie 2e Stuk medio 1923–1928*, 697–9. ARD chief van der Lely noted in his report that the formation of the PPPKI marked the first step for the creation of an "anti-imperialist (national-religious) bloc."

[18] PG to GG, June 18, 1928, in Kwantes, *De Ontwikkeling, 1928–Aug. 1933*, 54–5; Deputy adviser for native affairs to GG, July 19, 1928, in Kwantes, *De Ontwikkeling, 1928–Aug. 1933*, 79–85.

Two Strategies, Two Approaches

The Indies government watched PI and PNI carefully. The central question was what to do with this new group of intellectuals. Two different positions were offered by senior government officials.

W.P. Hillen, the governor of West Java, represented one position in the letter he sent to Governor General de Graeff on January 20, 1927.[19] He was concerned that "native" trust in the administrative officials had disappeared and the contact between the native population and the internal administration had been lost. He blamed the expansion of special government services such as government pawnshops and credit institutions as well as the educational expansion for the current sorry state. He also blamed the competition movement leaders offered to the administrative officials since the establishment of Sarekat Islam: "the rally man [movement leader] could criticize the government and the administration, normally unpunished." These developments brought about an enormous change "in the thought world of a simple native." "In the past he might once in a while talk pleasantly with his *wedana* [district chief] or *assistent wedana* [assistant district chief] at a village meeting" and he did what he was ordered to do. Now came non-officials, who disapproved whatever the government had decreed. Yet "*wedana* or *assistent wedana* sat by [at a rally] and did not shut up the speakers, [let alone] arrest them!" "Kromo [ordinary, i.e., uneducated and ignorant, native]" may not understand what was going on, but eventually he would conclude that his *wedana* was not such a powerful man as he had thought. These changes were felt most strongly in urban centers. "To maintain their influence," Hillen continued, "these leaders had to make beautiful hopes for what they would do for members, and thus emerged a class of professional leaders ... a sort of demagogues." They attacked "the loyal administrative official" and tried to "undermine" his authority. The paternalistic situation in earlier times [will] never come back, and the governors will be alienated further from the governed."

In his view "professional leaders" were almost by definition "professional revolutionaries." He simply did not believe any meaningful

---

[19] Governor of West Java to GG, Jan. 20, 1927, in Kwantes, *De Ontwikkeling, 1928–Aug. 1933*, 527–32. On W.P. Hillen, see also H.W. van den Doel, *De Stille Macht: Het Europese binnenlands bestuur op Japa en Madoera, 1808–1942* (Leiden: Uitgeverij Bert Bakker, 1994), 389, 399.

dialogue with "intellectuals" of study clubs then emerging on the horizon. Instead, he called for reinforcing the political policing apparatus, arguing that "the non-educated administrative officials were closer than those who had studied at the Osvia (Training School for Native Administrators) and that "when they achieve the rank of *mantri politie* [mantri polisi], they are of far more practical value than the 'educated' officials of the [same] rank."

Resident of Palembang J. Tideman, who would soon be posted to the Moluccas as governor, took a more liberal position on the issue in his letter to de Graeff dated March 2, 1927.[20] Like Hillen, he also located "the movement" in a larger context. He did not believe that the movement only resulted from instigation. He cautioned against equating "the large native movement" with "this excess, which locally went into revolt" and "leaders" with "instigators." What is needed, he argued, is to "give faith" to "the movement," if the government wanted to restore native trust. In his view, any effort for improvement should start with "ourselves," "like it is with the educator, who can maintain no order in the classroom." With "the dismissal of ringleaders and the help of disciplinary means," the teacher might succeed in restoring surface order in the classroom and having classes for some time. But "eventually his inability to win the trust of the youth will take its own revenge. Neither his own interest nor that of his pupils is served this way. It is not sufficient that he is just and gives good education. It depends on his intercourse with the pupils whether he can achieve [his] purpose." "If the boys in the classroom do not accept him as their teacher, there [will] develop fatal alienation for all." This was also the case with the government and the population, especially in a colony, he argued, because "the task of administration has a pedagogical side with it." For the administration to be effective, not only had it to be just and good, but also not to neglect its intercourse with the population and to make them understand that it was their interest to accept the administration. This meant, in his view, the government should work on "those who exercise influence on people's development."

The question was who these leaders were. In Tideman's view, it was not only those "so-called leaders," but also and "above all those people

[20] Resident of Palembang to GG, Mar. 2, 1927, in Kwantes, *De Ontwikkeling, medio 1923–1928*, 552–8.

[who are] influential in desa [villages], kampong [urban quarters], and doesoens [hamlets] who have little to do with politics and the like, but unconsciously influence the popular opinion greatly." He classified the "leaders" into three groups: the full-fledged educated intellectuals, the half-educated journalists and speakers at rallies who styled themselves as leaders with some self-overestimation, and the demagogues or misleaders. Tideman immediately wrote the third group off. It was his belief that the only thing the government should do was "to take coercive measures against them, as soon as the maintenance of peace and order demands such [measures]." He admitted the need for the "European" administration to keep in contact with *volkshoofden* or traditional chiefs. But "the evolution is passing by this category of leaders," he argued, "like the 'adat [custom]'" which was also losing its meaning. They would only play a secondary role in the development of Indonesian peoples in the future. "The more primitive the situation remains, the more the chiefs come to the fore." But once the "new zeitgeist" has reached the people's lives, "anyone who wants to devote his energies to the development of the Indies has to turn above all to the leaders of the first group, the so-called intellectuals." If they become ever more hostile against "our administration" and its measures, Tideman reasoned, their "pernicious sentiments will eventually drive out all sound thinking" and they "will slide down straight into the yawning abyss, that is the chaos, bringing with them their own country and people." But if they were to accept the government offers and lead "the youth and the masses of people" "along the just path of cooperation with the Netherlands," it should be possible to work in a constructive sense.

These two positions, as articulated by Governor Hillen and Resident Tideman, represented the conservative and the liberal thinking in the government in 1927. They disagreed on whether there was any possibility of bridging the chasm between the Dutch Indies state and the native society, whether there was any hope for the government cooperation with intellectuals for native development, and most fundamentally what was the task of the government in the Indies. Hillen was fundamentally pessimistic about the future of Dutch rule in the Indies and was primarily concerned with peace and order. He had little hope for native intellectuals as intermediaries with the native society. Tideman, on the other hand, took the question of "native development" seriously as ethical liberals did in the early twentieth century. He believed in native evolution and took the government to task in pedagogical terms.

But his liberal optimism was hedged by his notion of "leaders." If he were logical in classifying leaders, his third category should have been "non-intellectuals," not "demagogues and misleaders." But the beauty of his notion was precisely there, for if any intellectual turned out to be a troublemaker unwilling to work with the government, he/she could be immediately reclassified into the category of "demagogues and mis-leaders." And if there were not very many left in the first category, his hope for cooperation with intellectuals would turn out to be empty and he would end up in effect in the same position as Hillen's. It was the course nationalist politics took from 1927 to the mid-1930s, but in early 1927, neither Hillen nor Tideman knew what the future held for them and for the Indies.

Governor General de Graeff's position was closer to that of Tide-man's.[21] At the administrative conference in March 1927, which all the regional chiefs of Java and Madura attended, he stated his position about the study clubs thus: [He is aware] that these study clubs are watched with distrust by the administration. This is understandable, because those associations are left-oriented and do not hesitate to admit communist leaders in their midst. In his opinion, however, it does not mean that such associations, especially the Surabaya Study Club, are moving in the communist direction. One should rather see in it an outcome of the idealistic plan of such debating clubs to give each [school of] thought an opportunity to express its views. Since this center for the native political life looks more important for the moment than the organized parties, he urged the administrative chiefs not to take them negatively with distrust and to promote contact [with them]. Personally meeting [with them] and listening to their objections open-mindedly, one can eventually go further than taking a negative position.[22]

Governor General de Graeff pinned his hope on study club intel-lectuals represented by Soetomo. But soon after the administrative con-ference, the CID raided and confiscated Semaoen's Organizational Plan and the Convention at Hatta's residence in the Netherlands in June 1927 and the PNI was established in Bandung in July 1927. These de-velopments put the question of intellectuals in a new light. In the early

---

[21] GG to minister of colonies, Mar. 6, 1927, in Kwantes, *De Ontwikkeling, medio 1923–1928*, 559–69.
[22] Ibid., 568–9.

days after the revolts, the *hoofdparket* was highly vigilant against any sign of communism. The *hoofdparket* had learned from its sister agency, the CID, that PI activists such as Iwa and Hatta were in close contact with Semaoen and Darsono. It had also learned by early 1927 that Soeprodjo, PKI leader in Bandung, discussed with Tjipto Mangoenkoesoemo and Iskaq Tjokroadisoerjo of Bandung General Study Club the creation of a new party, Partij Sarekat Republiek Indonesia (Party of Indonesian Republic League) at the instruction of Tan Malaka and Soebakat. And it had learned that Semaoen and Hatta signed the "Convention" in December 1926.[23]

In the wake of the revolts in Java, the *hoofdparket* had also expanded the meaning of the term *communist*. In the report Attorney General Duyfjes sent to Governor General de Graeff in December 1926, he dwelt on the term *communist* and argued thus: "whatever their understanding of the Soviet regime, those who call themselves communists here in this country and act as leaders of this movement are in general professed supporters of the propaganda methods, which the Third International has prescribed in its struggle against Imperialism and Capitalism, especially for the East. In the present phase, therefore, it is not so much about the ultimate purpose that one theoretically has to aim at as about the means of struggle against the present power holders. Herein shows the Third International the way to the East, and one cannot close one's eyes to the fact that above all in the course of the recent years the number of youngsters who have consciously joined the core of the movement has increased alarmingly."[24]

He saw no reason "to make a sharp distinction between communists and nationalists." Going a step further than Hillen who said that "professional leaders" are almost by definition "professional revolutionaries," the attorney general said all the revolutionaries were communists. In his view study club intellectuals were closet communists. In the same report, he argued that Singgih, Soejoedi, and Iskaq Tjokroadisoerjo were active in an effort "to unite elements of the industrial proletariat and revolutionary intellectuals" in an anti-imperialist bloc, consisting of all the national revolutionary parties." Semaoen's Organizational Plan came

---

[23] PG to GG, April 11, 1927, Mr. 468x/27. Tan Malaka and Soebakat to Soeprodjo and Koesno, Singapore, August 17, 1926, Mr. 468x/27.
[24] PG to GG, Dec. 3, 1926, in Kwantes, *De Ontwikkeling, medio 1923–1928*, 510.

as no surprise to the *hoofdparket* and provided a most authentic piece of evidence to confirm the view it had held.[25]

Since Semaoen's Organizational Plan has been translated into English in its entirety by John Ingleson, we do not need to dwell on it for long. Semaoen set the goal of a new party as creating "a state within the state" on the basis of "self-help." He argued that "our freedom can only be achieved through the shedding of blood and tears" and that "a revolution will only succeed if it is well organized and if it takes place at all places simultaneously." The organization must be led by an executive board. "[W]e must begin with the creation of a solid core. We must set up a new organization with its headquarters, for example, in Bandung. A branch should be established at the capital of each residency to carry out above and underground action. It is not necessary that there be too many branches. For this organization must guide the people to a general and organized revolution. These must occur only one or two days apart. Today in place A, tomorrow in place B, the day after in place C, etc. It must spread in the form of a circle, grouped around fixed centers. Of greatest interest here is the capture of major towns because when these fall into our hands the countryside will follow naturally." We follow the Carbonarists in Italy and the Young Turks in 1908. "The beginning of the revolution must be made at a remote major town, or in its immediate vicinity, so that the colonial power's military power takes some time to get there. Meanwhile, the places weakened by the sending of the army to the first revolution are taken by surprise. If the organization of the revolution is such that at the major places the central thrust is directed towards occupation of the telegraph and telephone buildings, then such places can fall almost without bloodshed." And finally, he envisioned in the central executive

---

[25] Ibid., 509–10. Singgih, a leading member of the Surabaya Study Club, was then active "among young Javanese intellectuals and association leaders in central Java" and called for the formation of Persatoean Indonesia, Unity of Indonesia. E. Gobee, deputy adviser for native affairs, wrote in his report dated May 26, 1928 that Singgih was elected BO secretary at its congress in April 1928 and worked as editor of *Timboel* together with Radjiman Wediodiningrat. Given the fact that the BO in Solo under Radjiman and others formed a major royalist/loyalist force against the Sarekat Hindia/National Indies Party under Tjipto Mangoenkoesoemo and Hadji Misbach during 1919–20, one wonders how far right the political tectonic plate had to move to make Singgih "a revolutionary intellectual." See Deputy adviser for native affairs to GG, May 26, 1928, in Kwantes, *De Ontwikkeling, 1928–Aug. 1933*, 34–5. See also Resident of Yogyakarta to PG, Nov. 19, 1926, in ibid., 464–5.

"the commissioner for national trade unions" who is responsible for "the organization and care of trade unions" as well as "the development of national scouting, which is the core of the future national army" and "the organization of secret societies." [26]

Semaoen wrote his Organizational Plan in a moment of despair in the wake of the failed revolts in Java. Although it was titled Organizational Plan, it was in fact Semaoen's fantasy about organizing revolution in the political void. It contained no political and economic analysis of the Indies and no geo-political strategy as in Tan Malaka's *Naar de Republiek Indonesia*. As Hatta explained at his trial, Semaoen gave his original Malay language text to him in November 1926 in the hope that the PI executive would adopt it as the program for a new revolutionary party. Hatta translated the text into Dutch, but thought it unfeasible. He never submitted it to the PI executive. Semaoen's Organizational Plan did not form a basis for Hatta's phantom new party. Presumably the document was sitting somewhere in Hatta's apartment until it was discovered and confiscated by the CID. Nor was there any evidence that anyone who participated in establishing the PNI read it. But it was written by Semaoen, the former PKI chairman and Communist International agent. It contained such key concepts as "self-help" and "a state within the state" that informed the PI and the PNI party vision. It was plainly subversive. And it was available in Dutch. [27]

Semaoen's Organizational Plan provided an authentic and convincing framework in which Dutch Indies officials, especially the *hoofdparket*, interpreted the development of Indonesian nationalist politics. Attorney General Duyfjes argued in his letter to Governor General de Graeff dated October 28, 1927 that scouting organizations formed "the core of the future national army." His successor, J.K. Onnen, interpreted "the nature and development" of PNI in terms of the PI and the Organizational Plan in his letter to de Graeff dated June 18, 1928. [28] J.J. Schrieke, government representative to the Volksraad, also understood the establishment of the PNI in light of the Hatta-Semaoen Convention and the Organizational Plan and located this development

---

[26] The original Dutch text is in Kwantes, *De Ontwikkeling, 1928–Aug. 1933*, 884–8. Its English translation is in Ingleson, *Perhimpunan Indonesia*, 80–4.

[27] Kwantes, *De Ontwikkeling, 1928–Aug. 1933*, 51. See also John Ingleson's introduction in his *Perhimpunan Indonesia*, 80.

[28] PG to GG, Oct. 28, 1927, in Kwantes, *De Ontwikkeling, medio 1923–1928*, 639–47; PG to GG, June 18, 1928, in Kwantes, *De Ontwikkeling, 1928–Aug. 1933*, 51–7.

in a longer historical perspective. In the past the PKI did not succeed in revolutionizing the SI, he wrote, because it alienated its religious and bourgeois elements. Now, however, Soekiman was trying to rectify this mistake, he noted. "They say nothing unkind to principality administrations" and Singgih now lives in the principalities as an "agent de liaison." Schrieke concluded that the PNI signified the creation of "a national-communist bloc" in the Indies.[29]

The policy implication of this line of interpretation was plainly clear. As the attorney general put it, the enemy is "a relatively small core of determined members" intent on overthrowing "the established Western authority," and the only thing the government can do is to let them understand by repressive means the impossibility to achieve independence with violent means. He also noted that it would be impossible "to eliminate the core with internment and conviction and that the government should be ready to deal with "periodic outbursts."[30]

Governor General de Graeff, however, still sought for a way to engage nationalist intellectuals for "constructive cooperation." The job to figure out how to do it was given to Charles O. van der Plas, former Dutch consul in Jeddah (1921–26) and seconded to the office for native affairs (1927–31).[31] He was instructed to "conduct field investigations and discussions" and to report to the governor general what the government can do directly or indirectly "in order to neutralize and fight the revolutionary propaganda among the native population, in particular in Java and Madura, through better guidance of officials and population." He was to study what the government should do for "political

---

[29] Government representative to the Volksraad for general affairs to GG, Oct. 12, 1927, in Kwantes, *De Ontwikkeling, medio 1923–1928*, 630–9.

[30] PG to GG, July 17, 1927, Mr. 1060x/1927.

[31] Born in 1989 in West Java, van der Plas joined the Indies internal administration in 1911. In 1921 he was posted in Jeddah as consul for the Netherlands at the recommendation of Christiaan Snouck Hurgronje. Back in the Indies in 1927, he was seconded to the office of native affairs under E. Gobee and worked as acting adviser during Gobee's absence from December 1928 to mid-1929. He was bright and knew Javanese, Sundanese, Madurese, Malay (Indonesian) and Arabic. After his stint at the office of native affairs, he served as assistant resident of Blitar, East Java (1931–32), resident of cirebon, West Java (1932–36) and governor of East Java (1936–41). William H. Frederick, "The Man Who Knew Too Much: Ch. O. van der Plas and the Future of Indonesia, 1927–1950," in *Imperial Policy and Southeast Asian Nationalism, 1930–1957*, ed. Hans Antlov and Stein Tonnesson (London and New York: Routledge, 1995), esp. 35–7.

guidance of the people," that is government anti-revolutionary political propaganda.[32]

Van der Plas submitted his report to de Graeff in April 1928.[33] In his 173-page report, he accepted ARD chief van der Lely's thesis on the communist strategy to establish an anti-imperialist bloc with nationalist intellectuals. He agreed with the *hoofdparket* about the PI and its Communist International connections. It was beyond any doubt, he wrote, that nationalist intellectuals were under Moscow's influence. Iwa Koesoema Soemantri, Semaoen's representative in the Netherlands, was PI chairman in 1923. In response to the 5th world congress of the Communist International in 1924 which called for underground action, the September/October issue of *Indonesia Merdeka* published an article titled "Underground action." In November 1925 the PI leadership under Boediarto, Sartono, and Hatta wrote to the Communist International executive committee its support for the Communist International policy for the national revolutionary movements and appointed Semaoen and Iwa as its representatives. The PI also adopted "the Organizational Plan for our National Movement" as its program, he argued, and in December 1926 Hatta as PI chairman signed a "convention" with Semaoen as PKI representative in which the PKI accepted the PI leadership in the nationalist movement.

But van der Plas was more nuanced in his view about ex-PIers (former PI members) in the Indies. He noted that they organized study clubs, two major ones of which were Surabaya Indonesian Study Club and Bandung General Study Club. Indonesian Study Club was led by Soetomo, and he wrote that its "spirit" could best be understood in light of Soebroto in its leadership who opposed the expulsion of Noto Soeroto from PI in his Holland days. On the other hand, van der Plas argued that Bandung General Study Club "consistently strives for the implementation of the PI program, that is the Organizational Plan."

Van der Plas interpreted PNI, the incarnation of Bandung General Study Club, in this light. In his view, its organizational development

---

[32] First government secretary to deputy adviser for native affairs, Aug. 29, 1927, Mr. 1060x/1927. Attorney General Duyfjes was understandably skeptical about the entire project from the beginning. PG to GG, July 17, 1927, Mr. 1060x/1927.

[33] It was submitted to the governor general with Gobee's cover letter dated April 10, 1928, and is now available in Mr. 457x/1928. Van der Plas's preliminary report is in Mr. 121x/1928.

as well as the establishment of Jong Indonesia/Pemoeda Indonesia and National Scouting Organization clearly demonstrated that "the Moscow-PI program is implemented systematically." It was calling for the establishment of a people's party and the organization of "a state within the state." In the meantime, he noted, other associations were being infiltrated by ex-PIers through "the formation of cells": Soekiman Wirjosandjojo in PSI, Soejoedi, PNI leader in Yogyakarta, in the BO central committee, Anwari in Surabaya Indonesian Study Club. Sartono and Soekarno also joined *Bendera Islam* (Banner of Islam) as editors, a national Islamic newspaper published by Tjokroaminoto. And in December 1927 a federation of national political associations in the form of PPPKI was established under the leadership of Soekarno and Soekiman. He thus concluded that "the second offensive of Moscow has started," in accordance with the guidelines determined at the 5th world congress of the Communist International, as "a national liberation struggle" under the leadership of nationalists as agreed on in the convention between PI and PKI, and with "PNI as the center."

The question was how to meet this second offensive. Van der Plas mapped out the political terrain in Java and Madura, and located "counter-forces" in: Moehammadijah, which had been engaged in "constructive" activities since its foundation under Kyai Hadji Ahmad Dahlan and which opposed the communists and Sarekat Islam; Nahdatoeloelama (Nahdatul Ulama), an association of orthodox Islamic scholars established in Surabaya in 1926, which "sought the support, at least the friendship of the government" and "commended" the government for "its recent measures and undertakings in the field of divorce, religious administration of justice, and other matters related to the [Islamic] religion" and whose "influence over the masses is still very big"; autonomous administrations, princely courts of Java's Principalities, and *priyayi* (members of the Javanese official class), although he noted *priyayi* as counter-forces have been weakened, because more and more revolutionary and radical leaders are coming from high *priyayi* families and "the old-fashioned aristocrat-turned-bureaucrats" are outnumbered by "Western-educated native officials alienated from their own society and culture"; Javanists [and other] "local patriots," that is BO and Pasoendan, although they were more susceptible to PNI influence than to PKI, and Jong Java; and, finally, the Indonesian Study Club in Surabaya, "a counter-force of far more importance," whose members' nationalism is "beyond any doubt as much as that of the extremists in

Bandung and Batavia" and having done "[their] constructive work and
learned their responsibility and their own weakness distinguish them
from the doctrinaire revolutionaries."[34]

Van der Plas also noted two groups in the PNI: "the group of engineers with Dr. Tjipto Mangoenkoesoemo as the spiritual father" and
the group of lawyers, represented by Sartono, Iskaq Tjokroadisoerjo,
Soenarjo, and Soejoedi. The most important in the first group was
Soekarno, "a very gifted speaker, an upright and courageous man, who
carries the heart on his tongue, is often incautious, and if he gives his
trust, goes very far in it. As a student he wavered between the Islamist
and the modern nationalist line. The influence of Dr. Tjipto has made
a westernized man out of him, who has also abandoned Islam. I regard
him as a perfectly sound figure, no doubt—he said this himself—revolutionary of temperament and seized by a firm belief in the liberation of
Asia in the near future, but by his disinterestedness, his sensitivity and
sunny openness, someone who in the future, when he has become a bit
older and has learnt to work for a distant future, may be hoped to be
ready for fruitful cooperation." In contrast, van der Plas was negative
about PNI lawyers. Mr. R.M. Sartono, he wrote, was "a secretive, very
cool man, with an unfavorable appearance." "It seems to me that he is
personally the most dangerous among the leaders of this group." He also
found Mr. R.P. Iskaq Tjokroadisoerjo "very secretive, cool, and gloomy,"
Mr. Soenarjo "an embittered young man, though in my opinion [he can
be] easily influenced," and Mr. Soejoedi "idle and morally lax."

Van der Plas was well disposed to Soetomo, but saw him as no rival
with Soekarno. "I would only like to underline," he wrote, "that this
doctor is not a man of great political ideas or fixed lines." He should
be appreciated for his practical work and his "pragmatic" attitude. He
welcomed government support for his work to make Javanese economically independent, and his energy, pragmatism, and knowledge of the

[34] For the Moehammadijah and the Nahdatoel Oelama in the 1920s and 1930s, see
Michael Francis Laffan, *Islamic Nationhood and Colonial Indonesia: the Umma below
the Winds* (London: Routledge Curzon, 2003). Also see Deliar Noer, *The Modernist
Muslim Movement in Indonesia 1900–1942* (Singapore: Oxford University Press,
1973); Alfian, *Muhammadiyah: The Political Behavior of a Muslim Modernist Orga-
nization under Dutch Colonialism* (Yogyakarta: Gadjah Mada University Press, 1989);
Howard M. Federspiel, "The Muhammadijah: A Study of an Orthodox Islamic
Movement in Indonesia," *Indonesia*, no. 10 (Oct. 1970): 57–79.

situation in Java's countryside were highly important for Java's "social construction." So were other leaders of the Surabaya Study Club in his view. R.M. Hario Soejono, he noted, was "accommodating and prag- matic," a "strong supporter of Western education," "a man with whom a lot of good work can be done" and Mr. R. Ng. Soebroto is "an upright cooperator and because of his personality a strong support for the con- structive policy of the government." He also noted that Indonesian Study Club is against PSI, for its leaders such as Tjokroaminoto, Hadji Agoes Salim and Soerjopranoto did nothing for social construction, while Soetomo and others see PNI "theoretically purer and more logical," but "utterly sterile." And he wrote that Singgih as Javanist was distrusted by revolutionary nationalists and that Soekiman Wirjosandjojo was a "European hater" and "uprooted," from whom "no cooperation can be expected."

Having thus assessed intellectuals on center stage of nationalist politics, van der Plas proposed two-pronged strategy. First, the govern- ment should "meet all constructive work with sympathy" and convince native intellectuals that it is possible for them to work for national con- struction under the present administrative system. He did not approach the question of "cooperation" solely in terms of nationalists' participa- tion in the Volksraad and the local councils. He said that it was an important arena for political cooperation, but emphasized the impor- tance of cooperation in "concrete cases for peaceful national construction of native society in all its forms." If nationalist leaders accept Volksraad membership, "they would lose influence on radical elements who need their moderating influence most." He argued that the government should "meet every self-motivation in social and economic fields with sympathy," that government subsidies be given to Soetomo's Indonesian Study Club and Soewardi Soerjaningrat's Taman Siswa, and that a "Dutch-native school commission" for the development of national education should be established. Second, the government should "forcefully combat destructive action" and guarantee "the peaceful development" of the peoples in the Indies. And finally, he proposed to establish "a bureau for political affairs," with the chief official supported by small staff and making use of film, index card system, and other modern technology, to centrally direct this two-pronged strategy,

Van der Plas approached the question of intellectuals as a political management question. His strategy was built on his understanding of Indonesian nationalist politics, its terrain, its major forces, their balance of power, their political and ideological positions and their leaders. His analysis of "counter-forces," to which the *hoofdparket* paid little attention, was the best available in the Indies government, even though it is not hard to note his own biases in assessing personalities. He personally got to know many nationalist intellectuals, including Soewardi Soerjaningrat (Ki Hadjar Dewantara), Dr. Tjipto Mangoenkoesoemo, Dr. Soetomo and Ir. Soekarno. Born in 1891, van der Plas was in the same age group as Soetomo (b. 1888) and Soewardi Soerjaningrat (b. 1891), but 10 or 11 years older than Sartono (b. 1900) and Soekarno (b. 1901). In combination with his large ego, which perhaps Soekarno took care of nicely, this age difference might explain at least in part his patronizing assessment of Soekarno in contrast to his apparent dislike of Sartono and other lawyers who were trained in the Netherlands and had no reason to treat him differentially.

Van der Plas's proposed bureau for political affairs was crucial to his strategy, because it was meant to fill the void left by the office for native affairs which no longer had any good access to Indonesian nationalists and the political policing apparatus. The structure and style of his report reminds us of Dr. Rinkes's 1915 report on the SI. Rinkes, adviser for native affairs at that time, had reviewed major SI leaders in the report and had pinned his hope on Tjokroaminoto for guiding the SI "onto the path we hope or at least not objectionable to our authority." The office for native affairs under Dr. Rinkes had functioned as a de facto office for native political affairs and Rinkes had helped Tjokroaminoto establish his leadership in the SI.[35] Van der Plas might as well have aspired to be another Rinkes, to work with his Tjokroaminoto he found in Soekarno, to guide the nationalist movement under his leadership onto a constructive path, and to bridge the chasm between the government and the native population. But neither Deputy Adviser for Native Affairs Gobee nor Attoney General Duyfjes wanted their bureaucratic rival to emerge under van der Plas. If there was any chance for his proposal to be adopted as a government policy, it was if and when Soekarno would turn around and start working with the government as van der Plas hoped.

Governor General de Graeff made a statement in the Volksraad on May 15, 1928, to send the message of constructive engagement,

---

[35] Missive van den Adviseur voor Inlandsche Zaken, Nov. 30, 1915, Mr. 1263/16, Vb. 1 Sept. 1917, No. 33. See also Shiraishi, *An Age in Motion*, 69, 71–2.

as van der Plas suggested in his report.[36] He expressed his hope that "the healthy sense of self-preservation" would be "a strong dam against nationalism that moves in the extremist direction and against the invasion of false slogans." He then continued:

> One should not think that I am blind to the great difficulty which is in the way of those nationalists who, without denying their future ideals, show the insight that the realization [of their ideals] can be approached [in cooperation] with the government. Their position in the political struggle is delicate and difficult, it attracts a change in their character and personality, on their seriousness and in the firmness of their convictions, but the government is certain that in the long run the exchange will be fully honored. With genuine sympathy, the government continues to watch their efforts and work. It does this with an equally strong conviction as with which it stands aloof—and also vigilant—against those who, because of their utterly unfruitful position of non-cooperation, stand aloof to the government and to the fulfillment of its task.

In light of van der Plas's report, it should be clear that de Graeff had Soetomo's Indonesian Study Club and Soewardi's Taman Siswa primarily in mind when he expressed his sympathy for those who were willing to work with the government and that he had PNI in mind when he warned those who called for non-cooperation.

Yet it was PNI that emerged as the organizational focus for the government's hope for constructive engagement. The reason was simple and straightforward. As van der Plas put it, his strategy was predicated on two possibilities. If PNI remained small and marginal, such nationalists as Soetomo and Soewardi, who van der Plas believed were willing to work with the government in social and economic fields, would have more influence on the course of nationalist politics. But handling PNI was more complicated than handling PKI. For one thing, it was too early to write off Soekarno as a recalcitrant revolutionary and therefore hopeless for future constructive cooperation with the government. And for another, as Attorney General Onnen pointed out shortly after the governor general made his statement in the Volksraad, the time had

---

[36] Bijeenkomst tot opening van de zitting 1928–1929, gehouden op dinsdag 15 Mei 1928, Rede van Zijne Excellentie den Gouverneur-Generaal, *Handelingen Volksraad*, Zittingsjaar 1928–29, 4–5.

not come yet for an immediate drastic action against PNI. It largely depended on whether PNI would get to the masses through "destructive practical politics."[37]

This was the point de Graeff no doubt had in mind when he explained his position to his officials on August 20, 1928. He said that the government decided to "check" the PKI and "immobilize its core leadership" by means of internment and imprisonment, because it was "fed" from abroad. But the situation created by PNI action, in his view, was more serious and complicated. One should have no illusion that nationalist feelings among "the thinking part of the masses" could be suppressed by government intervention and that nationalist sentiments could be silenced. "The nationalist movement is [already] there, one can no longer get rid of it, however much one is against it, [and] one has to accept it as a fact." This does not mean, de Graeff added, that "the government should leave PNI action uncurbed under all circumstances." But "in assessing if and what measures are needed, he himself has to consider carefully what should be achieved with them and if and to what extent the opposition should be weighed against the possible useful effect expected of them." In his opinion the government has two coercive instruments available for PNI, criminal prosecution and internment. The PNI leadership, however, had been careful not to provide any excuse in which it could be successfully prosecuted by the *hoofdparket*. Internment thus remained the only coercive instrument available to the government. But it should be considered the last resort to address the PNI danger, when it becomes too threatening for the government to tolerate. Enough evidence needs to be marshalled "to justify internment decisions." It should also be the internment of a relatively small number of people which would be enough to destroy the PNI leadership. A second massive internment as applied to the PKI and SR was out of the question. And finally, he said, it should achieve its expected effect in a larger circle to exorcise any potential danger in PNI action. For the moment, the governor general did not believe all these conditions were in place to warrant internment measures against the PNI. He did not preclude the future possibility of interning Soekarno and others, but in his view it should be under an "entirely different" situation.[38]

---

[37] PG to GG, June 18, 1928, in Kwantes, *De Ontwikkeling, 1928–Aug. 1933*, 51–7.
[38] First government secretary to governor of Central Java, Aug. 20, 1928, in Kwantes, *De Ontwikkeling, 1928–Aug. 1933*, 101–6.

The government representative announced in the Volksraad on November 8, 1928, that the government would guarantee the freedom of speech "within the limits of public order," but warned that "it would not shrink from any means [to deal with] PNI and other leaders as soon as it learned that their words, by whichever persons and for whatever reasons, threatened to be translated into actions dangerous for peace and order. There are very many who now sigh within the prison walls and on the banks of the Digul [river], who misled by slogans they accepted uncritically had fallen into this misfortune. The government regards it as its high calling to watch not only for the freedom of speech but also for the freedom of those who could become its victims."[39] To put it differently, the government in effect made it clear that PNI leaders as well as other nationalist intellectuals would be held responsible not only for their words but also for the effects of their words on others. It was the effects that created an "entirely different" situation under which the question of PNI would be discussed from late 1928 to the end of 1929.

PNI Mass Action

The government position on PNI was thus that of "wait and see," largely because it was too early to draw any definite conclusion about its position in nationalist politics and it had not yet embarked on popular mobilization. But the leadership position it successfully established among nationalist intellectuals and its attempt to transform itself from a cadre party to a mass party made the government position increasingly problematic from mid-1928 onward. The reason was straightforward: learning from its past experience with the movement, there was a broad consensus in the government that "each agitation of whatever kind in the village must degenerate in resistance against the Netherlands authority and was harmful for a peaceful development of the people and the state authority."[40]

As we have seen earlier, PNI held its first national congress in May 1928 in Surabaya. It was a small cadre party then: in July 1928,

---

[39] Nov. 8, 1928, *Handelingen Volksraad*, 1627. See also Blumberger, *De Nationalistische Beweging*, 221.

[40] Nota resident van Banjoemas betreffende het gevoerde en te voeren beleid ten opzichte van de "extremistische" exponenten van de nationalistische beweging, Feb. 1927, Mr. 274x/1927, Vb. 19-6-28 lr. O10. For a similar statement, see also Deputy adviser for native affairs to GG, July 19, 1928, in Kwantes, *De Ontwikkeling, 1928–Aug. 1933*, 48–50.

there were nine party branches in Java and three outside Java. Eleven branches were established between the May 1928 congress and the year end with its membership reaching 2,787. The Jakatra (Batavia) branch had the largest membership of 869, followed by Bandung (564), Surabaya (482) and Yogyakarta (80). Local branches were led by young professionals as well as teachers at private schools, clerical workers, and traders. As Attorney General Onnen noted in his report to the governor general on June 18, however, PNI had not succeeded in enlisting enough propagandists and most of its branches had only a small number of cadre members.[41]

The PNI leadership was no doubt aware that if local activity were to take place outside its control, the entire party would be in trouble. It kept tight control over local activity and did its best to create a core of cadres it could trust. Regular courses were held to train second echelon leaders. People's universities were established in Batavia, Bandung, and Surabaya. A debating club was organized in Bandung to train propagandists. With its members acting as officials and advisers, PNI also established its footholds in existing trade unions and organized new ones. At rallies often held in movie theaters (such as Changhay Theater in Semarang), Soekarno was always on center stage. As PNI propaganda gained momentum, the party started to be transformed from a cadre party to mass membership in late 1928.[42]

This was a source of major concern for the government. As early as in October 1928, van der Plas wrote to Governor General de Graeff: "the influence of PNI will steadily grow and [the observation I made in April 1928] that a mass action it started would meet no or only weak opposition from other associations is largely established by the factual development." He wrote that the PNI nationalist propaganda would take a far deeper root in the long run than the communist without any real resistance from those educated and well-to-do and that given its influence on students, there would be a real danger "that a great part of intellectuals would join the recalcitrant nationalists in the future." Van der Plas also observed in the report that the central figure for this new mass action was Soekarno. At a rally held in Grisse in August 1928, Soekarno said, van der Plas reported, that "we will not dissipate any force in councils, while we have not enough hands for the propaganda

---

[41] Ingleson, *Road to Exile*, 58–61; PG to GG, June 18, 1928, in Kwantes, *De Ontwikkeling, 1928–Aug. 1933*, 51–7.

[42] Ingleson, *Road to Exile*, 62–8.

in the villages and the mountains. No, we will go into the hamlets and mountains for propaganda and to unify all brothers. Go into villages [and] mountains, the speaker called on his audience, and tell [people] that we Javanese, Madurese, Sundanese and so on are of one people, Indonesians ... Go home and tell everyone the spirit of Indonesia."[43]

Soekarno understood that it was part of his effort to prepare "the terrain" to confront the Dutch Indies state with Indonesian numbers, to make the government take seriously the native power which would find its expression in massive numbers PNI could mobilize. As he explained later to L.J.A. Roskott, chief official seconded to the *hoofdparket*, in 1930, what he meant by "a purposive nationalist mass action" was to put popular pressure on the government to obtain concessions such as the native majority in the Volksraad, the appointment of native members in the Council of the Netherlands Indies, abolition of governor general's extraordinary powers and the penal sanction, and eventually the achievement of Indonesian independence via the dominion status. But in the years from 1927 to 1929, before his arrest, he devoted himself in mobilizing masses in the revolutionary action. In October 1928, he wrote in his letter, "Well, you now understand what Bandung wants. Prepare and once again prepare, continuously agitate, so that before long when the great day of unity action dawns, [we] can go forward with great manifestation indeed. I propose to hold a great open air rally on this great day, followed with a great demonstration-procession.... That great uproar of open air rallies and uproarious processions is needed like rice for the political education of the masses. The masses are not a thinking head. Bringing the masses in motion in this manner, Gandhi, Lenin, Garibaldi, Young Egypt, Young China, and so on have succeeded in organizing the mass will with the powerful elan."[44]

---

[43] Rapport assistent-resident t/b van de wd. adviseur voor inlandse zaken over de politieke toestand, Oct. 25, 1928, in Kwantes, *De Ontwikkeling, 1928–Aug. 1933*, 115–20.

[44] Rapport assistent-resident t/b van de wd. adviseur voor inlandse zaken over de politieke toestand, Oct. 25, 1928, in Kwantes, *De Ontwikkeling, 1928–Aug. 1933*, 115–20; Hoofdambtenaar ter beschikking van den PG bij het Hooggerechtshof van Nederlandsch Indie, Geheim Verslag van het Vooronderzoek inzake de PNI leiders, May 13, 1930, Mr. 501x/1930. Soekarno's letter, dated October 5, 1928, is quoted in part by van der Plas in his Gegevens ten behoeve van een Regeeringsbeslissing inzake de PNI leiders, May 31, 1931, Mr. 547x/1930. Van der Plas did not say who Soekarno addresses his letter, but it could be van der Plas himself.

For local government officials, his call for mass action was tanta-mount to a threat to peace and order. As Soekarno and others attacked the government at PNI rallies, local government officials and police officers became increasingly sensitive to their propaganda and more frequently intervened in public meetings. As John Ingleson points out, it was in part because the government policy blurred "the dividing line between legitimate and illegitimate actions to the point where few knew where they stood." But it was also because the *hoofdparket* let PNI take mass action, while watching it carefully and looking for the right timing to intervene. As the attorney general put it, the time had not come yet in December 1928 for "rigorous police action" on PNI public rallies or a government ban on civil servants joining the PNI.[45]

Whether there were any clearly defined guidelines as regards what was admissible and what was not at political rallies, the question of authority was inherent in the very theatricality of the rally itself, because at issue were the effects on the audience of what Soekarno and other PNI leaders said at rallies and whether police intervened or not.[46] We can see this point at a PNI open rally held in Semarang in December 1928 in which the local PID chief and the police *wedana*, who attended the rally at the instruction of the resident of Semarang, banned Soekarno from continuing his speech after an interruption. Defending the police action, Governor of Central Java van Gulik argued to the governor general that if the police, after the first interruption and warning, had just given Soekarno a second warning and not banned him from conti-nuing his speech, "the intervention [interruption] would have been counter-productive of what was intended [to achieve], because it would have given the audience a [wrong] impression that the police looked powerless either against the courage or against the will power of the speakers.... I should also like to point out that the police action at such public rallies must satisfy this demand that it clearly gives the impression on the uneducated masses of audience that the Government maintains the Authority."[47]

Yet PNI continued its mass action in 1929, in the process of which it officially decided to transform itself from a cadre to a mass party. The second PNI congress held in Semarang in May 1929 agreed

---

[45] Ingleson, *Road to Exile*, 77–80; PG to GG, Dec. 15, 1928, Mr. 1181x/1928.

[46] For the question of authority and the theatricality of the rally in other contexts, see Shiraishi, *An Age in Motion*, 65–8, 159–65.

[47] Governor of Central Java to GG, Dec. 4, 1928, Mr. 1181x/1928.

on establishing trade unions and peasant organizations. Party leaders no doubt worried that new party members might go wild. They decided to establish a committee to ensure uniformity in the handling of subjects at branch cadre training courses and to impose tighter control over branch and lower level activities.[48]

After the congress, unions were established: Persatoean Motorist Indonesia (Indonesian Chauffeurs' Union) in Bandung; Sarekat Anak Kapal Indonesia (Indonesian Sailors' Union) in Tanjung Priok, Batavia; Persatoean Djongos Indonesia (Indonesian Servants' Union) and O.J.S. Bond Indonesia (Indonesian East Java Steamtram Workers' Union) in Surabaya. Reading clubs were organized for workers to read and discuss PNI organ *Persatoean Indonesia* (Unity of Indonesia) and other PNI literature. PNI membership expanded. It reached 1,700 in Batavia and 2,800 in Bandung. Three types of member meetings were organized: cadre training courses, extra cadre training courses, and debating club meetings. Its cadre training courses in Bandung, often presided over by Soekarno, attracted 800 to 1,000 members, and a series of PNI open rallies held in August 1929 attracted 2,500 in Yogyakarta, 800 in Palembang, 330 in Batavia, and 600 in Garut, West Java.[49]

The PNI propaganda actions alarmed the government and annoyed local administrative and police officials. The basic approach was one of warning, telling the PNI central leadership not to go beyond the limits the government could tolerate and showing where the "no trespass" signs were placed. The government clamped down on the SKBI and arrested Iwa Koesoema Soemantri in July 1929 and interned SKBI leaders and activists to Digul in December 1929 and Iwa to Banda Neira in March 1930. In another word, the government hit something which had gone into "no trespass" zones and sent the signal to Soekarno and the PNI to watch out. The government stated in the Volksraad on July 9, 1929— two weeks before it clamped down on the SKBI and arrested Iwa—that it was watching PNI carefully and that it would not hesitate to intervene if the PNI leadership did not meet three conditions: to use its forces for socially constructive work and guard against destructive actions; to maintain sufficient discipline over its party and to prevent any active resistance movement of its members; and to exercise caution in its recent

---

[48] Ingleson, *Road to Exile*, 90.
[49] Advocate General to GG, Oct. 9, 1929, in Kwantes, *De Ontwikkeling, 1928–Aug. 1933*, 282–9; Ingleson, *Road to Exile*, 94–6.

involvement in trade unionism. The government also warned PNI about its relationship with PI and Liga (Liga tegen koloniale onderdrukking, League against Colonial Suppression). And on August 6, 1929, after the suppression of SKBI and the arrest of Iwa, the government representative to the Volksraad again stated that the government would expect popular leaders to have sufficient sense of responsibility and warned that if disturbance and excesses were caused by their propaganda, the government would have to take severe measures. As far as the nationalist action was concerned, he continued, the government would tie all action to double demands: they carry out their activity within the limits of order and authority and that such an action leads to strong social or political constructive work.[50]

But PNI kept organizing open rallies, member meetings, and cadre training courses and continued its propaganda activities. Local officials demanded that the government take tougher measures against the party. Although his suggestion was turned down, the governor of Central Java proposed in August 1929 that the government ban civil servants from joining PNI. In October, the governor of West Java banned police officers from joining PNI and the army commander forbid soldiers and their family members and servants from participating in the party. In November Advocate General Verheijen instructed regional chiefs to report on rumors about disturbances, strikes, and so on. As John Ingleson rightly points out, this inquiry generated more rumors about PNI-led disturbances. Equally important, such rumors were a clear sign that memories of the 1926–27 revolts were returning to the popular mind. PNI rallies, member meetings, and cadre training courses, combined with tough police control over its activity, reminded people of PKI as well as all the consequences of its action—revolts, arrests, imprisonments and internments. The resident of Central Priangan, West Java, reported, for instance, that more than 100 PNI members handed over their membership cards to the police in Cimahi and Lembang in December, because they were afraid of "getting into trouble."[51]

---

[50] *Handelingen Volksraad*, Aug. 6, 1929. Also see Blumberger, *De Nationalistische Beweging*, 239.

[51] See Advocate General to GG, Sept. 16, 1929, in Kwantes, *De Ontwikkeling, 1928– Aug. 1933*, 275–9; Army Commander to GG, Oct. 30, 1929, in *De Ontwikkeling*, 303; Advocate General to Heads of Regional Administration, Nov. 6, 1929, in *De Ontwikkeling*, 308–9; Resident of Central Priangan to PG, Jan. 2, 1929, Mr. 20x/ 1930; Ingleson, *Road to Exile*, 104–6, 109.

Rumors of imminent disturbances also reminded Governor General de Graeff and Advocate General Verheijne of the communist revolts and prompted their decision to clamp down on the PNI. De Graaf wrote to Minister of Colonies de Graaff on January 9, 1930 that after December 15 rumors of imminent disturbances reported to the *hoofdparket* suddenly increased and that both authorities and private persons received anonymous warnings toward the end of December. He therefore concluded, he said, that revolts were in the making in the near future. Of particular importance in this connection, judging from ARD chief van der Most's January 3, 1930, report, was a Bandung PID report dated December 19, 1929. It reported that "according to Soekarno, the PNI central executive naturally cannot do anything, due to the vast number of its members, against the disturbances the members might cause as a result of their untenable living situation ... But it is certain that the central executive, nonetheless, would be suspected later that it has had a hand in those excesses because the riots are caused by [its] members." "Ir. Soekarno fears," the report continued, that "workers have already turned to that" and that the disturbances will take place on May 1, 1930. It is probably the work of former PKI members who have now joined the PNI and instigated others to the making of excesses. The disturbances will mean a disaster for the central leadership." The report, in other words, expected a repeat of the disturbances in late 1926.[52]

On December 24, 1929, the attorney general, with Governor General de Graeff's approval, sent a secret circular to regional chiefs, instructing to conduct house searches on PNI offices, its leaders' and propagandists' residences, and other possible hideouts such as local clubs, editorial offices, and schools on Sunday morning, at 6:00 a.m., on December 29, to confiscate all important documents, to interrogate PNI leaders and propagandists about party activities, and to report to him by telegraph about the result of house searches, especially information as regards its revolutionary action, its contact with abroad, and those who should be considered for internment. Ir. Soekarno (chairman; Bandung

---

[52] GG to minister of colonies, Dec. 25, 1929, in Kwantes, *De Ontwikkeling, 1928–Aug. 1933*, 318; GG to minister of colonies, Jan. 9, 1930, in Kwantes, *De Ontwikkeling, 1928–Aug. 1933*, 323–5; Chief of the ARD, Voorloopig Rapport, Jan. 3, 1930, Mr. 30x/1930. For more on De Graeff's thinking as shown in his letters to Idenburg, see Bloembergen, *De Geschiedenis van de Politie in Nederlands-Indie* (Amsterdam: University of Amsterdam Press, 2009), 286–9.

branch chairman), Mr. Gatot Mangkoepradja (second secretary; Bandung branch first secretary), Inoe Perbatasari (secretary of Indonesia Chauffeurs' Union), Maskoen (Bandung branch secretary), Mr. Iskaq Tjokroadisoerjo (first secretary; Bandung branch treasurer), Soepradinata and Soekemi were under arrest.[53]

Shortly after the government intervention, Kiewiet de Jonge, government representative to the Volksraad made a statement to underline no policy change to the nationalist movement. "The government policy toward the people's movement—I am authorized to make this announcement expressly—is and remains unchanged. What happened is the clear consequence of that policy. There is always a line drawn between evolutionaries and revolutionaries, between socially useful constructive work and socially dangerous destructive activity. The government has always warned that it shall not tolerate the revolutionary inclination swelling into serious threats. It has always put it as its duty to protect the seeds of sound growth in the native society against harm by popular violence. What is socially productive must be encouraged or at least permitted and what is socially destructive must be assailed and destroyed."

The government clamp down on the PNI thus signified not the refutation of its previous policy of constructive engagement. Translated in practical terms, it sent a signal to PNI and the public to announce that the government would not destroy PNI, not ban it, and not be hostile to the "well-intentioned, at least reformable, currents in PNI." The attorney general also confidently added: "The timely launched counter action has markedly purified the atmosphere and once again demonstrated at the same time that the great mass [of people], relying on their trust in the government, want as always to stay away from the relatively small group of sensational intellectuals and has accepted a government action against them as something self-evident." Reading government documents sent from the Indies, following nationalist politics via government reports, and writing about it in The Hague, Petrus Blumberger, chief cabinet secretary in the ministry of colonies, concluded his chapter on PNI that "the atmosphere in the popular movement was purified and cleared up anew, now that [the government] put

---

[53] PG to Heads of regional administration, Dec. 24, 1929, in Kwantes, *De Ontwikkeling, 1928–Aug. 1933*, 317–8. See also GG to minister of colonies, Dec. 25, 1929, *De Ontwikkeling*, 318.

an end to an inflammatory revolutionary action ... The evolution [of the nationalist movement] has to take other organizational forms."[54]

The Fiasco

If the government stated that the intervention "cleared up the atmosphere" and opened up a new possibility for "evolutionary" "socially constructive" nationalist efforts, it was expressing its hope more than the reality. For the policy of constructive engagement, as formulated by van der Plas, had been bankrupt since late 1929, when he had to admit that the "counter-forces" were no rival to PNI and that Soekarno, whom he had hoped to be willing to work with the government, turned out to be the driving force of PNI mass action. Though the government still maintained that there might be "well-intentioned, at least reformable currents in PNI," there was hardly any basis for the hope. But it was not just van der Plas's strategy that went bankrupt, but also the *hoofdparket*'s theory of nationalist politics, PNI as the vanguard of the second Comintern offensive that also went bankrupt in 1930.

In clamping down on PNI, the attorney general was convinced that PNI was organizing unrest and that the timely intervention prevented a repeat of the revolts in 1926 and 1927. But no evidence for the organization of unrest was found in house searches. This was something the *hoofdparket* had not expected in light of its experiences with PKI. It had hoped to obtain "compromising" correspondence, especially with individuals abroad, but nothing was found. In a few days, all but seven PNI leaders were released, and Soekemi, Inoe Perbatasari, and Iskaq Tjokroadisoerjo were also out of prison by the end of January. Mr. L.J.A. Roskott led the investigation. In his report dated May 13, 1930, he said that the four PNI leaders—Soekarno, Gatot Mangkoepradja, Maskoen, and Soepriadinata—could be prosecuted, but found it unadvisable because there was no convincing evidence available to support the case. The advocate general, in submitting Roskott's report to de Graeff, proposed that the government general invoke *exorbitant rechten*, extraordinary powers, to intern the four. The internal government debate thus centered on the question whether the four PNI leaders should be put

---

[54] PG to GG, Jan. 4, 1930, Mr. 20x/1930; Blumberger, *De Nationalistische Beweging*, 249.

on trial or interned. This question is discussed well by John Ingleson, and we only need to mention that the governor general eventually decided to prosecute them even if it meant risking their acquittal. What is more interesting for our discussion is how the *hoofdparket* reasoned to make its case for internment and how its theory became untenable.

The "theoretical" base for the internment was provided by ARD chief van der Most in his report dated May 13, 1930, which Advocate General Vonk submitted to de Graeff together with Roskott's report. Van der Most started his report with this paragraph: "The birth of Partai Nasional Indonesia (PNI) can be demonstrably considered as an outcome of efforts Perhimpoenan Indonesia (PI) and the Third International made in this country to establish a national revolutionary party alongside the communist organization (PKI)."

Van der Most's report consisted of quotations of quotations, all framed in a ready-made framework conveniently provided, as the paragraph above suggests, by Semaoen's Organizational Plan. He made his case thus:

> In 1926, PI chairman Mohammad Hatta wrote to Soedjadi, then official at the department of finance and now member of the PNI central executive and editor of *Persatoean Indonesia*, about his plan to create a new revolutionary party modelled after PI and asked him to obtain cooperation from former PI members. Soedjadi contacted Mr. Iskaq Tjokroadisoerjo and Mr. Boediarto, and made a draft statute for a new party, Sarekat Rajat Nasional Indonesia [SRNI] or Indonesian National People's League. PI in the meantime had been in communication with Moscow and in fact the plan for a new party was inspired by Moscow. In its letter to the PKI central executive dated May 4, 1925, the Comintern had urged PKI to cooperate with nationalists, and wrote that "a platform must be drawn up for the general national struggle, which must give first considerations to the interest of the peasantry and must also contain a program minimum for the workers. Sarekat Rajat must be separated from the communist party of Indonesia, and be converted into a genuine national revolutionary organization, working in conjunction with and under the intellectual leadership of the communists." As van der Lely noted in his report, the Comintern policy was to urge PKI to create an anti-imperialist bloc out of all the national revolutionary parties, and the policy change in PI, its leftward movement of intellectuals and nationalists, was in response to this communist move. This would have developed further, had not the government taken measures against the PKI in the wake of the revolts.

In April 1927, however, the plan to create a new party started anew with the meeting at Soekarno's residence, attended by Iskaq Tjokro-adisoerjo, Soenarjo, Boediarto, Tjipto Mangoenkoesoemo, J. Tilaar, Soedjadi (Sartono and Anwari were absent), which decided to estab-lish a committee for organizing a national congress, Rapat Besar Indonesia [Big Conference of Indonesia]. The PNI was established on July 4, 1927, with the draft statute Soedjadi, Boediarto, and Iskaq had prepared for the SRNI. It was headquartered in Bandung with Soekarno as chairman, Iskaq as secretary-treasurer, and Samsi Sastro-widagdo as commissioner. "It thus complied with the instruction of Mohammad Hatta that a new revolutionary association must be established as a loyal imitation of PI." Based on the PI policy of non-cooperation and self-activity, PNI announced in the August/September issue of *Indonesia Merdeka* that it would restore the na-tional movement and "inherit the political heritage of the late PKI."

The establishment of PNI thus marked "a beginning to execute in action the ideas [to create an anti-imperialist, national revolutionary bloc which had grown] in the bosom of PI under the influence of the Third International with an independent Indonesia as the ultimate goal." These ideas were further developed in the Organizational Plan for our National Movement, the document confiscated at the house search of Hatta's residence in July 1927. This Organizational Plan was drafted for a new party that was soon to be established. The PNI central leadership led the party in accordance with this Organiza-tional Plan. Mr. Iskaq Tjokroadisoerjo, for instance, "called for de-veloping [their] own forces, creating [their] own system and forming [their] own method to form a state within the state" at a PNI propa-ganda meeting held in Bandung in September 1927. Mr. Soejoedi also suggested to other PNI leaders in Yogyakarta in September 1928 to recruit staff of the Post, Telegraph, and Telephone service, again in line with the Organizational Plan to create an extended espionage service and obtain the secrets of the *Sana* [over there] group.

The PNI membership had reached 6,000 by the second congress in May 1929 and discussed trade unionism. As the attorney general noted in his report on the PNI congress, the party had been carrying out, along with above ground activity, "underground action (propa-gation of [its] principles and the recruitment of members, the place-ment of cells and spies in associations and government services, the covert influence over other organizations, etc.)."

PNI started to be active in trade unionism after the congress and established trade unions such as chauffeurs' union in Bandung, sailors' union in Tanjung Priok, and East Java Steamtram Workers' Union in Surabaya. PNI also carried out its propaganda activities at cadre training courses in Bandung and its vicinity. The Political Police Survey over November 1929 reported: "The cadre training meetings and extra courses in Bandung and its vicinity attract much interest. This is also increasingly the case in West Priangan, that is in Cianjur and Sukabumi. The crowd [who came to] the cadre training meeting held in [Sukabumi] on November 30 was so large (about 500 people) that there was not enough room for the crowd and another meeting had to be held again in the same evening. In Pekalongan also the number of participants increased to some extent. In Surabaya, Batavia, and Palembang, on the other hand, the picture of meetings remained unchanged, while in Wonokromo, Grisse, Semarang, and Yogyakarta there was no great interest [in PNI meetings]."

And along with PNI propaganda activities, numerous rumors spread about disturbances expected in the year of 1930: that the communists would return home from Boven Digul in 1930 in order to establish an utopia in the Indonesia ravaged in the war (Central Priangan); that the revolution would break out in 1930 and the communists would win decidedly (East Priangan), etc.

Van der Most did not forget to mention Iwa's contact with Sartono and Soenarjo as well as the fact that Daniel Kamoe, Wawoeroentoe, and Wentoek got in touch with Sartono in April 1929 after their return from Moscow. He argued that "foreign influence" over the PNI had to be neutralized.

Advocate General Vonk's proposal for the internment of Soekarno and three other PNI leaders was based on van der Most's analysis. In opposing Vonk's proposal, Deputy Adviser for Native Affairs Gobee criticized his report. He did not agree "that in processing and classifying these ['extensive, very incriminating policing'] data it is assumed as the starting point that the well-known 'organizational plan for our national movement,' presumably written by Semaoen, forms the secret guideline for the PNI action."

Though I accept that various parts of its action can be said for sure to have derived from it, it is dangerous to preconceive as van der Most does in his treatise that the effort of the association aims at pursuing the Organizational Plan in all parts, because one tends to take lightly what one sees but does not fit with this thinking, to find it unimportant, or to see it as camouflage. It seems necessary to see this movement in itself, not tied to any one association or plan

imposed on it from the outside, as an association which has adopted
a lot in its organization which it regards useful and necessary for the
achievement of its purposes and has learned from Western revolutionary action or revolutionary action contrived in the West for colonial countries, but has developed independently.

Gobee's criticism was devastating. It was precisely the kind of view
Governor General de Graeff needed not to be too wedded with the political policing view and to reach his own politically astute decision on
Soekarno and others. Advocate General Vonk was angry at Gobee. He
argued in his letter to de Graeff that the police did not seek "anything
which is not (yet) there." But he was obviously defensive, and as if
admitting the *hoofdparket* was less cautious than it should, reminded the
governor general that "the great cautiousness [of the *hoofdparket*] was
even part of the reason for the circumstances in which [we] were taken
by surprise by the unrest from November 12 and 13, 1926." He also
defended van der Most, saying that he instructed him to quote extensively from the Organizational Plan, because one could not get without
the Plan "any objective picture of [PNI] ... [its] birth and growth, [its]
goals and the weapons, [its] reality and camouflage." But he no longer
believed what he said. After this debate, Vonk, or for that matter any
of his successors as chief of the *hoofdparket*, never again relied on the
Organizational Plan for an analysis of nationalist politics. It was clear
that the government had to deal with nationalist parties and associations,
whether revolutionary or evolutionary, differently from the communists,
with or without international connections. The "No Trespass" signs
the government had posted to define the limits beyond which activists
should not go, it was clear, were not effective enough to force nationalists
to police themselves.

The central issue of the debate in which Vonk and Gobee articulated their opposing views was whether the four PNI leaders should be
prosecuted or interned. How to assess PNI and its revolutionary action
was closely related to this question. Governor General de Graeff was
not persuaded of the *hoofdparket*'s reasoning. On June 16, 1930, he announced in his speech opening the Volksraad's first session for 1930–31
that the government would prosecute Soekarno and the three other
PNI leaders for violation of Articles 153 bis and 169 of the Criminal
Code, while warning that if they were acquitted and continued their
activities as they had, he could not guarantee that he would not resort
to using his extraordinary powers in the future if he considered peace
and order threatened.

De Graeff also reaffirmed his policy at the administrative conference he chaired on May 5, 1931. He noted once again "the increasing notion of national desires and consciousness in all strata of the native population," and said that whether "one might deplore it or applaud it... because it goes in parallel with the modern colonial policy, one cannot but accept this course of affairs." At the same time, however, one could not deny that there was "uncertainty, confusion, mutual discord, and jealousy" in the organizational expression of national desires. In his view, therefore, "the native movement is in a period of transition and is seeking for self-reform and reorientation." The outcome would be of great importance, even decisive, for future development. His policy would remain unchanged: anything and everything provocative should be avoided; within the limits enforced by the law and the government, any effort of the native population for "self-realization" would be unhindered and meet government sympathy. The government would encourage everyone who attempts to realize his political ideals or his plans for economic construction and carefully avoid anything that might drive "the moderates" into the arms of the radicals. De Graeff then warned the conference audience that the time for "the tradition of ... autocratic administration, however well-intentioned it is, has irrevocably passed" and that the native administration has to listen to the voices that come from the population."

In September 1931, de Graeff also approved the introduction of *persbreidel* (press muzzling), an administrative measure to proscribe the publication of newspapers and periodicals for maintaining the peace and order, in addition to the *persdelict* (press offense) articles of 161 *bis* and 153 *bis* and *ter* of the penal code, a powerful weapon against recalcitrant journalists.[55] It was an act of concession for hardliners. Under de Graeff, the liberal wing of the government thus managed to protect their policy against the conservatives. But it was doomed anyway. Though de Graeff reaffirmed his policy of constructive engagement, he could only express his hope for a transition in the nationalist movement for "self-reform" and "reorientation," the foundation for which had been largely lost as van der Plas admitted as early as in late 1929. The fiasco also underlined the hollowness of the assumptions on which the *hoofdparket* pursued

---

[55] It took effect under Governor General de Jonge and worked as a potent weapon for preventive surveillance. For *persbreidel*, see Yamamoto, "Print Power and Censorship," chap. 7.

its investigation into PNI. It led de Graeff to question the wisdom of relying on the ARD-PID apparatus for political intelligence and briefly to entertain an idea for creating another intelligence apparatus on "the normal development of the political life" in the native society.

The government policy on the movement was thus clearly in transition. Senior government officials were deeply divided about what standpoint it should take toward nationalist intellectuals, how to deal with PNI, and how to think about Indonesian nationalism. The debates, however, took place within a very narrow limit set by the paramount importance all the senior government officials unanimously placed on maintaining peace and order, with their memories of the recent revolts and their fear of a repeat and within the institutional framework set by the constitution. To put it differently, de Graeff's policy of constructive engagement in effect amounted to a numbing proposition: nationalist intellectuals should be allowed to pursue their political ideals and plans for social and economic construction, as long as they remain within the limits set by the law and the government, do not attempt popular mobilization, do not threaten peace and order, and therefore remain insignificant. Soekarno posed a major challenge to this position, not only because of his ability for popular mobilization, but also because he counterpoised the government position with his "revolutionary" mass action to put popular pressure on the government and to obtain political concessions.

The trial of the four PNI leaders at the Bandung lower court lasted from August 18 to September 29, 1930. On December 22, 1930, Soekarno was sentenced to a 4-year imprisonment; Gatot Mangkoepradja, 2 years; Maskoen, 20 months; and Soepriadinata, 15 months. The sentences were confirmed on appeal by the Batavia court of justice on April 17, 1931. On August 31, 1931, de Graeff decided to give remission to Soekarno and three others. He called his decision "fait accompli" in light of his imminent replacement as Governor General by B.C. de Jonge on September 12, 1931. It was the last signal he sent to nationalist intellectuals that he still hoped for constructive cooperation. But it was not necessarily received as such. Soekarno was seen by Indonesians as a martyr for the nationalist cause and his remission as his personal triumph. Hillen called it "a certificate of approval" for the extremism. Soekarno had emerged as the symbol of Indonesian nationalism and had become a major concern for the government.

CHAPTER 5

Politics=Police

Bonifacius C. de Jonge replaced A.C.D. de Graeff as governor general of the Dutch Indies in September 1931. A long time protégé of Minister of Colonies H. Colijn, he was critical of "the hyper ethical direction" of the Indies government under de Graeff and was determined to deal with revolutionary endeavors in the Indies firmly and give more powers to the native officials. In his first speech in the Volksraad, he identified two major challenges the government was facing, "a rapid development with which the forces of the country could not have kept pace" and the world crisis. The crisis was indeed serious as evidenced by the collapse of the international gold standard and the Japanese occupation of Manchuria shortly after his arrival in the Indies.[1] Ch.O. van der Plas, who served Governor General de Graeff as an adviser for native affairs in 1927–31, was sent to Blitar, East Java, as assistant resident. E. Gobee, deputy adviser for native affairs under de Graeff, was promoted to adviser for native affairs, but had little access to de Jonge, even though he asked the new governor general to see him at least once every other month.[2] Instead, de Jonge thought highly of Attorney General R.J.M. Verheijen and relied on Dr. A.D.A. de Kat Angelino for native affairs, who obtained a doctorate for his dissertation on colonial policy, worked for the office of Chinese affairs (1931–33), and was seconded to the general secretariat as chief official (1933–34). De Kat Angelino believed in "retraditionalization" and saw the purpose of colonial policy in a

---

[1] S.L. van der Wal, ed., *Herinneringen van Jhr. Mr. B.C. de Jonge met brieven uit zijn nalatenschap* (Groningen: Wolters-Noordhoff, 1968), 78–9, 91, 103–4.

[2] De Jonge does not mention Gobee among the officials that he relied on, while the Schrieke brothers—J.J. Schrieke and B.J.O. Schrieke—were described as "fierce supporters of the previous regime." Ibid., 110.

"fruitful" synthesis of the East and the West."[3] He regarded nationalism as "sterile" and was of opinion that repressing nationalists and supporting traditional leaders was the way to go.[4] The center of gravity in the making of government native policy moved to the right, far more in tune with the thinking of the *hoofdparket*. A change in native policy was clearly in the air.

The start of the new administration under Governor General de Jonge coincided with the deepening of the great depression. The depression hit the Indies toward the end of the 1920s and dealt a crippling blow to its export economy. The openness of the Indies economy combined with the conservative monetary policy of maintaining the gold standard (until September 1936) directly translated the drastic fall in global market prices into a collapse of domestic prices. Prices in the Indies fell by 47 per cent and the depression lasted longer there than elsewhere. The Indies GDP per capita declined by almost 20 per cent in the depression years.[5] The sugar industry in Central and East Java was a major victim. From 1929 to 1933, the price of 100 kilograms of "superior" sugar tumbled from f. 5.66 to f. 3.66, and by the end of 1932 the equivalent of a whole year's Java sugar production remained stockpiled and unsold. Due to the forced cutbacks in production that the government imposed on sugar factories, the area under sugarcane cultivation declined from 200,000 hectares in 1930/31 to 34,000 in 1933/34. Sugar factories in operation fell from 179 to 45 in the same period. Land-owning peasants as well as agrarian workers were badly hurt and unemployed workers drifted to urban centers.[6] De Jonge was well aware that the depression could create a fertile ground for nationalist propaganda. In a time of serious economic difficulty, however, there was no room in his view for agitation for "unrealistic political ideals" but for sound economic management. He was in no mood to tolerate

---

[3] Sutherland, *The Making of a Bureaucratic Elite*, 132.
[4] Ibid., 117.
[5] Jan Luiten van Zanden and Daan Marks, *An Economic History of Indonesia, 1800–2012* (London: Routledge, 2012), 100–2.
[6] R.E. Elson, *Javanese Peasants and the Colonial Sugar Industry: Impact and Change in an East Java Residency, 1930–1940* (Singapore: Oxford University Press, ASAA Southeast Asia Publication Series No. 9), 233–5; John Ingleson, *The Road to Exile: The Indonesian Nationalist Movement, 1927–1934* (Singapore: Heinemann Educational Books, 1979), 175–6. See also Zanden and Marks, *An Economic History of Indonesia*, 100.

any sign of unrest caused by "irresponsible Indonesian political leaders." The depression also hit government finance. Government revenue plummeted from f. 523 million in 1929 to f. 380 million in 1930, to f. 257 million in 1933, and finally to f. 233 million in 1935, forcing him to cut down government spending from f. 515 million in 1929 to f. 482 million in 1931, to f. 378 million in 1933, and finally to f. 316 million in 1935. Government spending for education went down from f. 53 million in 1931 to f. 25 million in 1936. To cope with the deep cut in defense spending for the 1933 budget, de Jonge initiated army reorganization in 1932 while doing his best to maintain government spending on the navy.[7]

The depression, combined with de Jonge's conservative political instinct, ideological inclination, and authoritarian personality meant that maintaining peace and order would weigh far more in the government deliberation on native policy and favor tougher government measures on the nationalist movement. At the same time, it is important to remember the new administration was not only more conservative and tougher in its handling of native political affairs, but also and more importantly, determined to shape the native political terrain in such a way as to make nationalists "behave" and to achieve "constructive cooperation" in a way far more coercive than de Graeff had ever thought of.

The Course of Nationalist Politics

The senior nationalist politician Governor General de Graeff counted on most for the "purification" and "reorientation" of the native movement was Dr. Soetomo, the leader of Surabaya Indonesian Study Club. After the government intervention in the PNI at the end of 1929, Soetomo met with Sartono, Samsi Sastrowidagdo, Iskaq Tjokroadisoerjo, and other PNI leaders in March 1930 and called for the dissolution of PNI and the creation of a new party with more emphasis on Indonesian economic and social advancement. In July 1930, Ali Sastroamidjojo, who returned to the Indies in 1928 and was working with Singgih in Surakarta as a lawyer, moved to Surabaya and joined as an editor *Soeloeh Rajat Indonesia* (Torches of Indonesian People), a newspaper Indonesian Study Club published. In November 1930, Soetomo transformed his

---

[7] Wal, ed., *Herinneringen van Jhr. Mr. B.C. de Jonge*, 114–6.

Indonesian Study Club into Persatoean Bangsa Indonesia (PBI, Indonesian National Union). Its stronghold was in East Java, but it expanded influence in Central Java with Singgih who had quit BO as a central figure. It had 17 branches in July 1931.[8]

In Surabaya, where both Indonesian Study Club and PBI headquartered, the party found popular support among workers. Soetomo was convinced that organizing urban workers was important for the nationalist movement and that a labor movement should focus on industrial issues, workers' social and economic conditions and their consciousness of their rights. He brought financial and organizational assets his study club had built in Surabaya to the trade union movement. Its building provided space for the unions and their meetings. It drew on the support of lawyers, doctors, journalists, teachers, officials and prominent Chinese Indonesian businessmen for its expanding activities.[9] The study club established seven unions for private sector workers in Surabaya in a few months in 1930. Persatoean Personeel Drukkerij Indonesia (PPDI, Union for Indonesian Printers) and Sarekat Sekerdja Indonesia (SSI, Union for Indonesian Workers) were established in March 1930, Perkoempoelan Kaoem Kleermaker Indonesia (PKKB, Union for Indonesian Tailors) was established in April and joined by workers at European garment factories. In May, a new federation for local trade unions, Persatoean Sarekat Sekerdja Indonesia (PSSI, Federation of Indonesian Unions), was established in Surabaya. It was a trade union federation for the private sector workers, joined not only by those led by Indonesian Study Club, but also those originally established by PNI.[10]

The PNI central leadership under Sartono, however, decided not to go along with Soetomo to join forces. After the arrest of Soekarno, Sartono and Anwari, Soekarno's former classmate in Bandung, took over the PNI leadership and on January 9, 1930, instructed its local branches and members to cease all political activity in the name of the party. On April 25, 1930, after the Batavia court of justice confirmed the

---

[8] Ingleson, *The Road to Exile*, 122–5; Deputy adviser for native affairs to GG, June 30, 1931, in Kwantes, *De Ontwikkeling van de Nationalistische Beweging in Nederlandsch-Indie, Bronnenpublikatie 3de Stuk 1928–Aug. 1933* (Groningen: Wolters-Noordhoff/Bouma's Boekhuis, 1981), 575–7.

[9] Ingleson, *Workers, Unions and Politics: Indonesia in the 1920s and 1930s* (Leiden: Brill, 2014), 130–1.

[10] Deputy attorney general to GG, July 23, 1930, in Kwantes, *De Ontwikkeling, 1928–Aug. 1933*, 445–7; see also Ingleson, *Workers, Unions and Politics*, 135–6.

sentences to Soekarno and three other PNI leaders, Sartono convened a
PNI extraordinary congress and proposed disbanding the party. Twelve
branches out of 14 supported Sartono. On May 1, a new party, Partai
Indonesia (Partindo, Party of Indonesia) was established with Sartono
as chairman. Initially its branches were confined to Batavia, Bandung,
Pekalongan, and Yogyakarta. By June 1930, however, Soepriadinata, Iskaq
Tjokroadisoerjo (Menado), Soejoedi (Yogyakarta), Soenarjo (Medan),
and Ali Sastroamidjojo (Batavia) joined the party. The inaugural rally
was held in July 1930 in which self-help, cooperatives, and *swadesi* were
emphasized.[11]

PNI members who opposed the dissolution of the party established
their own associations. In Batavia, Soedjadi emerged as a leading oppo-
nent of the Sartono-led Partindo and established Perhimpoenan Kema-
djoean Kebangsaan Indonesia (Association for Indonesian National
Progress), which together with Abdoel Karim Pringgodigdo's Studieklub
Nasional Indonesia (Indonesian National Study Club) tried to rally PNI
members. In Bandung, Inoe Perbatasari established Indonesian People's
Study Club. A branch of Soedjadi's association was also established in
Surabaya with the name of Pendidikan Nasional Indonesia (Indonesian
National Education). All these groups called themselves Golongan
Merdeka (Free Group), and by the end of September 1931 branches
had come into being in Batavia, Bandung (with branches in Garut,
Cimahi, and Sukabumi), Yogyakarta, Surakarta, Surabaya, and some
other places, especially among "less educated, radical elements of the old
PNI." Their organ, *Daulat Ra'jat* (People's sovereignty), was started at
Soedjadi's initiatives.[12]

As Adviser for Native Affairs Gobee reported in his letter to Governor General de Jonge in November 1931, Golongan Merdeka had little
prospect to compete with Partindo and Soetomo's PBI without the support of Soekarno and/or Mohammad Hatta. But Hatta and Sjahrir, who
were still in the Netherlands, were behind Golongan Merdeka. Critical
of Sartono, Sjahrir called for the establishment of a new revolutionary
party in August 1931.

---

[11] Deputy adviser for native affairs to GG, June 30, 1931, Mr. 794x/31, which is also
available in Kwantes, *De Ontwikkeling, 1928–Aug. 1933*, 575–7.

[12] Ingleson, *The Road to Exile*, 144–54; Adviser for native affairs to GG, Nov. 6,
1931, in Kwantes, *De Ontwikkeling, 1928–Aug. 1933*, 589–90; Rapport van het hoofd
van de dienst der algemene recherche, July 29, 1932, in Kwantes, *De Ontwikkeling,
1928–Aug. 1933*, 649–50.

Soekarno's Return

Soekarno was released from prison at the end of 1931 and almost immediately emerged again as a dominant figure in the movement. The occasion for Soekarno's return was the Great Indonesia Congress (Congres Indonesia Raja) held in Surabaya on January 1–3, 1932. It was a sort of expanded PPPKI congress, for the Sarekat Ambon (Ambonese League), Partij Celebes (Celebes Party), Timorsch Verbond (Timorese Union), Perserikatan Kaoem Christen (Christians' League), Pakempalan Politik Katholik Djawa (Java Catholic Political Association), PPPI, Partindo, and other non-PPPKI members also sent their representatives there. The congress itself had little political significance. In the wake of the government intervention in PNI at the end of 1929, the PPPKI central executive decided to establish a new united front, but by the time the congress was held in December 1930, PSII (Partai Sarekat Islam Indonesia) had pulled itself out of the PPPKI and its central leadership was deeply divided between Soetomo and Sartono. As ARD chief van der Most observed, the congress could not provide any new view for the movement and demonstrated a deep division in the movement.[13]

Soekarno's appearance on the congress a day after his release from prison, however, was big news for Surabayans. The congress was scheduled to open at 8:00 a.m. on January 1, 1932, but people arrived early and waited for the show. The auditorium, which had the capacity for 1,600 people, was packed with more than 3,000 by 8:00. The yard and the street in front of the building were crowded with thousands more. It was an ideal occasion for Soekarno to start his activity again, because as Landjoemin gelar Datoe' Toemanggoeng noted, "all native political associations" except Golongan Merdeka, PSII, Partai Rajat Indonesia (Indonesian People's Party), Moluksch Politiek Verbond (Moluccan Political Union), and Persatoean Minahasa (Minahasa League) were officially represented at the congress. Landjoemin, one of the most seasoned native official observers of the movement, wrote: "Just before half past nine enthusiastic exclamations resounded, indicating the arrival of Ir. Soekarno. As soon as he entered the main entrance of the auditorium,

---

[13] Geheim verslag van het Indonesia Raja Congres van het hoofd van de dienst der algemene recherche, Jan. 23, 1932, in Kwantes, *De Ontwikkeling, 1928–Aug. 1933,* 599–605.

he was immediately shouldered and brought to the platform with bois-
terous cheers and gamelan sounds, where he stood still for a moment
and saluted the audience, which made the audience exuberant: Long Live
Soekarno! Dr. Soetomo offered him a chair, while his wife, sister and
niece, who accompanied him, sat beside them."[14]

The next day Soekarno gave his speech. Gobee sent a "fairly
complete and accurate rendering" of his speech in Dutch translation to
de Jonge.[15]

Brothers, my comrades of one nationality!

Yesterday evening I promised to give [you] a *wedjangan* (message,
instruction, teaching), which I have brought with me from the
Sukamiskin prison, where I stayed for two years in seclusion.

This *wedjangan* is the basis of every movement and the basis of every
work. Therefore, brothers, take this *wedjangan* to heart and listen
carefully.

Before I give [you] this *wedjangan*, I first of all express my heart-felt
thanks for the honor and tribute you showed me after my release
from the prison.

The honor and tribute which I receive from you all is not meant for
Soekarno personally, but for Soekarno as your leader with high ideals
and full of a fervent will to put himself at the service of the People
and Mother Indonesia, as Your leader, who holds the torch fast,
which is necessary to illuminate you all on the dark path, and which
so long as the body of Soekarno still has life, will continue to reach
Indonesia Merdeka.

He then talked about the trial of himself, Maskoen, Gatot Mangkoepradja and Soepriadinata. They were not tried as individuals, he said, but
as leaders, as part of the people, "all groups and strata of the people in
entire Indonesia," and therefore their trial was in fact "the trial of the
Indonesian People." He thanked for all the support he received at his

---

[14] Verslag van het Indonesia Raja Congres opgemaakt door den Patih ter beschikking,
Landjoemin gelar Datoe' Toemanggoeng, in Mr. 273x/1932. Part of the report is
included in Kwantes, *De Ontwikkeling, 1928–Aug. 1933*, 605–9.
[15] Rede van ir. Soekarno, uitgesproken op 2 januari 1932, in Kwantes, *De Ontwikkeling, 1928–Aug. 1933*, 609–16.

trial and imprisonment and introduced his wife "Indit Karnasi [Inggit Karnasi]" to the audience as "the true Indonesian Srikandi." He compared his release from prison to the return of Wasi Djajadara from his place of exile Argasonja in the wayang world. He continued:

> This is the example, brothers! I am glad that I am back again in the middle of you all, that I can be active again and fulfill my obligations, but my heart broke and grieved, when I learned that my former comrades, in principle and in view, now oppose each other, the one group united in Partai Indonesia and the other in Golongan Merdeka.
>
> It pains me, because this dispute can make the influence on the people disappear. Now the time has come to explain my own standpoint, it is time for me to give a *wedjangan* to all brothers, which I very much hope will really be taken to heart.
>
> Now listen to my message! I will not go into one or another party, I will not agree with one group or criticize the other.
>
> In short, I will not choose any party, but I will make every effort to bring these two groups together again.
>
> Count on it, as long as Soekarno is still called Soekarno, as long as his life is not yet taken away from him, as long as I still possess strength, I will always be active, I will toil, use my powers and my effort will not count to put these two wings on a body.
>
> I am convinced, brothers, that the dispute between PI [Partai Indonesia] and GM [Golongan Merdeka] is only a misunderstanding ... Brothers, as I said I am pleased to be able to see the People's face again, I am even more pleased, [that] when I came back from prison, I noticed that our national movement in Indonesia has so progressed and that the spirit has spread. If it continues in this way and the unity between PI and GM can be brought about again and more generally in the People's movement, then with steadfastness and seriousness Indonesia must certainly be free, though I cannot say when, about ten, fifty, a hundred, or a thousand years.

He compared the Partindo and Golongan Merdeka to Gatotkatja and Hamantasena, Bima's two sons in Javanese wayang stories. They fought because of misunderstanding, but after Dewi Soebadra reconciled them, their unity became stronger. Soekarno would try to do what Dewi Soebadra did.

This is my position, brothers. I do not want to confuse the situation any longer and therefore do not choose a party or the other.

Whenever you are asked by people who are not here today, tell them that Boeng Karno joins neither the group of PI nor GM, but Boeng Karno belongs to Golongan Merdeka and is of Partai Indonesia.

This is my message, brothers! I ask for your help, brothers, to bring this message to the People in the hamlets, the villages, and the mountains. In short, in all places, where people live, this message must be brought, so that by the blessing of the rising spirit the People will help achieve the goal of regaining unity.

Soekarno then turned to his "younger brothers," the youth in age as well as in spirit. He talked about "the young Italian fighter Garibaldi," who asked young men to sacrifice for "the fatherland Italy" in return for "sorrow, calamity, and mischief." Like Garibaldi, he asked young Indonesians to sacrifice for free Indonesia. He sacrificed himself twice for Mother Indonesia, he said, the first time when he established PNI and the second time when he was imprisoned in Soekamiskin. Now, he said, Mother Indonesia asks for his third sacrifice to achieve unity between Partindo and Golongana Merdeka and in the entire popular movement.

He called on the audience to remember this trilogy, or the message Trimoerti from Your Boeng (brother): "National Spirit," which must be fostered and deepened; "National Will," which results from this national spirit and "can accomplish, for example, this building, the national bank, a national newspaper and the like," as well as remove fetters such as *heerendiensten* (corvee labor for the ruler) and penal sanctions; and "National Act," which results from the power of national will. He said that he would not lose hope even if the second and the third stage could not be reached in a few years. But he would continue to work for unity, "to find the flower Widjajakoesoema [i.e., unity], which he will offer to our beloved Mother Indonesia." He concluded his speech thus:

I will not be conceited, brothers, because all events are determined by God. But with the help of the entire People, and the support of the youth, with the blessing of Father Soetomo, Kyai [Haji Mas] Mansoer and others, must unity be achieved.

Not tomorrow or the day after tomorrow, brothers, as long as Soekarno is still alive, he will keep propagating to spread the national will, and now too!

A people that cannot be one is like loose sand, which can be easily blown apart by the wind. If, however, this sand remains together, is pounded together into cement, namely the cement of the spirit, it can become strong concrete, that is the concrete of that national will, from which finally the national deeds originate.

Brothers, help [me], carry my voice to Aceh and Fak Fak, through the whole world, from region to region, from village to village, from hamlet to hamlet, from mountain to mountain, yes, even to the realm of spirits and fairy.

For this unity, brothers, I am "toh pati." Toh pati means that I am ready to sacrifice my life for it if the unity needs a sacrifice.

So it is, brothers, give me support and blessing!

Soekarno's message was clear. He would not join either Partindo or Golongan Merdeka, but work to restore the unity of the old PNI. He was convinced that a "national spirit" was present in the people. His "message" was to forge a "national will" out of "national spirit," to restore unity between Partindo and Golongan Merdeka and to achieve unity of a national movement under his leadership. Engineer Soekarno compared the movement to a process of turning loose sand into cement and cement into strong concrete. In this respect, he was inheriting the torch of the movement as represented by Tjokroaminoto and Tjipto Mangoenkoesoemo, who in their different ways tried to awaken a national spirit in the people's minds.

More important, however, for the purpose of our discussion here is the way in which he put his message. He asked the audience to convey his message to those who were not there. He envisioned his voice of hope spreading from one person to another, from Aceh to Fak Fak, from village to village, from mountain to mountain, and reverberating in the minds of all who conveyed his voice throughout Indonesia. As Pari men accepted Tan Malaka's authority and shared his vision and hope for a Republiek Indonesia as Djamaloedin Tamin had told them to do, people accepted Soekarno's authority and hope for Indonesia Merdeka when they came to the congress; they received his message, and they conveyed it to others. It did not matter, as he said, whether the national will could be forged within a few years. Soekarno would not lose hope as long as people were willing to receive his message and convey it to others, for they would tell others what he had told them and in this very act of joining in his voice a national will would surely be in the making. Soekarno was different from Tan Malaka in one important respect. Tan Malaka's written words could reach at most hundreds. Soekarno's voice could reach tens of thousands, who could then convey his voice to tens of thousands more. This was a problem for the government, for Soekarno's authority was derived from his voice as much as from his message.

Nationalist Politics, 1932–33

Whatever possibility there was for a "reorientation" of the nationalist movement under Soetomo, as Governor General de Graeff had hoped for, was lost with Soekarno's return. PPPKI held a conference in Solo on April 30 and May 1, 1932. Soekarno was invited—he simply could not be ignored—even though he was not affiliated with any party. He said at the conference that PPPKI was in crisis and had no internal solidarity; he called for its reorganization. Soetomo resigned from the chairmanship of the PPPKI advisory council and was replaced by Thamrin. Soekarno was authorized to submit a reorganization plan to a meeting scheduled to be held four months later. The PPPKI leadership shifted from Soetomo to Soekarno and Thamrin, while the support of Soetomo and his PBI for PPPKI was in serious doubt.[16]

However, Soekarno was not successful in his attempt at unifying Partindo and Golongan Merdeka. Shortly after Golongan Merdeka held a conference in Yogyakarta to establish Pendidikan National Indonesia (Indonesian National Education) or New PNI (PNI Baru) in December 1931, Sjahrir returned to the Indies. In March 1932, Golongan Merdeka held another meeting in Batavia under Sjahrir's leadership and called for "power formation" by means of non-cooperation and mass action. It also announced a plan to establish an association on nationalist grounds "as soon as a suitable leader is found."[17] That leader would be Hatta.

Two months later, in May 1932, the New PNI held its first congress in Bandung. It was chaired by Sjahrir. His emergence as New PNI leader, "one of the extremist core members of Perhimpoenan Indonesia ... in contact with extremist and communist associations," alarmed the

---

[16] Ingleson, *The Road to Exile*, 163–6. See also Verslag van de assistant wedana van de politieke inlichtingendienst te Soerabaja, May 9, 1932, in Kwantes, *De Ontwikkeling, 1928–Aug. 1933*, 627–34.

[17] Adviser for native affairs to GG, March 12, 1932, Mr. 303x/1932, part of which is included in Kwantes, *De Ontwikkeling, 1928–Aug. 1933*, 617–18.

hoofdparket. The attorney general wrote to the governor general in July 1932 that he saw a threat in New PNI and that Sjahrir and Hatta would try to infuse new life into the revolutionary movement that had been "moribund" since the dissolution of the old PNI.[18]

Hatta returned to the Indies in August 1932 and took over the New PNI leadership from Sjahrir. As its name, Indonesian National Education, suggests, New PNI emphasized cadre training, based on a pamphlet that Hatta wrote in late 1932, *Kearah Indonesia Merdeka* (Toward free Indonesia). A lengthy question and answer sheet was prepared by the central leadership to test members' knowledge of the text. Its organ, *Daulat Ra'jat*, which was renamed *Kedaulatan Rajat* (People's Sovereignty) in October 1932, was placed under the control of Hatta, Sjahrir, Boerhannoedin, Inoe Perbatasari, and Soebagio. New PNI had 12 branches in June 1932, which increased to 32 in February 1933, including 26 in Java.[19]

Partindo, on the other hand, increased its membership to 3,000 and established branches in Jember, Madiun, Semarang, Kroya, Sukabumi, and Bogor as well as Batavia, Yogyakarta, Surakarta, and Surabaya by February 1932. While the central leadership of the old PNI was held, as van der Plas would put it, by Tjipto's proteges and Leiden-trained lawyers, student activists from the Faculty of Law (RHS, Rechtshooge-school) in Batavia now formed the backbone of new Partindo cadres. They were active in PPPI (Indonesian Students Union), which was established in 1927 to oppose the idea of "association." They were the driving force behind the fusion of youth organizations such as Jong Java (Young Java), Pemoeda Indonesia (Indonesian Youth), Jong Celebes (Young Celebes), and Pemoeda Soematera (Sumatran Youth) into Indonesia Moeda (Young Indonesia) in December 1930. By the time the Partindo congress was held in Batavia in May 1932, PPPI activists such as Mohammad Yamin and Amir Sjarifoeddin had emerged as its leaders along with Leiden trained lawyers such as Sartono and Ali Sastroamidjojo in Batavia. This was partly because as Attorney General Verheijen com-

---

[18] PG to GG, July 29, 1932, in Kwantes, *De Ontwikkeling, 1928–Aug. 1933*, 647–8.
[19] Adviser for native affairs to GG, March 12, 1932, Mr. 303x/1932; PG to GG, July 29, 1932, in Kwantes, *De Ontwikkeling, 1928–Aug. 1933*, 647–8. See also John D. Legge, *Intellectuals and Nationalism in Indonesia: A Study of the Following Recruited by Sutan Sjahrir in Occupation Jakarta* (Ithaca, NY: Modern Indonesia Project, Cornell University, 1988), 21–38.

plained to Kiewiet de Jonge, government representative to the Volksraad, Faculty of Law professors were adamantly opposed to any disciplinary measures taken against their students for their political activism and to PID surveillance over students in the school.[20]

At the first Partindo congress held in Batavia in May 1932, Sartono, chairman, announced that Partindo was a political party with the goal of achieving a Free Indonesia and that its principles were "right of self-determination, Indonesian nationalism, self-help, and democracy." As Gobee noted, "the national sentiment dominated all expressions" in the congress, which was in sharp contrast to the "pragmatic" PBI congress held in the same month in Surabaya, in which the organization of national education was the major topic. By the second congress held in Surabaya in April 1933, Partindo membership had reached more than 20,000, with 43 branches in Java and Madura alone.[21]

New PNI and Partindo also destroyed PBI dominance in private sector trade unionism. We can see this development most clearly in the transformation of PSSI, a federation of private sector unions established under the PBI leadership into CPBI (Centraal Perhimpoenan Boeroeh Indonesia, Center for Indonesian Workers Unions) dominated by New PNI union activists at the Indonesian Workers Congress (Congres Kaoem Boeroeh Indonesia) held in Surabaya in May 1933. John Ingleson tells us this story well.

The PBI-led trade union movement in Surabaya did very well in 1931. By the end of 1931, the PSSI-affiliated unions had more than 5,000 members and PSSI established Sarekat Sekerja Indonesia (SSI, Indonesian Workers Union) in May 1931 as a general union for workers. But the federation got into trouble in 1932. In January 1932, Partindo decided to go into trade unionism and established unions in Surabaya as well as other places. In Surabaya they competed for workers in the

---

[20] Deputy adviser for native affairs to GG, Sept. 30, 1931, in Kwantes, *De Ontwikkeling, 1928–Aug. 1933*, 489–91; PG to GG, July 29, 1932, in Kwantes, *De Ontwikkeling, 1928–Aug. 1933*, 647–8. Attorney General Verhijen mentions the following as active in the Parindra Soemitro: Reksodipoetro (RHS), R. Soejono Hadinoto (RHS), R. Soedjono (GH), R. Koentjoro (RHS), Soegondo Djojopuspito (RHS), Soenarko (RHS), Tirtosoepono (RHS), Antapermana (RHS), and R. Hendromartono (RHS), in addition to Yamin and Amir Sjarifoedin. He also mentioned Jahja Nasoetion as a student activist, even though in fact he was not.

[21] Adviser for native affairs to GG, May 31, 1931, in Kwantes, *De Ontwikkeling, 1928–Aug. 1933*, 635–8.

same industries as PSSI. Partindo also created a trade union federation (Perserikatan Kaum Buruh Indonesia) in Surabaya in March 1932 and, along with other local trade union federations in other places such as Semarang and Yogyakarta, established a Radicale Vakcentrale Indonesia (Radical Trade Union Center of Indonesia) to coordinate union activities. In the meantime, New PNI activists in Surabaya adopted a strategy of taking control of unions from the inside. By late 1931 the majority of SSI executives were New PNI members and in January 1932 they withdrew the union from the PBI-controlled trade union federation. In response, PSSI announced in late 1932 that it would hold an Indonesian workers Congress in May 1933 to create a Java-wide federation and to regain its leadership in the trade union movement. In the half year in between, however, PSSI-affiliated unions became dominated by New PNI members.[22]

The New PNI trade union strongholds were in Surabaya and Semarang. The largest union of private sector workers, PBKI (Persatoean Boeroeh Kareta Api Indonesia, Union of Indonesian Railway Workers), increasingly came under the influence of the Surabaya and Semarang New PNI branches. PBKI grew rapidly in 1932 and 1933. In April 1932 it had nine branches in East Java and three in Central Java. In March 1933, it claimed a membership of 4,150 in over 20 branches. Its central committee was headquartered in the PBI office in Surabaya and initially most of its leaders were PBI members. But the private railway network centered on Semarang and Yogyakarta, and New PNI activists took over the Semarang PBKI branch leadership and built it into its largest branch in 1932 and 1933. New PNI union activists also recruited workers into smaller branches along the central Java lines of the Semarang based Netherlands Indies Railway (NIS) and the Yogyakarta based Sister Societies. No doubt the legacy of the VSTP was still there with railway workers in Semarang. As the PBKI grew so too did the New PNI Semarang branch.[23]

The Indonesian Workers Congress was held in Surabaya in May 1933 with Soekarno, Sjahrir and Soetomo as the main speakers. Two months before the congress, however, the Surabaya trade union activist and PBKI secretary Udin announced the reorganization of PSSI which put its leadership in the hands of nominees of PBKI and other unions

---

[22] Ingleson, *Workers, Unions and Politics*, 173–81.
[23] Ibid., 223–30, 235–42.

controlled by New PNI or Partindo activists. The congress completed the process of reorganization, dissolving PSSI and creating a new trade union federation, the CPBI. PBI newspaper *Soeara Oemoem* announced that PBI would have nothing to with CPBI. It withdrew its institutional, financial and professional support for trade unionism and instead, expanded its social and economic activities and started organizing Roekun Tani (Peasant Association) in rural areas of East Java.[24]

Reshaping the Terrain

The Wild School Ordinance

The government became increasingly alarmed at the rising influence of Partindo and New PNI in the nationalist movement. Unlike previous years (1927–29), in which its major concern was the PNI under Soekarno's leadership, this time it was a general upsurge of popular mobilization, both national and local, which alarmed the government.

One major issue in this context, as historians often note, was the wild school ordinance (*wilde scholen ordonnantie*). The ordinance was first introduced in 1923 to place non-subsidized, private, native education under government supervision in view of the establishment of SI schools in Semarang and Bandung and Taman Siswa schools in Yogyakarta in the early 1920s. The ordinance required teachers in private schools to report to local authorities and to provide all necessary information, and a teacher was prohibited from teaching if his/her teaching was found to be a threat to peace and order. The system was "repressive," not "preventive." The government tightened the regulation in 1925 and gave powers to local authorities to prohibit anyone from teaching who could be expected "to educate his pupils in a spirit harmful for peace and order." A change was made with a revised ordinance in 1932 to move to a preventive system. This was not just for political reasons. Hit by the depression, the government drastically reduced its educational spending. This led to the increase in private, unsubsidized schools in the early 1930s. The government tried to regulate such "wild schools" with the introduction of a new ordinance. It stipulated that all teachers in private schools should have permission from local authorities before they could

---

[24] Ibid., 230–5, 248–51. See also Adviser for native affairs to GG, May 29, 1933, in Kwantes, *De Ontwikkeling, 1928–Aug. 1933*, 766–7; PG to GG, June 1, 1933, in *De Ontwikkeling*, 767–9.

begin teaching and that in order to obtain such permission, they should have a certificate from a government or a government-subsidized private school and must not, in the opinion of local authorities, be a threat to peace and order. Now the ordinance became a direct threat to unsubsidized private schools and their teachers.[25]

Popular resistance to the new ordinance began in October 1932. On October 1, the day when it was enacted, Ki Hadjar Dewantara (Soewardi Soerjaningrat), the leader of Taman Siswa schools, sent a telegram of protest to Governor General de Jonge, warning of the strongest possible non-violent opposition. Three days later, he called for passive resistance and was supported by Thamrin, Soekarno, Soetomo and other nationalist leaders. Political parties and other "non-political" associations participated in protest action. PPPKI decided on mass action. Partindo called for resistance. PSII issued a statement for "spontaneous" protest meetings. PGHB (Persatuan Guru Hindia Beland, Union of Dutch Indies Teachers) demanded the ordinance be altered. Moehammadijah organized a conference in Yogyakarta and stated its total disagreement with the ordinance. BO announced if the ordinance were not withdrawn by March 31, 1933, it would pull out all its members from representative bodies, shut down its schools, and provide financial support to those victims of passive, nonviolent opposition. Pasoendan also announced that it would recall its members from the Volksraad if the ordinance were not withdrawn by March 21, 1933. Local committees were established with representatives from Taman Siswa, Partindo, New PNI, PSII, BO, Moehammadijah, Pasoendan and other parties and associations. Protest rallies and meetings were held in many places, often simultaneously, in the name of "moment action." Not only the opposition to the wild school ordinance but also economic hardships of the population, "*peroet krontjong* [stomach singing]" as Soekarno put it, were voiced.[26]

The widespread popular protest alarmed the government. Kiewiet de Jonge, government representative to the Volksraad, met with Ki Hadjar Dewantara in October 1932 and assured him that "bona fide private

---

[25] Ingleson, *The Road to Exile*, 205; Abdurrachman Surjomihardjo, "Taman Siswa and the 'Wild Schools'," in *Born in Fire: The Indonesian Struggle for Independence*, ed. Colin Wild and Peter Carey (Athens, Ohio: Ohio University Press, 1986), 39–45; Kenji Tsuchiya, *Indonesia Minzokushugi Kenkyu: Taman Siswa no Seiritsu to Tenkai* (Kyoto: Sobunsha, 1982); Ruth T. McVey, "Taman Siswa and the Indonesian National Awakening," *Indonesia* 4 (Oct. 1967): 128–49.
[26] Surjomihardjo, "Taman Siswa and the 'Wild Schools'," 39–45.

educational institutions need not worry about their position." The attorney general proposed a ban on open rallies and processions. The governor general, worried about widespread passive resistance, was ready to drop the ordinance if an initiative came from the Volksraad and wide schools were not "misused." R.A.A. Wiranatakoesoemah, regent of Bandung and Volksraad member, gave the government a way out. On December 8, 1932, he asked the government whether it was prepared to revise the ordinance in view of popular protest. The government replied on December 24 that it had no political intention with the ordinance and that it was intended to prevent any abuse in education. In January 1933, Wiranatakoesoema introduced a proposal for a temporary suspension of the ordinance. In February 1933 the governor general decided to suspend the implementation of the ordinance indefinitely.[27]

The government yielded on this issue because de Jonge was shaken by the mutiny of De Zeven Provincien which took place on February 5, 1933, because he did not want to make Ki Hadjar Dewantara "a Gandhi-figure," and because the movement could be "contagious" and might allow popular resistance to be organized around other issues. As Advisor for Native Affairs Gobee wrote, "people are held back in no small degree by the diffidence of the unknown. Once this kind of resistance is committed and people see the results and see the victims fall, then there lies a strong urge to follow."[28]

It was not, however, an unalloyed victory for the movement. It was a compromise negotiated between the government and the movement. The Indies government decided to make concessions to the movement on tacit understanding that Taman Siswa, Moehammadijah and other educational institutions police themselves to contain any threat to peace and order and prevent their teachers and students to be involved in "practical" party politics. This was what Kiewiet de Jonge meant when he told Ki Hadjar Dewantara that "bona fide" educational institutions such as Taman Siswa did not need to worry about their position. But it was an important victory, nonetheless, because the government agreed to allow a space there in the arena of education for the movement, where, as John Ingleson rightly notes, "thousands of national[ist] schools" "kept

---

[27] Ingleson, *The Road to Exile*, 205–7; Surjomihardjo, "Taman Siswa and the 'Wild Schools'," 39–45.
[28] Adviser for native affairs to GG, Dec. 29, 1932, in Kwantes, *De Ontwikkeling, 1928–Aug. 1933*, 676–83.

alive and promoted the national ideals for which these [non-cooperation] parties had stood."[29]

Indeed, all the "bona fide" school systems did well in the 1930s to constitute social and educational foundations for training future Indonesians on the basis of "secular" nationalism as well as modernist and orthodox Islam. Taman Siswa, which was founded by Ki Hadjar Dewantara (Soewardi Soerjaningrat) in 1922 in Yogyakarta to provide "national education" and which did not adopt government curriculum and receive any government subsidy, had 166 schools and 11000 pupils by 1932. Moehammadijah, established in 1912 in Yogyakarta as a modernist Islamic educational and social association by Kyai Hadji Ahmad Dahlan, had 834 mosques, 31 public libraries, and 1774 schools by 1938. Nahdlatoel Oelama, founded in 1926 by Kyai Haji Wahab Chasboellah with the support and blessing of Kyai Haji Hasjim Asjari to defend the interests and positions of orthodox Muslims, had 120 branches in Java and South Kalimantan by 1942.[30]

Rural Action

Another arena in which the government negotiated the limits for tolerance with the movement was party and other associational activities in the countryside. The situation, however, was different from one region to another.

In West Java, the government was particularly alarmed at Partindo and New PNI action in Batavia, Cirebon, and Indramayu. The governor of West Java, C.A. Schnitzler, reported to Governor General de Jonge in December 1932 that both Partindo and New PNI were active in Bandung and that their rallies were well attended, even though not very many joined the parties. He also noted that Banten, Buitenzorg (Bogor), and Priangan were "politically quiet," but that the situation in Batavia was "not that good." The major force there was Partindo, with its membership reaching 8,000 in the city and its vicinities, especially private estate areas. Since economic conditions were "the worst" there in private estates, there could be a possibility, in his view, that "as in 1926 the

---

[29] Ingleson, *The Road to Exile*, 207.
[30] On Taman Siswa, see Tsuchiya, *Indonesia Minzokushugi Kenkyu*. On the Moehammadijah, see Ricklefs, *A History of Modern Indonesia*, 215–6, 221–3. See also Laffan, *Islamic Nationhood and Colonial Indonesia: Islamic Nationhood and Colonial Indonesia: the Umma below the Winds* (London: Routledge Curzon, 2003).

political agitation [might] find a fertile soil here [...] for direct extremist action." In the residency of Cirebon, which he wrote was "completely quiet" in 1929, "the political agitation perturbed the rural population" hit by the depression. The situation was worst in Indramayu, he reported, not only because of economic hardships but also because both administration and police were understaffed. New PNI was most active there, focusing its propaganda on "the lowest strata of the population." Resident of Cirebon van der Plas was of opinion, Schnitzler continued, that if its activity expanded, it would pose a direct threat to peace and order and the governor suggested that rallies and meetings be banned.[31]

It is hard to tell whether the situation was indeed serious as Governor Schnitzler argued or whether it looked serious because van der Plas who happened to be posted there as resident wanted to show his expertise in managing native political affairs. In any event, he applied the strategy he had sketched out in his 1928 report to Governor General de Graeff, mobilizing "counter-forces" to contain, isolate, and neutralize "mala fide" revolutionary forces in Cirebon. He reported to Schnitzler in November 1932 that New PNI often successfully recruited teachers, especially village school teachers, into its ranks and that this made its propaganda effective among "little desa [village] men" in the countryside, already hit by cash shortage, reduction in sugar cane cultivation, lack of employment opportunities, fall in rice prices, and higher land taxes. He saw "potential danger" in mass action led by New PNI and Partindo at a time of the crisis brought about by the depression, which manifested itself, for instance, in the rise of "bands of forest thieves," the suppression of which mass arrests and field police and military patrols proved ineffective in Indramayu. As he wrote in his monthly political report in December, van der Plas "carefully as well as consciously" rallied the support of "trustworthy and order-loving elements, above all adat [customary law] elders and kyai" to fight New PNI. As he noted in his letter to Attorney General Verheijen in December 1932, this "counter action" proved successful and there were signs of New PNI members returning their membership cards to local authorities.[32]

In the Vorstenlanden, New PNI started its activity in Surakarta and Klaten in 1933, calling for resistance against taxes and *heerendiensten*

---

[31] Governor of West Java to GG, Dec. 7, 1932, in Kwantes, *De Ontwikkeling: 1928– Aug. 1933*, 669–71.

[32] Resident of Cirebon to PG, Dec. 17, 1932, in Kwantes, *De Ontwikkeling: 1928– Aug. 1933*, 671–4.

The Phantom World of Digul

(corvee labor for the state) in Surakarta countryside and establishing a branch of its youth organization, Soeloeh Pemoeda Indonesia (Torch of Indonesian Youth). Partindo was less active, but kept its presence in Solo with the establishment of Indonesia Moeda and Kepandoean Bangsa Indonesia (Indonesian National Scouting) branches.[33]

Far more important in Surakarta, however, was Pakempalan Kawoela Soerakarta (PKS or Association of Subjects of Surakarta) established in 1932, as ARD chief van der Most put it, at PBI "instigation." The central figure in the PKS was Singgih, a leading member of the PBI in Solo, who called for the transformation of PBI into a mass party and established a Comite Pakempalan Kawoela Soerakarta (PKS Committee) as the "contact body" between PBI and the local population. From the beginning, the Committee concentrated its efforts on rallying popular support in the Surakarta countryside, organizing open rallies in Demangan (residency of Surakarta), Pengging (residency of Boyolali), and Polanharjo (residency of Klaten), the old Insulinde stronghold under Haji Misbach in 1919–20.[34] The first branch was established in Polanharjo in November 1932, and the Committee was transformed into PKS in December, with Singgih as chairman, and Soeratman, chairman of the PBI Surakarta branch and a medical doctor, as vice-chairman.

In 1933 PKS expanded its activity beyond the territory under the Sunan's court to the Mangkunegaran territory and its rallies attracted wider popular interest. Villagers took the trouble to walk "miles" to attend rallies and to see "Goesti [Lord] Singgih." As its name suggests, PKS was an association of subjects in the Sunan's principality, not revolutionary, not even evolutionary, and did not question the established Dutch Javanese social and political order in Surakarta. Singgih openly called for the cooperation between PKS and Narpowandowo, an association of Kasunanan princes. At an open rally in the city in October 1932, for instance, all the audience sat on the ground, while PKS leaders and police officers were seated on chair, and one PBI leader remarked that he felt like being a "kandjeng [lord]."[35]

---

[33] Chief of the ARD, Overzicht van de Politieke Beweging in de Gouvernementen Soerakarta en Jogjakarta na het ingrijpen der Overheid tegen de links-extremistische organisaties in 1933 tot op heden, May 10, 1936, Mr. 602x/1936.

[34] See Shiraishi, *An Age in Motion*, 146–74.

[35] Chief of the ARD, Overzicht van de Politieke Beweging in de Gouvernementen Soerakarta en Jogjakarta, May 10, 1936, Mr. 602x/1936.

PKS was the most important power base for Singgih. Its financial contributions persuaded the PBI central leadership to hold its congress in Solo in April 1933 and made Singgih a major force in the party. Once his relationship with the PBI central leadership soured, however, Singgih approached the Sunan's court circle, especially Pangeran (Prince) Koesoemojoedo, Kraton Regent R.M.H. Woerjaningrat (Boedi Oetomo chairman), and Pangeran Soerjohamidjojo. The PBI influence in Surakarta rapidly declined. The Sunan's court and Pangeran Koesoemojoedo partly financed Singgih's journal, *Timboel,* and when PKS organized its congress in November 1933, it was held in a building made available by Pangeran Koesoemojoedo and Woerjaningrat and a "propaganda car" was hired with Narpowandowo's funding.[36]

Yet local authorities and the police were alarmed at PKS activity in the Surakarta countryside, and the resident of Surakarta had to warn Singgih and his associates to tone down their propaganda, because its members were turning to PKS branch leaders, and not to village officials, for guidance, and "recidivists" were often appointed as its branch leaders, and its activists called for the refusal to perform corvee duties and pay taxes.[37]

The situation in Yogyakarta was not very different, though neither BO nor PBI had any influence on Pakempalan Kawoela Ngajogjakarta (PKN, Association of Subjects of Yogyakarta), which Pangeran Ario Soerjodiningrat, a half-brother of Sultan Hamengku Boewono VII, established in 1930. Its stated purpose was to work for the good of the Yogyakarta principality and its royal house, welfare of its subjects, harmony of the native population of different statuses, and the achievement of self-rule on a democratic basis. It was royalist and anti-revolutionary. Soerjodingrat's idea originated from his conversations in 1928 with H.J. Kiewiet de Jonge, government representative to the Volksraad, about "the need for a party to express the interests of the 'middle class' Javanese in order to counter the movement of nationalists." At the first congress held in May 1931, two motions were passed, one asking

---

[36] Ibid.

[37] Ibid. The Mangkunegaran house, another royal court in Surakarta ever vigilant at any sign of Surakartan influence in its own territory, established its own Pakempalan Kawoela Mangkoenegaran (PKMN) in 1933 as a rival organization against the PKS. It was led by BO secretary Soedewo and retired Mangkunegaran officials, and its membership soon reached several thousand.

for reductions in the head tax and the other asking for concessions for government employees. Plans were announced for PKN to begin organizing agricultural cooperatives, to build a school in each village, and to establish a youth group and support a study fund for higher education. It employed all modern political techniques which had become common knowledge by then. PKN organized congresses, open rallies, member meetings, and cadre training courses. It established cooperatives and schools, purchased rice milling machinery, motor vehicles (for taxi and rental business) and a printing firm, and published its own organ, *Oetoesan Indonesia* (Indonesian Envoy). It grew huge in size, compared with any association of the day, with its membership reaching 34,000 half a year after its establishment at the end of 1930, 110,000 in May 1931, and more than 200,000 in May 1932.

As William O'Malley tells us, peasants who joined PKN, knowing that the party had spoken out against the head tax, felt that they no longer needed to pay it. Refusal to pay taxes or to listen to village heads began to happen more regularly after the PKN had passed a motion at its first congress to ask the Sultan to do away with the head tax. Local leaders, sensing the emergence of a new source of authority with which they were identified, challenged village officials. Incidents took place time and again in which Pangeran Soerjodiningrat was mentioned as *ratu adil*, just king, and there were rumors that those who were not PKN members would not be included when the new kingdom were established. Its huge size and its irregularities annoyed officials of the Indies government and the Sultan's principality. By 1933, officials put pressure on villagers to resign from PKN and to turn in their membership cards. They attended local PKN meetings and even broke up one. The governor of Central Java called Pangeran Soerjodiningrat "an untrustworthy socialist in duplicity" and hinted in his 1934 report that he might well be eligible for exiling from Yogyakarta. Under the assault, PKN began to decline. Membership dues ceased coming in to the PKN coffers. The cooperatives collapsed almost completely.[38]

In East Java, PBI expanded its presence in the countryside and the major issues were the terms of the contracts that the sugar factories

---

[38] William O'Malley, "Indonesia in the Great Depression: A Study of East Sumatra and Jogyakarta in the 1930s" (PhD diss., Cornell University, 1977), 309–34. See also Chief of the ARD, Overzicht van de Politieke Beweging in de Gouvernementen Soerakarta en Jogjakarta, May 10, 1936, Mr. 602x/1936.

had entered into with landholders for land that they could not use for sugar cane. Factories tried to annul contracts or revise them. They relied on village chiefs in making new arrangements. They also called in local government officials to mediate in their favor in their negotiations with landholders. In many places, peasants complied with factory managers, receiving a premium in return for the opportunity to renegotiate hire contracts and releasing factories from the obligation to pay full hire-fees for unwanted land. PBI took an active part in representing the peasantry in negotiating with factory administrators starting in 1932. As a vehicle for its work among the peasantry, it established a peasant organization, Roekoen Tani (RT, Peasants' Association) to promote peasant cooperation and advancement and to bring peasants "from the phase of darkness towards light." The RT stressed the need for peasants to unite to press their claims on sugar factories. Many landholders responded, turning to RT village organization for assistance in their dealings with factories. By 1933, in the words of the East Java governor, it had "annexed the whole political terrain of East Java."[39]

As a matter of fact, however, the PBI/RT success in recruiting members and promoting their interests in negotiations with sugar factories was uneven. The center of PBI/RT action was in the regency of Sidoarjo. PBI leaders such as Soetomo, Soebroto (chairman, PBI advice bureau for RT) and Pamoedji (PBI secretary) regularly visited the region, consulted with local RT leaders, and attended RT evening meetings. In those meetings, not only was the reduction in sugar cane planting areas discussed, but also questions of land taxes, village heads, salt and kerosene prices, dismissal of village officials, establishment of rice barns (lumbung), purchase of agricultural machines, conversion in the land tenure were raised. "The priyayi pays, they say, f. 15 income tax out of his f. 600 annual income," Resident of Surabaya A.H. Moreu reported, "[while] the peasant [pays] f. 16 land tax out of f. 100."[40]

The RT organized peasant shareholders in village communal land and represented them in negotiations with sugar factories. In the village of Sukorame, local RT executive members were called *loerah* [village

[39] Elson, *Javanese Peasants and the Colonial Sugar Industry*, 234–8. Resident of Surabaya to governor of East Java, June 26, 1933, in Kwantes, *De Ontwikkeling, 1928–Aug. 1933*, 802–9.
[40] Resident of Surabaya to governor of East Java, June 26, 1933, in Kwantes, *De Ontwikkeling, 1928–Aug. 1933*, 804.

chief], *tjarik* [secretary], and *kebajan* [messenger], as if they were village officials. But the resident of Surabaya argued that RTs were led by "entirely unfavorable elements (dismissed village heads and foremen [*mandoer*] of sugar factories)" and that those who were willing to renegotiate the terms of contracts with factories were afraid of being accused as "spies" by RTs and did not dare to come to the subdistrict head. In Sidoarjo, where "the most peace-loving relationship" had existed between factories and the population a year before, "the unrest manifested itself in the village" because of RT activities.[41]

One wonders whether phrases such as "recidivists" and "entirely unfavorable elements (dismissed village heads and foremen of sugar factories)" may signify wild forces in action. Historians have long noted their changing roles over centuries in Java. Onghokham talks about *weris* (spies), local toughs and brokers linking different social spheres and inhabiting the area between legality and criminality, who the regent relied on to maintain peace and order at the beginning of the twentieth century. Many of those people were "villagers of substance, some even headmen, but the ambivalence of their role as local political bosses, informers, and extortionists [and] their lack of prospects for advancement into the official class meant that there was little moral or material check on their doings."[42] PKI leaders also debated among themselves whether the party should and could abandon its nonproletarian support in the years leading to the rebellion with this type of people in mind. Darsono cautioned against their unreliability and Tan Malaka warned against 'anarchically inclined members." Those who disagreed with them, including Alimin and Moesso, called for agitation and deemed it imperative to secure the support of adventurers "who would be attracted to the party by its defiance of authority and not by class interests or by doctrine."[43] There is no reason to doubt that people variously called such as *kapetengan, djagabaja, djogodesa, bromotjorah, blateran,* and *weri* were in action.[44] But there is no way to know who of those were active in PBI/ RT, PKY, PKS and other associations in the 1930s. The only thing we

---

[41] Ibid., 803–4.
[42] Onghokham, "The Inscrutable and the Paranoid: An Investigation into the Sources of the Brotoningrat Affair," in *The Thugs, the Curtain Thief, and the Sugar Lord: Power, Politics, and Culture in Colonial Java* (Jakarta: Metafor, 2003), 36–7.
[43] McVey, *The Rise of Indonesian Communism,* 187–90, 297–300, and 320.
[44] Rush, *Opium to Java,* 115–6.

know for sure is that Dutch officials were worried about the challenge to government authority and that those such as *weri, bromotjorah* and "recivists" were names given to any individuals that signified a threat to peace and order.[45]

Nor for that matter were Dutch officials sure about the trustworthiness of village and native administrative officials. The resident of Surabaya, for instance, reporting that village chiefs and officials sat in the RT leadership initially, summoned the population for its meetings, collected fees, and distributed membership cards, wondered whether native officials were sympathetic for PBI/RT and argued that the best way to know their "spirit" was to look at what they read, *Pemimpin* (Leader) and *Onze Bode* (Our Messenger), "which have entirely adopted the tone of *Soeara Oemoem* [of PBI] and the former *Sinar Laoetan* of Indonesian Marine Union."[46]

With the approval of the resident of Surabaya, Assistant Resident of Sidoarjo F.H. Nieuwenhuyzen took measures to suppress "the unrest" and to "restore" "the peace of mind of the peasants." The PID was deployed to watch PBI and RT rallies and meetings. Native officials were

---

[45] For more on what Dutch officials were worried about—namely, the emergence of a new authority—see Frederick, *Visions and Heat*, 230–43, and Cribb, *Gangsters and Revolutionaries*. While *jago* in Indonesian history has been studied heavily, hardly any attempt has been made to locate its significance theoretically and in comparative perspective. Antonio Gramsci sheds some light on this point: "The petit-bourgeois [morti di fame] came originally from the rural bourgeoisie. Property gets broken up among large families until it vanishes altogether, but the members of this class are not prepared to work with their hands. In this way there is formed a famished stratum of aspirants to minor municipal appointments, as clerks, messenger, etc. This stratum constitutes a disruptive element in the life of the countryside, always thirsting for changes (elections, etc.), and furnishes the local "subversive" ... It allies itself especially with the rural bourgeoisie against the peasantry, and organizes the morti di fame to serve its interests. These strata exist in every region, and have ramifications in the towns, too, where they merge into the criminal underworld or into the shifting milieu which surrounds it. Many petty clerks in the towns originate socially from these strata, of the landowner who endures work under compulsion. The "subversivism" of these strata has two faces, one turned to the left and one to the right, but the left face is simply a means of blackmail; at the decisive moments they always move to the right, and their desperate "courage" always prefers to have the carabinieri on their side." Antonio Gramsci, *Selections from the Prison Notebooks of Antonio Gramsci* (New York: International Publishers, 1971), 272–3.
[46] Resident of Surabaya to governor of East Java, June 26, 1933, in Kwantes, *De Ontwikkeling, 1928–Aug. 1933*, 805.

instructed as to how to respond to questions and requests people would raise and how to maintain "the right standpoint" to parties. "The evening hours became hours of tension," the resident of Surabaya wrote.[47] And he argued that PBI was "hostile to the authority," not very different from Partindo and New PNI, despite its outward appearance of constructive work and that its associational life cultivated "recalcitrant" hate against the West. "The inland [*binnenlanden*] can tolerate no political agitation," he wrote, because of the economic "debacle," because the population was "emotional, primitive, and easy to incite," and because there was "no proper intelligence services and power instruments" available.[48]

Resident of Surabaya J.H.B. Kuneman summarized well the widespread sense among senior Dutch officials about the policy the government should take vis-à-vis rural action. Whether in West Java, the principalities, East Java or elsewhere, the entire rural area should be off the limits of any organizational action—loyalist, royalist, constructive, evolutionary, bona fide, destructive, revolutionary, and mala fide—because whatever stated intentions were, parties and associations would create a space for "recalcitrant" elements to act, people were "emotional, primitive, and easy to incite," and there were "no proper intelligence services" there.

Policy Shift

The introduction of the wild school ordinance provided an excellent opportunity for native associations and parties to unite and offer resistance to the government. Parties expanded their activity and influence. Rural action parties and associations organized often led to unintended resistance and challenges to the authority. Partindo membership expanded from 4,300 in May 1932 to 20,000 in July 1933, and under Soekarno its Bandung branch membership increased from 226 in August 1932 to 3762 in July 1933.[49] Governor General de Jonge was alarmed by the entire trend of events in the Indies and worried whether the situation was getting out of control.

It was under this circumstance that the munity on the Dutch warship *de Zeven Provincien* took place on February 4–10, 1933, in which

---

[47] Ibid., 806.
[48] Ibid., 809.
[49] Ingleson, *The Road to Exile*, 189.

a group of European and non-European NCOs and sailors revolted because of their dissatisfaction with government austerity measures.[50] The governor general convened an extraordinary meeting of the Council of the Netherlands Indies on February 8, 1933.[51] De Jonge was worried about the "infection" of the mutiny to the native society.[52] The attorney general seized the opportunity to argue that the political freedom the government had allowed to natives should be restricted to such a large extent that any undesirable consequences would not happen. In his view the freedom of political action should be denied entirely for army, navy and police personnel. For other vital services, it should suffice to require loyalty declarations, in addition to the ban on membership of certain associations.[53] Council Vice President C.W. Bodenhousen concurred and said that if there were no PNI, PKI or other extremist associations, no one would think twice about taking such measures as proposed by the attorney general. Unfortunately, however, "such disloyal societies do exist," and therefore he argued that it was obvious that one should have the courage to ban those subversive unions and then perhaps generally for all officials.[54] De Jonge said this proposal went far beyond what he had considered," but it "is attractive for its simplicity, its easy handling, and its underlying rational thought."[55] But he was not fully convinced of such drastic measures. He also observed that the general situation had not become serious enough to warrant such measures and that there would be objections to those measures in the Netherlands.[56]

After the Council meeting, the attorney general kept making his case to de Jonge. In his report to the governor general on February 10, he argued that the mutiny "can and will certainly stir up the courage and activity of other rebellious movements" and cautioned against the

---

[50] Prior to the munity, there were signs of unrest: in the wake of the governor general's decision to cut down navy budget in January 1933, protest meetings were organized, and the navy commander banned sailors' gatherings. Wal, ed., *Herinneringen van Jhr. Mr. B.C. de Jonge*, 158–60.

[51] Notulen buitengewone vergadering van de raad van Nederlandsch-Indie, Feb. 8, 1933, in Kwantes, ed., *De Ontwikkeling, 1928–Aug. 1933*, 684–93.

[52] Wal, *Herinneringen van Jhr. Mr. B C. de Jonge*, 162.

[53] Ibid., 689.

[54] Ibid., 689–90.

[55] Ibid., 689, 692–3.

[56] Ibid., 689, 692–3.

risk of contamination. He also observed in this connection that New PNI was revolutionary even if it did not pose a direct threat and that elements from the two disbanded parties—PKI and PNI—were joining it or finding resonance among those "non-intellectual and least balanced part of the population."[57] In his February 17, 1933, report, he argued in connection with an article about the munity published in *Soeara Oemoem* on February 6 that the government should demand Soetomo, "the leader of PBI and of course also the auctor intellectual of various subversive expressions of *Soeara Umem*," declare loyalty to the government as a civil servant, a physician attached to the government medical service.[58]

The Council of the Netherlands Indies met again on March 3, 1933, to discuss Attorney General Verheijen's proposal to dismiss Soetomo from government service. Advisor for Native Affairs Gobee disagreed, and argued that Soetomo's dismissal or his de facto forced resignation would drive the native movement to the far left and turn it into "a real anti-government movement."[59] The Council did not support the attorney general's proposal. Governor General de Jonge approved its recommendation on April 8, 1933. At the same time, however, he decided to handle the matter more systematically. As he said at the Council meeting in November 1933, the circumstances were becoming increasingly unfavorable toward the end of 1932 and the beginning of 1933. People were unhappy and taking action against salary cuts and the reduction of educational spending which led to the establishment of private schools. The situation was already tense, when the *Zeven Provincien* incident took place, and forced the government to face "the consequences of too generous a policy." This should not be tolerated, he said, and it is compulsory "for the government to tighten its reins."[60]

In his letter to Colonial Minister de Graaff on April 11, 1933, de Jonge spelled out the government's position.[61] First, all the civil servants should be prohibited from membership in any society with a revolutionary or non-cooperation principle [such as Partindo, New PNI,

---

[57] PG to GG, Feb. 10, 1933, in Kwantes, *De Ontwikkeling, 1928–Aug. 1933*, 695.
[58] PG to GG, Feb. 17, 1933, in Kwantes, *De Ontwikkeling, 1928–Aug. 1933*, 704–11.
[59] Advie van de raad van Nederlandsch-Indie, Mar. 3, 1933, in Kwantes, *De Ontwikkeling, 1928–Aug. 1933*, 711–14. See Yamamoto, "Print Power and Censorship," 284–6, for information on the government attack on Soetomo in 1933.
[60] Minutes, Raad van Nederlandsch Indie, Nov. 22, 1933.
[61] GG to minister of colonies, April 11, 1933, in Kwantes, *De Ontwikkeling, 1928–Aug. 1933*, 721–5.

and PSII]. Second, neither membership nor participation in societies with social-democratic principles would be allowed for all the members of the state coercive apparatuses (army, fleet, police). Third, civil servants would be required to take the oath of allegiance. And finally, all the board members of trade unions would be required to declare their loyalty to the government if they were civil servants.[62]

There was a broad consensus in the government that it should not risk any further chance of disturbance. Kiewiet de Jonge, the government representative to the Volksraad and a former ally of de Graeff, said in late April 1933 that as in the 1919 Afdeeling B affair, the 1923 railway strike, the 1926–27 communist "disturbances," and the 1929 PNI-led unrest, "today, in 1933, the course of events" was coming to a point of disjunction and that as the popular movement evolved, the general attitude of leading figures was becoming increasingly irreconcilable. If this development were allowed to go on, he warned, the situation would become untenable within 20 years, and the Indies would become like British India, but there was still time to intervene, decisively but cautiously, not to prevent the situation from developing in the direction in which it was going, but to change its pace. It is not that there were no potentially opposing forces. As a matter of fact, there were many moderates among the intellectuals and the nobility. But what made it impossible for these elements to assert themselves socially or politically was that anyone who dared to do so in press and popular meetings stirred up a constant campaign against his person. It was virtually impossible for a prominent figure to act as a leader of a loyal movement. Nor was it possible for a regent or a lower government official to support such a movement. They would not want to risk, in their own region and elsewhere, the undermining of their position and prestige. This was a frank admission on the part of the government that the constructive engagement, which Kiewiet de Jonge called "the liberal state idea," did not work and that the government would not allow the movement to develop in such a way to lead to disturbances or to allow the Indies turn into another British India.[63]

On June 27, 1933, the government banned civil servants from joining or working with associations that actively or passively acted

---

[62] Ibid.

[63] Government representative for general affairs to the Volksraad to GG, April 28, 1933, in Kwantes, *De Ontwikkeling, 1928–Aug. 1933*, 729–37.

against the Indies state. Partindo and New PNI were designated as such associations. The decree allowed civil servants to remain as members of a trade union if its executive board had at least a civil servant among its members. For a civil servant to serve on the board of a trade union, he was required to sign a declaration of allegiance to the state. Those who did not comply with the requirement were to be dismissed immediately and dishonorably from the state service.

Yet A.D.A. de Kat Angelino did not think the government had gone far enough. He submitted his note to the governor general in late June 1933.[64] He should have calculated that the government change in the Netherlands, in which H. Colijn whose protégé de Jonge was became prime minister and minister for colonies in May 1933, would make it easier for de Jonge to approve his proposal.[65] He called on the governor general to take further measures against Partindo and New PNI. His argument was straightforward: that the very nature of organized mass action would create problems, that it was precisely "the trade and peasant unions that embody the mass action," and that "organizing these forces is the task of PI [Partindo]." He said that Partindo and New PNI propaganda was hostile, and rhetorically asked what impression one would get if one had attended a series of public rallies and heard the word "imperialism," used synonymous with "the Dutch authority" and that of Indonesia Merdeka combined with "the fall of the Dutch authority." Partindo and New PNI were carrying out a revolutionary propaganda, creating almost unbelievable troubles and extremely dangerous trends in all layers of the population and almost in the entire Dutch Indies.[66] He argued that the depression worked for their favor, that there was a general sense of dissatisfaction among the population and that Imperialism, that is the government, was made into a scapegoat. As Dutch officials often said, he also argued that the stronghold of moderates which was already weak was further undermined by rising radicalism and that people left the safe self-restraint of regional activity and started to work on an Indonesian basis, change statutes to replace the pursuit of development with independence, Indonesia Merdeka. Even BO with its honorable tradition was "crying with the wolves in

---

[64] Nota van de algemene secretarie, end of June 1933, in Kwantes, *De Ontwikkeling, 1928–Aug. 1933*, 819–33.
[65] See Wal, ed., *Herinneringen van Jhr. Mr. B.C. de Jonge*, 169.
[66] Ibid., 825–7.

the forest and sometimes making noises."[67] Partindo and the New PNI influence on women and youth was also strong and getting stronger, he observed, and so it was with scouting and religious associations. It should be expected, he said, that the entire native associational life would be under the influence of fanatic, revolutionary associations. Their members were not very many, he wrote, but as initial timidity wore off, people would join in an influx. PBI would face difficult situations in which it would be confronted with a choice between isolation (and decline) and radicalization (and greater popularity).[68]

De Kat Angelino concluded that Partindo and New PNI should not be allowed to expand further. To this end, however, banning civil servants from joining Partindo and New PNI and imposing tougher control over their public meetings would not be enough. More drastic measures were needed, he argued. He confidently predicted that without further government measures there would be another "derailment" in the native political movement in the near future. In his view, "some simple guidelines" were needed to "purify" the movement and shift it from the revolutionary nationalism to the evolutionary nationalism, from the destructive to the constructive, and from the disloyal to the loyal. He argued that the government should make it clear that it would not allow any association on a non-cooperation principle to take political action. The ban obviously would not apply to such associations as PBI and Taman Siswa. The government should welcome all constructive socio-economic and educational activity, even if some of those associations adopt a non-cooperation principle. The government should also welcome all national awareness and action in the form of opposition, if it was to accept the legal framework and not to assume a revolutionary character.[69]

Shortly after De Kat Angelino submitted his note to Governor General de Jonge in June 1933, he visited West Sumatra together with Attorney General Verheijen and Director of Education and Religion B.J.O. Schrieke. Resident of West Sumatra B. H.F. van Heuven, after speaking with them, sent a proposal to the governor general to ban all the gatherings for Permi (Persatoean Moeslimin Indonesia, Indonesian Muslim Union), PSII, New PNI, and Partindo in West Sumatra in

[67] Ibid., 828.
[68] Ibid., 829.
[69] Ibid., 832–3.

early July.[70] The attorney general endorsed his proposal as well as the internment of H. Moechtar Loetfi, who was arrested on July 11.[71] The ban had been in place in effect, enforced by local adat chiefs, but the resident wanted to declare the ban on gatherings and provide the legal cover for it.[72]

On July 18, 1933, the governor general asked Deputy Attorney General Vonk for his opinion about applying the meeting ban to Partindo and New PNI.[73] On July 22, 1933, Governor of East Java J.H.B. Kuneman proposed the meeting ban to apply to Partindo and New PNI. He noted in his letter that Partindo and New PNI were getting more active in Surabaya since the Partindo congress in April, and observed that three open meetings, all heavily attended, were organized by Partindo in July alone, along with many closed cadre training meetings in different parts of the city, that Partindo membership in Surabaya now stood about 2000 and that the Surabaya branch of the PBKI railway workers union was under the control of Partindo and New PNI activists.[74] The attorney general followed up on the East Java governor's recommendation and proposed on July 31 that the government apply the meeting ban to Partindo and New PNI all over the Indies, in combination with the internment of their leaders as a preventive measure.[75]

---

[70] Aantekeningen van resident van Sumatra's Westkust over bespreking met procureur-general, A.D.A. de Kat Angelino en directeur van onderwijs en eredienst, July 9, 1933, in Kwantes, *De Ontwikkeling, 1928–Aug. 1933*, 834–7. For Partai Muslimin Indonesia (Permi) and its leaders, especially Iljas Jacub, Muchtar Luthfi and Djala-luddin Thaib, Kahin, *Rebellion to Integration: West Sumatra and the Indonesian Polity 1926–1998* (Amsterdam: Amsterdam University Press, 1999), 50–7. On the native officer most responsible for political policing in West Sumatra in the early 1930s, see also Blembergen, "The Perfect Policeman: Colonial Policing, Modernity, and Conscience on Sumatra's West Coast in the Early 1930s," *Indonesia* 91 (2011): 165–91.

[71] PG to GG, July 12, 1933, in Kwantes, *De Ontwikkeling, 1928–Aug. 1933*, 837.

[72] PG to GG, Medan, July 23, 1933, in Kwantes, *De Ontwikkeling, 1928–Aug. 1933*, 838–42.

[73] First government secretary to deputy PG, July 18, 1933, in Kwantes, *De Ontwik-keling, 1928–Aug. 1933*, 850–1.

[74] Governor of East Java to GG, July 22, 1933, in Kwantes, *De Ontwikkeling, 1928–Aug. 1933*, 851–5.

[75] PG to GG, July 31, 1933, in Kwantes, *De Ontwikkeling, 1928–Aug. 1933*, 855–7.

On the same day, July 31, 1933, Soekarno was arrested in Batavia. On August 1, the government announced its plan to intern him. On the same day, the Council of the Netherlands Indies met and endorsed the preventive measure of banning the meetings and the selective internment the attorney general proposed. Governor General de Jonge decided to apply the meeting ban on Partindo and New PNI and the decision took effect on the same day, August 1.[76] The Council of the Netherlands Indies met again on August 4, 1933 to endorse the attorney general's proposal to ban Permi and PSII in West Sumatra and intern some of their leaders to Digul.[77] On August 29, the governor general decided to surveille statements in the press more closely and to muzzle *Soeara Oemoem* and *Persatoean Indonesia*.[78]

In the meantime, de Kat Angelino sent another note to the governor general in August 1933, explaining his view on "the way in which political policy in the future could place the native political movement on a more real[istic] basis."[79] In his view, nationalism as represented by Partindo, New PNI, Permi and PSII was "anti-Western, anti-kafir, anti-capitalist, anti-imperialist, anti-Dutch and anti-regime" and as a matter of principle the government should ban all these parties as being in conflict with peace and order, prohibit [their] non-cooperation and mass action, and ban Partindo and New PNI from establishing their branches and associated unions and organizations. Trade unions should be "free" from [any] political influence. He also argued that some of the "revolutionary leaders" would attempt to organize "underground action" when they were banned from organizing meetings, but the political policing service should know what they might attempt to do underground. The government should not worry about their underground action, he argued. The most important thing was to ban their open action, for it was openness in his view that made their propaganda possible on a large scale

---

[76] Raad van Nederlandsch-Indie to GG, Aug. 1, 1933, in Kwantes, *De Ontwikkeling, 1928–Aug. 1933*, 858–9.

[77] Advies van de raad van Nederlandsch Indie, Aug. 4, 1933, in Kwantes, *De Ontwikkeling, 1928–Aug. 1933*, 860–3.

[78] GG to minister of colonies, Aug. 29, 1933, in Kwantes, *De Ontwikkeling van de Nationalistische Beweging in Nederlandsch-Indie, Bronnenpublikatie 4de Stuk Aug. 1933–1942* (Groningen: Wolters-Noordhoff/Bouma's Boekhuis, 1982), 21–36.

[79] Nota van de algemene secretarie, Aug. 1933, in Kwantes, *De Ontwikkeling, Aug. 1933–1942*, 1–20.

and gave the impression that the government would not be a match to the movement. Granting the right of association and assembly "in the Eastern society" could invite misunderstanding, he argued, because of the "fundamental differences between Western and Eastern society." It should not be allowed, not only for the sake of peace and order, but also for the sake of a "healthy and balanced development" of the native communities. To that end, it would suffice to revise the legal provisions concerning the exercise of the right of assembly to require prior notification to the local administration for the holding of political meetings (both open and closed), the permission for which the head of local government could refuse if he so desired. Nothing of the sort that had preceded the 1926 incident would be allowed. In any event the government was now well informed of the movement to such small details that there would be no surprise. In this way, he said, an important step would be taken in the direction in which sound political and socio-economic development should be pursued. One cannot help but note the enormous confidence de Kat Angelino had in the state capability of political policing and his contempt on Indonesian nationalism for its impotence, on which his entire native policy recommendation was built.

Governor General De Jonge made up his mind by the end of August 1933, to take the measures suggested by de Kat Angelino.[80] In the meantime, the attorney general proposed the internment of Soekarno in his letter to the governor general on August 19, 1933.[81] Soekarno's internment was a foregone conclusion, but the reasoning offered by the Council of the Netherlands Indies which met on October 13 reveals the foremost concern that the government had about Soekarno. The Council was convinced in view of his letters asking for the government pardon that he was a man of "weak and uncontrolled nature" and that even if he promised to moderate himself in the future, "he would be unable to resist the charm of the applauding audience."[82] To put it differently, the Council in effect concluded that it was his ability to establish rapport with the masses that was a threat and that Soekarno was a danger because he could unleash and be carried away by popular radicalism.

---

[80] GG to minister of colonies, Aug. 29, 1933, in Kwantes, *De Ontwikkeling Aug. 1933–1942*, 21–36.
[81] PG to GG, Aug. 19, 1933, in Kwantes, *De Ontwikkeling, 1928–Aug. 1933*, 870–82.
[82] Advies van de raad van Nederlandsch Indie, Oct. 13, 1933, in Kwantes, *De Ontwikkeling, Aug. 1933–1942*, 44–9.

The attorney general offered different reasons in his proposal to intern Mohamad Hatta, Shahrir and other New PNI leaders in his letter to the governor general dated December 22, 1933.[83] In his view, Hatta, a proponent of the cooperation between revolutionary nationalists and communists, was culpable beyond any doubt. He knew Hatta was a nationalist, but he argued that Hatta signed the convention with Semaoen in December 1926 to take over the nationalist leadership, that PNI was his "spiritual product" and that Hatta opposed Sartono and others in disbanding PNI, not only because it would confuse people, but also because if the movement were to go moderate, it would lose influence on the masses and "give Moscow the opportunity again to take control of the Indonesian masses." He wrote that Hatta and Sjahrir maintained a close relationship with P.L. Schmidt's Independent Socialist Party (Onafhankelijke Socialistische Partij, OSP) which was opposed to Moscow "stiff centralism" and that New PNI, like OSP, professed Marxist principles and aligned itself with OSP "as an anti-state association."

He cited an article that Sjahrir published in 1931 in the independent, revolutionary-socialist monthly, *De Nieuwe weg* (The New Way) with the title "The Indonesian Movement at a Dead Point, The Way Out," in which he argued that only a consciously revolutionary mass party, led and controlled by organization and discipline, would be able to lead the Indonesian people to its destination. In Verheijen's view, it was what New PNI, an "outpost of the masses," was all about, the party that was to lead to a future revolutionary mass party to be developed along the lines spelled out there in ideological and organizational terms, especially after Sjahrir's return and in anticipation of Hatta's arrival.

The attorney general also referred to an article that Boerhanoeddin, the party secretary, had published in *Daulat Rajat*, in which he said the struggle to achieve Free Indonesia should not only be "waged on stage," but also require "work in the dark." Verheijen took it to mean that Boerhanoeddin was suggesting underground action and suggested that Sjahrir, now in charge of the revolutionary trade union federation, CPBI (Indonesian Labor Union Federation), had withdrawn from the party central executive committee and handed over the party leadership to Hatta. After the government banned state employees from joining the

---

[83] PG to GG, Dec. 22, 1933, in Kwantes, *De Ontwikkeling, Aug. 1933–1942*, 189–206.

PBKI railway workers union, Verheijen said, a new union, SSO (Sarekat Sekerdja Oemoem, Union of General Workers) was established under the CPBI and New PNI leadership to organize railway and tramway workers, sugar factory workers, dock workers, as well as factory, port, and metal workers, printers, chauffeurs, coachmen and others who had not been organized in trade unions. It should not be a cause for alarm, he admitted, but cautioned that the government should not underestimate attempts at a "concentration of forces," because in the long run it might become impossible to fight revolutionary propaganda and agitation by banning gatherings once the movement was "anchored" in trade unions.

The attorney general concluded his letter to the governor general by saying that if "the government does not want to fall short in the exercise of its primary task—maintaining public peace and order," it should get to "the heart of the movement" directly and without delay and move against those who were undermining the public authority. "The history [of the 1926–27 revolts] taught us," he argued, the longer the government allowed "the criminals" to grow, the more disturbing and extensive they would become and that the government in the end would have to intervene. Something similar was going on now, which "according to my firm conviction" would eventually lead to similar— and "in itself undesirable for our good name as colonial power"—mass [internment] measures, "unless main troublemakers are eliminated in time." The attorney general thus made his case for interning Hatta, Sjahrir, and other New PNI central executive committee members (Maskoen, Boerhanoeddin, Soeka and Bondan).

In his letter to the governor general on January 24, 1934, Adviser for Native Affairs Gobee opposed their internment and instead proposed banning New PNI, even though he admitted that people of Hatta's mentality were dangerous, in comparison with whom a revolutionary figure such as Tjipto Mangoenkoesoemo would look like "a child."[84] De Kat Angelino disagreed with Gobee and wrote that they warned against a 'putsch' and called for a well-prepared revolutionary mass action, a thoughtful attitude on their part that reminded him of "one of the assassin" and that "good politics, which in the long run will

---

[84] Adviser for native affairs to GG, Jan. 24, 1934, in Kwantes, *De Ontwikkeling, Aug. 1933–1942*, 207–9.

create a healthy native movement" would not be achieved in the way Gobee proposed.[85]

The Council of the Netherlands Indies endorsed the attorney general's proposal on February 16, 1934 to arrest Hatta and others.[86] In its opinion, New PNI had been "walking right along the barbed wire," not doing anything other than what had been allowed in the past, but that intervention would be desirable to show once for all that the government had moved "the barbed wire." Hatta, Sjahrir, and others were arrested on February 24, 1934, for internment.

The "barbed wire" metaphor is useful to see the shift in the government policy to the movement, but it is misleading in capturing its precise nature. The "No Trespass" signs, which the Council called the barbed wire, were not moved. They remained there to mark the line beyond which one would have a good chance of being arrested, imprisoned, and exiled to Digul. But the government decision to intern Hatta and others created a new zone in which one could be arrested, imprisoned and interned to Digul, but this zone was not clearly marked. One could only tell it was there because it was infested with spies and informers and watched intensely by the political intelligence apparatus. Partindo, New PNI, and their substructures (*onderbouw*) were not treated as PKI and Pari were, but people were aware—and the police made them aware—that they were being watched by the police and that they risked arrest, imprisonment, and perhaps internment. This zone also expanded steadily: Partindo and New PNI were banned; trade unions, youth organizations, reading clubs, and other substructures associated with the parties were suffocated; Soekarno as well as Hatta and some other New PNI leaders were arrested and interned; who knows what to happen to those who might lead parties and associated organizations, whether noncooperation or cooperation? It was this condition under which Urip's equation, police=politics, was satisfied and which created the effect of "a diffidence of the unknown" as Gobee put it to contain the movement.

It should be no surprise then that the government took further measures in the months that followed, "the times of stress" according to

---

[85] Nota der Algemene secretarie, niet gedateerd, in Kwantes, *De Ontwikkeling, Aug. 1933–1942*, 211–16.
[86] Advies van de raad van Nederlandsch Indie, Feb. 16, 1934, in Kwantes, *De Ontwikkeling, Aug. 1933–1942*, 217–20.

de Jonge and his top lieutenants.[87] In September 1933, the government banned all teachers at government and government-subsidized schools from being members or attending meetings of Indonesia Moeda. In October the government banned state employees (that is state railway personnel) from joining PBKI (Indonesia Railway Workers Union), which had increasingly come under Partindo and New PNI.[88]

De Kat Angelino also followed up in November 1933 to make a case for a series of "desirable political measures" the government should take "to influence the political situation" and "combat excesses in the press and printed materials."[89] It was not because he and his colleagues in the government were worried about the native political situation. They knew that Partindo and New PNI were in disarray and that their trade unions and other associations were weak and insignificant. They were also in agreement that they could rely on the political intelligence apparatus. De Kat Angelino said that "thanks to the excellent functioning of the intelligence service under his leadership," the attorney general could now tell the government about New PNI shifting its center of revolutionary action.[90] Gobee wrote that Indonesians abroad played important roles in the preparation of revolts in 1926 and 1927, but now "the political investigation is so well equipped and calibrated for the task" that "history will not repeat itself in this way."[91] De Kat Angelino thus reasoned: once the government banned party newspapers, journals, and periodicals, they would publish pamphlets; if the government banned associations, they would hold meetings and gatherings; if the government interned core revolutionary party leaders, a new generation of leaders, already active in student and youth associations, would take over their positions; if the government required any association to obtain permission to hold an open public rally, they would organize a closed meeting; if the government allowed activists to keep teaching at schools,

---

[87] See Yamamoto, "Print Power and Censorship," 295–6, for the times of stress (*tyden van spanning*).

[88] Ingleson, *The Road to Exile*, 222–3.

[89] Nota (C) van de algemene secretarie, Nov. 1933, in Kwantes, *De Ontwikkeling, Aug. 1933–1942*, 103–9.

[90] Nota van de algemene secretarie, niet gedateerd, in Kwantes, *De Ontwikkeling, Aug. 1933–1942*, 215.

[91] Adviser for native affairs to GG, Jan. 24, 1934, in Kwantes, *De Ontwikkeling, Aug. 1933–1942*, 210.

they would influence school children. He concluded that "the [entire] terrain [must] be surveilled completely."

The Council of the Netherlands Indies endorsed de Kat Angelino's proposal on April 13, 1934, for the government to be active in all fields and to toughen "the legal arsenal against popular politics" such as extra-ordinary powers, muzzling the press, banning associations, requiring associations to obtain government permission to hold an open public meeting, possible travel ban and teaching ban.[92] The Volksraad approved the legal measures the government submitted as regards the right of association and assembly on February 20, 1935. Yet, there was a major drawback to the approach as we have seen. As P.J.A. Idenburg remarked after the Indies were lost to the Dutch, police "intelligence reporting" was sound and elucidative, but "the [police] considerations naturally emanated from a thought world" and "the police intelligence reporting did not—and also could not—make good the real policy of the governor general."[93] The government was as much a hostage of its own political intelligence as the Indies population, for without any other intelligence reporting, the *hoofdparket* under the attorney general, with its steady stream of considerations, speculations, stories and reports, provided the government with its only way of mapping the terrain and guided it in formulating its policy to the native movement.

In his final days as governor general, de Jonge attended the confer-ence with governors, residents, and regents of Java on August 18, 1936. The conference report[94] has this to say:

> The governor general has little to say about the political situation. In general, there is enough reason to be satisfied. Although a small upswing of unrest can be expected here and there, because the con-ditions abroad and the change in the administration in this country will probably give rise to something again, vigilance and if necessary deliberate and calm intervention can no doubt manage it. When he

---

[92] Advies van de raad van Nederlandsch Indie, April 13, 1934, in Kwantes, *De Ont-wikkeling, Aug. 1933–1942*, 226–35.

[93] P. J. A. Idenburg, "Het Nederlandse antwoord op het Indonesisch nationalisme," in *Balans van beleid: Terugblik op de laatste halve eeuw van Nederlandsch-Indië*, by H. Baudet en I. J. Brugmans (Assen, 1961), 149.

[94] Verslag conferentie van de gouverneur-generaal met gouverneurs, residenten en regenten op Java, Aug. 18, 1936, in Kwantes, *De Ontwikkeling, Aug. 1933–1942*, 349–56.

looks back at the past five years, he is surprised how little he has to do to maintain peace and order. But when he is here [in the conference] and finds himself among all the regents, this surprise disappears. After all, the good, quiet, patient people, administered by men of position and standing as regents, must be able to live in peace, if only one manages to curb the few malicious elements.

One wonders whether Harry J. Benda got his idea about the *beamtenstaat*, an "apolitical, administrative polit[y] par excellence" from such statements as this one. In any event, de Jong had enough reasons to be complacent about the nationalist movement. The governor of East Java reported in November 1933 on New PNI and Partindo affiliated trade unions, youth, scouting and other associations in Kediri, Madiun, Blitar, Surabaya, Jombang, Magetan, Besoeki, Bondowoso, Sitoebondo and other places.[95] The largest Partindo affiliated association was Indonesia Moeda (Young Indonesia) with 600 members. There were three Partindo affiliated trade unions with more than 100 members: PBKI (Indonesia Railway Workers Union) in Surabaya with 300 members, SKI (Sarekat Koetsier Indonesia, Indonesian Coachmen Union) in Madiun with 270 members, and PKT (Perkoempoelan Kaoem Tani, Peasant Association) in Jember with 227 members. New PNI related unions and associations were smaller. The largest youth organization was SPI (Soeloeh Pemoeda Indonesia, Torch of Indonesian Youth) with 90 members and the largest trade union was PKI (Persatoean Koesir Indonesia, Indonesian Coachmen Union) with 40 members. The governor also offered this observation: first, Partindo was far larger than New PNI; second, student, youth, and scouting organizations constituted a major base for Partindo; third, labor support was confined to artisans and the government ban on SBKA (Railway Workers Union) had a devastating effect, and finally Taman Siswa schoolteachers were active in New PNI and Partindo.

Chief of the ARD van der Most also reported on the political movement in Surakarta and Yogjakarta in May 1936:[96] In Surakarta, three New PNI leaders were arrested for speech and press offenses in June 1933; the arrest crippled New PNI and after the ban on meetings the party never recovered; by March 1934 its activities were reduced to the establishment of reading groups and publication of *Bedoeg* (Drum)

---

[95] Governor of East Java to GG, Nov. 9. 1933, Mr. 1403x/1933.
[96] Chief of the ARD, Overzicht van de politieke beweging in de Gouvernementen Soerakarta en Jogjakarta, May 10, 1936, Mr. 602x/1936.

and *Medan Pendidikan Rajat* (Forum for People's Education); the situation is not very different with Partindo; Indonesia Moeda meetings were forced to dissolve several times in 1933 because of political speeches. In Yogyakarta, Partindo and New PNI were more active than in Surakarta and carried out propaganda, organizing cadre training courses as a major instrument; New PNI established committees such as the Comite Pengetahoean Oemoem (Committee for Public Knowledge) and Comite Pengadjaran Rakjat (Committee for People's Education), but only a few attended their meetings. Youth groups such as Indonesia Moeda, Soeloeh Pemoeda Indonesia, and Persatoean Pemoeda Rajat Indonesia (Perpri, Indonesian People's Youth Union) were more active there, because there were many schools in Yogyakarta. After the meeting ban, Partindo did nothing, while New PNI attempted to organize meetings not very successfully. New PNI also attempted to organize cells in other organizations, but its activity stagnated in 1934. By 1935 its activists quit trade unions, even though the party central executive was now headquartered in Yogyakarta. Partindo in the meantime remained stagnant. Soejoedi stopped his activity. Peasant unions Partindo organized also stopped their activities. Partindo treasurer R.M. Soekardjo, active in the Royal Marine, was kicked out of the state service, imprisoned for a year for distributing "inflammatory pamphlets," and then interned in Digul.

R.A.A. Wiranatakoesoemah, regent of Bandung, reported at the August 1936 conference:[97] Partindo and New PNI were reduced to a small core group of members; nor were nationalist associations with the cooperationist character such as Pasoendan and Parindra active for that matter; the Pasoendan club house was closed because of a shortage of money; there was not much to say about trade unions or youth movements. The regent also said that religious associations in Bandung were largely under his control, that influential religious teachers trusted him, and that even though some politicians joined religious associations, it should not be a concern, because (any attempt at nationalist) political infiltration into religious associations would be resisted by their members.

---

[97] Verslag conferentie van de gouverneur-generaal (de Jonge) met gouverneurs, residenten en regenten op Java, Aug. 18, 1936, Mr. 954x/36, also included in Kwantes, *De Ontwikkelin: Aug. 1933–1942*, 349–56. For W.P. Hillen's frank assessment of Wiranatakoesoema, see H. W. van den Doel, *De Stille Macht: Het Europese binnenlands bestuur op Java en Madoera, 1808–1942* (Leiden: Uitgeverij Bert Bakker, 1994), 405. Hillen as governor of West Java had a good opportunity to observe Wiranatakoesoema as one of the regents in his territory.

We have now finally reached the point from which we can look back at the evolution of the government policy toward the movement, locate the policy in a larger strategic context, and contemplate what drove the Indies government in the direction that it chose after the 1926–27 revolts. Mapping out the native world to spell out how to meet the PNI offensive, Charles O. van der Plas identified "counter-forces" in Moehammadijah, Nahdatoel Oelama, autonomous administrations, the princely courts of Java's Vorstenlanden (principalities), and priyayi, "the local patriots" such as BO and Pasoendan, and Dr. Soetomo's Indonesian Study Club in Surabaya. He also identified two groups in the PNI leadership: "the group of engineers" represented by Ir. Soekarno and the group of lawyers, represented by Mr. Sartono, Mr. Iskaq Tjokro-adisoerjo, Mr. Soenarjo, and Mr. Soejoedi. Van der Plas was well disposed to Dr. Soetomo, but saw him as no rival with Soekarno. That was the reason he saw in Soekarno the hope to guide the movement on to a constructive path and the governor general decided to give remission to Soekarno and other PNI leaders and send the signal that he still hoped for constructive cooperation.

The liberal approach did not work out as de Graeff, van der Plas and others had hoped. But it is important to note that de Jonge, de Kat Angelino and others also shared an understanding in common about the native world as van der Plas had mapped out—or to be more precise, things eventually worked out as he had mapped out despite him—and built their strategy on it. The government reached a compromise with Taman Siswa in dealing with the protest against the wild school ordinance and made a deal with Taman Siswa, Moehammadijah and other educational institutions to allow them to keep their own spaces for education on condition that they stay away from nationalist party politics, self-police their own teachers and students, and in effect remain de facto "counter-forces" to contain popular politics. The government also opted on relying on *volksleiders* (traditional leaders)—adat chiefs and *zelfbesturen* in Sumatra and other Islands, the princely courts of Java's Vorstenlanden, and priyayi or more precisely aristocrat-turned-bureaucratic elite as represented by Regent of Bandung R.A.A. Wiranatakoesoemah—and no longer hoped much for cooperation with—and sometime was outright hostile to—moderate, cooperationist, bona fide forces (such as Dr. Soetomo's PBI, BO, and Pasoendan) because of their rural action which tended to invite "bad elements" and provoke unintended consequences. The terrain thus hedged, the remaining space was left for nationalist politics and political policing. De Jonge and his lieutenants did not entertain any hope for constructive cooperation with revolutionary, non-cooperationist, and mala fide nationalist forces, but were confident of the state's ability to police and control the space. Political policing measures that the government under de Jonge adopted were meant for this purpose and amounted in effect to deny all the forms in which Indonesian popular politics manifested itself in a systematic way: policing, intervening in and banning rallies and meetings, policing and muzzling newspapers and journals, policing and destroying trade unions as well as youth, women and scout organizations, banning government employees to join in any nationalist parties and organizations, interning a select number of party leaders.

It should also be clear by now that memories of the 1926–27 "disturbances" haunted the Indies government, especially senior Dutch officials, whether liberal or conservative, and drove the government policy on the movement in the direction it went. Governor General de Graeff decided to clamp down on PNI and arrest Soekarno and others because of wild rumors of coming disturbances. Governor General de Jonge decided to handle the movement systematically because he was worried about disturbances at a time when the Indies was hit hard by the depression, the government was forced to cut its budget drastically, and people were unhappy with their economic conditions. Anything that might lead to disturbance was revolutionary, and in this respect revolutionary/ evolutionary, cooperation/non-cooperation, mala fide/bona fide, radical/ moderate did not make much difference. It was not that the government was not confident in its ability to police and control Indonesian nationalist politics, above and underground. As both de Kat Angelino and Gobee said, the government had full confidence in the ability of the *hoofdparket* and its regional intelligence apparatus to police the movement. But the government was worried about uncertainties—wild forces which Soekarno could unleash in PNI and Partindo propaganda as well as his own inability not to be carried away with the forces he unleashed, wild forces which the rural action of even a royalist and/or a loyalist cooperation party (such as PKN and PBI) might let loose in the countryside, hidden forces which wrecked the PKI in the revolts. In this sense Digul signified a failure on the part of the Indies government to control wild forces, which explain why the government relied as much as it did on the political policing apparatus for maintaining peace and order and also why Minister of Colonies Ch. Welter wanted so much to abolish the camp in Digul in the final years of the Dutch rule when the Indies government, it appeared, finally attained peace and order.

CHAPTER 6

Politics in a Time of Normalcy

Thus, there arrived a time of normalcy in the Indies when politics was equated with police. The government made it impossible for non-cooperation parties and associations to remain active openly. Instead, there emerged in the mainstream of the nationalist movement cooperation parties and their associated organizations, represented by two parties, Parindra (Partai Indonesia Raya, Great Indonesia Party) and Gerindo (Gerakan Rakjat Indonesia, Indonesian People's Movement), which agreed to cooperate with the government in the Volkraad and other representative councils. There also emerged among Indonesian members in the Volksraad a movement to demand Indonesia's autonomy as demonstrated by Soetardjo Kartohadikoesoemo's petition, presented to the Volksraad in 1936, in which he asked for a discussion of self-government within the Dutch Indies constitutional framework. Lulled by the peace and order it maintained, confident in its ability to surveil the entire native political terrain and convinced of native loyalty to the empire, however, the government dismissed the cooperation parties as insignificant. The government also sat on Soetardjo's request for almost two years only to turn it down in 1938.[1]

This was not, however, a time of normalcy globally. The international gold standard system collapsed in 1931, even though the Netherlands left the system belatedly in 1937. In the same year of 1931, Japan occupied Manchuria and established Manchukuo. Adolf Hitler came to power in Germany in 1933. The civil war started in Spain in July 1936

---

[1] Susan Abeyasekere, "Relations between the Indonesian Cooperating Nationalists and the Dutch, 1935–1942" (PhD diss., Monash University, 1972); Susan Abeyasekere, "The Soetardjo Petition," *Indonesia* 15 (Apr. 1973): 81–107.

and ended with General Francisco Franco's victory in April 1939. The Sino-Japanese war started in July 1937. Japan occupied Kwangtung in October 1938 and Hainan Island in February 1939. German troops marched into Czechoslovakia in March 1938. Germany concluded a non-aggression treaty with the Soviet Union in August 1939 and divided Poland between the two in September. The war started in Europe.

Indonesian politicians might have thought that they could make a deal with the Indies government for cooperation and political support for the Dutch and the Dutch Indies government in return for political concessions in this time of crisis. Mohammad Husni Thamrin, a Parindra member in the Volksraad, together with Amir Sjarifoeddin of Gerindo and Abikoesno Tjokrosoejoso of PSII took the lead in creating a federation of political parties, GAPI (Gaboengan Politik Indonesia, Indonesian Political Federation) in May 1939 and called on all social, political, and economic groups to organize an Indonesian People's Congress in Batavia at the end of December 1939 as a first step toward the creation of an Indonesian Parliament. Neither the Dutch nor the Dutch Indies government were in the mood take this call seriously. Minister of Colonies Ch. J.I.M. Welter said in February 1939 that "My time is not that of great reforms and my place is not among the great reformers. I see my task as that of the guardian of precious inheritance which has been entrusted to us."[2] He was confident of popular support for the Indies government and said that "we listen to those who do not speak." Nor did Governor General Alidius Warmoldus Lambertus Tjarda van Starkenborgh Stachouwer, de Jonge's successor, feel the need to listen to the Indonesian demand. The attorney general warned the GAPI leadership not to threaten the government. Minister of Colonies Welter told the governor general to clamp down on *Indonesia Berparlemen*, the movement calling for the establishment of a parliament, before it got out of control.[3]

Soon thereafter, however, war came to the Netherlands. The Germans invaded the Netherlands on May 10, 1940. Four days later the

---

[2] Susan Abeyasekere, *One Hand Clapping: Indonesian Nationalists and the Dutch, 1939–1942* (Clayton: Centre of Southeast Asian Studies, Monash University, 1976), 25.

[3] Ibid., 37. It should be noted that by then de Kat Angelino had been back in The Hague and served as a close confident of Welter's.

Netherlands surrendered. The Dutch government in exile was established in London. On May 10, 1940, Martial Law was declared in the Indies and all public meetings of a political nature were banned. The governor general announced in June that no changes would be possible until after the war. The government representative in the Volksraad stated, "since the war broke out there has been greater solidarity among the population and greater loyalty to Holland. The political situation is peaceful and satisfactory."[4]

This is the picture, widely shared among historians, of above ground Indonesian nationalist politics and Dutch policy in the final years of Dutch colonial rule in the Indies.[5] It is wrong, however, to see cooperation parties and associations, especially Parindra and Gerindo as compliant, moderate, or insignificant. It is also wrong to see underground "parties," such as Young PKI (PKI Muda) and Pari, as lacking any "public influence," simply because their activities were invisible.[6] No doubt the native political terrain was under intense police surveillance as Politiek-Politioneele Overzichten van Nederlandsch-Indie (Political Police Overviews of the Netherlands Indies) demonstrate. Not very many Indonesians entered the terrain, where they were aware—and the police made them aware—that they were taking the risk of being watched, arrested, imprisoned and exiled to Digul. But there were people who did go into that terrain. There were also people who went beyond the "no trespass" signs, because once Partindo and New PNI were banned, it did not make much difference for an activist to be in the danger zone or to go into the zone marked by "no trespass" signs and join—whatever it meant—Pari and/or Young PKI.[7] Cooperation parties and organizations created a space, albeit small and under surveillance,

---

[4] Abeyasekere, "Relations," 198, 238, 265, 274.
[5] It should be noted, however, that the picture holds far less outside Java, especially in Sumatra. See Audrey Kahin, *Rebellion to Integration: West Sumatra and the Indonesian Polity 1926–1998* (Amsterdam: Amsterdam University Press, 1999). To look at the history of this period in a different way, see also Yamamoto, "Print Power and Censorship in Colonial Indonesia, 1912–1942" (PhD diss., Cornell University, 2011).
[6] See Legge, *Intellectuals and Nationalism in Indonesia*, 38–9.
[7] For instance, Saleh Rais, a Partindo activist in Batavia in touch with Djajadi, who was arrested in the police sweep against the Pari network, met with Soenarman when he was in Batavia for Young PKI. Harry A. Poeze, "The PKI-Muda 1936–1942," *Kabar Seberang*, no. 13–14 (1984): 166.

but legal all the same for activists. Cooperation parties had their head-quarters, branches, and other offices. They published their journals and newspapers. They organized rallies and gatherings. They ran schools, sporting clubs and cooperatives. Their leaders, activists, members and non-members came in and out of those places, read newspapers and journals, and attended rallies and meetings. All these activities were visible. The police watched all these activities and produced their reports. Underground activity, on the other hand, was by definition invisible. There were no doubt core party members, whose arrest could cripple their parties and lead to their collapse. Both those leaders and the police talked about party cells of three or five. But what most of those "cell" members did as party activity was to read underground party journals such as *Obor* of Pari and *Menara Merah* of Young PKI their leaders passed onto them occasionally. And in this danger/no trespass zone, even if one did not intentionally go beyond the "no trespass" signs, one would have an opportunity, once in a while, to see those underground publications, because in this zone organizational affiliations gave way to personal networks of fluid and constantly changing nature, in which people could be linked simultaneously with several parties, groups and associations, both above and underground, and in which even if some of the parties, groups and associations were weakened or destroyed, people could link up with others on the basis of ideological orientation, past party affiliation, school ties, family connections, personal friendship and many other reasons.

It should also be noted that conditions under which the terrain was organized were different from one region to another, because above-ground cooperation parties and their organizations as well as religious, educational and social associations which van der Plas called "counter forces" maintained their regional presence differently.

Parindra had a strong presence in Central and East Java, along with the two major religious and educational associations of Nahdatoel Oelama and Moehammadijah as well as the nationalist educational association, Taman Siswa, which Ki Hadjar Dewantara made sure to stay away from party politics. Parindra was established out of Soetomo's PBI and BO in 1935. Some of the former PNI/Partindo members also joined the party, including Soenarjo and Iskaq Tjokroadisoerjo. The party recognized its members in the representative councils as party representatives. Thamrin led its political committee in the Volksraad. Parindra leaders were "serious and measured men" if we borrow the phrase Gobee used to describe PBI leaders in 1934.[8] The party put emphasis on social, economic, and educational activities—clinics, cooperatives, schools and a national bank. Thamrin aside, most of its leaders were Javanese. Being a cooperation party and sending its members to the Volksraad and other councils did not really mean they were loyal to the colonial regime, either.[9]

Parindra's membership was 3,217 in 1936 and reached 11,246 in 1939. It published 11 newspapers. Its base, however, was largely confined to Central and East Java. In 1939, 55 out of 84 branches were in Java, while there were 10 in Kalimantan, 13 in Sumatra and 5 in Bali. The party also had 18 schools and its cooperatives had more than 20,000 members in East Java. Its peasant organization, Roekoen Tani, also had strong presence in East Java.[10] Surakarta also emerged as Parindra stronghold, mainly because BO had strong presence there—and the former BO chairman R.M.H. Woerjaningrat lived there—and because PKS under Singgih's chairmanship had 240 branches and 22,000 members at the end of 1935 in Surakarta.[11]

Yet the party with popular support, especially in the countryside, was suspect in the eyes of Dutch and native officials. Governor of East Java van der Plas noted in his report to the governor general dated March 22, 1937,[12] that self-help as represented by Roekoen Tani invited resistance from internal administration officials from the resident down to village heads because it was seen as interfering in their power positions, that "strict police control" imposed on Roekoen Tani member meetings prevented "the orderly elements" who would "reduce the danger of economic and in due course political power formation" from joining the association and in effect worked toward "a negative selection" and

---

[8] Adviser for native affairs to GG, May 8, 1934, in Kwantes, *De Ontwikkelin van de Nationalistische Beweging in Nederlandsch-Indie, Bronnenpublikatie 4de Stuk Aug. 1933–1942* (Groningen: Wolters-Noordhoff/Bouma's Boekhuis, 1982), 243–5.

[9] Abeyasekere, "Relations," 124.

[10] See Adviser for native affairs to GG, Feb. 4, 1936, in Kwantes, *De Ontwikkelin, Aug. 1933–1942*, 332–4; Abeyasekere, *One Hand Clapping*, 126–31.

[11] Chief of the ARD, Overzicht van de politieke beweging in de Gouvernementen Soerakarta en Jogjakarta na het ingrijpen der Overheid tegen de links-extremistische organisaties in 1933 tot op heden, May 10, 1936, Mr. 602x/1936.

[12] Governor of East Java to GG, March 22, 1937, Mr. 268x/1937, also included in Kwantes, *De Ontwikkeling, Aug. 1933–1942*, 413–9.

drove Roekoen Tani in a wrong direction. Based on his conversations with some "responsible" Parindra leaders regarding a police report, he wrote that there were villagers "with very bad reputation" in Roekoen Tani in a village in Sidoarjo—and he mentioned "*bromotjorah, konang konang*, gamblers or thieves," the kind of people James Rush talked about as inhabiting a twilight zone linking the official state sphere and the Java's village world in nineteenth-century Java[13]—and led the Parindra leadership to investigate the Roekoen Tani membership and presumably to purge those "with very bad reputations" from the association. To put it differently, van der Plas made sure the Parindra leadership would police their own party and its associations.

Gerindo was established in May 1937. In contrast with Parindra which was heavily Javanese both in leadership and membership with its base in Central and East Java, Gerindo's center of activity was in Batavia (with 600 members in April 1938) and the East Coast of Sumatra (where many ex-Partindo, Permi and PNI activists joined the party). Its central leadership included people such as Adnan Kapau Gani (b. in 1905 in Agam, West Sumatra; on the party central executive board in 1937–41), Amir Sjarifoeddin (b. in 1907 in Medan, East Coast of Sumatra; on the party central board in 1938–40), Wilopo (b. in 1909 in Purworejo, Central Java; on the party central board in 1939–41), Mohammad Tabrani (b. in Pamekasan, Madura; on the party central board in 1938–40), Asmara Hadi (b. in Bengkulu; on the party central board in 1937 and 1940–41), B. Soetan Besar (on the party central board in 1938–40) and Notosoedirdjo (on the party central board in 1938–40). The two colleges—the Faculty of Law (RHS) and the Faculty of Medicine (GHS, Geneeskundige Hoge School)—supplied many leaders, including A.K. Gani, Amir Sjarifoeddin, Wilopo, Mohammad Yamin (b. in 1903 in Sawahlunto, West Sumatra) and Soemanang (b. in 1908 in Yogyakarta). Gerindo was active in holding rallies and meetings, but not in social and economic areas. In September 1937, it had 13 branches in Java (of which 7 were in West Java) and 4 in Sumatra, while in November 1941, it had 75 branches, of which 24 were in Java, 37 in Sumatra, and 10 in Celebes and Borneo each. There were radical members in Gerindo in the East Coast of Sumatra, in which the central leadership

---

[13] See James R. Rush, "Social Control and Influence in Nineteenth Century Indonesia: Opium Farms and the Chinese of Java," *Indonesia*, no. 35 (Apr. 1983): 59.

had to intervene at the attorney general's demand that they control their local groups.[14]

What was it like, then, to be an activist in the Indies in this time of normalcy? What did it mean to be political? One way to approach is to examine what some of those activists did in those days in the danger/ no trespass zone the police was closely watching.[15]

Soemanang

Let us start with Soemanang. He was no doubt under police surveillance as his name appears occasionally in the monthly political police reports. He was also mentioned, along with Mohammad Yamin and Amir Sjari-foeddin, as one of the PPPI leaders who were behind the Indonesia Moeda (IM) congress organizing committee, when the government banned the IM congress scheduled to be held in Batavia in July 1936. This means that he had worked closely with Soekarni who served as IM chairman in 1934–36.[16] Unlike Mohammad Yamin and Amir Sjarifoeddin, however,

---

[14] Abeyasekere, "Relations," 138–40, 143–4. See also Michael van Langenberg, "National Revolution in North Sumatra: Sumatra Timur and Tapanuli, 1942–1950" (PhD diss., University of Sydney, 1976). Adviser for Native Affairs G.F. Pijper wrote to the governor general on October 10, 1938, during its first congress held in Batavia in July, that unlike PNI, which called for Indonesia Merdeka, Gerindo defined its objective as the promotion of social, economic and political freedom on the basis of popular nationalism, and that [even] Mohammad Yamin called it "loyal opposition," though he called for the establishment of peasant leagues (Sarekat Tani) as Parindra had established Roekoen Tani. He also noted the difference in political orientation between A.K. Gani on the one hand and Amir Sjarifoeddin and Wikana on the other. Adviser for native affairs to GG, Batavia, Oct. 10, 1938, Mr. 461x/38.

[15] It should be said that there were people who were "political" in different ways as Hindromartono and Djoko Said were in the labor movement, Soedyono Djojo-praitono in Taman Siswa, and Liem Koen Hian in journalism. See John Ingleson, *Workers, Unions and Politics: Indonesia in the 1920s and 1930s* (Leiden: Brill, 2014); Tsuchiya Kenji, *Indonesia Minzokushugi Kenkyu: Taman Siswa no Seiritsu to Tenkai* (Kyoto: Sobunsha, 1982); Yamamoto, *Censorship in Colonial Indonesia, 1901–1942* (Leiden: Brill, 2019).

[16] The police clamped down on the Indonesia Moeda (IM) central leadership in August 1936 before its congress was held, but Soekarni escaped arrest. Shortly after-wards, the IM headquarters moved from Batavia to Surabaya with Roeslan Abdoel-gani as chairman. Adviser for native affairs to GG, Feb. 4, 1937, in Kwantes, *De Ontwikkeling, Aug. 1933–1942*, 400–1. On Roeslan Abdoelgani (Ruslan Abdulgani) and his family, see William H. Frederick, *Visions and Heat: The Making of the Indo-nesian Revolution* (Athens: Ohio University Press, 1989), 26–7.

Soemanang managed not to draw too much attention from senior government and police officials.[17]

Soemanang was born in 1908 in Yogyakarta. His father was a senior courtier at the Paku Alam house, a minor royal house in Yogyakarta. He entered the Rechtsschool (RS, Law School) in Batavia in 1922 and was active in the youth organization, Jong Java. He graduated from the RS at the top of his class in 1928 and was immediately admitted to the RHS. It was the transitional era for the tertiary education in the Indies and the RHS was opened in 1924. It was initially located at Koningsplein Zuid 10, now Merdeka Selatan 10, and then moved to Pegangsaan Timur 17. Yamin and Amir Sjarifoeddin were one-year older than Soemanang. All three of them stayed in the dormitory, Indonesische Clubgebouw (Indonesian club house) at Jalan Kramat Raya 106, now called Gedung Sumpah Pemuda (Youth Pledge Building). Soemanang was active in Indonesia Moeda in 1928 when he entered the RHS. In his early RHS years, Soekarno's trial in 1931–32 was big news and Soemanang was said to be deeply impressed by Soekarno's defense

---

[17] Adviser for native affairs to GG, Aug. 11, 1936 in Kwantes, *De Ontwikkeling, Aug. 1933–1942*, 347–8. Amir Sjarifoeddin was elected as vice president of Partindo at its second congress held in Surabaya in April 1933. He was arrested in March 1933 for the article "Massa Actie [mass action]," written but unsigned by Mohammad Yamin and published in *Banteng* (Bull), the journal of Partindo's Batavia branch, in which Amir served as director. He was sentenced to 18 months in prison. The attorney general proposed to the governor general that he should be interned in October 1933 while he was still in prison. Eventually the proposal was turned down in 1935. Jacques Leclerc, "Amir Sjarifuddin, between the State and the Revolution," in *Indonesian Political Biography: In Search of Cross-Cultural Understanding*, ed. Angus McIntyre (Clayton, Victoria: Centre of Southeast Asian Studies, Monash University, 1993), 29–30. It is useful to remember how, and how precisely, senior Dutch officials understood Mohammad Yamin and Amir Sjarifoeddin when they were looking at those who could succeed Soekarno as revolutionary nationalist leaders. The governor of West Java described Yamin as "an extremist, who is mainly interested in popularity and success at public meetings," "a dubious and weak person," who would be "of no influence" once the meeting was banned. In contrast, he argued, Amir Sjarifoeddin was "an extremist in heart and soul, with a powerful own conviction and strong will to carry out the extremist propaganda systematically in every act" and "strong personality" who "would dare to maintain his position consistently." Governor of West Java to PG, Nov. 10, 1933, in Kwantes, *De Ontwikkelin, Aug. 1933–1942*, 170–1. See also PG to GG, March 14, 1935, Mr. 572x/35. This perhaps is part of the reason that van der Plas and P.J.A. Idenburg, secretary to the Council of the Netherlands Indies, approached Sjarifoeddin about establishing an intelligence network in the Japan-occupied Indies during the final days of their rule.

speech *Indonesia Menggugat* (Indonesia Accuses); Soemanang joined Partindo in 1931. It is said that he stayed in Bogor in those days and worked as a propagandist, visiting villages by bike to lead Partindo meetings among those who were largely peasants, traders, government officials, teachers and clerks.[18]

Shortly after he entered the RHS, he also started to teach at Pergoeroean Rajat, a People's School. It was established in December 1928 at Gang Kanali in Salemba, Batavia, combining Poestaka Kita (Our Library) and a study club called Persatoean Oentoek Beladjar (POB, Union for Learning). Poestaka Kita was originally established to provide library service and hold lectures on important topics, while POB was meant to provide foreign language and journalism studies. In 1929, Pergoeroean Rajat established a People's university (Volksuniversiteit) where courses were offered on languages such as Dutch, English, French and German as well as state law, world and Indies history, ethnology, sociology, book-keeping, and stenography. Lectures were also given there once a week by such people as Ki Hadjar Dewantara on national education, Dr. Sardjito on malaria, Dr. Poerbotjoroko on native languages, and Dr. Asikin on hygiene, as well as those given by RHS students. In the same year it also expanded its activity with the establishment of an elementary school, a *schakelschool* (upper elementary school), a *mulo* (junior high school), and in due course a teachers' training school in 1932 and a preparatory school for higher education in 1933. A foundation, Stichting Pergoeroean Rakjat (Institute for People's Education), was established in 1933. Pergoeroean Rajat had branches in Jatinegara (Batavia), Bandung, Yogyakarta, Solo, Madiun, Semarang, Surabaya, Palembang and Makassar in 1936.[19]

When Amir Sjarifoeddin was banned from teaching at Pergoeroean Rajat and then arrested for the transgression of press laws in 1933, Soemanang replaced Amir as Pergoeroean Rajat director for education. Although Pergoeroean Rajat was non-political, its leaders and teachers included many RHS students, who were active members of PPPI. In 1936, the chairman of Pergoeroean Rajat was Soemanang with vice-chairman Amir Sjarifoeddin. Reporting to the advisor for native affairs on the Pergoeroean Rajat congress held in Batavia in April 1936,

---

[18] I.N. Soebagijo, *Sumanang Sebuah Biografi* (Jakarta: TP Gunung Agung, 1980), 36.
[19] For more on Poestaka Rajat/Volksbibliotheken and its cultural political significance, see Yamamoto, "Print Power and Censorship," 93–4.

H. Aboebakar wrote that Soemanang, Amir Sjarifoeddin, Mohammad Yamin and Sanoesi Pane were central there.[20] It was Pergoeroean Rajat where Soemanang came to know many beyond the RHS and PPPI circles such as Moewardi,[21] Boentaran Martoatmodjo,[22] Soegiarti,[23] Maria Ulfah,[24] Assaat,[25] A.K. Gani, Amir Hamzah,[26] Sanoesi Pane,[27] and Wilopo.[28]

As part of Soemanang's self-training in written Indonesian, he wrote essays for *Pemandangan* (View) under Tabrani's editorship and *Tjaja Timoer* (Light of the East) under Parada Harahap. He published *Perantaraan* (mediation), a tabloid, and *Doenia Kita* (Our World) in 1937.[29] He mingled with writers and poets who were associated with the journal *Poedjangga Baroe* (New Poet), and Armijn Pane, a poet and Sanoesi Pane's brother, stayed with him for a time. He attended the congress of journalists' union (Persatoean Djoernalis Indonesia) held in Bandung in 1938. He took leadership in organizing the Indonesian Language Congress (Kongres Bahasa Indonesia) in Solo in June 1938 where Bahasa Indonesia was decided to be the "official language of

---

[20] Adviser for native affairs to GG, May 5, 1936; H. Aboebakar, Verslag van het Congres, Apr. 18, 1936, both in Mr. 459x/1936.

[21] Moewardi was born in Pati, Central Java, in 1907. He graduated from the STOVIA and would emerge as chairman of Barisan Pelopor in Surakarta in 1945.

[22] Dr. Boentaran Martoatmodjo was born in Purworejo in 1896 and would emerge as a leader of Barisan Pelopor in 1945.

[23] Soegiarti was soon to emerge as editor of *Poejangga Baroe* (New Poet).

[24] Maria Ulfah was born in 1911. She obtained law degree from Leiden University in 1933 and helped to establish the news agency Antara.

[25] Asaat was born in Agam, West Sumatra in 1904. He studied at the Faculty of Law with Soemanang. He was active in Jong Sumatranen Bond (Young Sumatran Bond) and Indonesia Moeda, joined Partindo and eventually obtained law degree in the Netherlands in 1939.

[26] Amir Hamzah was born in Langkat, East Sumatra in 1911. He is remembered as a poet and writer of the *Poedjangga Baroe* generation. For *Poedjangga Baroe*, see Heather Sutherland, "Pudjangga Baru: Aspects of Indonesian Intellectual Life in the 1930s," *Indonesia*, no. 6 (1968): 106–27; Keith R. Foulcher, *'Pujangga Baru': Literature and Nationalism in Indonesia 1933–1942* (Adelaide: Flinders University, 1980).

[27] Sanoesi Pane was born in Tapanuli, East Sumatra, in 1905. A writer, journalist, and historian, he was also active in Gerindo.

[28] Wilopo was born in Purworejo in 1909. He was so impressed by Soekarno when he personally met him that he immediately joined Partindo. He initially went to the Faculty of Engineering in Bandung for higher education, but after teaching at Taman Siswa school in Sukabumi, he transferred to the Faculty of Law in Batavia.

[29] Soebagijo, *Sumanang*, 37, 43.

unity." Its honorary chairman was Prof. Dr. Husein Djajadiningrat and the chairman was Dr. Poerbatjaraka, while Amir Sjarifoeddin served on the executive committee. People such as Soetan Pamoentjak (Volkslectuur), C. Hooykaas (Java Instituut), Sanoesi Pane, Ki Hadjar Dewantoro, and Adinegoro also attended the congress.[30]

In the mid-1930s, most likely in 1936, shortly before Gerindo was established, Soemanang came to know Albert Manoempak Sipahoetar, who was working for the news agency ARTA run by a Dutchman, Samuel de Heer, as well as for *Tjaja Timoer* under the editorship of Parada Harahap.[31] Soemanang invited Sipahoetar to join him in establishing a news agency, Antara. Adam Malik, a friend of Sipahoetar who had been entertaining a similar idea also joined him. Its office was initially located at Jahja Nasoetion's office, Kantor Expeditie "Pengharapan" (Expedition Office "Hope"), which they inherited when Jahja was interned to Digul because of his involvement in Pari. Sanoesi Pane also played a part in the news agency's establishment and gave it the name Antara. Soemanang got to know Adam Malik when Antara was established. The first issue of *Bulletin Antara* was published in December 1939 when Soemanang was 29 years old, Sipahoetar 23, and Adam Malik 20.[32] By then Soemanang had finally graduated from the RHS. For reasons not entirely clear—and one wonders whether he might have sensed that he had come too close to the zone marked by "no trespass" signs—he resigned from Antara shortly thereafter and opened a law firm with Sartono in January 1940. He also became editor-in-chief of *Pemandangan*, replacing Tabrani, when he was appointed as head of Government Publicity Service (Regeerings Publiciteits Dienst) in October 1940. Van der Plas should have been watching Soemanang

[30] Ibid., 53–5. Both congresses were part of Gerindo social and cultural activities. See Verslaggever, Verslag van het eerste congres van de politieke partij "Gerakan Ra'jat Indonesia" (Gerindo), gehouden van 20 t/m 24 Juli 1938 te Batavia, Mr. 461x/38. On the Language Congress and the different views that informed the debate on the national language in the late 1930s, see Yamamoto, "Print Power and Censorship," 314–7, 373–84. Adi Negoro and Muhammad Yamin were brothers.
[31] Albert Manoempak Sipahoetar was born in Tarutong, East Sumatra, in 1914. He published a newspaper, *Sinar Marhaen* (Light of Marhaen), in Pematang Siantar in 1932, edited *Zaman Kita* (Our Time) in Pematang Siantar in 1933, worked in Medan for another newspaper named *Pewarta Deli*, moved to Batavia in 1936 with Adam Malik and was working at the office of *Tjaja Timoer* when he met with Soemanang.
[32] Soebagijo, *Sumanang*, 43–5, 48–50.

carefully, for he invited Soemanang as part of his delegation to visit Australia together with Adinegoro (editor-in-chief of *Pewarta Deli* [Deli Reporter] in Medan) and Soemarto Djojodihardjo (editor-in-chief of *Soeara Oemoem* in Surabaja) in October 1941 when the war was about to start in Asia.[33] And yet when the war came to the Indies in December 1941, Soemanang was arrested anyway along with his former colleagues at Antara.

Adam Malik

Adam Malik inherited the news agency Antara from Soemanang in 1939 at the age of 20, but as we can see in the fact that he inherited the office from Jahja Nasoetion, his background was very different from Soemanang's. Born in 1917 in Pematang Siantar, East Coast of Sumatra, as the son of a wealthy merchant who was the only owner of Buick sedan there in the 1920s, Adam Malik attended a Dutch native school and then went to a religious school in Bukit Tinggi, West Sumatra, where he read *Pewarta Deli*, *Seruan Azhar* (Azhar's Call) which was published in Cairo, and *Medan Moeslimin* (Muslims' Field), a journal published in Solo under the editorship of Haji Misbach. Adam Malik studied at the religious school in Bukit Tinggi for a year, moved to and studied at another religious school, Al-Masrullah, in Tanjung Pura, East Coast of Sumatra, for two years, and then started to help his father's business when he was 15. It was about this time that he started to be active in the movement, joining Hisboel Wathan, the scout movement under Moehammadijah, which Adam Malik says was the only semi-political organization active in Pematang Siantar in those days. He then joined in establishing Indonesia Moeda and Perkoempoelan Sopir-sopir Indonesia (Association for Indonesian Drivers), participated in Partindo in the East Coast of Sumatra in 1930, served as member of the Partindo Medan leadership in 1931, then chairman of its Pematang Siantar branch, and came to know Partindo activists in East Sumatra such as Djaoehari Salim, Hamid Loebis, Mohammad Djoni and Jakoeb Siregar as well as Mohammad Yamin and Amir Sjarifoeddin when they came to the East Coast of Sumatra for Partindo propaganda. He also published his writings in *Pelita Andalas* (Andalas lamp), a Partindo organ. Shortly after

---

[33] Ibid., 60–1, 65.

Partindo was disbanded in 1934, Adam Malik, together with Sipahoetar who had been a friend of his since the Pematang Sinantar days, moved to Batavia, where they got in touch with the man they had come to know well as a Partindo activist, Jahja Nasoetion, who had his office at Buiten Tijgerstraat (now Jl. Pinangsia) 38, Kota. Adam Malik did not know, he says, that Jahja was in the Pari network and under police surveillance. But he was arrested all the same in the police sweep against Pari in 1936 when he was selling used books in Pasar Senen.[34] He met with Pandoe Kartawigoena, a student activist, in the Struiswijk prison. As Adam Malik put it, Pandoe "had joined a youth organization which was part of the Pari underground movement." Pandoe told him about Soekarni, his activist friend who was serving as chairman of Indonesia Moeda and who would emerge as Tan Malaka's top lieutenant after the war.[35]

One wonders, however, whether Adam Malik was doing history back there, equating the underground with Pari in light of their future association with Tan Malaka. Both Pandoe Kartawigoena and Soekarni were active in Perpri (Persatoean Pemoeda Rajat Indonesia, Youth Union of Indonesian People). It was a non-official youth organization of Partindo stablished in July 1932 in Semarang. Its central leadership was consisted of Soetomo Djauhar Arifin as chairman, Soedimoeljono as deputy chairman, Mantoro Tirtonegoro as secretary, and Mohamad Soenarman in charge of propaganda. The first issue of its journal, *Revolutioner*, was confiscated by the police, Soetomo Djauhar Arifin was sentenced to 18 months and Soedimoeljono to one-year imprisonment for the transgression of press laws. Ngademo replaced Soetomo Djauhar Arifin as chairman and Soenarman became his deputy. In 1933, Perpri under their leadership expanded its activity and established branches in Batavia (under Saleh Rais) and Surabaya. It also organized cells, it is said, in schools and factories. It held a secret congress in July 1934 in Surakarta, at which Mantoro Tirtonegoro was elected chairman and Ngademo

---

[34] He says he was arrested in 1935. However, the year should be 1936, given the fact that Jahja Nasoetion was arrested on May 11, 1936.

[35] Adam Malik, *Mengabdi Republik, Jilid 1: Adam Dari Andalas* (Jakarta: Gunung Agung, 1979), 188; Sumono Mustoffa, *Sukarni: Dalam Kenagnan Teman-Temannya* (Jakarta: Pernerbit Sinar Harapan, 1986), 179–81. See also Hermawan Sulistyo, "Biografi Politik Adam Malik: Dari Kiri ke Kanan," *Prisma, Edisi Khusus 20 Tahun Prisma 1971–1991* (Jakarta: LP3ES), 81–101.

was put in charge of propaganda. The congress decisions, including the decision to take steps to organize cells in preparation for "the illegal struggle program," were sent to Soekarni, only to be intercepted by the police. The Batavia PID chief identified Soekarni as a liaison between the Perpri central leadership in Yogyakarta and Partindo Batavia branch chairman Saleh Rais. He also reported that the two letters the police confiscated at the Partindo office in Batavia underlined the importance of "organizing secret underground action" and talked about "girls should learn works female spies did in Europe," a youthful fantasy of student activists which Matu Mona and others would soon represent in fantastic spy stories such as *Spionnage-Dienst* (Espionage Service). Perpri leaders and activists were rounded up by the police in December 1934: eleven members were detained, including Soekarni, Pandoe and Saleh Rais in Batavia, Soenarman, Soedimoeljono, and Ngademo in Yogyakarta, and those in the central leadership such as Mantoro, Djoko Hasan and Sahoedoro. After being strongly reprimanded by the police, Soekarni, Pandoe, Soenarman, Soedimoeljono and Ngademo were released in September 1935. Three executive members were sent to the court. Mantoro Tirtonegoro was sentenced to an 18-month imprisonment; Sahoedoro, a year; and Djoko Hasan's case was dismissed.[36]

Adam Malik was released from prison in 1936. He was not a part of the Perpri network but got to know people in it via Pandoe and more generally those in the movement, especially in the PNI/Partindo/New PNI network in Batavia. He met former Partindo activists at Mandailing Club and attended a theater that staged such plays as Nyai Dasimah and Gagak Hitam (Black Raven). As he put it, he established the news

---

[36] The attorney general sent residents of Bandung, Batavia, Semarang, Surakarta, Yogyakarta and Surabaya an instruction on December 27, 1934, to carry out house searches at Perpri headquarters, branch offices, and their members' houses. Two letters the Partindo Batavia branch chairman sent to the Perpri central executive committee, dated August 22 and November 8, 1934, were confiscated. Though only three from the central executive committee were prosecuted, others were detained for nine months from January 1935 to September 1935. After the police raid, the Perpri headquarters were moved from Yogyakarta to Solo. PG to GG, Jan. 16, 1935, Mr. 2x/35, also in Kwantes, *De Ontwikkeling, Aug. 1933–1942*, 290–2; Chief commissioner of police/chief of Afdeeling PID, Alg. Politie te Batavia to resident of Batavia, Weltevreden, Dec. 21, 1934, Mr. 2x/35; PG to assistant resident of Batavia, Sept. 17, 1935, Mr. 1018x/35; PG to assistant resident of Yogyakarta, Sept. 17, 1935, Mr. 1018x/35. See also Poeze, "The PKI-Muda 1936–1942," 163.

agency Antara in December 1937, "with the assistance of" Soemanang, Sanoesi Pane, Amir Sjarifoeddin, Mohammad Yamin, Djohan Syahroezah and others.[37]

Adam Malik joined Gerindo when it was established in 1937. It was a step backward from Partindo, he says, but without a party, "rallies and meetings could not be held." It was "led by Soekarno's younger colleagues such as A.K. Gani, Amir Sjarifoeddin, Wilopo, and Sartono" and behind those "honorable" people, "young political activists like Wikana and me could show radical postures."[38] He also says that Gerindo was a vehicle "to accommodate various views and streams from various political parties that were banned by the Dutch colonial government, that is Partindo, PNI, New PNI, Pari and PKI" and that it was led by Wilopo, Amir Sjarifoeddin, A.K. Gani, Mohammad Yamin, and S.K. Trimoerti who was called Yu Tri.[39]

Adam Malik published *Negara* (Country) and *Tujuan Rakjat* (People's Goal) as Gerindo journals with Pandoe Kartawigoena and Djohan Sjahroeza. He also says Soekarni, Koesnaeni, Wikana, Maroeto Nitimihardjo, and others helped in the publication, though it is unlikely that Soekarni who was a fugitive in Kalimantan was part of the activity. It was in those days that Soemanang suggested that Gerindo establish a "national" news agency. Adam Malik, Sipahoetar and Sanoesi Pane joined him to establish Antara with "an old Royal typewriter and a second-hand Roneo stencil machine." In 1939, Adam Malik took over its leadership. He was 21 years old. Shortly thereafter, he was also appointed to the Gerindo central executive committee.[40]

When he wrote his memoirs, he knew what had happened to him and his friends in the postwar post-independence years. He therefore tended to organize his story in view of what he knew would happen in his later life. He sees the direct lineages from Pari to Partai Murba and from Young PKI (PKI Muda) Moesso established in Surabaya to PKI under Aidit. He says that Young PKI Moesso "nurtured" in Surabaya sent Wikana to join the news agency Antara, that Amir Sjarifoeddin— who would announce in 1948 that he had been a PKI member since

---

[37] Malik, *Mengabdi*, 21–3, 188–94, 219–21.
[38] Ibid., 25.
[39] Ibid., 196.
[40] Ibid., 199–201. Mustoffa, *Sukarni*, 183.

the prewar days—occasionally helped him as adviser and that there were "quiet contests going on in the shadow between Moesso's communist followers inside and outside the country, especially those who came from the Netherlands, and Pari followers led by Tan Malaka."[41]

He also downplays his partnership with Djohan Sjahroezah, most likely because Sjahroezah emerged as a leading figure of Socialist Party together with Soetan Sjahrir in the postwar years. Sjahrir's nephew and married with a daughter of Haji Agoes Salim, Djohan Sjahroezah was born in Muara Enim, South Sumatra, in 1912. After graduating from the ELS (European elementary school) in Medan, he proceeded via the MULO to the AMS in Batavia. He followed courses one of the Golongan Merdeka groups organized and joined New PNI. In 1932 he served as secretary at its Batavia branch under chairman Sjahrir. In the same year he entered the Faculty of Law, wrote for *Daulat Ra'jat*, the New PNI journal, and was active in PPPI. Soon he was arrested, convicted, and sentenced to an 18-month imprisonment for the transgression of press laws for the article he wrote for *Indonesia Raja* (Great Indonesia), the PPPI journal. He spent his time in 1933–34 in prison and by the time he was out, the government had clamped down New PNI and sent Hatta, Sjahrir, Bondan and others to Digul. Upon his release from prison Djohan refused to sign a letter promising not to be active in politics, and as a result he was not allowed to return to the Faculty of Law. He worked for the news agency Arta, and in 1937 joined Soemanang, Adam Malik, Pandoe Kartawigoena and others in founding the news service Antara.[42]

In those days, even though activists had different ideological inclinations and preferences, there hardly were any clearly defined ideological party differences. Adam Malik knew Djohan was in contact with New PNI people and may be aware that Wikana was in association with Widarta and active in Young PKI. As Adam Malik says, however, Antara distributed illegal pamphlets, both Pari's *Obor* and PKI's *Menara Mera* (Red Tower), often sent to the same addresses.[43] He was arrested

---

[41] Mustoffa, *Sukarni*, 183. It is highly unlikely Amir Sjarifoeddin joined Young PKI shortly after its establishment. See Leclerc's persuasive argument in "Amir Sjarifuddin."
[42] Anderson, *Java*, 417–8; Legge, *Intellectuals and Nationalism in Indonesia: A Study of the Following Recruited by Sutan Sjahrir in Occupation Jakarta* (Ithaca, NY: Cornell Modern Indonesia Project Publications, 1988), 61–2.
[43] Leclerc, "Amir Sjarifuddin," 183.

together with Wikana, Pandoe, and Amir Sjarifoeddin in June 1940 for distributing *Menara Merah*.[44] He was also arrested when the war came to the Indies along with his Antara friends.

Jahja Nasoetion and the Pari Underground[45]

It is not clear whether Adam Malik joined the Pari underground in the final years of Dutch rule as he says he did, but it is important to note that by the time he was out of prison and Jahja Nasoetion was waiting in prison to be sent to Digul, Pari had undergone a substantial transformation from the original Pari that Tan Malaka, Soebakat and Djamaloedin Tamin had established in 1927.

Born in Kotanopan, Tapanuli in 1907, Jahja Nasoetion was arrested in May 1936 when he was resident in Batavia. He started his work as a trader in Sibolga, North Sumatra, moved to Ipoh on the west coast of Malaya to work as a batik trader for eight months, moved back to the Indies, this time to Pekalongan to work as a batik trader, and finally moved to Batavia. He started becoming active in the movement as a Sarekat Islam member on the East Coast of Sumatra in the 1920s, joined PNI, and after it was disbanded in 1930, moved to Ipoh. When he was back to Pekalongan, he joined Partindo, served as secretary at the West Java regional leadership in 1932, and worked as its Batavia branch course leader in 1933 when he came under police surveillance and was brought to the attention of the *hoofdparket*. He also worked as director and editor-in-chief of *Persatoean Indonesia* [Unity of Indonesia],

---

[44] Anderson, *Java*, 47. See also Harry A. Poeze, *Politiek-Politioneele Overzichten van Nederlandsch-Indie, deel IV, 1935–1941* (Leiden: KITLV Press, 1994), 336.

[45] The following account is, unless otherwise noted, based on: Chief of the ARD, Geheim Rapport (Onderwerp: De Partai Republiek Indonesia, PARI, en hare actie in 1935 en 1936), Apr. 29, 1936, Mr. 446x/1936; PG to GG, May 6, 1936, Mr. 446x/1936; PG to GG, April 23, 1937, Mr. 403x/37; Chief of Afd. PID, Surabaya, Oct. 13, 1937, Geheim Rapport No 466/P.I.D./I.Z. betreffende het aandeel in de actie der "Partai Repoebliek Indonesia" afgekort "Pari," van: I. Malim Loebis alias Djaoes alias Husdeshagen alias Josee Toledo alias Si Pandjang alias Dawood Hawatt alias Bang Amat, II. Marinus Siringoringo, Mr. 1157x/37; PG to GG, Aug. 25, 1937, Voorstel tot internering van de Pari-propagandisten Djamaloedin Ibrahim en Jahja Nasoetion c.s., Mr. 822x/37; PG to GG, Dec. 15, 1937, No. 3917/A.P. Voorstel tot interneering van de Pari-propagandisten Malim Loebis alias Djaoes en Marinus Siringoringo; Proces-Verbaal (Jahja Nasoetion), Mr. 116x/38.

the Partindo organ, and member of the Partindo central executive board and established an "Expediteur" office Pengharapan (Hope). He was close to Amir Sjarifoeddin. He took care of Adam Malik and Sipahoetar when they moved to Batavia. He distributed *Obor*, the Pari Manifesto, and other Pari writings. He had contacts with Djaoes alias Dawood alias Malim Loebis in Surabaya and Djamaloeddin Ibrahim in Sukabumi. Abdoelhamid who was resident in Batavia and Siringgo Ringgo, a sailor, based in Surabaya who worked as liaisons to connect Jahja and Djamaloeddin Ibrahim with Djaoes, and Djaoes passed onto him Pari writings such as *Obor*, *Tongkat* (Stick) and *Sabit* (Sickle).[46]

It was in early 1935 when the Batavia PID learned that Jahja was associated with Pari. He told a police spy that out of the original 13 Pari founding members 7 still remained, that there were 6 Pari "agents" in the Indies, 1 each in Batavia, Semarang, Yogyakarta, Surabaya, Soengei Gerong (Palembang), and Balikpapan and that each "agent" organized a "cell" of 4 men, that is 1 "agent" and 3 "sub agents." Jahja also told him, the spy reported, that he had established cells among students, soldiers, sailors and port workers, and the ARD did identify a KNIL infantry sergeant in Bandung as a possible Pari activist. Jahja talked about a "coup d'état" "at the beginning of a possible world war or under the worsening depression" and let the spy read the June and July 1935 issues of *Obor*. The ARD also obtained intelligence about Soebono, a Partindo activist in Batavia, who was making Pari propaganda among the most "conscious" Partindo members. By late 1935 the ARD concluded that Jahja Nasoetion's house in Kota and the house of antique dealer Djakman at the Rijswijkstraat were centers of Pari activities.

In April 1936, other spies reported to the Batavia PID that "cells" had been organized at the state railway factory shop in Manggarai, the Meteorological Observatory, the General Motors workshop in Tanjung Priok and several other places in Bandung, and that there were Pari

---

[46] It is not clear who wrote the Pari brochures, but *Sabit*, now filed in Mr. 403x/37, looks similar in style and content to the statement Djaoes wrote in prison with his blood. The writer argues that "*semangat* (spirit)" is being killed by film and music, *bangsawan* and *ketoprak* theaters, gambling, liquors, opium, morphine, cannabis, prostitution and syphilis, that sugar, oil, mining and other syndicates are thieves, and that educational, religious and language institutes allied with the Dutch are killing the "spirit" of children of the Indonesian nation.

supporters in Cirebon, Tulungagung, Kroya, Kebumen, and Yogyakarta. The Batavia PID also obtained the January/February issue of *Obor*. The police learned that Soebono went to Bangka in February 1935 to travel to Singapore and then on to China to see Tan Malaka. The *hoofdparket* suspected that Djakman's brother worked as a contact with the Pari leadership abroad, because he regularly travelled to Singapore for trade. It also concluded that Jahja had contact with Noekman bin Mohamad Pasak who had been in contact with Mohamad Arief Siregar in 1933 and that the Pari "central executive committee" was represented by a man called Machmoed alias Li The Sang from Padang.

It took a while for the ARD to identify Machmoed, but eventually it found that it was Djamaloeddin Ibrahim alias Abdoerrachman bin Djamal alias Raman alias Ramantoen alias Mahmoed alias Oesman alias Ahmad alias Slamet alias Radjo. Born in Fort de Kock in 1903 and former teacher in the Padang Panjang schools, he met Tan Malaka in Singapore in 1926. He was resident in Sukabumi when arrested. He graduated from the Thawalib school in Payakumbuh and worked in Singapore as a trader in batik and antique and as a sailor on board the SS *Marella* between Singapore and Australia in 1929. He was recruited by Djamaloedin Tamin and Kandoor Soetan Rangkajo Basa to join the Pari in Singapore in 1930. He visited Tan Malaka in Amoy and personally knew Djaoes. He returned to Fort de Kock in 1931, but because of the arrest of Pari leaders in 1931, he moved back to Singapore. He then went back to the Indies in 1933, first to Surabaya, then to Bandung, and again moved to Batavia in 1934. Instructed to publish *Obor* in May 1935—it is not clear who instructed him—he published it, starting with no. 5, in June 1935, followed by nos. 6, 7, and 8. The 5th issue was handwritten, but the 6th to 8th issues were typewritten by a typewriter he borrowed from Jahja Nasoetion.

In the meantime, the Surabaya PID also obtained intelligence in early 1935 that an illegal organization was there, led by a man the police could not identify, but distributing Pari writings such as *Lapaar* (Hunger), *Persembahan* (Offerings), *Doeka* (Grief), and *Sembah Doeka* (Worship and grief). In the subsequent months the Surabaya PID obtained information regularly about a Pari cell—that included Malelo Siregar alias Djago Neneng, Ali Basah Siregar, Tjipto Soehardjo and Bajo Djambo Siregar—that Malelo Siregar visited Malang and Kediri for Pari propaganda in May and June 1935, that Tjipto Soehardjo established an association called Sport Organisatie Indonesia (SOI) in

Surabaya, many members of which were New PNI members, and that Pari branches were in Batavia, Semarang, Yogyakarta, Bandjarmasin, as well as Surabaya. The Surabaya PID also obtained the October 1935 issue of *Obor*.

The *hoofdparket* also obtained fragmentary information about Pari activity in the outer islands; they knew that New PNI leader in West Sumatra, Leon Salim, was in contact with Djamaloedin Tamin via Kandoor gelar Soetan Rangkajo Basa now in Digul, that New PNI member Soetan Noer Alamsjah in Medan was in contact with Pari in Singapore, via New PNI member Rahimy, who was originally from Fort de Kock and now resident in Singapore, that Pari man, Loetan bin Madjid who was from West Sumatra and now resident in Singapore went to Lampung for Pari propaganda in April 1936, that Ray alias Banray from Bandjarmasin went to Surabaya for Pari propaganda in 1934 and that Young PNI member Joesoef Mawangkang in Makassar was in contact with Pari in 1935. None of the information was verified. But spy reports suggested an expansion in Pari activity in 1935–36.

The attorney general sent instructions on May 6, 1936 to the residents of Batavia, Priangan, Banyumas, and Surabaya and the assistant resident of Yogyakarta to arrest Pari activists and supporters and carry out house searches. Jahja Nasoetion, Soebono, Djamaloeddin Ibrahim, Malelo Siregar, Ali Basah Siregar, Tjipto Soehardjo and others were arrested in a week. Djaoes escaped the arrest.

The Surabaya PID learned about Djaoes's presence in Surabaya and arrested him only after their interrogation of Malelo Siregar and Alibasah Siregar who Djaoes recruited. Djaoes alias Malim Loebis alias Husdeshagen alias Josee Toledo alias Si Pandjang alias Dawood Hawatt alias Bang Amat was a son of German mining engineer and his mistress. At the time of his arrest, he was in possession of *Obor* in carbon paper as well as such Pari writings as *Sabit* and *Tongkat*. Djaoes was probably the last of the Pari cadres Djamaloedin Tamin sent to Tan Malaka for training. He was arrested in Hong Kong with Tan Malaka in October 1932. At his arrest, he used Filipino Joose Toledo as his name, but Tan Malaka calls him Dawood in his memoirs. Dajoes came to see Tan Malaka in Shanghai, stayed there with him for about seven months, and left for Hong Kong before him. While in prison, Djaoes told Helen Jarvis, he had a chance to talk with Tan Malaka at the prison hospital about where to go. He left Hong Kong about a month before Tan Malaka headed for Canton, hoping to get in touch with a contact Tan

Malaka gave him. But he could not find the contact, and eventually he found his way back to Surabaya.[47]

After his arrest in Surabaya, Djaoes absolutely refused to talk to the police and went on a hunger strike. The attorney general instructed the Surabaya PID chief to send him to an asylum for observation, where he wrote a statement titled *Soerat Poesaka jang berharga besar! Dari seorang jang mati dalam tahanan* (Very valuable letter of inheritance! From someone who died in prison) with his blood.

The *hooftparket* knew that Pari was not a serious threat to peace and order as ARD chief van der Most noted in his report dated April 29, 1936. But not a few of those arrested had to be sent to Digul anyway. Nineteen people were arrested in West Java, 10 of whom were sent to Digul. One of them was Soedarmin bin Soeparmin, who born in Kebumen in 1914 joined in the establishment of scouting organization Kepandoean Anak Marhaen Indonesia (KAMI, Indonesian Marhaen Childrens Scouting), served on the central executive committee of the Perpri, taught at Probi (Pergoeroean Rajat Oentoek Bangsa Indonesia, People's School for Indonesian Nation), and had served as the commissioner of the Partindo Manggarai branch. He obtained two issues of *Obor* and Tan Malaka's *Massa Actie* from Djamaloeddin Ibrahim and recruited a few to Pari, such as Abdoelsalam who was born in Madiun in 1904, joined Partindo in Batavia in 1932 and taught at Probi, Abdoelhamid who born in Sawah Lunto in 1907 was a Parindra activist and worked as a liaison between Jahja Nasoetion and Djaoes, and Namin alias Naming bin Hardjo Moestono who born in Banyumas in 1913 used to be a member of Partindo and worked for *Persatoean Indonesia*, the Partindo organ, which Jahja Nasution and Joesoef Jahja published. They were linked with each other in a network which was nestled in Partindo, Perpri, Pergoeroean Ra'jat and some other associations and through which *Obor* was passed around. It was what joining the Pari meant.

The arrest and internment of Jahja Nasoetion, Djamaloeddin Ibrahim and Djaoes marked the transition for Pari.[48] Djamaloeddin Ibrahim and Djaoes were the last who were recruited by Djamaloedin Tamin and trained by Tan Malaka. Jahja Nasoetion marked the arrival of new Pari

[47] Tan Malaka, *From Jail to Jail*, trans. with intro. by Helen Jarvis (Athens: Center for International Studies, Ohio University, 1991), 2: 214, 224.
[48] Harry A. Poeze, *Tan Malaka: Strijder voor Indonesie's Veijheid: Levensloop van 1987 tot 1945* ('s-Gravenhage: Martinus Nijhoff, 1976), 169.

activists who emerged from among Partindo members and who had no direct contact with Tan Malaka, but read, heard, imagined and admired him, nonetheless.

In the meantime, Tan Malaka himself left Amoy at the end of August 1937 and moved, after a brief stay in Rangoon, to Singapore where he settled down as an English teacher at Chinese schools with the help of his Chinese friends. His knowledge of Chinese languages and customs helped. He had no contacts with Indonesia for a long time after 1932, but now, he wrote in his memoirs, "in my free time, and in secure places, I was able to 'talk' with certain Indonesians. The astute reader will know what I mean. Indonesia was now close by and offered many more possibilities for me than had my recent places of residence." One does not need to look far for its evidence. Matu Mona published two *Patjar Merah* (Scarlet Pimpernel, literally Red Love) novels in Medan in 1938: *Spionnage-Dienst (Patjar Merah Indonesia)* [Espionage service (The Scarlet Pimpernel of Indonesia) and *Rol Patjar Merah Indonesia c.s.* (The Role of the Scarlet Pimpernel of Indonesia and his company), in which the Scarlet Pimpernel (alias Vichitra, Tan Min Kha, Putting Ulap, and Ibrahim el Molqa) works with Paul Mussotte [Moesso], Ivan Aliminsky [Alimin], Semaunov [Semaoen], Darsonov [Darsono], and Djalumin [Djamaloedin Tamin]. Noriaki Oshikawa says that especially the first book incorporates many events and places which closely resemble Tan Malaka's own recounting of events and places in his autobiography published after the war and that Matu Mona obviously had a reliable source of information among those close to Tan Malaka or in Pari. Equally important, the stories clearly sent the message that "nothing is more important to him [Patjar Merah, that is Tan Malaka] than the liberation of his country," "he would resist Moscow's assumption that it could lay claim to all the world's independence movements in the name of internationalism," and that it was "in sharp contrast to the uncertainty of the other nationalists—Darsonov, Mussotte, Semounov, and Aliminsky—who comply with Moscow's instructions even though they question its authority."[49] Tan Malaka himself says in his memoirs, recalling he came across a book in a second-hand bookstall in Padang

---

[49] Noriaki Oshikawa, "Patjar Merah Indonesia and Tan Malaka," in *Reading Southeast Asia* (Ithaca, NY: Southeast Asia Program, Cornell University), 32. See also Poeze, *Tan Malaka*, 486; and Jarvis, "Introduction," in Tan Malaka, *From Jail to Jail*, 1: lxxii–lxxiii.

in 1942, "It was *Patjar Merah* by Matu Mona. This was the first time I had come across either the book or the author."[50] Tan Malaka had long been transformed into a sign of hope for national liberation which Patjar Merah literally embodied, but the stories sent the same message as *Obor* about Pari.[51] In April 1942, after Singapore fell to the Japanese, Tan Malaka left for Penang by train. He crossed the Straits of Malacca to Belawan, Medan and then crossed the Sunda Straits to arrive at Java.[52]

Amir Hamzah Siregar, Sajoeti Melik and S.K. Trimoerti

By the time the police started to investigate a Pari network in 1935, a new communist "center" had emerged in Singapore with Communist

---

[50] Tan Malaka, *From Jail to Jail*, 2: 130. But Oshikawa is cautious and only speculates that the two may have met. Oshikawa, "Patjar Merah Indonesia," 30n46. This fantasy about Tan Malaka as the Scarlet Pimpernel was kept alive even after he emerged on the center stage of national politics in the early days of revolution. See, for instance, Tamar Djaja, *Trio Komoenis Indonesia (Tan Malaka, Alimin, Semaoen) berikoet Stalin dan Lenin* (Bukit Tinggi: Penjiaran Ilmoe, 1946). For the fantastic stories published in Medan's *Pewarta Deli* about the Pari underground, Tan Malaka, and Djamaloedin Tamin, and the evolution of popular fantasies incorporating Tan Malaka as a legendary hero, see Yamamoto, "Print Power and Censorship," 324–55.

[51] Stories similar to Matu Mona's *Patjar Merah* were published on February 12, 1938 in *Pewarta Deli*, a Medan newspaper, under the title "Partai Republic Indonesia (Republic of Indonesia Party)" and referred Tan Malaka as the Scarlet Pimpernel. A newspaper in Batavia, *Pemandangan*, also ran an article, entitled "Patjar Merah dari Party Republic Indonesia tertangkap [The Scarlet Pimpanel of Indonesian Republic Party arrested]", on April 8, 1938. Oshikawa, "Patjar Merah Indonesia." Sintha Melati wrote in her memoirs that, "in the service of the underground: the struggle against the Japanese," the term *pacar merah* (*patjar merah*) referred to underground activists and Matu Mona's Pacar Merah story (*Spionnage-Dienst*) was used as a reading for the underground PKI. Anton Lucas, ed., *Local Opposition and Underground Resistance to the Japanese in Java 1942–1945* (Melbourne: Centre of Southeast Asian Studies, Monash University, 1986), 137, 144. For a possible origin of *patjar merah* in the 1930s Indies, see Jacques Leclerc, "Afterword," in Lucas, *Local Opposition*, 356, in which he says that, between April and August 1935, *Indonesia Berdjoang* under Pamoedji's editorship used Patjar Merah as the pen name of the editor in charge of articles dealing with the Soviet Union, and that the word derived from Tsar Merah (Red Tsar), an Indonesian translation of Christian Windecke's *De Roode Tsaar* (Utrecht, 1932), a Dutch adaptation of a German mystery novel in which Stalin is the hero, and which is filled with intelligence officers and intrigues. For *roman picisan* (pitjisan) in 1930s Medan, see Nobuto Yamamoto, "Medan no roman pichisan: 1930-nen dai matsu Indonesia bunka chizu to taishu shosetsu wo meguru seiji," *Hogaku Kenkyu* 68, no. 11 (1995): 147–79.

[52] Tan Malaka, *From Jail to Jail*, 2: 90, 111, 118.

International and Indies connections. In 1934, the MCP (Malayan Communist Party) briefly kept contacts with the Comintern bureau in Shanghai after it was revived. The constitution the party central committee adopted in March 1934 defined MCP as an "affiliate" of the Comintern. In June 1934, the MCP also received, according to the Straits Settlements Special Branch, a document that urged the party to recruit its members from among the working classes of all nationalities in Malaya. In those days there was a group of about fifty Indonesians as fugitives in Singapore, who included a small group of "pure communists with an 'international' outlook" and who helped the MCP to prepare the propaganda in Malay. Amir Hamzah Siregar was one of "the more dangerous members of this group of the locally resident 'international' communists" from the Indies and the Special Branch noted in 1934 that the party issued documents of a comprehensive character in Malay in which communist principles were explained "in understandable Malay of Indonesian origin with a minimum of party jargon and international terms."[53]

The attorney general reported to the governor general on January 15, 1935, about Amir Hamzah Siregar after his arrest in Surabaya in late December 1934 thus: the British Straits Settlements authorities informed the *hoofdparket* in October 1934 that Amir Hamzah Siregar alias Jimmy Taylor alias Elias bin Hassan alias Amat alias Monica was instructed by the MCP to carry out propaganda in the Indies. "[A] convinced communist" known to be "in contact with communist leaders in different countries in the Far East," the attorney general wrote, Amir Hamzah Siregar was in New York, went to China to establish contacts with the Chinese Communist Party, but unsuccessful in the mission, he moved to British Malaya and established contacts with MCP. Upon this intelligence, the Indies police arrested him when he arrived in Palembang in the same month. But he was released because he did not carry any incriminating documents with him. He went on to Batavia where he was again arrested, interrogated and released. He went to Semarang and Yogyakarta where he got in touch with ex-Digulist Kartopandojo and his brother Moefandi/Boedihardjo, and then on to Surabaya where he stayed with Alibasa Siregar, "editor in chief of *Lapar* (hungry)," and met

---

[53] Cheah Boon Kheng, *From PKI to the Comintern, 1924–1941: The Apprenticeship of the Malayan Communist Party* (Ithaca, NY: Southeast Asia Program, Cornell University, 1992), 18–9, 72–3.

with Achmad alias Mandojono, New PNI activist, and was arrested in December 1934 there. He also wrote an article titled "Beberapa Atoeran Oentoek Konspirasi [Some rules for conspiracy]" in *Warta* (News) published by the Bureau for PKI Abroad (Buro Loear Negeri Partai Komoenis Indonesia), an office established in the Netherlands in 1934.[54]

But if one reads his interrogation report and listens to him even with a great deal of caution, one can see someone who looks very different from the kind of seasoned underground communist operative the attorney general makes him out to be. A native of Tapanuli, born in 1909 he entered the second-class native elementary school in Sibolga at the age of 6 years old and moved to a Dutch native school in Padang Sidempuan, because his father was transferred there. After graduation he went to a Seventh Day Adventist Mission School in Singapore because a relative was there. He was kicked out of the school in a few years for the transgression of school discipline. By then, however, he had learned English. He joined a circus (Rodeo Circus), went to Rangoon, Madras, Bombay, Calcutta and other places in India and worked as a ticket office clerk. In those days he was called Jimmy Taylor or Jimmy Marcel. After staying there for five years, he became a seaman on a British cargo ship in 1930 and went back to Singapore in 1931. He was called Amat or Amir then. In the late 1931 and early 1932 the ship visited Surabaya where he got in touch with Ronomarsono, ex-Digulist, to learn about his brother, Abdul Hamid Siregar, who had been sent to Digul. Shortly thereafter he left for Singapore and then went on to New York via Shanghai. He lost his job when the Malay seamen on the ship went on strike and he was part of it. He found a job as a hotel boy with the

---

[54] PG to GG, Jan. 15, 1935, Mr. 63x/1935. The Bureau for PKI Abroad was part of the attempt to revive PKI in which, according to Poeze, Roestam Effendi, a CPN member in the Dutch Lower House, played an important role. Poeze, "The PKI-Muda 1936–1942," 159. See also PG to consul generaal of the Netherlands in Singapore, Jan. 15, 1935, Mr. 63x/1935; Advocate General to GG, June 26, 1935, Mr. 888x/35; commissioner of police, Rapport, Jogjakarta, May 5, 1935, Mr. 888x/35; Poeze, "The PKI-Muda 1936–1942," 159–60; Cheah, *From PKI to the Comintern*, 17–20, 72–3. Advocate General H. Marcella reported in his letter to the governor general on June 26, 1935 that Alimin had instructed Amir Hamzah Siregar to go into the Indies (which is incorrect) and that he earlier had visited Surabaya as a sailor and established contacts with ex-Digulist Ronomarsono and made contact with Karto-pandojo and Moefandi in Solo via Ronomarsono (which is correct, although the intention behind their meetings is a matter of interpretation). Amir Hamzah Siregar was interned to Digul in August 1935.

name Monica. It was in this period in New York in 1932 that he came
across a communist pamphlet and became interested in communism. He
studied communist literature and joined the party as Monica. He also
became an executive member of a local chapter of the League against
Imperialism and Colonial Oppression and a member of the International
Union of Seamen and Harbor Workers. He never wrote anything for
Warta or for any journal and newspaper.

He left New York entirely on his own will and without any instruction from the party. In Singapore he called himself Elias bin Hasan. He
came to know two members of MCP. Both were Totok Chinese, he said
in his interrogation, even though it is hard to imagine Amir without
any Chinese communicating with Totok Chinese who had no English
and no Malay. In any event, one of them gave him instructions to visit
the Indies to observe the situation there and so he went in October
1934 to the Indies. He went to Batavia via Palembang. He then went
to Semarang and stayed there for a month. He briefly visited Yogyakarta
and then went to Surabaya, stayed there for half a month and was
arrested. To his credit he never mentioned the names of his contacts in
Singapore and did not say he was on the MCP payroll. But he was tailed
once he got to the Indies and all the ex-Digulists he got in touch with
were also under police surveillance. He met Moefandi in Semarang, and
through him, met with Kartopandojo, Sismadi Sastrosiswojo and other
ex-Digulists. He told them that Moesso and Alimin were still with the
Communist International and asked whether there was any possibility
of establishing a MCP branch somewhere in Java.[55]

It should be noted that Amir Hamzah Siregar departed New York
of his own will, that he was in Shanghai because his ship stopped over
there, and that he was identified as the author of an article in *Warta*,
most likely because it was signed with Siregar. It is unlikely that he met
with Alibasa Siregar, let alone stayed with him, because Alibasa was in
the Pari underground. The fact that he got in touch with ex-Digulists
and asked them about the possibility of establishing a MCP branch
shows how unseasoned he was as an underground operative. One is
tempted to see Amir Hamzah Siregar as a young unmarried man floating,

---

[55] Proces verbaal (Amir Hamzah Siregar), Mr. 888x/35. Amir Hamzah Siregar was
interrogated by police commissioner Leopold Alexander Burer and police *wedana*
Raden Salamoen. Though the interrogation records are in Dutch, Salamoen most
likely interrogated him in Malay and wrote the records in Dutch.

as Mohamad Arief Siregar, wondering in and out of the Indies and stumbling on something fateful that changed his life.[56]

Shortly after Amir Hamzah Siregar was interned in Digul, the *hoofdparket* looked into the situation of 800 ex-Digulists and 2,500 "ex-communist convicts" who were arrested in the wake of the revolts but released after serving their prison terms. The *hoofdparket* found that the great majority of both groups stayed away from politics, but that approximately 45 ex-Digulists and 180 "ex-communist convicts" were under close surveillance. Only a very few were sent back to Digul, including "promoters and core members of the communist criminal organization discovered" in Kediri and Madiun in 1935 and "Firdos [Firdaus] alias Haroenrasjid," a former associate of Haji Misbach, for his attack on the government in the journal *Adil* (Just) he edited. Moefandi alias Boediardjo who Amir Hamzah Siregar had contacted was sternly reprimanded, but allowed to stay in Java. The *hoofdparket* suspected two ex-Digulists in Cirebon were involved in the dissemination of *Gagak Solo* and *Kaoem Pembrani* [Brave fold], pamphlets Young PKI issued, but it was not yet aware of the connection between the pamphlets and the new underground communist party. The *hoofdparket* also noted that there were not very many—20 among ex-Digulists and 6 among "ex-convicts" —who joined or were in sympathy with Partindo and New PNI and that most of them were in Batavia and Sumatra's west coast.[57]

Apparently the *hoofdparket* in this investigation did not uncover any attempt other than Amir Hamzah Siregar's to establish transnational links with ex-Digulists and other former PKI members. But the ARD learned from the investigation into the Amir Hamzah Siregar's case that the man who was also part of the Indonesian resident group of communists in Singapore and who most likely instructed Amir Hamzah Siregar

---

[56] Citing sociologist Usman Pelly, Loren Ryter says that the term *preman* in part came from *vrijman* or free man in early twentieth-century Deli and that it derived from "youths who don't want to be bound to any dependencies, including a job or a contract." Loren Ryter, "Pemuda Pancasila: The Last Loyalist Free Men of Suharto's Order?" in *Violence and the State in Suharto's Indonesia*, ed. Benedict O'G. Anderson (Ithaca, NY: Southeast Asia Program, Cornell University, 2001), 129. Amir Hamzah Siregar can be called *vrijman* in this sense.

[57] Deputy attorney general to GG, Batavia, Sept. 4, 1936, Onderzoek naar gedragingen enz. van ex-bannelingen en uit de gevangenis ontslagen communistische veroordeelden, Mr. 262x/37.

to go to the Indies on behalf of MCP was Sajoeti Melik alias Boediman alias Amat.[58] In July 1935, he was arrested by the British Special Branch on banishment warrant.

Born in 1908 as a son of a village head (*bekel jajar*) in Sleman, Yogyakarta and a protégé of Haji Misbach's, Sajoeti Melik was introduced to Marxism and communism by H.A. Zurink when he was a student at the teachers' training school in Solo. He was kicked out of the school because of his activism, taught at Sarekat Rajat school in Ambarawa, and at the age of 15 became secretary of the PKI Cilacap section in March 1924 (where section chairman Soekirno was on the PKI central executive committee). He got to know PKI leaders in those days, including Moesso who he called "instigator" and "messenger" contemptuously while recalling Aliarcham and Soebakat warmly in his interview as his teachers.[59] He also says he visited Bandung in April 1926, met Soekarno and read Tan Malaka's *Naar the Republiek Indonesia*. He was arrested after the revolts and interned to Digul in 1927. He was chairman of the PKI Cilacap section and Sarekat Pegawai Pelaboean dan Laoetan (SPPL, Dockworkers and Sailors Union) when he was arrested. He spent six years in Digul, where he learned English and French.

When he was released from Digul and came back to Java in 1933, Sajoeti Melik was 25 years old. He heard that there was an Indonesian who had come back from the US. He went to Singapore via Buleleng, Bali, worked as a coolie in Singapore and met with Amir Hamzah Siregar who introduced him to those active in "an anti-colonial movement" in Singapore—Chinese, Vietnamese, Filipinos, Malays, "even some" French and British. It was called the "Anti-Imperialism League." He soon became its chairman, because as he put it, he was "Malay"

---

[58] PG to consul general of the Netherlands in Singapore, Jan. 15, 1935, Mr. 63x/1935. It is not clear how the *hoofdparket* learned about Sajoeti Melik. Amir Hamzah Siregar did not mention his name in the interrogation as far as it was recorded. Given Sajoeti's close relations with Kartopandojo, the *hoofdparket* might have figured out that it was Sajoeti's network, to which Amir linked.

[59] Sajoeti describes Moesso, whom he met in 1924 as "revolutionary" in the sense "nekad [utterly determined]" and "without calculation" as if instigating only to rebel. When he came back from Russia in 1948, however, Sajoeti says Moesso was "very loyal to implement the instruction of his boss" and that he was "pesuruh [messenger]," different from Tan Malaka, who knew how to use his own brain. Arief Priyadi, ed., *Wawancara dengan Sayuti Melik* (Jakarta: CSIS, 1986), 276–7, 297–8.

and because he was seen to have enough experiences given his Digul
past. When he was in Seremban, he sent a letter to his activist friend
in Singapore, which was intercepted by the Special Branch and led to
his arrest in 1935. He spent a year in Singapore prison and was then
banished to Java in 1937, where he was detained again, only to be released in the same year.[60]

After his release, he went back to Yogyakarta, worked as a batik
trader, met with S.K. Trimoerti at Parindra and Gerindo meetings. They
were married in 1938 in Solo at the house of ex-Digulist Kartopandoyo,
one of the people Amir Hamzah Siregar contacted in 1934 who must
have been a good friend of Sajoeti's, given the fact that when both
Trimoerti and Sajoeti were in prison, their baby son was trusted to him.[61]

S.K. Trimoerti was born in 1912 in Boyolali, Surakarta. Her
father, R. Ng. Salim Banjaransari Mangunsuromo, was a courtier in the
Surakarta Court. She attended a second elementary school and a girls'
teachers training school (Meisjes Normaal School). After graduation, she
briefly taught in Solo and then moved to a girls' school in Banyumas.
It was there in Banyumas that she started to attend meetings the BO
organized. In August and September 1932, Soekarno visited Central
and East Java for Partindo propaganda. She attended a Partindo rally
in Purwokerto. She saw and heard Soekarno for the first time. She
quit her teaching job, went to Bandung, joined Partindo, and stayed at
Ashurama Republik Indonesia to study directly under Soekarno.[62] She
also taught at Pergoeroean Rajat and wrote for *Fikiran Rakjat* [People's
thought], a Partindo journal, at Soekarno's encouragement. After Soekarno's arrest, she briefly went to back to Klaten, Surakarta, and in
1935 moved to Yogyakarta where she joined in the establishment of
Persatoean Marhaeni Indonesia (PMI, Indonesian Marhaeni Union)
as secretary and published *Suara Marhaeni* (Marhaeni's Voice) as its
journal. It is not clear whether she joined Perpri, but it should be no
surprise if she knew some of its activists, given the fact that Perpri was
headquartered in Yogyakarta and was meant to be a Partindo unofficial
youth organization. By the time Gerindo was established in 1937, she
had moved to Semarang, where she worked for a journal, *Soeloeh Kita*

[60] Priyadi, ed., *Wawancara dengan Sayuti Melik*, 15–7.
[61] Ibid., 18–9.
[62] Mustoffa, *Sukarni*, 208.

(Our torch). She joined the party in 1937 and was elected a member of its central committee in 1939 along with A.K. Gani (general chairman), Sartono (first chairman), Atmadji (first secretary), S.I. Widjaja (second secretary) as well as Asmara Hadi, Adam Malik, Mohammad Joesoef and Sakirman (members).

After their marriage, Sajoeti joined Trimoerti in Semarang and published newspaper *Pesat* (Fast). Sajoeti joined Parindra and taught at its youth group, Soerya Wirawan (Reporters' sun). Trimoerti took the initiative, together with Kadarisman, a Gerindo activist, to create the Federation of Indonesian Private Sector Unions (Gabungan Sarikat Sekerja Particulier Indonesia, GASPI) in early 1941 and was joined by Muhamad Ali, an ex-Digulist and former VSTP activist.[63] They were a hub of movement activists in Semarang and they kept in contact with those associated with Parindra, Gerindo and other associations and organizations, including the underground Young PKI. They knew nationalist intellectuals such as Mohammad Yamin, Amir Sjarifoeddin, and Sartono personally. They knew Subandi/Widarta of Young PKI (PKI Muda), even though it is hard to believe the statement Sajoeti made that in 1941 Amir Sjarifoeddin led the PKI central committee and that Widarta was "his assistant."[64] They knew Ibnu Parna who was active in Semarang and led Sarekat Marhaen Revolutioner (Samare, Revolutionary Marhaen League), which he called a "wild communist group.[65] It is not clear whether Sajoeti or Trimoerti were members of Young PKI and what it meant to be a member, but Anton Lucas and Harry Poeze say that when Young PKI was established, Soenarman, one of its most active propagandists, contacted Trimoerti in Semarang and that she was helpful in establishing a Semarang branch of Centraal Persatoean Boeroeh Indonesia (Center Union for Indonesian Workers) in 1939.[66] Lucas also says that Sajoeti Melik published *Pesat* articles that Widarta wrote under different pen names. He also says that when PKI in Surabaya planned to disseminate a party manifesto to resist the Japanese invasion in the

---

[63] Ingleson, *Workers, Unions and Politics*, 315.

[64] Priyadi, ed., *Wawancara dengan Sayuti Melik*, 262.

[65] Sajoeti Melik says the PKI underground was under Amir Sjarifoeddin, that Akoma (Angkatan Komunis Muda)/Samare, which Ibnu Parna led, was not in the same line with the PKI underground and that Ibnu Parna was "very close" to Tan Malaka in the early days of the revolution. Ibid., 44–5.

[66] It is not clear what it means, however, for CPBI was practically dead by then.

Indies in the wake of the fall of Singapore, Widarta got in touch with
Trimoerti and Sajoeti Melik.[67] But we can only be sure that they were
a hub among radicals and in communication with Young PKI, and not
that they were part of the Young PKI underground.[68]

Soekarni, Wikana, and Young PKI (PKI Muda)[69]

While Amir Hamzah Siregar got in touch with ex-Digulists when he
visited Java in 1934, Moesso carefully avoided getting in direct contact
with ex-Digulists when he came to Surabaya in 1935. It is not clear
how long he stayed in the Indies, but Harry Poeze believes it was "a
longer stay" than the ARD thought, given the fact that Tamzil, an Indonesian student in the Netherlands who was active in CPN (Communist

---

[67] Sajoeti says in his interview that he strongly disagreed with Widarta (who he calls
Subandi from Surabaya) and the PKI action in Semarang (instead of "the action of
the PKI Semarang branch/section"), because he says it was irresponsible and would
provoke the Japanese. See Priyadi, ed., *Wawancara dengan Sayuti Melik*, 27–8, 242–6.
[68] Resident of Banyumas, Rapport over de ontwikkeling, uitbreiding en ontdekking
van de Communistische samenspanning in het gewest Banjoemas, Mr. 428x/1937;
Cheah, *From PKI to the Comintern*, 19–20; Poeze, "The PKI-Muda 1936–1942,"
163–4; Arief Priyadi, ed., *Wawancara dengan Sayuti Melik*, 10–27, 39, 247–53; Lucas,
Local Opposition, 17–20; Soebagijo, *S.K. Trimurti: Wanita Pengabdi Bangsa* (Jakarta:
Gunung Agung, 1982), 43–4; Ipong Jazimah, "S.K. Trimurti Pejuang Perempuan
Indonesia," *Sejarah dan Budaya: Jurnal Sejarah, Budaya, dan Pengajarannya* 10, no. 1
(2016): 45–53. Lucas says the Semarang cell of Young PKI included Trimoerti and
Sajoeti as members, but there is no evidence to support his statement. Sajoeti vehe-
mently opposed the dissemination of the PKI manifesto that Subandi/Widarta brought
to them. See Priyadi, ed., *Wawancara dengan Sayuti Melik*, 21, 26–7. Widarta played
a central role in (re)building the PKI underground under the Japanese and in the
early days of revolution. He worked at the BPM refinery in Plaju, Palembang, to
organize workers in the late 1930s and wrote for *Pesat* after he came back to Java.
Lucas, *One Soul One Struggle: Region and Revolution in Indonesia* (Sydney: Allen and
Unwin, 1991), 56. Ibnu Parna established Angkatan Komunis Muda (Young Communist Force) in 1946 in support of Tan Malaka.
[69] Unless otherwise noted, the following account is based on Amir Hamzah Siregar's
statement, included in Chief of the ARD, Geheim overzicht van de in 1936 te
Soerabaya voorbereide oprichting eener nieuwe 'Partai Kommunist Indonesia' (Feb.
1937), which was attached to a letter that the attorney general sent to the governor
general on February 4, 1937, Mr. 127x/1937; PG to GG, Sept. 15, 1936, Ext. 30-
8-37 Lt. G.177; PG to GG, Apr. 19, 1938, Mr. 146x/38; Assistant wedana bij de
PID, Hoofdbureau van Politie Semarang, Process Verbaal (Soenarman), Nov. 19,
1936, Mr. 146x/38; PG to GG, Jan. 4, 1938, Mr. 146x/28; Poeze, "The PKI-Muda,
1936–1942," 160–5.

Party of the Netherlands), visited the Indies "to control his [Moesso's] progress."[70] As we have seen earlier, Tan Malaka, Soebakat and Djamaloedin Tamin established the Pari, a new party, in Bangkok, after the 1926–27 revolts. They had been opposed to the party plan to revolt and called for organization and discipline. Alimin and Moesso had been part of the leadership driving the party to revolt. They were sent to Moscow for the Comintern endorsement for the plan. Tan Malaka tried to dissuade them from doing so, but they ignored him and went to Moscow. They came back to Singapore from Moscow and were arrested in Johore on December 18, 1926, by which time the revolts in Java had been suppressed. Expelled from Singapore, they went back to the Soviet Union via China to discover that their once rejected policy was now justified in spite of the fact that the revolution had proved an utter failure.[71] As Ruth McVey tells us in *The Rise of Indonesian Communism*, Alimin and Moesso represented the type of "daring leaders."[72]

Alimin Prawirodirdjo started his movement career with joining the CSI in the 1910s when he stayed in Surabaya at Tjokroaminoto's boarding house. He was also associated with Tjipto and joined the Insulinde. He was active in trade unionism and organizing printers, seamen and dockworkers of Batavia. He also joined the ISDV and in 1918 served as chairman of its Batavia branch and a member of the central party executives. He was arrested for his involvement in the Afdeeling B affair. Upon his release from prison, he revived the pawnshop workers' union and joined Moesso and Sosrokardono in a shortlived attempt to revive the CSI organ *Oetoesan Hindia* and eventually he chose to join the PKI by mid-1924 by appearing in China as the PKI delegate to a Comintern sponsored conference.[73]

Moesso, like Alimin who he had known since his school days, joined the CSI and lived for a time at the Tjokroaminoto boarding house in Surabaya and met Soekarno there. He joined, like Alimin, several associations such as the Insulinde, the Sarekat Islam, and the ISDV.

---

[70] Poeze, "The PKI-Muda 1936–1942," 165.

[71] McVey, *The Rise of Indonesian Communism*, 205–6, 346, 352.

[72] Ibid., 194.

[73] Alimin, born in Surakarta in 1889, was adopted at the age of nine by G.A.J. Hazeu, a student of Snouck Hurgronje and future adviser for native affairs. He attended European schools in Batavia and became fluent in French, English and Dutch, in addition to Javanese and Sundanese. Though Hazeu hoped he would join the government service, McVey says, Alimin instead went into politics, starting a newspaper, *Djawa Moeda*, and joining the Boedi Oetomo and the CSI. Ibid., 168–9.

He was said to be bright, a daring agitator, and a good organizer and writer, and "affected a rough-and-ready style in his public appearance." At the trials of the Afdeeling B affair, Alimin confessed he had lied to save Tjokroaminoto when confronted with evidence, but Moesso had refused to do so, "exhibiting a damn-the-consequences attitude." This was the reason Djamaloedin Tamin believed that Moesso was incapable of any underground work and that the Moesso who organized the underground PKI in Surabaya was fake. Upon his release from prison, Moess joined PKI, revived its Batavia branch, and in December 1924 emerged as an executive member of a secretariat of Red Indonesian Labor Unions headquartered in Surabaya. He served as head of Sarekat Postel and as editor of the local communist newspaper *Proletar*, worked as the major leader of the Surabaya-based communist labor campaign.[74]

Upon their return to Russia in 1927, Alimin and Musso attended the Lenin school for a few years.[75] They were then sent to China where they were instrumental in establishing a Malay section of the Anti-Imperialist League in June 1928, and they attempted to establish contacts with students from the Dutch Indies and British Malaya at Al-Azhar University in Cairo, apparently with some success. Two newspapers students published, *Pilihan Timor* (Choice of the East) and *Seruan Azhar*, were read in Malaya. After the Comintern sixth congress in July–August 1928, they studied at Moscow University and then left for Asia again to work for the Pan-Pacific Trade Union Secretariat (PPTUS) and the Comintern Far Eastern Bureau in Shanghai.[76] In 1931, Alimin got in touch with Tan Malaka and persuaded him to work for the Far Eastern Bureau, even though Tan Malaka denied this when he was interrogated by the British.[77] A letter intercepted in October 1931 revealed that a Dutch East Indies Bureau (DEIB) was established with the objective of

---

[74] Moesso was born in 1897 in Pegu, a village in the residency of Kediri. He attended high school and teacher training school in Batavia, where he was a friend of Alimin and a protégé first of Hazeu and then the educator and theosophist, D. van Hinloopen Labberton. McVey, *The Rise of Indonesian Communism*, 169–70, 275–6. See also Djamaluddin Tamim, *Sedjarah PKI*, Unpublished mimeograph, n.d.

[75] McVey, *The Rise of Indonesian Communism*, 202.

[76] Cheah, *From PKI to the Comintern*, 10; Poeze, "The PKI Muda 1936–1942," 158.

[77] In his memoirs, Tan Malaka remains silent about his activities over the two years that spanned from late 1929 to 1932. Harry Poeze and Helen Jarvis have a different take on this lacuna. See Poeze, *Tan Malaka*, 416–7; and Jarvis, "Preface," in Tan Malaka, *From Jail to Jail*, 1: xii–xiii.

reestablishing the PKI.[78] But Tan Malaka was arrested in Hong Kong in October 1932. In his interrogation Tan Malaka insisted that he was only interested in developing Pari as an "organization of the Javanese and Sumatran proletariat with the ultimate object of driving the Dutch from the N.E.I." and denied that he was "in the pay of Moscow" or that he had accepted Hilaire Noulens' offer in 1931 of proceeding to Burma with Alimin [Dirdja].[79] In any event, Tan Malaka never contacted the Comintern.[80]

In the meantime, the representatives meeting of the South Seas Communist Party (SSCP) held secretly in Singapore in April 1930 under Nguyen Ai Quoc's leadership decided to dissolve the party and to set up two new organizations, the MCP and the Indochinese Communist Party (ICP), both under the direct control of the Comintern Far Eastern Bureau. The parties of Siam, the Dutch Indies and Burma were to be sub-departments under MCP as a provisional measure. The Far Eastern Bureau also established a "Southern Section" in Hong Kong. But with the arrest of Hilaire Noulens in Shanghai and Nguyen Ai Quoc in Hong Kong in 1931, the Far Eastern Bureau was destroyed, and its Southeast Asian network shattered.[81]

A new link was established between MCP and the new Far Eastern Bureau in 1934. Cheah Boon Kheng says that between March and October 1934, "Dr. Ling," "a Comintern agent with impressive credentials from Shanghai" was in Singapore to reestablish contact with the MCP.[82] It is believed that he attended the sixth plenary session of the MCP central committee in March 1934, where the party drew up a new constitution. The Straits Settlements Special Branch also believed that "Dr. Ling" was "in touch with the headquarters of the International Seamen and Harbor Workers in Amsterdam and supposedly with the Comintern apparatus in Shanghai." The Special Branch also believed that

---

[78] Cheah, *From PKI to the Comintern*, 11, 137; see also Ban Kah Choon, *Absent History: The Untold Story of Special Branch Operations in Singapore 1915–1942* (Singapore: Raffles, 2001), 155.

[79] Cheah, *From PKI to the Comintern*, 137. See also Takeshi Onimaru, *Shanghai Noulens Jiken no Yami: Senkanki Ajia ni okeru Chika Katsudo no Network to Igirisu Seiji Joho Keisatsu* (Tokyo: Hayama Shuppan Kobo, 2014).

[80] Poeze, "The PKI Muda 1936–1942," 158–9.

[81] Cheah, *From PKI to the Comintern*, 16–7; see also Ban, *Absent History*, 129; Onimaru, *Shanghai Noulens Jiken no Yami*.

[82] Cheah, *From PKI to the Comintern*, 18.

he "left Singapore about 15 October 1934 by means and by a route at present unknown."[83] If "Dr. Ling" did go to the Indies, the timing is intriguing, because this was when the Special Branch noted that Indonesian communists were working for MCP and when Amir Hamzah Siregar, who received "regular payments" from MCP from November 1933 to September 1934, was also traveling to Java in the same month via Palembang. The ARD, however, was apparently kept in the dark about "Dr. Ling" as we have seen.[84]

In the Netherlands, in the meantime, Roestam Effendi was elected for the parliament as a CPN representative in 1933 (and served as a member of the Lower House till 1940). He was instrumental in drafting the CPN's eighteen-point program for PKI as the base for a new mass movement and establishing a Biro Luar Negeri PKI (Bureau for the PKI Abroad) in 1934 and attended the Comintern seventh congress in 1935 where the new popular front line was established. In these years Dutch and Indonesian communists worked together to revive PKI. Alimin and Moesso often visited the Netherlands, it is said, and maintained contacts with Indonesian students and seamen there.[85]

It was in this context in which Moesso came back to Surabaya, the city in which he spent many years in the 1910s and 1920s. Jacque Leclerc speculates—and it is plausible—that it was in part to deny Pari the PKI's mantle and to announce that PKI was there, both in exile and in the Indies.[86] While in Surabaya, Moesso sent a series of articles with the name of Ganda to *Indonesia Berdjoang* (Indonesia Fights), which led its editor in chief Pamoedji (who was also active in Sarekat Tani) who had known Moesso personally since the early 1920s to identify him as such. Pamoedji introduced Moesso to his deputy, Achmad Soemadhi. Pamoedji and Achmad Soemadhi introduced Moesso to Djokosoedjono, New PNI member active in the trade union movement who served as chairman of PBKP (Persatoean Boeroeh Kereta Api) and CPBI (Centraal Persatoean Boeroeh Indonesia) and Pamoedji's cousin, who in turn introduced him to Mas Roeskak, a clerk with the Post Telegraph and

---

[83] Ibid., 27.

[84] Ibid., 20.

[85] Lucas, *Local Opposition and Underground Resistance*, 3–4: Poeze, "The PKI-Muda 1936–1942," 159.

[86] Jacque Leclerc, "Underground Activities and their Double (In the Context of Amir Sjarifuddin's Relationship with Communism in Indonesia)," *Kabar Seberang*, no. 17 (1986): 86.

Telephone service and active in Partindo.[87] Moesso also got in touch
with Siti Larang, the widow of Sosrokardono, who once served as
Tjokroaminoto's top lieutenant at CSI and who Moesso had known well
since they stayed together at Tjokroaminoto's boarding house. Pamoedji
was arrested for the transgression of press laws in November 1935 and
sentenced for one-year imprisonment. The remaining four established
a PKI provisional central committee with Mas Roeskak as chairman,
Ahmad Soemadhi as secretary, Mrs. Sosrokardono and Djokosoedjono
as commissioners. Moesso and Soemadhi translated the CPN program
into Indonesian. Moesso also wrote a pamphlet to criticize Tan Malaka
and Pari and gave the committee 150 guilders for party activity. He
left Java in May 1936, Ahmad Soemadhi said in his interrogation, on
board the SS *Tjisaroea* of the Java-China-Japan line and went back
to Russia via Shanghai. While Moesso was still in Surabaya, Tamzil
(b. 1908 in Kota Gedang), who had stayed in the Hague since 1932
when he was a student, visited Batavia in April 1936 without Moesso's
knowledge, met members of the provisional party, gave the party 300
guilders, and went back to the Netherlands in mid-1936.[88]

---

[87] Djokosoedjono was born in Blora in 1909 and lived in Surabaya. He worked for
a year as administrator of *Soeloeh Ra'jat Indonesia* in 1927, moved to *Soeara Oemoem*
as administrator, and then joined *Persatoean Cooperatie Indonesia* as administrator in
1930. He also served as director of Among Siswa school in Kranggan, Surabaya, for a
time. He then joined New PNI and served as chairman of the New PNI-dominated
PBKI railway union central executive in 1933 when it was destroyed. Ingleson,
Workers, Unions and Politics, 237. See also Poeze, "The PKI-Muda 1936–1942," 172.
ARD chief van der Most wrongly identified Djokosoedjono as a former chairman
of SKBI in Surabaya. His name does not appear on the list of SKBI leaders van der
Most himself compiled in 1929. See "Staat van leiders en hun antecedenten," which
is appended in PG to GG, May 15, 1929, Mr. 627x/1929.

[88] Soe Hok Gie says two Indies Chinese, Tan Ling Djie and Liem Koen Hian, also
joined Young PKI. Soe Hok Gie, "Simpang kiri dari sebuah djalan (kisah pemberontakan Madiun September 1948" (MA thesis, Universitas Indonesia, Fakultas Sastra,
Djurusan Sedjarah, 1969), 20–1. For more on Liem Koen Hian, see Yamamoto,
"Print Power and Censorship," 446–62. Born the son of a wealthy businessman in
1896 in Banjarmasin, he worked as a journalist in many places in the Indies and led
a series of newspapers in Surabaya in the 1920s and 1930s. He established Partai
Tionghoa Indonesia (PTI, Chinese Party of Indonesia) in 1932 with *Sin Tit Po* as its
official news organ. In 1933, however, he quit Sin Tit Po, moved to Batavia to study
at the School of Law (RHS), came to know such nationalists as Mohamad Yamin,
Sanoesi Pane and Amir Sjarifoedin, and joined Gerindo in 1937. He went back to
Surabaya in 1939 to work as editor-in-chief of *Sin Tit Po*, only to give the job to
Tan Ling Djie in the same year and return to Batavia.

When the party, now remembered as the illegal PKI or Young PKI (PKI-Muda), was established, it was defined as a part of the Communist Party of the Netherlands (CPN), until such time as it could be recognized as an independent section by the Comintern. The party started its activity after Moesso's departure. Poeze says that Ahmad Soemadhi found an energetic propagandist in Mohamad Soenarman Wirjoatmodjo. He and Ngademo who Soenarman recruited got in touch with activists they had known since the Perpri days: Soedimoeljono and S.K. Trimurti in Semarang, Mantoro Tirtonegoro in Yogyakarta, and Ismail in Surabaya. Ngademo also met with Soekarni and Saleh Rais in Batavia in August 1936.[89]

Out of five committees the central committee planned to establish —peasants, trade unions, youth, women, and cells—the party was successful, the ARD believed, in establishing a youth organization which was called Indonesian Communist Youth under Soenarman's leadership. Five hundred copies of *Kalzan* and 300 copies of *Gagak Solo-Dahlia Opera* (Solo Raven-Dahlia Opera) were printed and in part circulated. In two months, at the latest by mid-September 1936, the ARD learned from two informers, one in Batavia and the other in Semarang, that Partindo activist Ngademo from Surabaya circulated *Kalzan* in the two towns. The attorney general sent his secret circular to the regional chiefs on October 1, 1936, that the ARD had learned from informers that two communist brochures, camouflaged as an advertisement for Kalzan (which was the Dutch Communist Party program to promote the formation of an anti-imperialist popular front of all nationalist organizations) and a program of Dahlia-Opera (in which Tan Malaka and Pari were criticized) were circulated by Ngademo and Ali Hanafiah. The attorney general instructed regional chiefs to arrest anyone involved in the distribution and circulation of these brochures and to pay special attention to the proliferation of communist propaganda material in Perpri and Partindo circles. In February 1937, by which time the ARD investigation had come to a provisional conclusion, ARD chief van der Most reported that about 30 members were under arrest, including Achmad Soemadhi,[90] Mas Roeskak, Mrs. Sosrokardono, Djokosoedjono, Ismail

---

[89] Poeze, "The PKI-Muda 1936–1942," 163–4.

[90] Achmad Soemadhi was born in Grisse in 1910. He taught at Pergoeroean Ra'jat in Batavia Centrum for four years but was banned from teaching in 1934. He then moved to Surabaya, joined *Indonesia Berdjoang* as editor, and published *Berita*. Mr. 146x/38.

alias Achmad Ismail,[91] Ali Hanafiah, and Soenarman[92] in Surabaya, Soedimoeljono[93] in Semarang, Soegoro[94] in Sukabumi, and Harjono[95] and Saleh Rais[96] in Batavia and that Ngademo alias Joesoef Effendi (Surabaya) and Soekarni (Batavia) were still at large. Soetomo Djauhar Arifin was also arrested right after his release from prison in September 1937. Members, or more precisely those who were suspected to be members of Young PKI and its youth organization, largely came from among Partindo and Perpri activists. The government decided to intern 12 out of 30 arrested in Digul, including Roeskak, Djokosoedjono, Ahmad

---

[91] Ismail Widjojo was born in Semarang in 1914. He joined Partindo in 1933 and served on the executive of its Semarang branch in 1934–36. He moved to Surabaya in 1936 and worked for *Indonesia Berdjoang*, then later for *Berita*. Chief of Afd. PID, Alg. Politie Soerabaja, Rapport No. 526/PID/Ind. Zaken, Overzicht van de door den communist Moeso gestichte (nieuwe) PKI te Soerabaja, Nov. 5, 1937, Mr. 146x/38.

[92] Mohamad Soenarman was born in Kendal in 1914. After serving nine months in prison from December 1934 to September 1935 for his Perpri activity, he taught at Pendidikan Rajat school in Surabaya and worked for a while as deputy editor in chief of *Waktoe* (Time). Mr. 146x/38.

[93] Soedimoeljono was born in Solo in 1913 and after he graduated from a six-year private Dutch native primary school and a two-year native craft school lived in Semarang. He taught at Pergoeroean Ra'jat for a year and joined both Perpri and Partindo in 1932–33. He was elected as second chairman of Perpri in June 1933 and detained for nine months in 1935. Resident of Semarang to GG, Feb. 17, 1938, Mr. 146x/38.

[94] Soegoro, also known as Slamet Atmoprasodjo and S. Hendrojono, was born in Yogyakarta in 1914. He taught at Taman Siswa school in Situbondo but was banned from teaching in 1934. Chief of Afd. PID, Semarang to resident of Semarang, Oct. 14, 1936, Mr. 146x/38.

[95] Harjono bin Hardjokoesoemo was born in Boyolali in *ca.* 1907. He joined New PNI in 1932 in Solo and was elected its Magelang branch chairman in 1933. He moved to Batavia in 1934 where he served as chairman of its central executive committee. He was arrested and served in prison for ten months for the transgression of press laws for the article he published in *Daulat Ra'jat*. Controleur voor de Politie te Batavia, Process Verbaal, Feb. 28, 1938, Mr. 146x/38.

[96] Saleh Rais bin Moehammad Gazali was born in Batavia in *ca.* 1900. He worked as a clerk of Chinese food and drink store. When he was chairman of the Partindo Djakatra branch, he was arrested and served in prison for a year for his Perpri activity. In July 1936 he met Ngademo and Ali Hanafiah, who came from Surabaya and most likely agreed to distribute *Kalzan* pamphlets. A police informant got a copy, passed it on to a police officer at the Batavia PID in September, and soon Saleh Rais was under arrest. A well-known activist, he was also arrested in May 1936 as a suspected Pari member because of his "friendship" with Jahja Nasoetion. Chief of Afd. PID, Batavia, Sept. 27, 1937, Mr. 146x/38.

Soemadhi and Soenarman. Van der Most was not aware that Pamoedji was a member, because he had been under arrest after he joined the party and before the police investigation started.[97] Ex-Digulist Harjono alias Hardjokoesoemo was also arrested in connection with the arrest and externment of Johannes Hermans Philippo, a Dutch activist since the ISDV days, in 1937 for handing *Kalzan* to Philippo.[98]

The Semarang PID assistant wedana tells us how Soenarman went about carrying out communist youth propaganda. He got in touch with Soedimoeljono in Semarang in April 1936. In August, Soedimoeljono went to Surabaya, met with Ngademo, former PPPI and Perpri activist, and, shortly thereafter, gave *Kalzan* to a police informer. He also showed *Kalzan* and *Dahlia Opera* brochures to Iman Tegoeh, chairman of the Parindra Semarang branch and Soekarman, chairman of the New PNI Semarang branch. The police informer eventually managed to get the brochures from Soedimoeljono and gave them to the wedana.[99] The most convincing evidence of Soedimoeljono's culpability was his distributing PKI bulletins clandestinely.

The ARD understood that Soenarman relied on the former Perpri activist network for his propaganda. The PID Surabaya chief put it this way in connection with the arrest of Soetomo Djauhar Arifin.[100] Moesso revived the PKI clandestinely as part of the Comintern decision at the third International to form "an anti-imperialist popular front of all political nationalist organizations." To establish a new communist mass youth organization to replace all of the existing youth organizations was part of the motivation for this endeavor. Soetomo Djauhar Arifin was arrested on suspicion that he worked for the unification of the native youth movement to steer it to the communist direction. The PKI made it an integral part of its mission to revolutionize native youth. Soenarman, under de facto PKI leader Ahmad Soemadhi, was assigned to work on this task, namely the creation of Kommunistische Jeugd Internationale

---

[97] Anton Lucas says Pamoedji, a Dutch-educated teacher and journalist, was left with rebuilding the underground PKI while serving as a member of the Gerindo Surabaya branch leadership and circulating *Menara Merah*, a pocket-sized pamphlet which carried articles on the international situation. Lucas, *One Soul One Struggle*, 55.

[98] Proces Verbaal (J.H. Philippo), July 26, 1937, Exh. 30-8-37 Lt. G.177.

[99] Assistant wedana of Afd. PID, Hoofdbureau van Politie Semarang, Process Verbaal, Nov. 19, 1936, Mr. 146x/38.

[100] Chief of the Afdeeling P.I.D., Algemeene Politie Soerabaja, March 3, 1938; Chief of Afdeeling PID to resident van Soerabaja, March 8, 1938, Mr. 469x/38.

(sic, Communist Youth International) as part of the formation of a popular front in the Indies. When Soenarman learned in April 1936 that Indonesia Moeda, the "highly politicized revolutionary youth organization," planned to hold a youth congress in July 1936, he decided to seize the opportunity for the establishment of a communist youth. He traveled to Solo, Semarang, Batavia and Buitenzorg (Bogor). He met with the chairman of the Indonesia Moeda central committee, Soekarni, now fugitive, in Batavia to ask him to join in his endeavor. He saw Taman Siswa teacher Soegoro alias Hendrojono in Buitenzorg for the same purpose, while he established a preparatory committee for the youth congress in Surabaya with himself as chairman, Soetomo Djauhar Arifin as secretary/treasurer, and Ngademo, now fugitive, as propagandist.

But the story Soetomo Djauhar Arifin told in his interrogation and in his letter to the governor general is more nuanced, and it is enlightening to see what it was like to be in the political "underground" in the late 1930s.[101] Now remembered as poet and writer of short stories and drama, Soetomo Djauhar Arifin was born in the village of Krandegan, Madiun in 1916. His father was a peasant. After graduating from the second native school in sub-district Delopo, Madiun, he went to Semarang to stay with his older brother who was working at a land tax office, and he attended a school for typesetters in Semarang. When he graduated from the school at the age of 18, he joined Partindo, because he was impressed by Soekarno who was imprisoned to "defend the nation." He attended Partindo cadre training courses and meetings diligently. He went to the party club house "almost every week" and waited for any party work he could do. In a few months, he found himself working for the Partindo Semarang leadership. Yet he still felt that was not enough and that he could still do a lot more.[102] He was full of energy, which was driving him towards something that he himself did not know.

It was in those days that preparations for establishing a Perpri branch in Semarang started. Partindo allowed its members to join other associations if they were not political parties, while Perpri did not prohibit its members from joining a political party. Soetomo Djauhar Arifin joined the preparatory committee for a Semarang branch. When the

---

[101] Eigenhandig Geschreven verklaringen van: Soetomo Djauhar Arifin; Proces Verbaal (Soetomo Djauhar Arifin), Algemeene Politie Soerabaja Afdeeling Politieke Inlichtingen Dienst, 469x/38.
[102] In the original, he wrote: "Rasanya, masih koerang boeat saja pekerjaan itoe, masih banjak tenaga saja menganggoer!"

branch was approved in August 1932 by the Perpri headquarters, he was chosen as its vice chairman along with Soedimoeljono as chairman. A month later, in September 1932, he was elected as first secretary of the Partindo Semarang branch. He also served as secretary of action committee to oppose the "wild school" ordinance.

When the Perpri congress was held in Semarang, Soetomo as Perpri Semarang branch vice president called on youth in congress bulletins to come to the congress "with this radical and revolutionary spirit." He also published the journal, *Revolusioner* (Revolutionaries). He was chosen as vice president of the central committee of the Perpri for 1933–34 at the congress. But on the day the congress ended, he was arrested for the transgression of the press laws in connection with *Revolusioner*. He was sentenced to a 21-month imprisonment, received a 3-month remission in August 1934 and was released in January 1935 after serving 18 months in prison.

In those days, as he wrote in his letter to the governor general, he wanted to do whatever as he pleased. He wrote for *Sendjata Ra'jat* (People's Weapon), the Partindo Semarang branch journal, as an editorial committee member, but other and more senior members on the editorial committee revised, softened, and often refused his written pieces for publication. He thought they were "old" and not daring. This was a reason he published *Revolusioner*. As he put it, the stuff which had long been inside the volcano could no longer be kept there, and "now erupted!" He said what he had long wanted to say in the journal. He also gave a speech at the first public rally Perpri held on the occasion of its congress. But the police interrupted his speech and dissolved the rally. Senior activists were angry at him, even though he thought they should be angry at the police.

Shortly after he was released from prison in January 1935, he moved to Surabaya in April 1935 to serve as secretary of the Partindo central committee. By then Partindo was in serious trouble. As he put it, it was not dead, but it was not alive, either. It could not hold meetings. The headquarters could not maintain communications with its branches. Soetomo as secretary accompanied Partindo chairman Soediro to visit branches in East and Cetral Java to see the financial and membership situation in each branch and meet with branch leaders to exchange views. They were cautious not to get hit by the meeting ban which did not allow more than five people to get together. Back in Surabaya, however, Soediro and Soetomo were arrested all the same in June 1935 and sent to Yogyakarta prison. Soetomo was in prison for two months.

After he was released, he went back to Surabaya. He was hurt, however, because "friends" said that he was still too much a kid to serve on a party central committee. He no longer wanted to serve on the committee. He stepped down in August 1936 as Partindo secretary, even though he kept working on editing a party annual report.

In June 1936 Soetomo started a new journal, *Pedoman Masjarakat Baroe* (Guideline for New Society), with Tegar as director and editor-in-chief and Soetomo as administrator. He wanted to work as administrator, because, as he put it, he did not want to do any work that might send him back in prison. Yet he was arrested for the transgression of press laws again—although it is not clear whether it was because of *Pedoman Masjarakat Baroe* or *Sedjarah Partindo* (Partindo history), or the Partindo annual report he edited. He was sentenced to 18-months imprisonment and after being given a 3-month remission, got out of prison in September 1937.

Upon his release from prison, Soetomo was immediately brought to Surabaya, arrested there again by the PID, and interrogated in connection with Young PKI under Ahmad Soemadhi and the communist youth front Soenarman was presumably working on. He wrote in his letter to the government general that Soenarman never told him the intent of the preparatory committee for the youth congress, that if friends [i.e., Soenarman] had frankly invited him to join a communist movement, he would have said yes, and that he was saying this not because he did not want to be sent to Digul—in fact, he said that he would rather be sent to] Digul than go through all the repeated suffering he had experienced in prison. One naturally wonders whether he meant what he said, but one thing is clear: Digul was very much on his mind, perhaps for the first time in his life.

Then Soetomo told his story about how he got involved in the preparatory committee for youth congress. He had moved to Surabaya in 1935 to serve as Partindo secretary. Soenarman came from Yogyakarta to Surabaya in 1936, and he visited the newspaper *Indonesia Berdjoang* office in Djagalan. Soetomo met him there and helped him find a job as teacher at Pendidikan Ra'jat school. Soetomo had known Soenarman since the Perpri days. They met often in Surabaya. Soenarman did not have a position at the *Indonesian Berdjoang* office, but he visited often. Soetomo also went to the office practically every day, because the Partindo office was also there in the *Indonesian Berdjoang* office. One day both Soenarman and Soetomo read an article in *Indonesia Moeda* which called for the organization of a youth congress (*kongres pemoeda*).

Both loved the idea. As Partindo secretary, Soetomo volunteered to work for the preparatory committee as secretary and treasurer, while Soenarman would serve as chairman. But Soenarman, Soetomo and Ngademo (who was supposed to work as propagandist) did not have a chance to meet and discuss the matter, because shortly after his meeting with Soenarman, Soetomo was arrested for the third time for the transgression of press laws. In any event, the purpose of the congress was straightforward. There were many youth organizations—Indonesia Moeda, Soeloeh Pemoeda Indonesia, Himpoenan Pemoeda Islam Indonesia, Jong Islamieten Bond and others. Soetomo wanted to call on all the youth groups to unite and work in the social field, such as fighting illiteracy, opium, and gambling. But he denied he planned to establish a communist youth front and said that Soenarman never mentioned it in his conversations with him.

Soetomo also explained his relations with other people who Surabaya PID officers had suspected of having Young PKI and communist youth connections. When Soetomo came to Surabaya to work as Partindo secretary in 1935, its office was located at Kramatgantoeng 62, where the *Indonesia Berdjoang* office was located. In those days Achmad Soemadhi was editor of *Indonesian Berdjoang*. Soetomo came to know him well because they met every day in the office. He also came to know Tamzil in 1936 in the *Indonesia Berdjoang* office. Partindo chairman Soediro brought him there and introduced him to Soetomo as a friend from PI (Perhimpoenan Indonesia). Soetomo came across him again when he was on the way to the Partindo/*Indonesia Berdjoango* office; Tamzil told him he would be happy to financially support the publication of a newspaper if he had a plan. Soetomo also met with Soekarni at the Partindo/*Indonesia Berdjoango* office in 1936. He came with Ngademo and introduced himself as someone from Indonesia Moeda. Soetomo also met Soedimoeljono often, because he was working for *Indonesia Berdjoango*. In 1938 the government decided to intern him in Surabaya, which presumably required him to stay in Surabaya and report to the police regularly.

Pamoedji survived the Dutch colonial regime, only to be arrested together with Amir Sjarifoeddin, Sajoeti Melik and others as part of the PKI underground in the early years of Japanese occupation. He was executed in 1944. It is not clear Soekarni joined Young PKI, even though Poeze says that Soekarni called on all Indonesian youth to form a popular front (*volksfront*) in June 1936 in the *Indonesia Moeda* journal, that shortly after its appearance, large scale house searches of Indonesia

Moeda executive committee members took place, and that "the link with the discovery of a revived PKI seems here quite obvious."[103] Adam Malik on the other hand says that, as we have seen, Soekarni was part of the Pari network. What we can be sure about is that he was active in Indonesia Moeda and Perpri circles and that he escaped arrest when the police clamped down on the Indonesia Moeda central leadership in 1936.

Born in 1916 in Blitar, Soekarni went to Dutch native elementary school and junior high school.[104] He had known Soekarno's family since he was small. After graduation of junior high school, he went to Bandung to join Soekarno as one of his cadres in Asrama Indonesia Merdeka along with S.K. Trimoerti. He joined Indonesia Moeda in 1930. He was also associated with Pergoeroean Ra'jat, and Darwis Tamin recalls that one day in 1935 Soekarni was furious at Soekarno because of the news in *Bintang Timur* that Soekarno asked Governor General de Jonge for pardon.[105] In any event, Soekarni came to know people teaching at the Pergoeroean Ra'jat, including Amir Sjarifoeddin, Soemanang, and

---

[103] Poeze, "PKI Muda 1936–1942," 164. Deputy Attorney General Marcella reported to the governor general on June 22, 1936, that in connection with the article published in the second issue of *Indonesia Moeda* that called on the youth to be the vanguards of the people, he instructed the police to arrest the writer and proposed de Jonge ban the Indonesia Moeda congress to be held in July in Batavia. He also noted "an intensified revolutionary action" among students belonging to PPPI, as evidenced in the article titled "Hendak kemana, stoeden Indonesia? [Where do you want to go, Indonesian students?]" published in the April 1934 issue of *Indonesia Raja* and argued that the *Indonesia Moeda* article was a clear evidence of the increasing influence of this action. He did not mention, however, who the writer was. Nor is there any evidence that the hoofdparket connected the *Indonesia Moeda* article to Young PKI. Since the ARD most likely learned the presence of a new underground communist organization sometime in July–mid-September 1937, it seems too early for the government to decide clamping down on IM because of its connection with the communist underground. See PG to GG, June 22, 1936, No. 1818/A.P., Mr. 603x/36, which is also included in Kwantes, *De Ontwikkeling, Aug. 1933–1942*, 343–4. Adviser for Native Affairs Gobee noted in his report to the governor general dated August 11, 1936 that Deputy Attorney General Marcella mentioned three PPPI activists, Soemanang, Mohammad Yamin, and Amir Sjarifoeddin, as advising Sarwoko, the chairman of the Indonesia Moeda congress organizing committee, but argued that it did not mean that the entire IM was under PPPI influence. Kwantes, *De Ontwikkeling, Aug. 1933–1942*, 348.

[104] Unless otherwise noted, the following account is based on Mustoffa, *Sukarni*.

[105] Mustoffa, *Sukarni*, 168.

Mohammad Yamin. Soekarni also taught elementary school children at the Pergoeroean Ra'jat school.

Indonesia Moeda (IM) was founded in September 1930 as a fusion of regionally based youth organizations. Then IM became radicalized and opened its membership to non-students and led to the election of Soekarni in the fifth congress held in Solo in December 1934. Soekarni served as IM chairman, except for the period he spent in jail from December 1934 to September 1935 because of his Perpri activity together with Pandoe Kartawigoena, Djokosoedjono, and others. Roeslan Abdoelgani, who led the IM Surabaya branch when Soekarni was IM chairman, says that he often came to Surabaya and brought "underground" brochures including Tan Malaka's writings with him. When the police clamped down on the IM leadership in 1936, because of his article calling for a popular front in its journal, most of its members, including Pandoe Kartawigoena, Jamal Ali, and Wardoyo were arrested. But Soekarni escaped the arrest.[106] In the absence of chairmanship Roelan Abdoelgani was elected chairman by referendum. Soekarni disagreed with Roeslan's moderate line, visited him in disguise in December 1936 and asked him, as he put it, to maintain IM as "radical-revolutionary." As Poeze says, Soekarni was no doubt influenced by the idea of popular front, CPN pamphlet Moeso and Soemadhi translated into Indonesian, Tan Makala's writings and Ngademo's talk about Young PKI, but no doubt he read all those writings and listened to all those talks as he pleased.[107] Shortly after he visited Roeslan Abdoelgani, he was gone to Kalimantan and stayed there as a fugitive till 1940 with the cover name of Maidi and working for the BPM topography service.[108]

As we have seen, Adam Malik learned about Soekarni when he met with Pandoe Kartawigoena in prison. He says both Soekarni and Pandoe were active in Perpri since its establishment in 1934 and that Perpri was under police surveillance because it had relations with Pari. There is no evidence, however, to support Adam Malik's statement about

---

[106] For an article published in *Indonesia Moeda*, the booklet *Baroto Yoedho* and some other writings published in PPPI journal *Indonesia Raja*, calling for the formation of a *volksfront* and organization of youth as "avant-gardes," see Chief of the ARD, Geheim rapport, Batavia-Centrum, 22 Juni 1936, Mr. 603x/36; Deputy PG to GG, June 22, 1936, Mr. 603x/36. This document is included in Kwantes, *De Ontwikkeling, Aug. 1933–1942*, 343–7.

[107] Mustoffa, *Sukarni*, 74–6; Poeze, "The PKI-Muda 1936–1942," 173–4.

[108] This reminds us of what Widarta did in the 1930s after he joined the illegal PKI.

the connection between Pari and Perpri and/or Soekarni's participation in Pari. More interesting and important to note is the way in which Adam Malik says Pandoe Kartawigoena described Soekarni: Soekarni was central, because "he carried instructions and messages from those who had been there for a long time, whether they had already gone to the place of exile or were still in hiding" and that "he had names and addresses he could trust, who could serve as links or as pillars to develop organizations in each region."[109] In short he was a major hub to connect the old and the young and those above and underground.

The ARD apparently did not know that Wikana was also part of the Young PKI underground. Adam Malik says that Young PKI was based in Surabaya under Pamoedji's leadership and let Wikana join the news agency Antara and that there were "quiet contests in the dark between communist followers of Moesso's, whether inside the country or outside, especially those who came from the Netherlands, competing with followers of Pari led by Tan Malaka."[110] This is doubtful, because "radical-revolutionary" activists were on the same terrain with the same enemy to fight, even if they were aware of the difference between the two lines represented by Tan Malaka and Moesso. And indeed, as Adam Malik reports, the news agency Antara did distribute both Pari's *Obor* and *Menara Mera* of the illegal PKI and Wikana, Adam Malik, and Pandoe Kartawigoena were arrested in distributing *Menara Merah.*

Born in Sumedang, West Java, in 1914, Wikana came from a priyayi family.[111] His father was Raden Haji Soelaiman, a migrant from Demak and one of his brothers, Wiranta, was exiled to Digul where, it is now remembered, he wrote a novel, *Antara Hidup dan Mati atau Boeron dari Boven Digul* (Between life and death or running away from Digul).[112] Wikana went to ELS (European primary school) and MULO.

[109] Mustoffa, *Sukarni*, 179–81.
[110] Ibid., 183.
[111] Unless otherwise noted, the following account is based on: Andry Anshari, "Wikana Tragedi Seorang Pahlawan," https://www.qureta.com/post/wikana; Bonnie Triyana, "[Sejarah Yang Dihilangkan] Mencari Wikana yang 'Dihilangkan', Menemukan Kembali Elan 'Revolusi Pemoeda.'" *Perpustakaan Online Genosida 1965–1966* online, Aug. 20, 2017, https://genosida1965wordpress.wordpress.com/2017/08/20/sejarah-yang-dihilangkan-mencari-wikana-yang-dihilangkan-menemukan-kembali-elan-revolusi-pemoeda/; Hendri F. Isnaeni, "Anak Menak Revolusioner," *Historia* online, Aug. 19, 2010, https://historia.id/ persona/articles/anak-menak-revolusioner-Dr1x6. All citations accessed August 10, 2018.
[112] See Wiranta, *Boeron dari Digoel* (Magelang: Tamboer Press, 2000).

He then joined Soekarno in Bandung and was trained by him as a Partindo cadre, along with Asmara Hadi, Soekarni, S.K. Trimoerti and others. In those days he often wrote for *Fikiran Rakjat*, a newspaper Soekarno edited, and was also active in Taman Siswa school.

He moved to Surabaya in 1935 where he worked as editor of *Pedoman Masjarakat Baroe*, a weekly, which Soetomo Djauhar Arifin started. He then moved to Batavia in 1938 and worked as editor of *Kebangoenan* (Awakening), a newspaper. In the meantime, Partindo was disbanded in November 1936 and Gerindo was established in May 1937. He was elected chairman of Gerindo Youth Front (Barisan Pemuda Gerakan Rakyat Indonesia) established in 1938 and sat on the editorial committee of political monthly, *Toedjoean Rakjat* (People's Destination), together with Amir Sjarifoeddin, Asmara Hadi, and Sipahoetar. In the same year he was also elected Gerindo second secretary. Soemarsono who came to know Wikana when he joined Gerindo says that he was seen as "senior" among Gerindo youth. In 1939, however, Wikana was replaced by Ismail Widjaja as chairman of Gerindo Youth Front, because A.M. Hanafi (Anak Marhaen Hanafi) says Wikana was forced to resign by A.K. Gani, Gerindo chairman.

Along with his Gerindo membership, Wikana was also active in the Young PKI underground. It is said that he was close to Widarta who was responsible for Young PKI activity in West Java. He worked as "agent" in circulating *Menara Merah* in West Java which Pamoedji edited and printed in Surabaya. It was a pocket-sized pamphlet.[113] It called for a popular front against fascist Germany and Japan. It also attacked Tan Malaka and Pari.[114] In June 1940 he was arrested for the circulation of *Menara Merah*, published in the name of Comite Partai Kommunist Indonesia, along with Amir Sjarifoeddin, Adam Malik and Pandoe Kartawigoena. When the war came to the Indies, he was rounded up together with some 500 activists and sent to Garut. He was released from the camp in Garut together with Soekarni, Adam Malik, Pandoe, S.K. Trimoerti and others, after the Dutch surrender in March 1942.[115]

---

[113] Anton Lucas, *One Soul One Struggle*, 55.

[114] Poeze, "The PKI-Muda 1936–1942," 169.

[115] Poeze, "The PKI-Muda 1936–1942," 170. Asmara Hadi, who was also arrested on December 10, 1941 and sent to Garut via Sukabumi, told his wife to inform Soemanang and Sartono of his arrest. But Soemanang himself was arrested and sent to Garut. Asmara Hadi, *Dibelakang Kawat Berdoeri* (Djakarta: Pemandangan, 2002), 9, 13.

All those mentioned above were under police surveillance. Some were arrested, imprisoned and sent to Digul, while some others were arrested and imprisoned but not sent to Digul, and yet others managed not to be arrested. But they were all well networked: they knew each other and, if not, they could get to know each other via their mutual friends. They attended and met with one another at Parindra and Gerindo meetings. Not a few played leadership roles in Gerindo and Parindra as well as in their youth, scout and other associations. Not a few also edited and/or contributed their writings to newspapers and journals. In a way serving as an editor-in-chief meant to take responsibility and to possibly go to jail for the transgression of press laws on behalf of other, anonymous writers. Many taught at private schools. Education consti-tuted an arena, a space in which they could be political, as long as they did not openly work for political parties and its affiliated organizations, while rallies and meetings, newspapers and journals, and parties and associations were intensely watched. They all understood that they were in the danger zone when they attended meetings, let alone gave speeches, wrote for or edited newspapers or played leadership roles in parties and their affiliated organizations.

EPILOGUE

In the wake of the 1926–27 communist revolts, the Dutch Indies government embarked on fashioning a new regime, a *beamtenstaat* of "peace and order." The government organized large-scale arrests, imprisonment, and internment to destroy the PKI: 13,000 were arrested, 4,500 imprisoned, and by the end of the 1930s more than 1,300 were interned in Boven Digul. A greatly expanded political policing apparatus with the ARD in the *hoofdparket* as its nerve center became the prime instrument of surveillance and control of the Indonesian nationalist movement.

In this new regime of order, Digul occupied a crucial place. One can see this in the code Soebakat invented for Pari's internal communication, in which "General Hospital" signified Digul, while "Hospital" meant prison and "Abu" the police. In Soebakat's imagined political landscape, the Indies was policed by "Abu," dotted with "Hospitals," and Digul was the terminal destination. To maximize the effect of police-prison-Digul on the people in order to encourage them to self-police and to remain within the limits set by the government, Dutch officials posted "no trespass" signs that warned against the PKI, SR (Sarekat Rakjat), VSTP, Comintern (Communist/Third International), Pan Pacific Trade Union Secretariat, Anti-Imperialist League, Moscow, and Tan Malaka and impressed an association between transgression and Boven Digul on the popular consciousness. The internment of SKBI, Pari and Young PKI leaders and activists in Digul as well as Iwa Koesoema Soemantri's internment in Banda Neira helped to serve this purpose.

Digul also offered an analogy for how the Indies government went about organizing the terrain in the Indies. There were two camps in Boven Digul: Tanah Merah (Red Land) and Tanah Tinggi (High Land). In Digul the population was classified into five categories: the willing-to-work who served as hamlet heads and clerks in the local government office, nurses in the hospital, workers for the malaria control service, clerks and coolies in the harbor warehouses, technical workers in the power center and the telephone office, and manual laborers in the fields, all government employed; the self-employed who made their living as fishermen, vegetable farmers, store and stall owners, barbers, bakers, tailors, shoemakers, photographers, private teachers; the relief-recipients or invalids, people with serious chronic illness such as incurable malaria and tuberculosis, mental disturbance and insanity caused in most cases by their long isolation, solitude, and homesickness; the naturalists who refused to perform any work for the government and received free food rations in natura from the government; and finally the recalcitrant who were interned in Tanah Tinggi, Digul's Digul, so to speak, whose insertion in Digul made life in Tanah Merah look and feel normal. In this scheme of things, normalcy appeared in relativity: and as such, the Indies appeared normal compared to Digul, just as Tanah Merah appeared normal compared to Tanah Tinggi.

The main human categories that informed the way that life was organized in Digul—the willing-to-work, the self-employed, the naturalists, and the recalcitrant—were isomorphic in structure with the way in which the Indies government mapped out its terrain: *volksleiders* (traditional leaders), bona fide/willing to cooperate/moderates, mala fide/not willing to cooperate/revolutionaries, and recalcitrant/extremists/those who were gone into the zone marked with "no trespass" signs. To put it in a different way, we can understand above-ground Indonesian nationalist politics, both cooperationist and non-cooperationist, only if we also look at the revolutionary underground, however phantom-like it may have been; we can understand Tanah Merah with its willing-to-work, self-employed, and naturalists only if we also look at Tanah Tinggi and its ghostlike recalcitrant inhabitants.

In the wake of the revolts, and when confronted with the rise of the PNI under Soekarno, Charles O. van der Plas identified two sets of "counter forces": on the one hand, autonomous administrations, princely courts of Java's Principalities, and priyayi—that is, those willing to work—and on the other hand, Moehammadijah, Nahdatoel Oelama, Taman Siswa, "local patriots" such as BO and Pasoendan, and Soetomo's Indonesian Study Club—that is, the self-employed. Furthermore, he identified two groups within the PNI leadership: "the group of engineers" represented by Soekarno and the group of lawyers Sartono and others represented. While van der Plas was well disposed towards Soetomo, he saw in Soekarno the hope, however delusionary it was, of becoming self-employed and guiding the movement onto a more constructive path. Governor General de Graeff's liberal policy depended on the hope van der Plas entertained, but it was torpedoed by the wild rumors of impending disturbances which forced the government to intervene in PNI.

With the arrival of de Jonge as de Graeff's successor, the government policy toward the movement shifted. Nonetheless, Governor General de Jonge, de Kat Angelino and others shared the view of the terrain that van der Plas had mapped out, and built their strategy based on that same perspective. The government reached a compromise with Taman Siswa, Moehammadijah, and other educational institutions to allow them to keep their own space without government intervention on the condition that they stay away from political parties and party politics, that they self-police their own teachers and students, and that they in effect remain de facto "counter forces" to contain revolutionary, non-cooperationist, mala fide, and of course recalcitrant forces. The government also opted on reliance on traditional leaders (adat chiefs) and autonomous administrations in Sumatra and other Islands, the princely courts of Java's Principalities, and the *priyayi*, or more precisely, the aristocrats-turned-bureaucratic elite as represented by the Regent of Bandung R.A.A. Wiranatakoesoemah. They no longer expected much of, and were sometimes outrightly hostile to, moderate, cooperationist, bona fide forces (such as Dr. Soetomo's PBI, BO, and Pasoendan) because these forces' rural actions tended to create space for "bad elements" and in any case could provoke unintended consequences.

The terrain thus hedged, the remaining space was left for nationalist politics and political policing. Governor General de Jonge and his lieutenants did not entertain any hope for constructive engagement with revolutionary, non-cooperationist and mala fide nationalist forces as well as the recalcitrant, but they were confident of the state's ability to police and control the space. The political policing measures the government under de Jonge adopted were meant for this purpose and amounted in effect to denying all the forms in which Indonesian popular politics manifested itself in a systematic way: policing, intervening in and banning rallies and meetings, policing and muzzling newspapers and journals, policing and destroying cells of trade unions as well as youth, women's and scout organizations, banning government employees from joining any nationalist parties or organizations, and interning a select number of party leaders to Digul. It was under these circumstances that Hurip's equation, police=politics, was satisfied.

Memories of the 1926–27 revolts haunted the Indies government, especially its senior officials, and drove the government policy toward the movement even further down the road in the direction it had chosen. Governor General de Graeff decided to clamp down on PNI and arrest Soekarno and others because of wild rumors of coming disturbances. Governor General de Jonge sought to handle the movement systematically because he was worried about disturbances at a time when the Indies was hit hard by the depression. The government considered anything that might threaten disturbances to be revolutionary. It was not that the government was not confident of its ability to police and control nationalist politics, both above and under-ground. The government was fully confident of the ability of its political policing apparatus. Still, the government was worried about "wild forces" which Soekarno unleashed in PNI and Partindo propaganda and hidden forces which rural action of even a bona fide cooperationist party and association could let loose in the countryside. In this sense Digul was there as a reminder that the Indies government was once failing to control wild forces.

In retrospect, the government's political policing strategy worked to maintain peace and order in the Indies in a time of crises emanating from world developments. But keeping external forces out of the Indies turned out to be beyond the power of the Netherlands and the Netherlands Indies. There is a memorable passage in Tan Malaka's *From Jail to Jail* about the sea he crossed to Java in 1942: "The real sea is both the quiet and calm sea and the raging, surging sea. To love the sea is to love it not only in its calmness but also when its waves seethe and heave."[1] The sea here has both literal and figurative meanings. He experienced both the calm and the raging sea in crossing the Sunda Straits. His crossing also signified the historical shift from a time of normalcy in which peace and order reigned supreme in the Indies and he himself was a fugitive to a time of war, Japanese occupation and revolution. It was the Japanese war machine that ultimately destroyed the Dutch power. The Indies political policing apparatus was of no use in the war. In anticipation of the Japanese military landing on Java, the attorney

---

[1] Tan Malaka, *From Jail to Jail*, Volume 2, 140. There were others who warned the Indies government that it should not be lulled by the semblance of peace and order for the long-term significance of Indonesian nationalism. Regent of Magelang R.A.A. Danoesoegondo said at the administrative conference held on August 18, 1936, that the government should not count too much on the present peace which can be the calm before the storm. Verslag conference van de gouverneur generaal met gouverneurs, residenten en regenten op Java, Aug. 18, 1936, Mr. 953x/36.

general ordered the destruction of all political intelligence records and the dispersal of its staff to the countryside.[2]

In retrospect, the government strategy worked to maintain peace and order in the Indies not because it destroyed the nationalist movement, but because of the combination of political strategy, political policing, and the creation of no-trespass and danger zones. The government marked a terrain with no-trespass signs and arrested, imprisoned and interned to Digul those recalcitrant who dared to venture into this no-trespass zone. The government interned Soekarno in Ende and Hatta and his people in Digul, and then Banda Neira, while policing and intervening in rallies and meetings, journals and newspapers, and parties and organizations to warn the natives that there was a danger zone and to effect a diffidence of the unknown, as Gobee said, among those leaders and activists.

But life in this time of normalcy produced its own share of boredom and restlessness, which ended up fueling the hope among Indonesians that the Indies could not and would not remain immune to the developing world crisis and there would be yet another opportunity to attain their dream of Indonesia Merdeka. No doubt the intense policing led many to stay away from the danger zone, let alone the terrain marked with no-trespass signs. Instead, these people worked in the fields of education and labor movements, the space the government allowed Indonesian educational institutions and labor unions to maintain on the condition of self-policing. The police also watched intensely the political leaders on the center stage of open rallies and newspapers and forced them to watch themselves and behave. Behind those people, however, activists—younger, less well-known, perhaps less mature, but certainly more impatient and daring—came to know each other as well as their seniors. They attended rallies and meetings, read and wrote journal and newspaper articles, and circulated pamphlets and booklets among themselves, while being fully aware that they too were under intense police surveillance. Their numbers were small, no more than a few thousand. The political intelligence, with its spies and informers, made sure these people would not grow into big hubs and together start developing any organization of significance. Nevertheless, they were there, and their ranks were constantly replenished by new entrants produced by the

---

[2] Frederick, *Visions and Heat*, 86.

expansion of the Indies educational system. It was these young activists, soon to be called *pemuda* (youth), who would emerge as the driving force for myriads of revolution in the early days of the revolution.[3] In retrospect it was hope, expressed in such terms as Republiek Indonesia (Tan Malaka), Indonesia Merdeka (Soekarno) and Indonesia Frij (Hatta) with different nuances and visions,[4] and perhaps more important, the energies pent up in this age of normalcy that drove not a few Indonesians—mainly urban, middle-class, and school-educated youth immortalized by the character of Hurip in Pramoedya Ananta Toer's story "Kemudian Lahirlah Dia (And then he was born)"—into politics.

What remains is for us to sketch briefly what happened to those who appeared on stage in this book. The life stories of those who were on center stage—Amir Sjarifoeddin, Mohammad Hatta, Sjahrir, Soekarno and Tan Malaka—are already well known, thanks to their biographies and memoirs. What follows then are potted biographies, alphabetically ordered, of other figures whom we looked at closely in this book.

With "a fine sense of how far one could go (which was farther than many politicians dared)," Ruth McVey recalls, Adam Malik was "a central figure in the formulation of Guided Democracy and a close counsellor of Soekarno." Having decided to go against Soekarno in the crisis that accompanied Suharto's extended coup in 1965–66 and which witnessed the killing of tens of thousands of communists and alleged communists, Adam Malik was "not thereby completely discredited in the eyes of his former colleagues." "For many of his old leftist associates he remained a patron: a leader who would still receive and could occasionally aid them, who could still speak their language, if only in private," and who still managed—"in spite of his evident wealth, Western admirers, and service to a counter-revolutionary regime"—to "embody what remained of the Generation of '45, the fading memories of a radical and optimistic youth."[5] He served as minister for trade and minister in charge of the implementation of the Guided Economy under Soekarno. After Suharto seized presidential power in March 1966, Adam

---

[3] Benedict R. O'G. Anderson, *Java in a Time of Revolution: Occupation and Resistance, 1944–1946* (New York: Cornell University Press, 1972).

[4] See Robert E. Elson, *The Idea of Indonesia: A History* (Cambridge: Cambridge University Press, 2008).

[5] Ruth T. McVey, "In Memoriam: Adam Malik (1917–1984)," *Indonesia*, no. 39 (1985): 145.

Malik took up the position of minister of foreign affairs and formed, together with Suharto and Sultan Hamengku Buwono IX, a triumvirate. He served as vice president from 1978 to 1983.

Alimin Prawirodirdjo returned to Indonesia from the Soviet Union via Yenan and Vietnam in July 1946. He was instrumental in reestablishing the PKI and led the Sajap Kiri (Left Wing) and the FDR (Front Demokrasi Rakjat, People's Democratic Front) in 1946–48. He survived the Madiun affair. He openly disagreed with Aidit when he seized the party leadership, but was still elected as a member of the new Politburo in 1951 as the "grand old man."[6] In 1956, he circulated a statement among PKI leaders in which he strongly denounced the party leadership for its "class collaboration" and for bringing it to the level of "an ordinary bourgeois party that no longer teaches class consciousness." When Donald Hindley met him in May 1960, he was "old, senile, ailing, lonely, no longer visited by Party members, and obsessed with what he considered to be the Party leadership's flouting of the elementary principles of Marxism-Leninism."[7]

Hendrikus Colijn ended his prime ministership in 1939. After the Dutch surrender to Germany, he disagreed strongly with the transfer of the Netherlands government in exile in London and wrote a booklet in which he called for accommodation, accepting the reality of German occupation. When the Nazis banned Dutch political parties, including the Anti-Revolutionary Party (ARP), however, he changed his position and rejected the Dutch Union. He was arrested in 1941 and taken to Berlin for his support for the resistance against Germany. In 1942 he and his wife were taken to a remote mountain hotel in Ilmenau in Thuringia, where he died in 1944.[8]

"A close friend of Sjahrir and a key figure linking various underground groups in Jakarta and the provinces,"[9] Djohan Sjahroeza worked in Hatta's office when Hatta came back from exile in 1942. He moved to Surabaya in 1943 where he worked for union organization at the

---

[6] Jacques Leclerc, "Aidit and the Problem of the Party in the Year 1950," *Kabar Seberang*, no. 17 (1986): 107.

[7] Donald Hindley, *The Communist Party of Indonesia 1951–1963* (Berkeley: University of California Press, 1966), 105.

[8] Enne Koops, "Hendrikus Colijn (1869–1944): Premier tijdens de crisisjaren 1930: 'Gaat u maar rustig slapen.'" Historiek (online), accessed Aug. 5, 2018, https://historiek.net/hendrikus-colijn-premier-crisisjaren/69176/.

[9] Anderson, *Java in a Time of Revolution*, 126.

BPM (Bataafse Petroleum Maatschappij), while remaining in close communication with Sjahrir as well as members of the underground PKI and other "radicals" outside Sjahrir's network such as Adam Malik, Chaeroel Saleh, Soekarni, Pandoe Kartawigoena and Maroeto Nitimihardjo.[10] He also led the Pathuk group in Yogyakarta, members of which included Sjam Kamaruzaman, who was to play a fatal role in the September 30, 1965, coup.[11] Djohan Sjahroeza came back to Jakarta in the early days of revolution, worked with Hatta and Sjahrir, and was instrumental in establishing an oil workers' union which served as the nucleus of SOBSI (Sentral Organisasi Buruh Seluruh Indonesia, Central All Indonesia Workers' Organization) established in 1946. He was also instrumental in founding Partai Rakyat Sosialis (Paras, Socialist People's Party), in its fusion with Amir Sjarifoeddin's Partai Sosialis Indonesia (Parsi, Indonesian Socialist Party) to create Partai Sosialis (PS, Socialist Party), and in its break-up and the formation of PSI (Partai Sosialis Indonesia, Indonesian Socialist Party).[12]

Andries Cornelis Dirk de Graeff went back to the Netherlands after he stepped down as governor general in 1931. He served as minister of foreign affairs in 1933–37 in the second and third Colijn cabinet and tried to steer the Netherlands toward the neutrality policy when the League of Nations failed, the Versailles treaty system collapsed, and Nazi Germany embarked on rearmament.[13]

Djamaloeddin Ibrahim, suffering from tuberculosis, was kept in prison in Cipinang. Because the doctor treating him refused to have him sent to Digul, the government transferred him to the Cisarawa hospital in Bogor, where he died, still in detention, shortly before the Japanese invasion.[14]

---

[10] Mrazek, *Sjahrir: Politics and Exile in Indonesia* (Ithaca, NY: Southeast Asia Program, Cornell University, 1994), 242.

[11] John Rosa, *Pretext for Mass Murder: The September 30th Movement and Suharto's Coup D'etat in Indonesia* (Madison: University of Wisconsin Press, 2006), 122.

[12] J.D. Legge, *Intellectuals and Nationalism in Indonesia: A Study of the Following Recruited by Sutan Sjahrir in Occupation Jakarta* (Ithaca, NY: Cornell Modern Indonesia Project, 1988), 63–5; William H. Frederick, *Visions and Heat: The Making of the Indonesian Revolution* (Athens: Ohio University Press, 1989), 160.

[13] C. Fasseur, "Graeff, jhr. Andries Cornelis Dirk de (1872–1957)," in *Biografisch Woordenboek van Nederland*, Huygens ING, last modified Nov. 12, 2013, accessed, http://resources.huygens.knaw.nl/bwn1880-2000/lemmata/bwn2/graeff.

[14] Audrey Kahin, *Rebellion to Integration: West Sumatra and the Indonesian Polity* (Amsterdam: Amsterdam University Press, 1999), 67.

Iwa Koesoema Soemantri moved from Banda Neira to Makassar in February 1941 and returned to Java in March 1942. He was associated closely with his former PI friends and younger activists such as Ahmad Soebardjo, Soekarni, and Wikana in the Asrama Indonesia Merdeka (Free Indonesia Asrama) sponsored by Admiral Tadashi Maeda in the Naval Liaison Office during the war. He served as minister of social affairs in the first cabinet of the Republic in August–November 1945. He was instrumental in the establishment of Partai Buruh Indonesia (Indonesian Labor Party) in which he served as an executive member in 1946. Allied with Tan Malaka in 1946, he was imprisoned in connection with the July 3, 1946, affair from 1946 to 1948. He joined Partai Murba in 1949. He served as minister of defense in Ali Sastroamidjojo cabinet in 1953–55, minister of higher education and science in 1961–62 and ministerial aide to President Soekarno in 1962–66.[15]

B.C. de Jonge went back to the Netherlands and retired to his Dennenoord estate in Oosterbeek after he stepped down from the governor general in 1936. In 1940 when the Netherlands was under German occupation, he was approached by Jan Edward de Quay to lead as a "strong man" the Dutch Union, which called for partial collaboration with the Germans. De Jonge apparently declined the offer.

A.D.A. de Kat Angelino (1891–1969) spent his war years in the Netherlands. He was appointed a member of the Netherlands Academy of Sciences in 1942. He served as a Dutch delegate to the Far Eastern Commission in 1945–48. After the Linggarjati agreement he understood that restoring the Dutch control over Indonesia was hopeless and therefore worked with G.A. Ph. Weyer, the former chairman of the Indies entrepreneurs' association, to develop a plan, ultimately unsuccessful as it turned out, to protect Dutch investments in Indonesia with the participation of British and American business in the Republic as a leverage. After the publication of *Balans van Beleid* (Balance of Policy) in 1961 in which he contributed a chapter, he established, together with J.W. Meyer Ranneft and G.A. Ph. Weyer, de Commissie voor bronnenpublicatie betreffende de geschiedenis van Nederlandsch-Indië 1900–1942 van het Historisch Genootschap (Commission for source

---

[15] Anderson, *Java in a Time of Revolution*, passim; Tan Malaka, *From Jail to Jail*, 3: 316; Iwa Kusuma Sumantri, *Indonesia Minzokushugi no Genryu*, passim.

publication concerning the history of the Netherlands Indies 1900–42 of the Historical Society), from the publications of which we still benefit.[16]

Matu Mona, a pseudonym of Hasbullah Parinduri, is now remembered as a writer. When the Dutch surrendered to the Japanese in 1942, he was in Sukamiskin prison for the transgression of press laws for publishing an article in *Tjendrawasih* under his editorship. In the war years he was associated with theatrical groups in Jakarta and periodically wrote for *Pandji Poestaka*. He served as spokesman for Surakarta head-quartered Division XII in 1946 and fought as a guerrilla in East Java in 1948. In post-independence Indonesia, he worked as editor-in-chief of Banda Aceh daily *Tegas* (1950–53) and weekly *Penyebar* in Medan (1954–59), and deputy editor-in-chief of journal *Selecta* in Jakarta (1960–87).[17]

Moesso returned to Indonesia in August 1948. Immediately acknowledged as "the old master (*de oude heer*)" as Jacque Leclerc put it, he drew up a resolution calling for the reorganization of the communist forces into a unitary party.[18] The plenary meeting of the PKI central committee adopted the resolution in the same month and the new politburo of the enlarged PKI was announced in September. Shortly thereafter, however, the Madiun affair began. The government moved against the rebel forces swiftly, capturing Madiun in two weeks and crushing the rebellion in two months. Moesso was killed in a skirmish at the end of October 1948.[19]

Jahja Nasoetion came back from Digul to Java via Australia in February 1946. Jahya, together with A.J. Patti, established Partai Kebangsaan Indonesia (Indonesian National Party) in Mackay, Queensland. In Australia he was also engaged to Chamsinah Ali Dachlan, the daughter of another Digulist Mohammad Amin (a Bantenese who survived Digul most likely as a "naturalist" given the fact that he named another daughter of his Siti Natura), and married her in September

---

[16] P.J. Drooglever, "Kat Angelino, Arnold Dirk Adriaan de (1891–1969)," in *Biografisch Woordenboek van Nederland*, Huygens ING, last modified Nov. 12, 2013, http://resources.huygens.knaw.nl/bwn1880-2000/lemmata/bwn3/kat.

[17] Soebagijo, *Jagad Wartawan Indonesia* (Jakarta: Gunung Agung, 1981), 222–6. Soebagijo says *matumona* means "start" or "have just started" in the language of South Tapanuli.

[18] Leclerc, "Aidit and the Problem of the Party," 115.

[19] Ibid.; Hindley, *The Communist Party of Indonesia*.

1945, keeping his pledge that he would marry her when Indonesia be-
came Independent. After their return to Indonesia, Jahja joined Partai
Murba. Adam Malik, it seems, took care of him and his family well.
Jahja died in 1962.[20]

Charles O. van der Plas was appointed to the Council of the
Netherlands Indies, the highest advisory body in the Dutch Indies in
mid-1941 by Governor General Tjarda van Starkenborgh Stachouwer.
He was ordered by the governor general a few weeks before the Dutch
surrender on March 8, 1941 to make arrangements for the underground
organization the Dutch might leave behind and contacted Amir
Sjarifoeddin. Van der Plas left the Indies for Australia on March 6,
1942. He spent his war years in Australia, where a Netherlands Indies
government-in-exile was established. At the end of the war, he represented the Netherlands Indies government in Mountbatten's Southeast
Asia Command and was the first senior Dutch official to return to Java
with Allied forces. Although he was forced to resign in December 1945
as Council of the Netherlands Indies member and as acting director
of the department of internal administration for his statement about
the government's readiness to take part in preliminary discussions with
Republican leaders, he was retained as a special adviser to Van Mook
and eventually in 1947 was appointed commissioner for administrative
affairs of East Java and served in this capacity until December 1949.
In 1951–52 he advised the Food and Agricultural Organization (FAO)
on its operations in Saudi Arabia, worked on the agricultural project in
Greece in 1956–58 and Laos in 1960–61. He also worked in Gambia
from 1954, promoting a community development project for small
farmers for more than 10 years. He retired from the FAO at the age
of 70 in 1961, but kept working in Gambia with the support of the
Dutch Organization for International Assistance (NOVIB) until 1974.
He died in 1977.[21]

Sajoeti Melik or Mohamad Ibnu Sayuti spent a good part of his
Japanese and revolutionary years in prison. He was imprisoned in 1942–
43 by the Japanese occupation authorities, but released at Soekarno's

---

[20] Chamsinah Ali Dachlan, "15 Tahun Aku Hidup di Pengasingan Digul," *Femina* 23,
no. 32 (Aug. 1995).
[21] Frederick, "The Man Who Knew Too Much: Ch. O. van der Plas and the Future
of Indonesia, 1927–1950," in *Imperial Policy and Southeast Asian Nationalism, 1930–
1957*, ed. Hans Antlov and Stein Tonnesson (London: Routledge, 1995).

request and worked as the latter's secretary, in which capacity he typed the text of the proclamation of Indonesian independence on August 17, 1945. He was imprisoned by the Republic in 1946–48 in connection with the July 3, 1946, affair, during which time he typed part of Tan Malaka's manuscript of *From Prison to Prison* in prison on Tan Malaka's behalf.[22] He was imprisoned again in 1948–49 by the Dutch. Though he supported Soekarno, he went against Nasakom (nationalism, religion and communism), argued that Soekarno's Marhaenism was different from Marxism-Leninism, and was attacked by PKI in the final years of Soekarno's Guided Democracy. He served as a Golkar (Golongan Karya) member of the DPR/MPR in 1971–81.

Soekarni worked in the news agency Antara and the Domei news agency during the occupation. He was also in charge of Asrama Angkatan Baru Indonesia (Asrama of the New Generation of Indonesia) and was one of the organizers of the plan to abduct Soekarno and Hatta to force them to declare independence. Initially known to be close to Sjahrir, he joined Tan Malaka by the end of 1945, worked as one of the organizers of the Persatuan Perjuangan congress and was imprisoned by the Republic from March 1946 to September 1948 in connection with the July 3, 1946 affair. He served as president of Partai Murba from its foundation in 1948 to his death in 1971. As the PKI rose to power, Partai Murba was suspended in 1965 and he was imprisoned. Released from prison in October 1966, he rehabilitated the party and was appointed to the Supreme Advisory Committee in 1967.[23]

Soemanang worked as an editor of *Pemandangan/Pembangoenan* (View/Building) and *Asia Raja* (Great Asia) and as a senior official in the general affairs bureau of Jawa Hokokai (Java Service Association) during the Japanese occupation. In the early days of the revolution he published newspaper *Nasional* and weekly *Revue Politik* in Yogyakarta. He participated in the establishment of Partai Nasional Indonesia (PNI) in January 1946. He served as minister for economic affairs in the Wilopo cabinet in 1952–53. Herbert Feith wrote in the 1950s that Soemanang as minister for economic affairs was known to brush off "requests for privileges" which came either from PNI or individual PNI

---

[22] Arief Priyadi, *Wawancara dengan Sayuti Melik* (Jakarta: CSIS, 1986), 274. His wife, S.K. Trimoerti, was minister of labor then, and she sent him a typewriter.
[23] Tan Malaka, *From Jail to Jail*, 3: 349; Anderson, *Java in a Time of Revolution*, passim.

businessmen. In the years thereafter, he served as parliamentary member and director at the IMF to represent Indonesia.[24]

Soetomo Djauhar Arifin (1916–59) is now remembered as a poet, dramatist, storyteller, and writer. He worked in the cultural affairs office during the occupation and in the ministry of information after independence until his death. His writings include poems, drama, short stories and a novel (*Andang Teruna* [Cadets], 1941).[25]

Djamaloedin Tamin was transferred from Digul to Australia in 1943. After he learned the proclamation of Indonesian independence, he established Komite Indonesia Merdeka (Free Indonesia Committee) in September 1945 and became its chairman. He came back to Jakarta on March 13, 1946, left for Solo on March 20 to join Tan Malaka, and was arrested on March 31 there, four days after Tan Malaka himself was arrested in Madiun. He saw Tan Malaka under house arrest, and Tan Malaka advised him to join the PKI then being reestablished by Sardjono and other ex-Digulists. But Tamin's attempt to join the party was rejected by Sardjono and others out of hand. He became an active member of Partai Murba and founded Pusaka Murba (Murba's Heirlooms) in Jakarta in 1977. He died in Jakarta in 1977.[26]

Tan Malaka's life in his final three years from 1945 to 1949 is well-known. But what Ruth McVey has to say about him is worth quoting for its deeper insights:

> Tan Malaka seems to have been a revolutionary exile whose train to the Finland Station never departed, even when he found himself in the midst of revolt. Perhaps, by the time of the independence proclamation, his hard life had left him played out as well as suspicious. But as a symbol of uncompromising struggle for independence, he was powerful, and his significance lay not so much in what he did as what other political leaders thought he might do, or what might be done in his name. He was jailed in March 1946, not for his actions but to get him out of the way. In July he was asserted to have mentored an attempted coup, even though he was in prison at the time

---

[24] Herbert Feith, *The Wilopo Cabinet, 1952–1953: A Turning Point in Post-Revolutionary Indonesia* (1958, Jakarta: Equinox, 2009), 216; I.N. Soebagijo, *Sumanang, Sebuah Biografi* (Jakarta: TP Gunung Agung, 1980).

[25] Soetomo Djauhar Arifin, *Andang Teruna* [Cadets] (Jakarta: Balai Pustaka, 1941). http://ensiklopedia.kemdikbud.go.id/sastra/artikel/Soetomo_Djauhar_Arifin

[26] Tamin, *Sedjarah PKI*; Tan Malaka, *From Jail to Jail*, 3: 355–6. Jarvis, "Introduction," in Tan Malaka, *From Jail to Jail*, 1: c–ci.

Epilogue 303

and had no evident link to it ... He remained unnudged but also unreleased, until the outbreak of the Madiun Affair in September 1948 led the republic's leaders to consider that he might be useful in their hour of need to split the ranks of the PKI. But once the Dutch had overrun the republic and captured Sukarno and Hatta, the possibility arose that Tan Malaka, who was underground with some TNI troops and guerrillas in the Kediri area, might yet assert leadership of the revolution. Order was therefore given for his death, thus finally settling the matter of his potential threat or usefulness.[27]

S.K. Trimoerti worked for Putera (Pusat Tenaga Rakjat, Center of People's Strength) and Jawa Hokokai at Soekarno's request in the war years and served as minister of labor in the Amir Sjarifoeddin cabinet in 1947–48. She was also on the executive committee of the Labor Party (Partai Buruh). She went back to study economics at the University of Indonesia in the mid-1950s and declined Soekarno's offer to serve as minister for social affairs in 1959. She was active in the women's movement, joining in the establishment of Gerwis, a women's movement, in 1950, but left the movement in 1965, long after it was transformed into Gerwani, Indonesian Women's Movement, under PKI. In the 1970s she served on Dewan Nasional (National Council) and Dewan Perancang Nasional (National Planning Council). She was part of Petisi 50 in 1980 to protest Suharto's misuse of Pancasila. In her final years she was steeped in mysticism. She died in 2008.[28]

Wikana joined Ahmad Soebardjo in the Naval Liaison Office and the Asrama Indonesia Merdeka during the Japanese occupation. He was involved in the kidnapping of Soekarno and Hatta on the eve of the proclamation of independence, and emerged as a major figure of the '45 Generation. He was a founding member of Pesindo (Pemuda Sosialis Indonesia, Socialist Youth of Indonesia) together with Chaeroel Saleh and Soekarni and served as minister of youth affairs in the Sjahrir cabinet in 1946–48. In the PKI under Aidit, however, he was marginalized as one of the "old" PKI leaders who openly disagreed with the new leadership on matters of party strategy in 1950 and the first to be publicly disciplined. In the third Pesindo congress in November 1950, he was not reelected to the executive committee and in December 29

---

[27] Ruth McVey, review of "Harry A. Poeze, *Verguisd en vergeten: Tan Malaka, de linkse beweging en de Indonesiische Revolutie, 1945–1949*," *Indonesia*, no. 86 (2008): 171–4.
[28] Soebagijo, *Jagat Wartawan*, 397–402; Anderson, *Java in a Time of Revolution*, 454.

he was made to resign from a study group organized by Partai Murba which the PKI leadership denounced as Trotskyites. He was dropped from the PKI central committee at the fifth national congress in 1954, even though he was returned to it in 1959. He was in China when the September 30 movement took place on October 1, 1965. He came back home, nonetheless, and about a year later in 1966 he was arrested and never returned.[29]

Widarta emerged as the leader of the underground PKI during the Japanese occupation and is said to have recruited Aidit dan Lukman into the party. In the early days of the revolution, he was sent by Amir Sjarifoeddin as his envoy to the three regions (tiga daerah) on Java's north coast and played a crucial role in the social revolution there. But he opposed the government policy of "diplomasi" under Sjahrir and Amir Sjarifoeddin and openly demanded that the party debate the issue. He was kidnapped by the party, sentenced to death at the party court chaired by Amir Sjarifoeddin, and executed in 1947.[30]

Djaoes (Djaos, Dawood) survived Digul. He came back to Java after Tan Malaka was arrested in 1946 but never saw him again. Helen Jarvis, who interviewed him in 1980, writes that he lived in Tanggerang, was active in the associations with prewar activists, but had fading memory.[31]

Kandoor St. Rangkayo Basa also survived Digul and worked as a staff member of the Hatta cabinet.[32]

Djokosoedjono and Ahmad Soemadhi emerged as members of the general secretariat of the PKI unified under Moesso's leadership in 1948.[33]

Soenarman was also back in Java in 1946, but we do not know what happened to him after his return.[34]

Pandoe Kartawigoena was associated with Barisan Buruh (Workers' Front) after the proclamation of independence and was imprisoned in

[29] Anderson, *Java in a Time of Revolution*, 455–6; Tan Malaka, *From Jail to Jail*, 3: 359–60, Hindley, *The Communist Party of Indonesia*, 24–5, 64–5, 104; Leclerc, "Aidit and the Problem of the Party"; Rosa, *Pretext for Mass Murder*, 118–22.
[30] Anton Lucas, *One Soul One Struggle* (Melbourne: Centre of Southeast Asian Studies, Monash University, 1986), passim.
[31] Tan Malaka, *From Jail to Jail*, 3: 306.
[32] Personal communication with Audrey Kahin, Mar. 3, 2020.
[33] Harry A. Poeze, *Verguisd en Vergeten: Tan Malaka, de linkse beweging en de Indonesische Revolutie, 1945–1949* (Leiden: KITLV Press, 2007), 2: 1113.
[34] Ibid., 221.

1946–48 in connection with the July 3, 1946 affair. He joined Partai Murba and remained close to Adam Malik.[35]

Abdul Hamid Siregar survived Digul and joined Akoma (Angkatan Komunis Muda, Young Communist Force) in the revolutionary years.[36]

Mohamad Arief Siregar and Malelo Siregar came back to Indonesia with Djamaloedin Tamin and joined Partai Murba.

What happened to W.P. Hillen, A.E. van der Lely, B.R. van der Most, Amir Hamzah Siregar, Ali Basa Siregar, Soedimoeljono, Tjipto Suhardjo, and M. Visbeen remains to be told.

---

[35] Tan Malaka, *From Jail to Jail*, 3: 327.

[36] Poeze says that Abdul Hamid Siregar was arrested together with Sarosan and S.K. Trimurti in 1947 in connection with their action in Akoma (which was led by Ibnu Parna) against the PKI-dominated Dewan Perdjuanganand Lasjkar Rakjat in Magelang. Poeze, *Verguisd en Vergeten*, 2: 793.

BIBLIOGRAPHY

The Bibliography lists the sources referred to explicitly in the book.

Archives

The main collection used was that of the former Ministry of the Colonies, held in the Algemeene Rijksarchief, The Hague. Unless otherwise specified, documents identified as Mr. (*mailrapport* or mail report) and Vb. (*verbaar*) are from this collection. Other archives consulted were the collection of the Royal Institute for the Tropics, Amsterdam and the Arsip Nasional, Republic of Indonesia, Jakarta.

Official Publications

Handelingen Volksraad. 1928.

Indisch Verslag 1931: II. Statistisch Jaaroverzicht van Nederlandsch-Indie over het Jaar 1930. Batavia: Landsdrukkerij, 1931.

Mededeelingen der Regeering omtrent Enkele Onderwerpen van Algemeen Belang. Weltevreden: Landsdrukkerij, 1928.

Onderzoek naar De Mindere Welvaart der Inlandsche Bevolking op Java en Madoera: VIIIb. Overzicht van de Uitkomsten der Gewestelijke Onderzoekingen naar 't Recht en de Politie en daaruit gemaakte Gevolgtrekkingen. Deel II. Slotbeschouwingen. Batavia: Ruygrok, 1912.

Periodicals

De Indische Gids.

De Nederlandsch-Indische Politiegids, 1932–34.

Regeeringsalmanak, 1919–41.

Vereeniging van Hoogere Politie-Ambtenaren, 1916–1936: Jubileum-Nummer van de Nederlandsch-Indische Politiegids bij Gelegenheid van het 20 Jarig Bestaan van de Vereeniging. Batavia: n.p., 1936.

Printed Works, Theses and Other Sources

Abeyasekere, Susan. *One Hand Clapping: Indonesian Nationalists and the Dutch, 1939–1942*. Monash Papers on Southeast Asia, No. 5. Clayton, Victoria: Centre of Southeast Asian Studies, Monash University, 1976.

———. "Partai Indonesia Raja, 1936–42: A Study in Cooperative Nationalism." *Journal of Southeast Asian Studies* 3, no. 2 (1972): 262–76.

———. "Relations between the Indonesian Cooperating Nationalists and the Dutch, 1935–1942." PhD dissertation, Monash University, 1972.

———. "The Soetardjo Petition." *Indonesia*, no. 15 (April 1973): 81–107.

Adam Malik. *Mengabdi Republik, Jilid 1: Adam Dari Andalas*. Jakarta: Gunung Agung, 1979.

Alfian. *Muhammadiyah: The Political Behavior of a Muslim Modernist Organization under Dutch Colonialism*. Yogyakarta: Gadjah Mada University Press, 1989.

Anderson, Benedict R. O'G. *Imagined Communities: Reflections on the Origin and Spread of Nationalism*. London: Verso, 1983.

———. *Java in a Time of Revolution: Occupation and Resistance, 1944–1946*. New York: Cornell University Press, 1972.

———. *The Spectre of Comparisons: Nationalism, Southeast Asia and the World*. London: Verso, 1998.

Anderson, Benedict R. O'G., ed. *Violence and the State in Suharto's Indonesia*. Ithaca, NY: Southeast Asia Program, Cornell University, 2001.

Anderson, David M., and David Killingray, eds. *Policing and Decolonisation: Politics, Nationalism and the Police, 1917–65*. Manchester: Manchester University Press, 1992.

Anshari, Andry. "'Kalau Harus Mati, Saya Pilih Mati Di Tanah Air' – Wikana." 2015. http://hmifisipusu82.blogspot.com/2015/12/wikana-tragedi-seorang-pahlawan.html, accessed on August 10, 2018.

Antlov, Hans, and Stein Tonnesson, eds. *Imperial Policy and Southeast Asian Nationalism, 1930–1957*. London: Routledge, 1995.

Arendt, Hannah. *The Origins of Totalitarianism*. New edition. New York: Harvest/HBJ, 1975.

Arnold, David. "Police Power and the Demise of British Rule in India, 1930–47." In *Policing and Decolonisation: Politics, Nationalism and the Police, 1917–65*, ed. David M. Anderson and David Killingray. Manchester: Manchester University Press, 1992.

Arnold, Eric A. Jr. *Fouche, Napoleon, and the General Police*. Washington, DC: University Press of America, 1979.

Ban, Kah Choon. *Absent History: The Untold Story of Special Branch Operations in Singapore 1915–1942*. Singapore: Raffles, 2001.

Barker, Joshua. "State of Fear: Controlling the Criminal Contagion in Suharto's New Order." In *Violence and the State in Suharto's Indonesia*, ed. Benedict

R. O'G. Anderson, 20–53. Ithaca, NY: Southeast Asia Program, Cornell University, 2001.

Benda, Harry. *The Crescent and the Rising Sun: Indonesian Islam under the Japanese Occupation, 1942–1945.* The Hague: W. van Hoeve, 1958.

———. "The Pattern of Administrative Reforms in the Closing Years of Dutch Rule in Indonesia." *Journal of Asian Studies* 25, no. 4 (1966): 589–605.

Benda, Harry J., and Ruth T. McVey, eds. *The Communist Uprisings of 1926–1927 in Indonesia: Key Documents.* Modern Indonesia Project, Translation Series. Ithaca, NY: Southeast Asia Program, Cornell University, 1960.

Bloembergen, Marieke. "The Dirty Work of Empire: Modern Policing and Public Order in Surabaya, 1911–1919." *Indonesia* 83 (2007): 119–50.

———. *De Geschiedenis van de Politie in Nederlands-Indie.* Amsterdam: University of Amsterdam Press, 2009.

———. "The Perfect Policeman: Colonial Policing, Modernity, and Conscience on Sumatra's West Coast in the Early 1930s." *Indonesia* 91 (2011): 165–91.

———. *Polisi zaman Hindia-Belanda: Dari kepedulian dan ketakutan.* Translated by Tristam P. Moeliono, Anna Wardhana, Nicolette P.R. Moeliono and Tita Soeprapto Mangoensadjito. Jakarta: Penerbit buku Kompas, KITLV, 2011.

Blumberger, J.Th. Petrus. *De Nationalistische Beweging in Nederlandsch-Indie.* Haarlem: H.D. Tjeenk Willink & Zoon, 1931.

Boekhoudt, W. *Rapport Reorganisatie van het Politiewezen op Java en Madoera (Uitgezonderd de Vostenlanden, de Particuliere Landerijen en de Hoofdplaatsen Batavia, Semarang en Soerabaja), 1906–07.* Batavia: Landsdrukkerij, 1908.

Bruckenhaus, Daniel. *Policing Transnational Protest: Liberal Imperialism and the Surveillance of Anticolonialists in Europe, 1905–1945.* New York: Oxford University Press, 2017.

Castles, Lance. *Religion, Politics and Economic Behavior in Java: The Kudus Cigarette Industry.* Cultural Report Series No. 15. New Haven, CT: Southeast Asia Studies, Yale University, 1967.

Centraal Kantoor voor de Statistiek in Nederlandsch-Indie. *Statistisch Jaaroverzicht van Nederlandsch-Indie: Jaargang 1925.* Weltevreden: Landsdrukkerij, 1926.

———. *Statistisch Jaaroverzicht van Nederlandsch-Indie: Jaargang 1926.* Weltevreden: Landsdrukkerij, 1927.

———. *Statistisch Jaaroverzicht van Nederlandsch-Indie: Jaargang 1927.* Weltevreden: Landsdrukkerij, 1928.

Cheah, Boon Kheng. *From PKI to the Comintern, 1924–1941: The Apprenticeship of the Malayan Communist Party.* Ithaca, NY: Southeast Asia Program, Cornell University, 1992.

Cheesman, Nick. *Opposing the Rule of Law: How Myanmar's Courts Make Law and Order.* Cambridge: Cambridge University Press, 2015.

Colombijn, Freek, and J. Thomas Lindblad. *Roots of Violence in Indonesia: Contemporary Violence in Historical Perspective.* Singapore: Institute of Southeast Asian Studies, 2002.

Comber, Leon. *Malaya's Secret Police 1945–60: The Role of the Special Branch in the Malayan Emergency.* Clayton, Victoria: Monash Asia Institute; Singapore: Institute of Southeast Asian Studies, 2008.

Couperus, Louis. *De Stille Kracht.* 1900. Amsterdam: L.J. Veen, 1989.

Cribb, Robert. *Gangsters and Revolutionaries: The Jakarta People's Militia and the Indonesian Revolution 1945–1949.* 1991. Jakarta: Equinox Publishing, 2009.

Cribb, Robert, and Audrey Kahin. *Historical Dictionary of Indonesia.* Second edition. Lanham, MD: The Scarecrow Press, 2004.

Dachlan, Chamsinah Ali. "15 Tahun Aku Hidup di Pengasingan Digul." *Femina* 32, issue 23 (1995): 10–4.

Dahm, Bernhard. *Sukarno and the Struggle for Indonesian Independence.* Ithaca, NY: Cornell University Press, 1969.

Darwin, John. *The Empire Project: The Rise and Fall of the British World-System 1830–1870.* Cambridge: Cambridge University Press, 2011.

Dekker, P. *De Politie in Nederlandsch-Indie: Hare Beknopte Geschiedenis, Haar Taak, Bevoedheid, Organisatie en Optreden.* Soekaboemi: Drukkerij "Insulinde," Tweede Druk, 1938.

Doel, H.W. van den. *De Stille Macht: Het Europese binnenlands bestuur op Java en Madoera, 1808–1942.* Leiden: Uitgeverij Bert Bakker, 1994.

Djojoprajitno, Sudijono. *PKI-SIBAR contra Tan Malaka.* Jakarta: Jajasan Massa, 1962.

Drewes, G.W.J. "Balai Pustaka and its Antecedents." In *Papers on Indonesian Languages and Literature,* ed. in Nigel Phillips and Khaidir Anwar, 97–104. London: Indonesian Etymological Project, SOAS, University of London, 1981.

Elson, Robert E. *Javanese Peasants and the Colonial Sugar Industry: Impact and Change in an East Java Residency, 1830–1940.* Singapore: Oxford University Press, 1984.

———. *The Idea of Indonesia: A History.* Cambridge: Cambridge University Press, 2008.

Ensering, Else. "Afdeeling B of Sarekat Islam: A Rebellious Islamic Movement." In *Conversion, Competition and Conflict : Essays on the Role of Religion in Asia,* ed. Dick Kooiman, Otto van den Muijzenberg and Peter van der Veer, 99–122. Amsterdam: Free University Press, 1984.

Fasseur, C. "Nederland en het Indonesische nationalism: de balans nog eens opgemaakt." *Bijdragen en medeelingen betreffende de geschiedenis der Nederlanden* 99, no. 1 (1984): 21–44.

Federspiel, Howard M. "The Muhammadijah: A Study of an Orthodox Islamic Movement in Indonesia." *Indonesia,* no. 10 (October 1970): 57–79.

310

Feith, Herbert. *The Wilopo Cabinet, 1952–1953: A Turning Point in Post-Revolutionary Indonesia*. 1958. Jakarta: Equinox, 2009.

Foster, Anne L. *Projections of Power: The United States and Europe in Colonial Southeast Asia, 1919–1941*. Durham, NC: Duke University Press, 2010.

Foucault, Michel. "Security, Territory, and Population." In *Ethics: Subjectivity and Truth: The Essential Works of Michel Foucault 1954–1984*, volume 1, ed. Paul Rabinow, trans. Robert Hurley et al., 67–72. London: Allen Lane, 1997.

Foulcher, Keith R. *'Pujangga Baru': Literature and Nationalism in Indonesia 1933–1942*. Asian Studies Monograph No. 2. Adelaide: Flinders University of South Australia, 1980.

Frederick, William H. "The Man Who Knew Too Much: Ch. O. van der Plas and the Future of Indonesia, 1927–1950." In *Imperial Policy and Southeast Asian Nationalism, 1930–1957*, ed. Hans Antlov and Stein Tonnesson, 34–62. London: Routledge, 1995.

———. *Visions and Heat: The Making of the Indonesian Revolution*. Athens: Ohio University Press, 1989.

Friend, Theodore. *The Blue-Eyed Enemy: Japan against the West in Java and Luzon, 1942–1945*. Princeton: Princeton University Press, 1988.

Furnivall, J.S. *Netherlands India: A Study of Plural Economy*. First published 1939. Digital reprint, Cambridge: Cambridge University Press, 2010.

Goscha, Christopher E. *Thailand and the Southeast Asian Networks of the Vietnamese Revolution, 1885–1954*. Nordic Institute of Asian Studies monograph series, 79. Richmond, UK: Curzon, 1999.

———. *Vietnam: A New History*. New York: Basic Books, 2016.

Gramsci, Antonio. *Selections from the Prison Notebooks of Antonio Gramsci*. New York: International Publishers, 1971.

Groen, Petra. "Colonial Warfare and Military Ethics in the Netherlands East Indies, 1816–1941." *Journal of Genocide Research* 14, nos. 3–4 (2012): 277–96, DOI: 10.1080/14623528.2012.719365.

Hack, Karl. *Defense and Decolonization in Southeast Asia: Britain, Malaya and Singapore 1941–68*. Richmond, UK: Curzon Press, 2001.

Hadi, Asmara. *Dibelakang Kawat Berdoeri*. Djakarta: Pemandangan, 2002.

Hering, Bob. "From the Files of Empire." *Kabar Seberang*, nos. 13–4 (1984): 177–91.

Hijzen, Constant Willem. "The Perpetual Adversary: How Dutch Security Services Perceived Communism (1918–1989)." *Historical Social Research* 38. no. 1 (2013): 166–99.

———. *Vijandbeelden: De Veiligheidsdiensten en de democratie 1912–1992*. Amsterdam: Boom, 2016.

Hindley, Donald. *The Communist Party of Indonesia 1951–1963*. Berkeley: University of California Press, 1966.

Honna, Jun. "Military Ideology in Response to Democratic Pressure during the Late Suharto Era: Political and Institutional Contexts." In *Violence and the State in Suharto's Indonesia*, ed. Benedict R. O'G. Anderson, 54–89. Ithaca, NY: Southeast Asia Program, Cornell University, 2001.

Hoorweg, A. "Gewapende Politie." In *Vereeniging van Hoogere Politie-Ambtenaren, 1916–1936: Jubileum-Nummer van de Nederlandsch-Indische Politiegids bij Gelegenheid van het 20 Jarig Bestaan van de Vereeniging*, 41–4. Batavia: n.p., 1936.

Idenburg, P.J.A. "Het Nederlandse antwoord op het Indonesisch nationalism." In *Balans van beleid: Terugblik op de laatste halve eeuw van Nederlandsch-Indië*, by H. Baudet en I.J. Brugmans, 121–51. Assen, 1961.

Ingleson, John. *Perhimpunan Indonesia and the Indonesian Nationalist Movement, 1923–1928*. Monash Papers on Southeast Asia, no. 4. Clayton, Victoria: Center for Southeast Asian Studies, Monash University, 1975.

————. *Road to Exile: The Indonesian Nationalist Movement, 1927–1934*. Asian Studies Association of Australia Southeast Asia Publications Series 1. Singapore: Heinemann Educational Books, 1979.

————. *In Search of Justice: Workers and Unions in Colonial Java, 1908–1926*. Singapore: Oxford University Press, 1979.

————. "Sutomo, the Indonesian Study Club and Organized Labour in Late Colonial Surabaya." *Journal of Southeast Asian Studies* 39, no. 1 (February 2008): 31–57.

————. *Workers, Unions and Politics: Indonesia in the 1920s and 1930s*. Leiden: Brill, 2014.

Isnaeni, Hendri F. "Anak Menak Revolusioner." *Historia* online, August 19, 2010. https://historia.id/persona/articles/anak-menak-revolusioner-Dr1x6, accessed August 10, 2018.

Iwa Kusuma Sumantri. *Indonesia Minzokushugi no Genryu: Iwa Kusuma Sumantri Jiden*. Translated by Kenichi Goto. Tokyo: Waseda Daigaku Shuppanbu, 1975.

Jarvis, Helen. "Introduction." In Tan Malaka, *From Jail to Jail*, translated and introduced by Helen Jarvis, volume 1. Athens: Ohio University Center for International Studies, 1991.

Jazimah, Ipong. "S.K. Trimurti: Pejuang Perempuan Indonesia." *Sejarah dan Budaya: Jurnal Sejarah, Budaya, dan Pengajarannya* 10, no. 1 (2016): 45–53.

Jedamski, Doris. "Balai Pustaka: A Colonial Wolf in Sheep's Clothing." *Archipel*, no. 44 (1992): 23–46.

Jones, Alun. "Internal Security in British Malaya, 1915–1935." PhD dissertation, Yale University, 1970.

Jong, Cornelis Gijsbert Eliza, de. *De Organisatie der Politie in Nederlandsch-Indie. Proefschrift ter verkrijging van den graad van doctor in de rechtsgeleerdheid aan de Rijksuniversiteit te Leiden*. Leiden: "Luctor et Emergo," 1933.

Kahin, Audrey. *Rebellion to Integration: West Sumatra and the Indonesian Polity 1926–1998*. Amsterdam: Amsterdam University Press, 1999.

Kahin, George McT. *Nationalism and Revolution in Indonesia*. Ithaca, NY: Cornell University Press, 1952.

Kat Angelino, A.D.A. de. *Colonial Policy*. Translated by G.J. Renier. Chicago: University of Chicago Press, 1931.

Kwantes, R.C., ed. *De Ontwikkeling van de Nationalistische Beweging in Nederlandsch-Indie, Bronnenpublikatie, 1ste Stuk 1917–medio 1923*. Uitgaven van de Commissie voor Bronnenpublikatie betreffende de Geschiedenis van Nederlandsch-Indie 1900–1942 van het Nederlands Historisch Genootschap, no. 8. Groningen: H.D. Tjeenk Willink, 1975.

———. *De Ontwikkeling van de Nationalistische Beweging in Nederlandsch-Indie, Bronnenpublikatie 2e Stuk Medio 1923–1928*. Uitgaven van de Commissie voor Bronnenpublikatie betreffende de Geschiedenis van Nederlandsch-Indie 1900–1942 van het Nederlands Historisch Genootschap, no. 9. Groningen: Wolters-Noordhoff, 1978.

———. *De Ontwikkeling van de Nationalistische Beweging in Nederlandsch-Indie, Bronnenpublikatie 3de Stuk 1928–Aug. 1933*. Uitgaven van de Commissie voor Bronnenpublikatie betreffende de Geschiedenis van Nederlandsch-Indie 1900–1942 van het Nederlands Historisch Genootschap, no. 10. Groningen: Wolters-Noordhoff/Bouma's Boekhuis, 1981.

———. *De Ontwikkeling van de Nationalistische Beweging in Nederlandsch-Indie, Bronnenpublikatie 4de Stuk Aug. 1933–1942*. Uitgaven van de Commissie voor Bronnenpublikatie betreffende de Geschiedenis van Nederlandsch-Indie 1900–1942 van het Nederlands Historisch Genootschap, no. 11. Groningen: Wolters-Noordhoff/Bouma's Boekhuis, 1982.

Laffan, Michael Francis. *Islamic Nationhood and Colonial Indonesia: The Umma below the Winds*. London: Routledge Curzon, 2003.

Lamb, Nicole. "A Time of Normalcy: Javanese 'Coolies' Remember the Colonial Estate." *Bijdragen tot de Taal-, Land-, en Volkenkunde*, no. 170 (2014): 530–56.

Langenberg, Michael van. "National Revolution in North Sumatra: Sumatra Timur and Tapanuli, 1942–1950." PhD dissertation, University of Sydney, 1976.

Leclerc, Jacque. "Afterword: The Masked Hero." In *Local Opposition and Underground Resistance to the Japanese in Java 1942–1945*, ed. Anton Lucas, 323–68. Melbourne: Centre of Southeast Asian Studies, Monash University, 1986.

———. "Aidit and the Problem of the Party in the Year 1950." *Kabar Seberang*, no. 17 (1986): 102–28.

———. "Aliran Komunis, the Communist Current: Sejarah dan Penjara, The Past and Prisons." *Kabar Seberang*, no. 17 (1986): 53–71.

———. "Amir Sjarifuddin, between the State and the Revolution." In *Indonesian Political Biography: In Search of Cross-Cultural Understanding*, ed. Angus McIntyre, 10–41. Clayton, Victoria: Centre of Southeast Asian Studies, Monash University, 1993.

———. "Underground Activities and their Double (In the Context of Amir Sjarifuddin's Relationship with Communism in Indonesia)." *Kabar Seberang*, no. 17 (1986): 72–98.

Legge, J.D. *Intellectuals and Nationalism in Indonesia: A Study of the Following Recruited by Sutan Sjahrir in Occupation Jakarta*. Cornell University, Modern Indonesia Project, no. 68. Ithaca, NY: Cornell Modern Indonesia Project Publications, 1988.

———. *Sukarno: A Political Biography*. Third edition. Singapore: Archipelago Press, 2003.

Lely, A.E. van der. "Handhaving der openbare rust, orde en veiligheid." First published in *Rijkseenheid*, January 1932. Reprinted in *De Nederlandsch-Indische Politiegids*, no. 1932 (June 1932): 191–3.

Locher-Scholten, Elsbeth. "State Violence and the Police in Colonial Indonesia *circa* 1920: Exploration of a Theme." In *Roots of Violence in Indonesia*, ed. Freek Colombijn and J. Thomas Lindblad, 81–104. Singapore: Institute of Southeast Asian Studies, 2002.

Lucas, Anton. *One Soul One Struggle: Region and Revolution in Indonesia*. ASAA Southeast Asia Publications Series no. 19. Sydney: Allen and Unwin, 1991.

Lucas, Anton, ed. *Local Opposition and Underground Resistance to the Japanese in Java 1942–1945*. Melbourne: Centre of Southeast Asian Studies, Monash University, 1986.

Luttikhuis, Bart, and A. Dirk Moses. "Mass Violence and the End of the Dutch Colonial Empire in Indonesia." *Journal of Genocide Research* 14, nos. 3–4 (2012): 257–76. DOI: 1-.1080/14623528.2012.719362.

Maddison, Angus. "Dutch Colonialism in Indonesia: A Comparative Perspective." In *Indonesian Economic History in the Dutch Colonial Era*, ed. Ann Booth, W.J. O'Malley and Anna Weidemann, 322–35. New Haven, CT: Yale University Southeast Asian Studies, 1990.

Matu Mona. *Akibat Perang*. Jakarta: Gapura, 1950.

———. *Spionnage-Dienst: Patjar Merah Indonesia*. Medan: Centrale Courant en Boekhandel, 1939.

McCoy, Alfred W. *Policing America's Empire: The United States, the Philippines, and the Rise of the Surveillance State*. Madison: University of Wisconsin Press, 2009.

McVey, Ruth T. "In Memoriam: Adam Malik (1917–1984)." *Indonesia*, no. 39 (1985): 145–50.

———. Review of *Verguisd en vergeten: Tan Malaka, de linkse beweging en de Indonesiische Revolutie, 1945–1949*, by Harry A. Poeze. *Indonesia*, no. 86 (2008): 171–4.

————. *The Rise of Indonesian Communism.* Ithaca, NY: Cornell University Press, 1965.

————. "Taman Siswa and the Indonesian National Awakening." *Indonesia,* no. 4 (1967): 128–49.

Melati, Sintha. "In the Service of the Underground: The Struggle against the Japanese in Java." In *Local Opposition and Underground Resistance to the Japanese in Java 1942–1945,* translated and annotated by David Bouchier, ed. Anton Lucas, 121–321. Melbourne: Centre of Southeast Asian Studies, Monash University, 1986.

Mrazek, Rudolf. "Boven Digoel and Terezín: Camps at the Time of Triumphant Technology." *East Asian Science, Technology and Society: An International Journal* 3, nos. 2–3 (2009): 287–314.

————. *Sjahrir: Politics and Exile in Indonesia.* Ithaca, NY: Southeast Asia Program, Cornell University, 1994.

Mustoffa, Sumono. *Sukarni: Dalam Kenagnan Teman-Temannya.* Jakarta: Pernerbit Sinar Harapan, 1986.

Neijtzell de Wilde, A. "De Nederlandsch-Indische Politie." *Koloniaal Tijdschrift* 13 (1924): 126–30.

Nieuwenhuys, R. *Oost-Indische Spiegel.* Amsterdam: Querido, 1978.

Noer, Deliar. *The Modernist Muslim Movement in Indonesia 1900–1942.* Singapore: Oxford University Press, 1973.

Noer, Deliar, ed. *Portrait of a Patriot: Selected Writings by Mohammad Hatta.* The Hague: Mouton, 1972.

Oates, William A. "The Afdeeling B: An Indonesian Case Study." *Journal of Southeast Asian History* 9, no. 1 (March 1968): 107–16.

O'Malley, William J. "Indonesia in the Great Depression: A Study of East Sumatra and Jogjakarta in the 1930s." PhD dissertation, Cornell University, 1977.

Onghokham. "The Inscrutable and the Paranoid: An Investigation into the Sources of the Brotoningrat Affair." In *Southeast Asian Transitions: Approaches through Social History,* ed. Ruth T. McVey. New Haven, CT: Yale University Press, 1978. Reprinted in Onghokham, *The Thugs, the Curtain Thief, and the Sugar Lord: Power, Politics, and Culture in Colonial Java,* 3–73. Jakarta: Metafor, 2003.

Onimaru, Takeshi. *Shanghai Noulens Jiken no Yami: Senkanki Ajia ni okeru Chika Katsudo no Network to Igirisu Seiji Joho Keisatsu.* Tokyo: Hayama Shuppan Kobo, 2014.

Onraet, Rene H. *Singapore: A Police Background.* London: Dorothy Crisp, 1947.

Oshikawa, Noriaki. "Patjar Merah Indonesia and Tan Malaka: A Popular Novel and a Revolutionary Legend." In *Reading Southeast Asia,* ed. Takashi Shiraishi, 9–39. Translation of Contemporary Japanese Scholarship on Southeast Asia, vol. 1. Ithaca, NY: Southeast Asia Program, Cornell University, 1990.

Penders, C.L.M., ed. *Mohammad Hatta, Indonesian Patriot: Memoirs*. Singapore: Gunung Agung, 1981.

Pluvier, J.M. *Overzicht van de Ontwikkeling der Nationalistische Beweging in Indonesie in de jaren 1930 tot 1942*. 's-Gravenhage: W. van Hoeve, 1953.

Poeze, Harry A. "From Foe to Partner to Foe Again: The Strange Alliance of the Dutch Authorities and Digoel Exiles in Australia, 1943–1945." *Indonesia*, no. 94 (October 2012): 57–84.

————. "The PKI-Muda 1936–1942." *Kabar Seberang*, no. 13–4 (1984): 157–75.

————. "Political Intelligence in the Netherlands Indies." In *The Late Colonial State in Indonesia: Political and Economic Foundations of the Netherlands Indies, 1880–1942*, ed. Robert Cribb, 229–45. Leiden: KITLV Press, 1994.

————. *Tan Malaka, Strijder voor Indonesie's Veijheid: Levensloop van 1987 tot 1945*. 's-Gravenhage: Martinus Nijhoff, 1976.

————. *Verguisd en Vergeten: Tan Malaka, de linkse beweging en de Indonesische Revolutie, 1945–1949*, deel I–III. Verhandelingen van het Koningklijk Instituut voor Taal-, Land- en Volkenkunde 250. Leiden: KITLV Press, 2007.

Poeze, Harry A., ed. *Politiek-Politioneele Overzichten van Nederlandsch-Indie, deel I, 1927–1928*. The Hague: Martinus Nijhoff, 1982.

————. *Politiek-Politioneele Overzichten van Nederlandsch-Indie, deel II, 1929–1930*. Dordrecht, Holland: Foris, 1983.

————. *Politiek-Politioneele Overzichten van Nederlandsch-Indie, deel III, 1931–1934*. Dordrecht, Holland: Foris, 1988.

————. *Politiek-Politioneele Overzichten van Nederlandsch-Indie, deel IV, 1935–1941*. Leiden: KITLV Press, 1994.

Priyadi, Arief, ed. *Wawancara dengan Sayuti Melik*. Jakarta: CSIS, 1986.

Reid, Anthony. *The Blood of the People: Revolution and the End of Traditional Rule in Northern Sumatra*. Kuala Lumpur: Oxford University Press, 1979.

Ricklefs, M.C. *A History of Modern Indonesia since c.1200*. Third edition. Stanford, CA: Stanford University Press, 2001.

Rosa, John. *Pretext for Mass Murder: The September 30th Movement and Suharto's Coup d'Etat in Indonesia*. Madison: University of Wisconsin Press, 2006.

Rose, Mavis. *Indonesia Free: A Political Biography of Mohammad Hatta*. Ithaca, NY: Cornell Southeast Asia Program, Cornell University, 1987.

Rush, James R. *Opium to Java: Revenue Farming and Chinese Enterprise in Colonial Indonesia, 1860–1910*. Ithaca, NY: Cornell University Press, 1990.

————. "Social Control and Influence in Nineteenth Century Indonesia: Opium Farms and the Chinese of Java." *Indonesia*, no. 35 (1983): 53–64.

Ryter, Loren. "Pemuda Pancasila: The Last Loyalist Free Men of Suharto's Order?" In *Violence and the State in Suharto's Indonesia*, ed. Benedict R. O'G. Anderson, 124–55. Ithaca, NY: Southeast Asia Program, Cornell University, 2001.

Said, Mohammad. *Pertumbuhan dan Perkembangan Pers di Sumatera Utara*. Medan: Waspada, 1976.

Salim, I.F.M. *Vijftien Jaar Boven-Digul: Concentratiekamp in Nieuw-Guinea, Bakermat van de Indonesische Onafhankelijkheid*. Amsterdam: Contact, 1973.

Scherer, Savitri. "Sutomo and Trade Unionism." *Indonesia*, no. 24 (1977): 27–38.

Schmitt, Carl. *Political Theology: Four Chapters on the Concept of Sovereignty*. Translated by George Schwab. Chicago: University of Chicago Press, 1990.

Shiraishi, Takashi. *An Age in Motion: Popular Radicalism in Java 1912–1926*. Ithaca, NY: Cornell University Press, 1990.

────. "A New Regime of Order: The Origin of Modern Surveillance Politics in Indonesia." In *Southeast Asia over Three Generations: Essays Presented to Benedict R. O'G. Anderson*, ed. James T. Siegel and Audrey R. Kahin, 47–74. Ithaca, NY: Southeast Asia Program, Cornell University, 2003.

────. "The Phantom World of Digoel." *Indonesia*, no. 61 (1996): 93–118.

────. "Policing the Phantom Underground." *Indonesia*, no. 63 (1997): 1–46.

Siegel, James T. "Thoughts on the Violence of May 13 and 14, 1998, in Jakarta." In *Violence and the State in Suharto's Indonesia*, ed. Benedict R. O'G. Anderson, 90–123. Ithaca, NY: Southeast Asia Program, Cornell University, 2001.

Sinclair, Georgina. *At the End of the Line: Colonial Policing and the Imperial Endgame, 1945–80*. Manchester: Manchester University Press, 2006.

────. "'The Sharp End of the Intelligence Machine': The Rise of the Malayan Police Special Branch 1948–1955." *Intelligence and National Security* 26, no. 4 (2011): 460–77.

Sinclair, Georgina, and Chris A. Williams. "'Home and Away': The Cross-Fertilisation between 'Colonial' and 'British' Policing, 1921–85." *Journal of Imperial and Commonwealth History* 35, no. 2 (2007): 221–38.

Sjahrir, Soetan. *Out of Exile*. Translated with an introduction by Charles Wolf, Jr. New York: John Day, 1949.

Smith, Simon. "General Templer and Counter-Insurgency in Malaya: Hearts and Minds, Intelligence, and Propaganda." *Intelligence and National Security* 16, no. 3 (2001): 60–78.

Soe Hok Gie. "Simpang kiri dari sebuah djalan (kisah pemberontakan Madiun September 1948)." MA thesis, Universitas Indonesia, Fakultas Sastra, Djurusan Sedjarah, 1969.

Soebagijo, I.N. *Jagad Wartawan Indonesia*. Jakarta: Gunung Agung, 1981.

────. *S.K. Trimurti: Wanita Pengabdi Bangsa*. Jakarta: Gunung Agung, 1982.

────. *Sumanang, Sebuah Biografi*. Jakarta: Gunung Agung, 1980.

Steinberg, David J., ed. *In Search of Southeast Asia: A Modern History*. Revised edition. Honolulu: University of Hawai'i Press, 1987.

Stockwell, A.J. "Policing during the Malayan Emergency, 1948–60: Communism, Communalism and Decolonization." In *Policing and Decolonisation:*

Politics, Nationalism and the Police, 1917–65, ed. David M. Anderson and David Killingray. Manchester: Manchester University Press, 1992.

Stoler, Ann Laura. *Along the Archival Grain: Epistemic Anxieties and Colonial Common Sense*. Princeton: Princeton University Press, 2009.

—―. *Capitalism and Confrontation in Sumatra's Plantation Belt, 1870–1979*. New Haven, CT: Yale University Press, 1985.

Sukarno. *Sukarno: An Autobiography as Told to Cindy Adams*. Hong Kong: Gunung Agung, 1966.

Sulistyo, Hermawan. "Biografi Politik Adam Malik: Dari Kiri ke Kanan." *Prisma: Di Atas Panggung Sejara, Dari Sultan Ke Ali Moertopo, Edisi Khusus 20 Tahun Prisma 1971–1991*, 81–101. Jakarta: LP3ES, 1991.

Suminto, H. Aqib. *Politik Islam Hindia Belanda: Het Kantoor voor Inlandsche Zaken*. Batavia: LP3ES, 1985.

Surjomihardjo, Abdurrachman. "Taman Siswa and the 'Wild Schools.'" In *Born in Fire: The Indonesian Struggle for Independence*, 39–45. Athens: Ohio University Press, 1986.

Sutherland, Heather. *The Making of a Bureaucratic Elite: The Colonial Transformation of the Javanese Priyayi*. Asian Studies Association of Australia Southeast Asia Publications Series 2. Singapore: Heinemann Educational Books, 1979.

—―. "Pudjangga Baru: Aspects of Indonesian Intellectual Life in the 1930s." *Indonesia*, no. 6 (1968): 106–27.

Tamar Djaja. *Trio Komoenis Indonesia: (Tan Malaka, Alimin, Semaoen) berikoet Stalin dan Lenin*. Bukit Tinggi: Penjiaran Ilmoe, 1946.

Tamin, Djamaluddin. "Sedjarah PKI." Unpublished mimeograph. N.p., n.d.

Tan Malaka. *From Jail to Jail*. Three volumes. Translated and introduced by Helen Jarvis. Ohio University Monographs in International Studies, Southeast Asia Series, No. 83. Athens: Center for International Studies, Ohio University, 1991.

—―. *Menudju Republik Indonesia*. Jakarta: Jajasan "Massa," 1962. An Indonesian translation of Tan's *Naar de 'Republiek Indonesia'*.

—―. *Naar de Republiek Indonesia*. Canton (Guangzhou): n.p., 1925.

Thomas, Martin. "Albert Sarraut, French Colonial Development, and the Communist Threat, 1919–1930." *Journal of Modern History* 77, no. 4 (2005): 917–55.

—―. *Violence and Colonial Order: Police, Workers and Protest in the European Colonial Empires, 1918–1940*. New York: Cambridge University Press, 2012.

Thomas, Martin, Bob Moore, and L.J. Butler. *Crises of Empire: Decolonization and Europe's Imperial States*. Second edition. London: Bloomsbury, 2015.

Tim Penyusun Pembuatan Buku Sejarah Perintis Kemerdekaan Departemen Sosial RI Tahun 1976/77. *Citra dan Perjuangan Perintis Kemerdekaan Seri Perjuangan Ex Digul*. Jakarta: Direktorat Jenderal Bantuan Sosial Departemen Sosial, 1977.

Toer, Pramoedya Ananta. "Kemudian Lahirlah Dia." In *Cerita dari Blora: kumpulan cerita pendek*, 49–66. Kuala Lumpur: Wira Karya, 1994.

———. *Rumah Kaca*. Jakarta: Hasta Mitra, 1988.

Toer, Pramoedya Ananta, ed. *Cerita dari Digul*. Jakarta: Kepustakaan Populer Gramedia, 2001.

Triyana, Bonnie, Jay Akbar, M.F. Mukthi, and Hendri F. Isnaeni. "Mencari Wikana," *Majalah Historia*, 2016, http://bukuliat.blogspot.com/2016/09/mencari-wikana-bonnie-triyana-jay-akbar.html. Accessed on August 10, 2018.

Tsuchiya, Kenji. *Indonesia Minzokushugi Kenkyu: Taman Siswa no Seiritsu to Tenkai*. Kyoto: Sobunsha, 1982. (Translated into English as *Democracy and Leadership: The Rise of the Taman Siswa Movement in Indonesia* [Honolulu: University of Hawai'i Press, 1982].)

Van Till, Margreet. *Banditry in West Java 1869–1942*. Singapore: NUS Press, 2011.

Verslaggever Boven Digul [Mas Marco Kartodikromo]. "Riwajat Boven Digul (I)." *Persatoean Indonesia*, no. 33, November 15, 1929.

———. "Riwajat Boven Digul (III)." *Persatoean Indonesia*, no. 35, December 15, 1929.

———. "Riwajat Boven Digul (IV)," *Persatoean Indonesia*, no. 36, January 1, 1930.

Veur, Paul W. van der, ed. *Towards a Glorious Indonesia: Reminiscences and Observations of Dr. Soetomo*. Translated by Suharni Soemarmo and Paul W. van der Veur. Athens: Ohio University, Center for Southeast Asian Studies, 1987.

Wal, S.L. van der, ed. *Herinneringen van Jhr. Mr. B.C. de Jonge met brieven uit zijn nalatenschap*. Groningen: Wolters-Noordhoff, 1968.

Widjojoatmodjo, Abdulkadir. *Riwajat Kepolisen di Hindia Ollanda dengan Ringkas: Lezing dengan hadlirat j.m. toen Resident Prijangan Tengah dalam Congres Inlandsche Politie Bond ke-tiga di Bandoeng pada boelan April 1927 tanggal 17*. Semarang: Typ Khouw Beng Wan, 1927.

Williams, Michael C. *Communism, Religion, and Revolt in Banten*. Monographs in International Studies Southeast Asia Series, No. 86. Athens: Ohio University, Center for International Studies, 1990.

———. *Sickle and Crescent: The Communist Revolt of 1926 in Banten*. Ithaca, NY: Cornell Southeast Asia Program, Cornell University, 1982.

Wiranta. *Boeron dari Digoel*. Magelang: Tamboer Press, 2000.

Xarim M.S., Abdoel. *Pandoe Anak Boeangan*. Medan: Uitgevers Genootschap "Aneka," 1933.

Yamamoto, Nobuto *Censorship in Colonial Indonesia, 1901–1942*. Leiden: Brill, 2019.

————. "Medan no roman pichisan: 1930-nen dai matsu Indonesia bunka chizu to taishu shosetsu wo meguru seiji." *Hogaku Kenkyu* 68, no. 11 (1995): 147–79.

————. "Print Power and Censorship in Colonial Indonesia, 1912–1942." PhD dissertation, Cornell University, 2011.

————. "Teikoku Seiji kara Kokusai Seiji he: 1920-nen dai Tonan Ajia ni okeru Chiiki Kokusai sistemu no tenkan." *Hogaku Kenkyu* 86, no. 7 (2013): 67–92.

Zanden, Jan Luiten van, and Daan Marks. *An Economic History of Indonesia, 1800–2012.* London: Routledge, 2012.

INDEX